Personnel

Contemporary Perspectives
and Applications

The West Series in Management

Consulting Editors:

Don Hellriegel—Texas A&M University
and
John W. Slocum, Jr.—The Pennsylvania State University

Personnel

Contemporary Perspectives and Applications

2nd Edition

ROBERT L. MATHIS
University of Nebraska at Omaha

JOHN H. JACKSON
University of Wyoming

WEST PUBLISHING COMPANY
St. Paul   New York   Los Angeles   San Francisco

A study guide has been developed to assist you in mastering concepts presented in this text. The study guide reinforces concepts by presenting them in condensed, concise form. Additional illustrations, examples, and readings are also included. The study guide is available from your local bookstore under the title, *Study Guide, Readings, and Exercises to Accompany Personnel: Contemporary Perspectives and Applications, Second Edition*, prepared by Sally A. Coltrin.

COPYRIGHT © 1976 By WEST PUBLISHING CO.
COPYRIGHT © 1979 By WEST PUBLISHING CO.
                         50 West Kellogg Boulevard
                         P.O. Box 3526
                         St. Paul, Minnesota 55165

Library of Congress Cataloging in Publication Data

Mathis, Robert L   1944–
    Personnel.

    (The West series in management)
    Includes bibliographical references and
indexes.
    1. Personnel management. I. Jackson, John
Harold, joint author. II. Title.
HF5549.M3349 1979   658.3   78-27343
ISBN 0-8299-0199-X
3rd Reprint—1979

Jo Ann Mathis
who manages me

To

R. D. and M. M. Jackson
who have been
successful managers of
people for many years

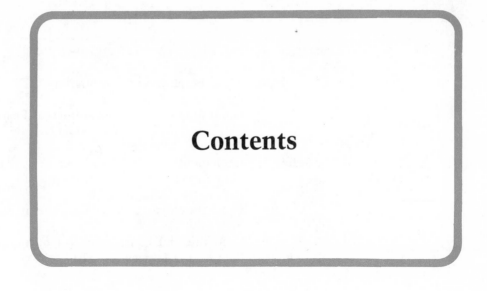

Contents

vii

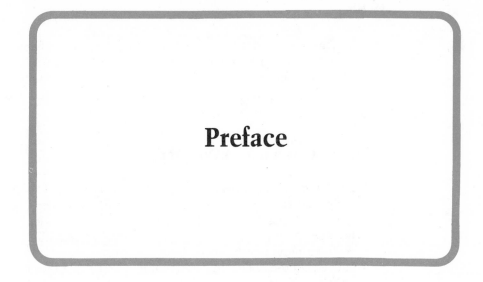

Preface

We Need Education in the Obvious
More Than Investigation of the Obscure

Oliver Wendell Holmes

This second edition, like the first one, approaches the study of personnel management from the position that *both* the practical aspects of personnel and the underlying reasons and theories behind the practices are important. Certainly not everyone who reads this book will be a personnel manager. Indeed, most students who take a personnel course never become personnel specialists. However, everyone who works in any organization comes in contact with personnel management—both good and bad. Further, anyone who does become a manager must be able to manage personnel activities. To one degree or another, every manager is a personnel manager, and his or her actions in this area can have major consequences for the organization.

A unique feature of the book is specifying the "interface" between operating managers and the personnel unit. If every manager must be concerned with personnel management, the division of labor between operating managers and the personnel unit is very important. This division will vary depending on the size of the organization, its technology and history, and other factors, but the main point is that there exists a group of personnel activities for which individuals in the organization have to take responsibility. How this responsibility is divided is the "interface" concept used throughout the book.

xiii

This book examines the major activities in personnel or "Human Resources" management completely but concisely. We are gratified by the reception the first edition received and feel the changes and additions suggested by users of the first edition have made the book even better.

NEW AND REVISED FEATURES

Personnel is a rapidly changing area of study. Two of the most important forces causing such changes are court decisions and revision of governmental regulations. The authors have made a concerted effort to include the most up-to-date legal information possible. The coverage of equal employment has been completely revised and expanded so that two entire chapters focus on equal employment (Chapters 4 and 5) instead of only one chapter as in the first edition. Emerging privacy legislation is discussed as it applies to reference checking (Chapter 8) and as it relates to personnel record keeping (Chapter 17). This edition also includes revised coverage of age discrimination and retirement concerns to reflect changes in these areas (Chapter 14). Finally, the revised practices of the Occupational Safety and Health Administration are detailed (Chapter 15).

The organization of the book has been slightly altered by discussing training and development before discussing appraisal and compensation. The nature of communication is now included with the human behavior topics (Chapter 3). Also, there are expanded chapters on personnel coordination, personnel records, and personnel research (Chapters 16 and 17). Restructured and expanded coverage of unions, collective bargaining, and grievance resolution is included (Chapters 18 and 19).

In addition to the modifications mentioned above, the authors have revised or added several content sections, including the following: new content on personnel in international and matrix organizations (Chapter 2); new material on the legal aspects of job analysis (Chapter 6); expanded discussions of manpower planning and internal versus external recruiting (Chapter 7); a completely rewritten section on career planning (Chapter 10); and a new section on the legal aspects of performance appraisal (Chapter 12).

The last several chapters contain a large amount of new or revised information on personnel coordination using policies and rules (Chapter 16), personnel records and computerized employee information systems (Chapter 17), the unionization process (Chapter 18), and personnel in the future (Chapter 20).

Taken together, all of the changes and additions represent the authors' efforts to have this book be timely and current, while preserving the readability and positive features of the first edition.

Building upon the favorable response to the first edition, this edition also contains some new design features. Two obvious ones are the addition of a second color and the addition of "Idea Checks" in the form of short questions following major content sections.

Many instructors utilize cases in the teaching of personnel management. To aid this instructional orientation, a short case that poses a problem opens each chapter in this edition. At the end of each chapter a follow-up to the opening case describes how material in the text is useful in analyzing the opening case problem. Another case problem is then presented for analysis. Other features included are learning objectives and chapter-ending questions that focus on mastery of the material.

The availability of a unique study guide, written by Sally Coltrin, further enhances this book as a learning tool. The study guide contains chapter summaries, review questions, readings, and exercises. The inclusion of one or two short readings and exercises represents a significant improvement over traditional student supplements and provides instructors a widely varied package of resources.

We feel that this edition contains a practical view of personnel management that integrates both the contributions from the behavioral sciences and the legal issues that have raised personnel or human resources management from a narrow record-keeping function to a mainstream organizational activity.

ACKNOWLEDGMENTS

Producing any book requires assistance from other people. Helpful comments and contributions have come from the following persons: James M. Black (University of South Carolina), Diane C. Hale (Rider College, New Jersey), James C. Hodgetts (Memphis State University), Thomas T. Johnston (Nassau Community College, New York), Patricia Linenberger (University of Wyoming), Ernest C. Miller (California Polytechnic State University), Tai K. Oh (California State University, Fullerton), and Stephen Rubenfeld (Texas Tech University). A special thanks is due the author of the accompanying student supplement, Sally Coltrin (University of North Florida), who provided numerous suggestions, and whose supplement significantly enhances the learning experiences available with this book.

Kathy Maris, Lori Ray, and Peggy C. Ritchey deserve acknowledgment for their secretarial assistance. Tom Billesbach, a graduate student at the University of Nebraska at Omaha, provided invaluable assistance in many and varied areas. Finally, JoAnn Mathis deserves special recognition for content and editorial suggestions and typing assistance.

The authors wish to note that many of the examples used to illustrate concepts reflect real situations, but specific references to existing organizations or people is merely coincidental. We feel this edition has fulfilled what we perceive to be a real need in the study of Personnel Management.

RLM
Omaha, Nebraska

JHJ
Laramie, Wyoming

To the Reader

This book is designed to aid you, the reader, as you learn more about personnel management. As you use this book, you may find value from the following tips:

1. Familiarize yourself with the learning objectives at the beginning of each chapter. The learning objectives indicate what you should know after reading and studying a chapter.

2. Outline each chapter for study purposes by noting the main, second level, and in-paragraph headings.

3. Read the case at the beginning of the chapter which illustrates the type of problems the information in the chapter would help you resolve.

4. As you read the chapter, notice the idea check questions and see if you can answer them. Each idea check relates directly to one of the learning objectives. If you cannot correctly and completely answer an idea check, go back and re-read the section immediately preceding the idea check.

5. After reading the chapter, answer the review questions. Also, if your instructor has requested you to use the student supplement, read the summary in that supplement and answer the sample questions in it.

6. Review the opening case, and then read the case follow-up and see if you can identify how the chapter material helps in analyzing the case problems.

7. Read the short ending case and answer the questions on it by applying ideas from the chapter.

If you let this book and the learning features in it aid you, your study of personnel management will be easier and more enjoyable. With the knowledge you acquire, you will be able to become more effective in your chosen career field.

Personnel Management and the Human Resource

section 1

New approaches to personnel management have emerged to meet the demand for effective ways to manage people in organizations. These approaches use analysis of human behavior to help organizations improve existing working environments and plan those of the future.

These approaches did not just happen. They are the product of 25 years of development. In the last ten years dramatic developments in the field have altered its traditional image. This text provides perspectives on important traditional, current, and emerging practices to help the reader develop a practical, realistic, and modern view of personnel management.

This first section (1) examines differing views of personnel management, (2) defines and places personnel management in an organizational context, and (3) examines basic human considerations of motivation, leadership, group behavior and communication.

Chapter 1 presents three debates on the nature of personnel management. The two perspectives in each debate provide the basis for understanding different views of personnel management in different organizational settings. The "interface" concept is used to reconcile these three debates.

An *interface* is a *point of contact* between a specialized personnel unit in an organization and other managers. This concept provides a basis for

1

understanding what personnel management *is*, and why it differs in various organization situations.

Chapter 2 places personnel management in an organizational context and views an organization as an open system. The four subsystems of an organization are technology, structure, people, and tasks. Personnel's role in the organization and the effects of two of these variables, technology and structure, are discussed.

Chapter 3 examines the human resource by considering four basic intraorganizational processes: motivation, leadership, group behavior, and communication. Knowledge of each of these behavioral processes is fundamental to managing human resources in organizations.

chapter 1

The Nature of Personnel Management

When you have read this chapter, you should be able to:

1. Discuss the three sets of views about the nature of personnel management.

2. Reconcile the different views into a definition of personnel management that emphasizes managing the human resource.

3. List and in one sentence identify the seven personnel interfaces.

Pulled Both Ways

William Anderson, plant personnel manager for Amalgamated Products in Dallas, Texas, is the center of a controversy—and he does not even know it. The vice-president of personnel and the vice-president of manufacturing are arguing over an issue that will affect him. The company had received attention from the Occupational Safety and Health Administration (OSHA) because of its excessive accident rate, especially at the Dallas plant. The vice-president of personnel feels William must be told in no uncertain terms that the plant must be ready to pass a safety inspection at any time and that William, as plant personnel manager, will be held responsible for the results.

Unfortunately, the vice-president of manufacturing does not agree. He has continually emphasized that safety is the job of the line supervisors and is not a Plant Personnel Department job. As he put it to the personnel vice-president last week: "You do the hiring and put up the safety posters, and the supervisors will run their departments."

William has a problem, and it's even greater than he thinks. It involves the basic nature of personnel management; what it is, who should practice it, and how it is "best" handled in all kinds of organizations.

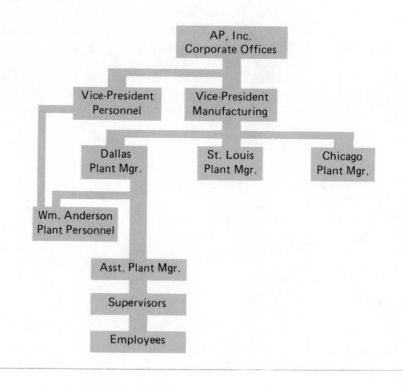

Successful management of human resources is one of the keys to the effective operation of an organization. Numerous public relation documents describe people as the most important resource a firm has available. A highly trained and competent work force represents a distinct competitive advantage for some organizations. As an example, IBM Corporation has been extremely successful in the computer industry due, in large part, to its ability to attract and retain skilled employees and managers. It is significant that IBM also has the reputation of having sound forward-looking personnel management policies and practices.

Some individuals may assume that personnel management is primarily a "business" profession or activity. However, managers in organizations in both the private and public sectors must tap their human resources if they are to be successful. Large corporations, banks, universities, advertising agencies, small retail stores, hospitals, manufacturing firms, and governmental agencies all must tap the talents of their people if the organizations are to accomplish their objectives. A production supervisor, a hospital administrator, a grocery store manager, a mayor—any manager in any organization—will succeed in getting the job done only if that manager can deal with people problems.

But the days when a "concern for people" is all that is necessary for success in personnel matters are long past. Dealing with people's needs, expectations, and legal rights in work organizations has become more demanding and complex. Laws and regulations at federal, state, and local levels impose limitations on what managers can and cannot do as they manage employees. Nondiscriminatory recruiting, selection, and promotion criteria must be identified and used. Appropriate programs for training people to perform their jobs well require consideration of a number of interrelated human and organizational concerns. Sound, coordinated, and legal wage and salary systems must be designed and implemented so that employees are fairly compensated for their efforts. Personnel policies that help rather than hinder the accomplishment of work must be implemented. These areas are a few of the concerns of personnel management.

Who is a personnel manager? What exactly is personnel management? Which managers should do what jobs in managing people? These questions will help define the subject area. A usable definition of personnel management will be developed through the following discussion of different views of personnel.

VIEWS OF PERSONNEL MANAGEMENT

Different viewpoints about the nature of personnel management are examined here. These viewpoints stem from various questions. For example, who should do the personnel work in an organization—a specialized unit or all of the managers? There are individuals who argue each extreme, as well as points of view in between. In the case of William Anderson, presented at the start of this chapter, the vice-president of manufacturing felt the supervisors should be responsible for safety, while the vice-president of personnel thought safety should be plant personnel's job. Typically, such a difference of opinion is hardened when each opposing advocate insists that his viewpoint is the only correct one.

The different views discussed here represent extreme positions. Although not everyone who considers the following questions takes an extreme position, extremes are used to present the issues clearly. The three issues are:

1. Who is a personnel manager?
2. How does human nature affect personnel management?
3. What is personnel management?

In most situations when two distinctly different views are voiced, there are sound points made by each. As you will discover, the answers to these questions reject the extremes and emphasize the need for reconsidering the various viewpoints. This resolution incorporates the sound points made at the extremes but rejects the notion that one view is totally correct.

Who Is a Personnel Manager?

On the question, *Who is a personnel manager?*, there is much continuing debate. One side contends that personnel management is limited to only one part of the organization, the personnel department. This is the *personnel specialist view*. The other side believes that all managers are personnel managers, and it is only through the effective use of human resources by all managers that work gets done. This is the *all managers view*. As Figure 1–1 shows, the continuum of views ranges from personnel specialists to all managers.

FIGURE 1–1   Who is a personnel manager?

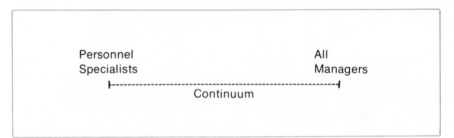

Personnel   All
Specialists   Managers
|--|
              Continuum

Personnel specialist view. **The** personnel specialist view holds that personnel management is composed of certain duties which are best performed in one unit of the organization, usually labeled the personnel department. This department is the part of the organization which "handles people," in the same manner as the finance department handles the management of capital and cash. The personnel unit specializes in the management of conditions and events affecting the people in an organization. Figure 1–2 shows a typical organization chart. Personnel is shown on the chart as a distinct unit, just as marketing, finance, and purchasing are separate specialized units.

Personnel specialists deal with people in areas such as employment, counseling, wage and salary administration, safety, benefits, training, and labor relations. The personnel unit assists, advises, and supports the other parts of the organization in matters dealing with employees. With top management, this unit may formulate personnel policies, audit and control personnel activities, and research innovative personnel programs.[1]

The personnel specialist view has sometimes been stretched to include in personnel those people-related activities which do not conveniently fit anywhere else in the organization, such as the company bowling league. This dumping of less important duties has been called the "trash can" approach to personnel.[2] This extremely "functional" approach may force the personnel unit to concentrate on very minor aspects of personnel management.

Consider the Plains Manufacturing Company, a medium-sized manufacturer of machine products. At Plains the personnel department spends much of its time planning social and recreational outings for employees, coordinating bowling leagues, and devising new gimmicks to get more employee suggestions in the suggestion box. However, the firm's personnel manual and job descriptions have not been revised in five years. Plains is not unusual either; personnel units in numerous firms are still at this level of organizational busy work.

A major problem is that personnel management may become narrowly defined as *only* those areas with which a "personnel" department directly deals. For example, the personnel department at Plains Manufacturing

FIGURE 1–2 Personnel as a special unit in Amalgamated Products.

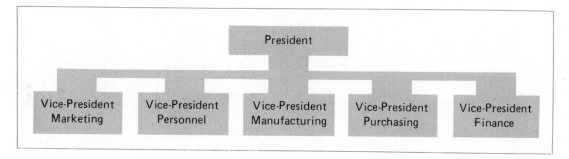

Company may make wage surveys, but it does not work with middle-level managers on allocation of production bonuses because that is the production department's job rather than personnel's.

"All managers" view.   The other side of this argument suggests that personnel management is spread throughout the organization. All managers are viewed as personnel managers. Sales managers, head nurses, manufacturing supervisors, corporate treasurers, college deans, and retail store managers are personnel managers because their jobs are vitally connected with human resources. Their effectiveness is closely tied to their employees' effectiveness.

Some evidence for this view can be offered. Managers typically play a large role in the selection of many employees, especially upper level ones. Furthermore, an operating manager is in a key position to determine how well employees do their jobs.

In reality, both of these views have sound bases up to a point. Some personnel activities require the use of a personnel specialist or they can be done by a specialist to save an operating manager time and effort. For instance, it is unrealistic to expect an accounting department supervisor to be extremely knowledgeable about Equal Employment laws and various benefit plans. Likewise, having an employment specialist screen a large number of applicants down to five or so relieves the department manager from devoting too much time to interviewing, time that might be better spent on accounting activities. As will be emphasized later, personnel specialists and operating managers must work together to manage personnel activities by each doing what they can do best.

The "all managers" view may preclude having a personnel department at all and suggests that the scope of personnel management is much broader than what one department can handle. Because the responsibilities for employees and their problems are so widely distributed in an organization, one department possibly cannot and should not be "in charge" of all these responsibilities.

How Does Human Nature Affect Personnel Management?

A second disagreement about personnel management is, *How does human nature affect personnel policies and activities?* One extreme perspective says that management can initiate standardized techniques for handling all people. These techniques will be effective because people will do what is expected of them for their own benefit. For example, this *"rational view"* might argue that if a training program has been well designed, it will be effective because people will benefit from it, and therefore will welcome it. The other view holds that individual human nature and processes must be incorporated in the design and operation of personnel management activities. For example, establishing a rationally designed training program would not necessarily guarantee that the trainees would understand or approve of the training. Therefore, human behavior must be considered in designing the training program. This has been labeled the *situational view*. Figure 1–3 shows the continuum of views on this debate.

Rational view.   According to the extreme rational view of personnel management, there can be universally applicable truths about managing people. "Principles" which can be used to determine management actions exist. The type of organization, the people involved, or the organizational setting do not greatly affect the validity of these principles. For example, such a principle might state: one manager can directly and successfully manage only about six people regardless of the type of people or work involved.

Such rational principles emphasize organizational uniformity, conformity, and predictability. The principles also assume that people will be just as rational and predictable as the organization expects them to be. The rational view is summarized as "everything done from the perspective of the organization and not from the worker's perspective."[3]

Situational view.   The other side of this issue focuses on the behavior of people in organizations. Some people criticize the rational approach for being rigid and too prescriptive. They argue that the type of organization, the type of position, and employees' individual qualifications and personalities have such a great impact on personnel decisions that management principles have very little value. At a minimum, human nature will disrupt or alter orderly rational principles.

The proponents of this viewpoint stress the system-wide effects of personnel management activities. They claim that the organization is really an interrelated set of subsystems; and thus, a change in one personnel activity will have an effect on the total organization. For example, new performance appraisals will ultimately affect compensation, train-

FIGURE 1–3   Human nature and personnel management.

People Are Rational and Similar		Individual Differences Are Critical
├───────────────	Continuum	───────────────┤

ing, and promotion activities. Some might argue that these complexities make designing rational personnel systems almost impossible.

The resolution of these extremes recognizes that organizations need a reasonable degree of standardization and uniformity. However, what is appropriate for one organization and its employees may not be best suited to another. Additionally, focusing heavily on individual differences is not realistic because of the need for coordination in an organization. Some accommodation to individuals must be given, but this must be balanced with the overall needs of the organization as well.

What Is Personnel Management?

There is a third question which must be dealt with: *What is personnel management?* One side of this debate claims that personnel management is a very practical and applied field. Thus, it should focus on the development of very practical techniques for meeting personnel problems. This is the *techniques view*. The opposing side holds that personnel management possibly should not be considered a field at all. In fact, this argument challenges the idea that personnel management as an area of study even exists. Proponents feel that understanding basic human nature through analytical studies in psychology, sociology, or anthropology is more appropriate than talking about techniques. This is characterized as an *analytical view*.

The debate often is a split between practicing personnel managers on the one hand and researchers and scholars on the other. The disagreement is over the nature of personnel management knowledge and practice. Figure 1–4 illustrates this continuum.

The techniques view. **The techniques side is concerned with the applied aspects of personnel management. Emphasis is solely on the needs and concerns of organization managers and personnel managers as they deal with the daily problems and demands of their jobs.**

FIGURE 1–4   What is personnel management?

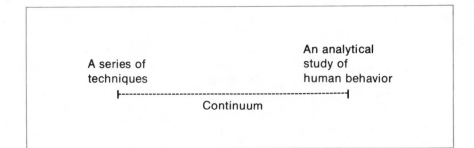

This techniques approach may offer numerous multistep lists for handling any personnel problem. These lists typify an overconcern with techniques and not enough concern with understanding reasons why problems exist or why a certain approach may work. A good example of the extreme technique approach follows:

Five Steps for Handling Contract Grievances[4]
1. Check for procedural compliance.
2. Perform preliminary research.
3. Conduct an orderly first-step meeting.
4. Research the problem, then decide.
5. Present your decision.

Analytical view. Certain behavioral scientists fault the techniques approach as being excessively concerned with "how to" issues which do not consider the variability of employee behavior. Techniques are sometimes viewed as "recipes" for dealing with any and all personnel problems.

Some analytical proponents challenge the idea that personnel management is even a field of study. "Indeed personnel is rapidly becoming an anachronism when used to describe an academic field. It is viewed as too applied and untheoretical, and in the better universities practically no Ph.D. candidates are being trained as personnel men."[5]

This perspective is that personnel management is filled with "harmless chaps who spent their careers worshiping files, arranging company picnics, and generally accomplishing nothing whatsoever of any fundamental importance."[6] Thus, the analytical side of this debate suggests that personnel management emphasizes the unimportant and is too technique-oriented and that personnel managers are too concerned with day-to-day problems. The extreme side of this view contends that personnel professionals should be concentrating on the "humanization" of work, the creation of a climate of "openness," and the demise of the "bureaucratic structure" instead of job descriptions, application blanks, and company handbooks.

To resolve these differing views, it is vital to see personnel management as a combination of analytical studies from which specific applications are derived. The rather bland "list-following" urged by some techniques must be tempered with the knowledge gained from analytical studies. In a similar manner, analytical studies that are not easily translated or are not realistic for application are of little value to personnel specialists and other managers.

Can you discuss the three sets of views about Personnel Management?

RECONCILING DIFFERENT VIEWPOINTS

In Figure 1–5, the debates just presented are summarized graphically. Views on the left side focus on day-to-day administration of traditional personnel activities in a rather rational and technique-oriented manner with authority for personnel-related activities limited to the personnel department. On the right side of Figure 1–5 personnel management is seen as based on an analytical evaluation of people, their behavior, and the organization itself, and all managers are personnel managers because they must interact with people on a continual basis.

Reconciling these divergent frameworks is important because elements of each have some value in the study of personnel management. Such reconciliation can be accomplished by using the concept of personnel unit/manager interface.

Personnel Unit/Manager Cooperation: The Interface Concept

An interface is a surface of contact between two entities.

> INTERFACES, as defined here, are areas of contact between the personnel unit and other managers in an organization.

These contacts are at points focusing on the management of the human resources of an organization.

As shown in Figure 1–6, the activities themselves are the concern of both personnel specialists and operating managers. Unless their contact, or interface, is focused on who is most qualified to perform various parts of a personnel activity, the activity is likely to be mismanaged. In the

FIGURE 1–5   Reconciling differing viewpoints.

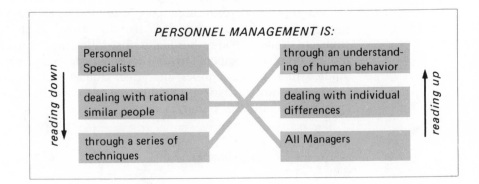

PERSONNEL MANAGEMENT IS:

reading down

Personnel Specialists

dealing with rational similar people

through a series of techniques

through an understanding of human behavior

dealing with individual differences

All Managers

reading up

FIGURE 1-6   Interface between personnel unit and other managers.

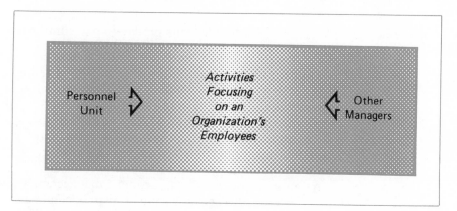

opening case the conflict between vice-presidents is not likely to lead to effective management of safety activities. Only by cooperatively deciding who can best perform which part of safety activities will the safety activities themselves be sound.

These activities must be carried out by the most appropriate organizational entity—either managers or the personnel unit. The key word is *appropriate.* Personnel activities should be performed by those who can do them most effectively. Who is "most appropriate" may vary from organization to organization based on such items as size, tradition, and the person who has specific expertise. However, *someone* must manage the "people-related" activities. Thus, personnel management is a concern of *both* the managers *and* the personnel unit in an organization.

The size of an organization is a key consideration in determining who will do what. In a very small organization, such as a small retail store, no specialized personnel unit may exist. Instead, the owner-manager will hire the clerks, handle the payroll, train new employees, and perform any other needed personnel activities. However, a large retail chain will usually have a specialized personnel unit.

The scope of each personnel activity managed by the personnel unit or individual managers varies among organizations. For example, in a large manufacturing plant, the personnel administrator may interview and select employees. However, the sales manager may interview and select the salespersons, but only after the personnel unit has handled the campus recruiting effort. The important point is that activities must be performed by those who can do so most effectively in that particular organization.

The prime focus of personnel management must be on the effective management of an organization's human resources. The personnel activities in any organization draw the personnel unit, if there is one, and the managers into a partnership. Much of the success or lack of it depends upon how effectively the partners coordinate and cooperate with each other.

Reconciling the personnel specialist vs. "all managers" view. The interface approach can be used to resolve the first debate concerning who is a personnel manager. The view that there are certain personnel activities or parts of certain activities which are more appropriately handled by a specialist in a personnel unit is valid in certain situations because of the knowledge and expertise of those specialists' activities. Further, some are best centralized for uniformity. Yet, as the "all manager" view states, if one assumes that the management of human resources pervades the entire organization and is a vital part of a manager's job, it follows that there are personnel aspects to all managers' jobs.

As an example, both a department manager in a retail store and an interviewer in the personnel unit must cooperate and interrelate when hiring clerks. The personnel unit has the expertise to advertise the job effectively and comply with Equal Employment requirements, while the department manager may be in a better position to evaluate an applicant's sales background.

Reconciling the rational vs. situational views. The interface approach can also be used to resolve the second debate. The rational approach to people and organizing deals well with one part of the relationship, since a certain amount of uniformity, conformity, and predictability is essential for the organization to operate. However, the contributions of the situational view are valuable for understanding the situational and behavioral characteristics involved. By emphasizing the management activities themselves and the relevant contributions of both approaches, valuable parts of the rational view of personnel management can be preserved, and important insights from modern research can be added.

Reconciling the techniques vs. analytical views. The third debate can also be resolved using the interface concept. Research on personnel activities (the analytical view) such as recruiting, training, or compensation allows procedures based upon research information to be developed for solving day-to-day problems. This application-orientation is the practical side of the issue. The interface concept suggests that the emphasis should be on *understanding* personnel problems in order to *manage* personnel activities effectively.

Value of the interface concept. The major intent of the interface approach that this book uses is to *identify people-oriented activities* that must be performed in all organizations. The responsibility for proper management of personnel activities such as interviewing, training, or performance appraisal in a given situation is placed on both managers and personnel specialists.

A manager must consider both the situation and the personnel involved to determine the most appropriate approach for handling problems. For example, assume that the appraisal of a nurse's performance is the activity under consideration. The interface approach suggests that various methods of appraisal might be used; but there are analytical considerations as well as considerations in technique. The head nurse and/or personnel administrator must choose the most appropriate appraisal method, given the situation and the nurse involved. This approach differs greatly from prescribing an appraisal technique for "any situation," or from examining appraisal problems in the absence of having to solve them. It also requires cooperation between the head nurse and personnel specialists, but the end result is a much more adaptable and effective personnel system.

How can various views of personnel management be reconciled?

The interface idea will be developed throughout the book by beginning each chapter with an interface showing particular personnel activities and who typically performs what portion of them. However, these interface illustrations are not attempts to indicate "the one way" all organizations can or should perform the activities. They illustrate how these activities can be divided.

Personnel Management Defined

The reconciliation of the various viewpoints emphasizes that personnel management is a *set of activities* that must be effectively managed. Thus,

> PERSONNEL MANAGEMENT is the effective use of human resources in an organization through the management of people-related activities.

A key portion of this definition is that any organization must adapt to the needs of its employees, as well as to have the employees meet basic organizational requirements. The definition also emphasizes the personnel activities themselves, and *not* who performs them. All organizations must deal with the specific personnel activities of work analysis, staffing, training and development, appraisal, compensation, maintenance, and union relations.

Can you define personnel management?

PERSONNEL INTERFACES

Major personnel activities at the interface between the personnel unit and managers are presented in the center portion of Figure 1–7. These activities include the following:

work analysis
staffing
training and development
appraisal
compensation
maintenance
(union)

(The union interface overlaps the environment because the union is an organized semi-external force not present in all organizations.) The personnel unit, if one exists, and individual managers must cooperate to effectively manage the employees and their work within each of the seven activities.

Environmental forces which affect every aspect of any organization are shown in Figure 1–7 as an external circle surrounding the organization. These forces include legal, societal, and interorganizational factors. The development of an organization as a system open to environmental factors and the relationship of the personnel unit to the total organization are concepts discussed in Chapter 2. A critical environmental force, equal employment laws, and other governmental legislation are capsuled in Chapters 4 and 5.

Intraorganizational forces of leadership, motivation, and group behavior are more general organizational processes concerned with human behavior. They are shown in Figure 1–7 flowing through the entire organization and affecting all interfaces. These processes are broad dimensions rather than specific personnel activities and are discussed in Chapter 3.

A brief overview of each of the seven interfaces follows:

Work analysis interface. The *work analysis interface* focuses on the concept of a job as a unit of work. The specialization of narrow jobs versus the humanization of broader jobs is one consideration in job design. Once the unit of work is established, jobs can be analyzed and job descriptions and specifications can be written. The nature of these activities and their implications for human behavior are discussed further in Chapter 6.

Staffing interface. The *staffing interface* emphasizes the recruitment and selection of the human resources of an organization. Manpower planning and recruiting precede the actual selection of people for positions in organizations. Choosing the right person for the job involves the

FIGURE 1–7   Model of personnel activities.

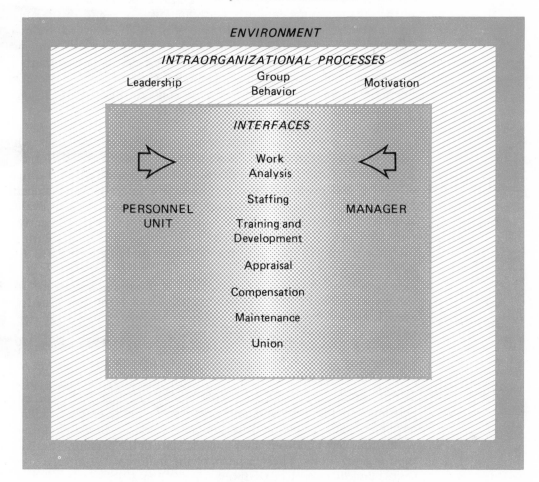

use of such data sources as application blanks, interviews, tests, background investigations, and physical examinations. The staffing interface is examined in Chapters 7 and 8.

Training and development interface.   The *training and development interface* consists of many facets. Included under training are the orientation of the new employees, the training of personnel to perform their job duties, and the retraining of employees as their job requirements change. The development and growth of more effective employees is another facet of this interface. Finally, organizational development, a behaviorally oriented philosophy/strategy, is included in this interface as an approach which is used to make organizations more flexible and variable for the present and the future. All of these facets of the training and development interface are examined in Chapters 9, 10, and 11.

Appraisal interface.   The *appraisal interface* focuses on the performance of the organization's employees. An appraisal is useful in making wage and salary decisions, in specifying areas in which additional training and development of employees are needed, and in making placement decisions. The approaches to appraisal and the types of appraisal methods are integral parts of implementing an appraisal system. The behavioral consequences of appraisal are also a primary concern throughout the appraisal interface, which is discussed in Chapter 12.

Compensation interface.   The *compensation interface* deals with rewarding people through pay, incentives, and benefits for performing organizational work. The behavioral side of compensation and the meaning of equity and reward to the employee are underlying considerations. Building on job analysis from the work interface, the job evaluation activity determines the relative worth of each job. Also, incentive systems and benefits, as special types of compensation, fall within this interface. Compensation activities are discussed in Chapters 13 and 14.

Maintenance interface.   The emphasis of the *maintenance interface* is somewhat different than the others. Instead of being concerned with a specific aspect of personnel management, the maintenance interface emphasizes consistency, stability, continuity, and an acceptable work environment. The physical and mental health and safety of employees are key parts of this interface. The Occupational Safety and Health Act of 1970 (OSHA) has caused concern in the health and safety management aspect of this interface. Finally, the maintenance interface is concerned with personnel coordination and personnel records and research. In addition to developing and implementing policies, managers must communicate with employees and keep abreast of the state of the personnel activities in their organizations. These aspects of the maintenance interface are presented and discussed in Chapters 15, 16, and 17.

Union interface.   The *union interface* is considered last because the union is an organized, semi-external force which influences the organization, the personnel unit, managers, and all of the other interfaces. An understanding of this interface requires an overview of the development of an organized labor movement in the United States, the current state of unions, and the international dimension of unions.

The prime union/organization interface occurs at two levels. One interface with unions at the formal organizational level of the company is formed when the union becomes the agent representing the organization's employees. Once an organization is unionized, a contract must develop through union/organization discussions and collective bargaining in which behavioral considerations play a vital role. At another level, the on-going union/organization relationship focuses on settling disputes and grievances which arise during the labor agreement. Because effective union relations may play a significant role in the management of human resources, a discussion of unions is vital to understanding this aspect of personnel management. The union interface is discussed in Chapters 18 and 19.

Can you briefly identify the seven interfaces?

The final chapter "Emerging Directions in Personnel," examines some of the emerging characteristics and challenges of personnel management. The need for professional managers to deal with personnel activities is highlighted and examined. Also, some future concerns in each of the above interfaces are discussed.

PERSONNEL ACTIVITIES: A SURVEY

A cost or budget analysis can reveal the relative degree of responsibility for various activities that a specialized personnel department holds within the total organization. If a firm assigns costs to an activity, then the percentage of costs assigned to the personnel unit may be one means of measuring the extent of that unit's involvement in the organization.

A 1977 survey of 240 organizations with a total of 347,478 employees, taken by the American Society for Personnel Administration and the Bureau of National Affairs, collected data on the relative allocation of the cost of the various personnel activities between the personnel unit and the rest of the organization. Figure 1–8 shows a comparison of these personnel unit costs by size and industry.

In the survey, almost half the organizations are manufacturing firms, one-third are nonmanufacturing companies, and the remaining 16 percent are health care, education, and government organizations. The survey shows that the typical personnel department has one employee for every 100 employees on the company payroll.

Figure 1–8 indicates the personnel record keeping and Equal Employment Opportunity and affirmative action activities in which the personnel unit has some or full responsibility. At least 90 percent of the surveyed organizations include insurance benefits, recruiting, hiring, orientation for new employees, discipline, wage and salary administration, and promotion, transfer, and separation in the personnel department.

The survey also demonstrates clearly that what is as important as *who* does these activities is that they do get done. That is, of course, the thrust of this book. For certain activities the personnel department in smaller

FIGURE 1–8   Comparison of personnel activities by industry and company size.

% of Companies with All or Some Costs Allocated to Personnel Department

Activity	All Companies (N = 227)	Type of Industry			Number of Employees			
		Mfg. (N = 117)	Nonmfg. (N = 76)	Nonbus. (N = 34)	Up to 249 (N = 33)	250-499 (N = 57)	500-999 (N = 61)	1,000 or more (N = 76)
Personnel records and reports	99	99	100	100	100	99	100	100
EEO/affirmative action	95	95	99	92	88	96	96	98
Insurance benefits administration	95	94	99	94	97	89	98	97
Recruiting/hiring	92	92	91	97	88	88	93	96
New employee orientation	92	93	89	95	82	89	97	93
Employee relations/discipline	92	92	90	94	94	90	95	90
Wage and salary administration	92	92	96	89	85	89	97	95
Promotion/transfer/separation procedures	91	89	92	100	85	86	95	96
Employee communications	88	88	89	85	84	81	90	92
Pension plan administration	87	84	92	89	91	74	93	91
Personnel research	86	81	93	91	73	79	92	94
Vacation/leave procedures	85	84	84	88	88	80	86	86
Health and medical services	79	86	79	59	85	74	84	79
Performance evaluation	78	71	82	92	66	76	82	80
Supervisory training	78	73	85	79	63	72	84	84
Recreation/social/recognition programs	77	77	84	59	81	70	79	77
Management development	76	71	83	76	63	65	80	85
Community relations/fund drives	74	85	71	45	78	77	77	68
Counseling programs	71	74	70	64	73	70	76	67
Pre-employment testing	70	65	74	83	59	58	74	82
Safety programs	69	81	58	56	82	72	69	63
Human resource planning	66	63	76	53	54	61	66	75
College recruiting	63	59	70	62	45	61	59	75
Tuition aid/scholarships	61	64	61	56	60	56	55	70
Executive compensation	57	50	67	59	42	44	67	66
Union/labor relations	56	63	43	62	36	60	54	63
Management appraisal/MBO	54	52	54	59	42	55	49	62
Skill training	51	50	59	39	39	42	49	64
Food services	41	58	33	3	36	42	39	45
Payroll processing	40	30	57	38	39	42	44	36
Suggestion systems	39	36	44	36	36	37	41	40
Security/plant protection	32	45	22	3	48	30	27	28
Administrative services (mail, messenger, etc.)	20	28	14	6	33	23	20	12

(Source: ASPA = BNA survey "Personnel Activities, Budgets and Staffs: Preliminary Data," *Bulletin to Management* #33, December 8, 1977, p. 3. Used with permission.)

organizations is less likely to be involved, and one can assume that if they are being done, other managers are doing some of them. In conclusion, the survey reinforces the importance of viewing personnel management using the interface approach.

REVIEW AND PREVIEW

The objectives of this chapter are to provide an examination and definition of personnel management and to present a brief overview of the personnel interfaces. The effective management of human resources is absolutely necessary for an organization to continue and grow. The prime mission of personnel management is the effective use of, and adaptation to, people in all types of organizations—business firms, hospitals, governmental entities, and others. Therefore, a workable accommodation between the organizational necessities of productivity and coordination and the employees' needs and goals must be developed.

Conflicting views about the essence of personnel management have been advanced and examined. The three sets of different viewpoints discussed in this chapter focus on separate aspects of personnel management. These divergent views can be reconciled by emphasizing that personnel management is a *set of activities* which must be performed if people are to accomplish work in modern organizations.

The theme of this chapter and this book is effective management of the interfaces, or points of contact, between personnel specialists and the management group. This theme is reflected in the definition of personnel management as the effective use of human resources in an organization through the management of people-related activities. Seven interface activities form the core of personnel management: *work analysis, staffing, training and development, appraisal, compensation, maintenance,* and *unions.*

Before turning to the individual interfaces, personnel management should be placed in an organizational context. Chapter 2 provides this organizational perspective.

Review Questions

1. Each set of differing viewpoints on personnel is concerned with a slightly different aspect of personnel management. What are the three sets and with what is each concerned?
2. Define personnel management and explain how the three sets of differing viewpoints can be reconciled into your definition.
3. What are the seven personnel interfaces and what is the nature of each?

OPENING CASE FOLLOW-UP

This case illustrates how the differing views can actually occur and how a misperception of personnel management can cause problems. The vice-president of manufacturing is working from a narrow functional view of personnel. On the other hand, the vice-president of personnel appears to have a somewhat different view of personnel. Since safety is related to production efficiency, the vice-president of manufacturing has some valid reasons for his view. Also, safety does have some "people" dimensions and the vice-president of personnel probably feels that the personnel manager should have the responsibility for safety activities.

What has been overlooked is that the safety activity must be handled by someone and coordinated effort is necessary. All parties involved need to focus on the *activity* and who can best perform the various components of a good safety effort. Unless the personnel manager can generate that form of cooperation and understanding, continued confusion and ambiguity are likely to continue, to the overall detriment of the organization. There is no "right" answer as to who should always do these things. But *someone* must.

Case: Phillips Furniture

In 1969, Mr. Albert Phillips opened his own retail store and sold unpainted furniture. His store was located in Lakeside, a small city in the southeastern part of the United States. Although his business was somewhat slow at first, it grew steadily.

Many more sales, stock, and clerical personnel were hired. However, it soon became evident that Mr. Phillips was not able to effectively service all of his customers. Warehouse space was also badly needed.

Phillips Furniture Store was situated in a central location, and Mr. Phillips was hesitant about relocating. As an alternative to relocating, Mr. Phillips opened a satellite store in an outlying district to attract a new source of customers, as well as to provide better service to his current customers. Mr. Phillips eventually expanded his business into several neighboring towns until he had a total of six stores. When Martin Furniture, a small manufacturing firm which supplied some of the furniture for Phillips, became financially unstable, Mr. Phillips was able to gain control of the manufacturing plant.

At the end of last week, you were called into Mr. Phillips' office, and Mr. Phillips said, "_____ (Your name), I have been pleased with your progress with us as a management trainee since you graduated six months ago." He explained that he felt that the company had gotten large enough to need a personnel manager. Previously, all managers handled most of their own personnel activities, usually on a "casual" basis. Mr. Phillips told you that with the acquisition of the manufacturing firm, "It's time for us to get our personnel activities organized, and you're the person to do it."

When asked why, he said, "I reviewed your personnel file and noticed you had a course in personnel management listed on your transcript." Faced with both the challenge and the promotion, you accepted. Now you are trying to decide "What am I, now that I'm a personnel manager?"

QUESTIONS

1. How would the interface concept help you in defining your role at Phillips Furniture?
2. On what activities would you tell Mr. Phillips you intend to focus? Why?
3. What would be your first actions, and why?

Notes

1. Fred Foulkes and H. M. Morgan, "Organizing and Staffing the Personnel Function," *Harvard Business Review* (May-June, 1977), pp. 143–144.

2. Dalton E. McFarland, *Cooperation and Conflict in Personnel Administration,* (New York: American Foundation for Management Research, 1962), p. 48.

3. Stephen J. Carroll, "Graduate Student Attitudes toward Personnel Management and the Future Development of the Field," *Academy of Management Proceedings,* 32nd Annual Meeting (Boston: August 13–16, 1972), p. 232.

4. Keith B. Krinke and Jerome M. Nelson, "Five Steps For Handling Contract Grievances," *Supervisory Management* (September 1977), pp. 14–20.

5. George Strauss, "Organizational Behavior and Personnel Relations," in *A Review of Industrial Relations Research,* Vol. I (Madison, Wis.: Industrial Relations Research Association, 1971), p. 14.

6. Herbert E. Meyer, "Personnel Directors are the New Corporate Heroes," *Fortune* (February 1976).

chapter 2

The Organization and Personnel

When you have read this chapter, you should be able to:

1. Define organization and describe why an organization should be viewed as an open system.

2. Name the four organizational subsystems and discuss how they are interrelated.

3. Define and discuss the concepts of authority and line-staff.

4. Describe personnel's role in organizations.

5. Discuss how personnel's role is affected by varied organizational environments.

Succeed, Grow?

In 1974, Frances Marvin faced a crisis in her life. Her husband died unexpectedly of a heart attack, and Frances had to decide what to do about the successful business her husband operated in Massachusetts: Marvin Pipe Fabricators (MPF). At the age of 47, Frances, with little previous work experience, decided to try to run MPF. Fortunately for Frances a strong organization existed at MPF, and with the help of some devoted employees, Frances has led MPF to several profitable years of operation.

A crucial business decision faces Frances now. Demand for the firm's pipe products has grown to the point that demand exceeds MPF's ability to supply goods. Her sales manager just returned from Central America where additional raw materials can be purchased. Further, the government of Mexico is willing to make low-cost loans if MPF will build a new plant there. Pipe at that plant could be produced and shipped to the United States for 8 percent to 10 percent less than the pipe produced at MPF's current plant.

However, such a drastic expansion would mean a drastically revised organization for Frances, the transfer of six to eight top managers who would have to be replaced at the main plant, and numerous other "headaches." Frances faces decisions both about personnel and about the nature of her organization.

Managing human resources is a part of every managerial job in every organizational unit. Personnel activities typically performed by managers include appraising people's performance, designing jobs, and orienting and training employees. Managers in all types of organizations—business, government, military, nonprofit, and others—need a working knowledge of personnel management. Because personnel management takes place in organizations, an understanding of the nature of organizations is necessary to analyze its role, even though the role of a personnel unit may vary from organization to organization.

THE ORGANIZATION

Since prehistoric times, the human need to group together for protection, food, shelter, and companionship has raised the dilemma of organizing group efforts to get work done. Similarly, the associated problems of getting along in large groups or organizations has arisen.

Anthropologists note that prehistoric peoples banded together in small family groups and tribes for mutual assistance and protection. From this simple beginning an organizational system developed, sometimes based on physical strength, religious ideas, family, age factors, or sex. Men commonly hunted; women usually reared the children and took care of household chores. The level of coordination required to meet most daily needs was simple. As the complexity of work tasks increased, problems of organizing to accomplish new goals grew. Personnel problems associated with the processes of organizing and managing people to get work done accompanied the development and expansion of organizations.

Organization Defined

An ORGANIZATION is a set of stable social relations deliberately created with the intention of accomplishing some goal or purpose, generally existing with an authority structure, and influenced considerably by its technology and the environment in which it operates.

This definition does not include spur-of-the-moment social arrangements with short-term purposes, such as a group of passengers trapped in a bus in a snowstorm who must reach safety to survive. That is not an organization as defined here.

To move toward organizational goals, the coordination of the activities of a number of people is necessary. Some means must be developed to divide the work. Also, members of the organization must accept guidance by certain other members to realize the benefits of coordination. Applying the above ideas: a hospital is an organization attempting to provide health care through the combined efforts of administrators, doctors, nurses, and technicians. Administrators primarily act to direct and coordinate the efforts of the hospital employees. An organizational structure is established by staffing a hospital with an administrator, director of nursing, director of housekeeping, and chief surgeon to guide the hospital's efforts to provide quality health care. The number of beds and the type of laboratory and X-ray equipment also affect the overall organization and operation of the hospital.

What is an "organization"?

Organizations as Systems

Many approaches have been used in the past to try to understand organizations and how they operate, but change has taken place in the study of organizations. At one time, they were thought of in terms of a "universal organizational design," complete with a set of principles. The rational approach discussed in Chapter 1 was of this type. Those ideas have generally been combined under the title of "Classical Organization Theory."

Until the early 1960s, organizations were usually viewed as closed systems, which corresponds to classical organization theories. Environmental effects on the organization were minimized, so organizational analysis was oversimplified and focused primarily on processes within the organization.

Classical theory is criticized for being too restrictive and inadequate, considering the type of organization and the environment in which a modern organization operates. The current trend in organization design is to build the organization to fit the situation, so that the organization can deal successfully with its environment. Some of the rationalist "principles" may apply and some may not, depending on the circumstances. No one universal organizational design will fit all situations. As an example, in some manufacturing firms a quality-control inspector reports to the plant manager. In others, quality control may not be a separate job because employees check the quality of their own work.

Systems Approach.   The systems approach is currently popular because it provides a useful way to emphasize the whole organization and the interrelationships of its parts. The major implication of the systems approach is that an organization must be examined as a whole, including its parts or "subsystems," and as a part of the environment around it. For example, a public university is a system with subsystems (colleges of business, arts, engineering, etc.) and is part of a state system including other public universities in the state. Combining the subsystems or parts (the various colleges) creates the university as a whole.

System Components.   Regardless of size, purpose, or makeup, a system, whether biological, such as the human body, or social, such as a business organization, has four major components: *inputs, transformation processor, outputs, and feedback.*[1] Figure 2–1 shows the relationship of these components to each other and the organization as it might apply to a bank.

Open Systems.   In the concept of the systems approach, the organization is an open system, or a "living" entity which takes energy from its environment, processes it, and returns outputs to the environment. In other words, it is a "Transformation system" which changes inputs into outputs.

Basically, the difference between an open system and a closed system is that the open system affects and is affected by its environment. The closed system tries to operate as a self-contained unit with little regard for its environment. Note in Figure 2–1 some examples of external forces that affect the internal operations of a bank.

FIGURE 2–1 Simple bank system and its components.

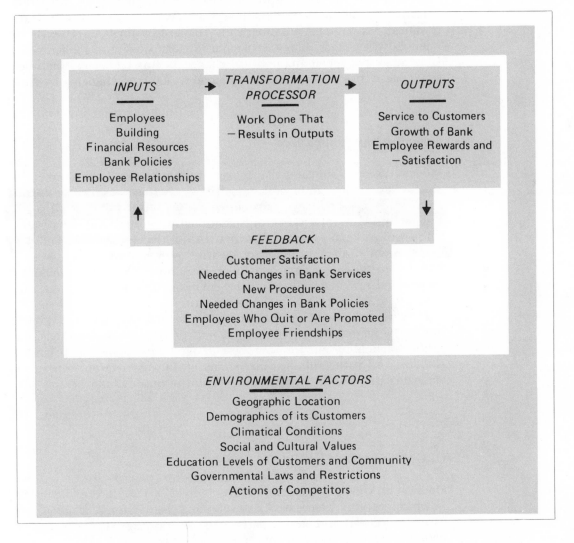

It is important to realize that as an open system, the organization is continually dependent upon inputs from the environment. Too much managerial concern with the internal aspects of an organization, such as coordination, control, or job design, ignores the system's relation to its environment. This nearsightedness may be fatal to the existence of the organization. For example, a bank that does not consider a free checking account plan offered by another bank may lose customers.

The most important argument for an open systems approach to studying organizations is the increasingly complicated and unstable environment in which most organizations exist. For example, the passage of laws on equal employment opportunities (EEO) and occupational safety and health (OSHA) has had significant impact on how organizations operate. Selection and promotion of employees and working conditions in many organizations have been dramatically changed by these laws. With the rapid growth of technology, geographical expansions into foreign countries, and rapid social and political change, organizations and their personnel activities are constantly pressured to adjust to changing environments.

Organizations Summarized

Modern research indicates that recognizing the external environment is crucial in designing an organization. The systems approach suggests that an organization is (1) part of a larger system and (2) a whole comprised of subsystems—the total set of organizational parts constitutes a system. The organizational system takes inputs from the environment and processes them through technology into an output. This output is then returned to the larger environment. For example, a business firm takes money and raw materials from the environment and turns them into products to sell back to the environment.

How to best design organizations is dependent upon analyzing a number of factors. When viewing organizations in a systems mode, the futility of holding out for "one best design" becomes evident. Understanding the nature of the subsystems of an organization is basic to analyzing the internal operation of the entire organization.

Why view an organization as an open system?

ORGANIZATIONAL SUBSYSTEMS

One way to view an organization is as a "lively set" of interrelated parts in which everything feeds back on everything else.[2] Figure 2–2 shows four variables that are interacting parts of an organization. The interrelated nature of the four components, indicated by the arrows, shows that a change in one of the variables can result in a change in any or all of the others.

In this model, *task* refers to the work individuals do, that is, their jobs. *Technology* is the sum of the methods (machines, processes, ideas about production) used to get the work done. *Structure* is the way the organization is put together to get work done. *People* obviously are the part which brings the rest of the model together—the human spark for the organization. And the entire organization must always consider the demands of the environment in which it exists.

This model reflects the view that an organization is a dynamically linked whole, not just a collection of parts. A manager may be able to

FIGURE 2–2 Organizational subsystems.

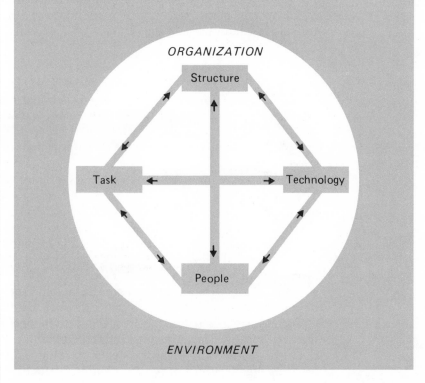

(Source: Adapted from Harold J. Leavitt, *Managerial Psychology*, 3d ed. (Chicago: University of Chicago Press, 1972), p. 264. Copyright University of Chicago Press. Used with permission.)

change any of the four variables but must realize that all components are interrelated. Because of this, changes in one part will probably affect the other three.

For example, as adjustments in technology are made, other portions of the organization may need to be restructured or realigned. Consider the payroll department at Coastal Petroleum Company when a computer was brought in for the first time to process payroll. First, people had to be trained. New specialists were hired, which resulted in new social groupings—new car pools, lunch groups, and so on. The tasks changed because an interaction with the computer was now required. New facilities were needed to accommodate more equipment. In addition, the technology an organization uses can determine the structure that will be most effective. As an organization increases in size a new layer of management may be needed. The structure which worked well with 25 bookkeepers may not work well with the new computer staff.

Managers must be aware of some basic considerations within each of the four variables of technology, structure, people, and tasks. The variables of structure and technology are discussed in separate sections in this chapter. The people variable is the focus of Chapter 3 and the task variable is examined in Chapter 6.

Technology

The technology used by an organization is broader than just machines. One definition of technology is "the types and patterns of activity, equipment and material, and knowledge or experience used to perform tasks."[3] Figure 2–3 illustrates the parts of this definition of technology in a food store.

Technology can affect the shape and complexity of an organization. The technology needed to package a deodorant spray is different than the technology required to manufacture color televisions. More time, money, parts, and machines are needed to make a color television. Changes in tasks or products may require considerable expenditures to change the technology used. However, refusal to keep up with technological changes may hurt the success of an entire organization. The plight of the U.S. steel industry, with its many obsolete or old factories, illustrates the importance of keeping up with technological advances.

Technology also requires both specialized manpower, which results in the need for more organization, and more planning. The overall result is the increased need for organizations to do what individuals alone cannot do; thus organizations grow and require a structure.

Structure

Structure in an organization serves the same purpose as the skeleton does for the human body; to hold it together to function well.

Just as the human skeleton has various sizes of bones, an organization

FIGURE 2–3   Technology.

Components	Food Store Example
Type of activity	Shelf stocking, bottle refunding
Patterns of activity	Store layout, check-out lines
Equipment	Carts, cash registers
Materials	Sacks, groceries
Special knowledges	Meat cutting
and experiences	Produce buying

is composed of structural units, such as divisions and departments. In any organization there is a cohesive force, which is exhibited as "company policy," "group will," or "organizational mind." This force helps to overcome the differences among individuals and groups within the larger organization. An example of such cohesiveness is found in police department cutbacks experienced in some cities where some officers are willing to work some days without pay or work fewer days in order to reduce layoffs.

Structural Growth.   **All organizations have structure.** The growth of an organization's structure generally begins when a very small organization adds more people. Suppose an individual has an idea: stores carrying merchandise selling for 5¢ and 10¢. The stores are enthusiastically received and the entrepreneur must eventually move to a larger building, hire more employees, and open new stores. Soon the founder becomes overburdened because it is impossible for one person to direct effectively all of the stores. The entrepreneur must get organized! Figure 2–4 contains a brief story of such an entrepreneur—Frank W. Woolworth. Eventually conditions may be such that more managers must be hired to manage the additional stores. Thus, some sort of division of duties begins.

Organizations "coordinate" the efforts of human resources by placing some direction on people's behaviors. Whenever two or more people get together—for any purpose—some form of hierarchy is born in that group.

Structure is often based upon real or assumed differences in the abilities and contributions of individual members to achieve the groups goals. With the development and recognition of someone "in charge," a group's or organization's hierarchy is established. Thus, the foundation of an organizational structure based upon formal authority is laid.

What are the four organizational subsystems, and how are they related?

FIGURE 2–4   Frank W. Woolworth

> Frank W. Woolworth, founder of the world's most famous five-and-ten-cent stores, once indicated that the turning point in his career came when he suffered a breakdown that confined him to a hospital. "Before that," he said, "although I had several stores, I felt it was up to me to do everything myself. I was sure that there was nothing I couldn't do better than any of my employees—even dressing windows and opening boxes of merchandise. During my long absence, I found things had gone along quite well. After that, I changed my tactics, I let others attend to the ordinary running of the business and devoted myself to working out plans for expansion—and we made much greater progress."

(Source: Forbes, February 6, 1978, p. 95.)

Authority

> AUTHORITY is defined as the right to use resources to accomplish goals.

This right can be derived in two ways: through *formal* designation or through *informal* designation. Formal authority exists originally in the governing body of an organization. For example, if the organization is a corporation, ultimately the stockholders hold formal authority for making decisions. However, this formal authority is delegated to the board of directors and the president, who then delegates some of this authority to various vice-presidents, who in turn delegate authority to operating managers, and so on. Figure 2–5 illustrates a variety of organizational authority structures.

A manager attains formal authority by accepting a position as a manager. Unquestionably, when Carolyn Carter agrees to become manager of the accounting department, she acquires the right to direct it. It is even possible under certain circumstances for her to fire anyone who will not accept her formal authority. Although this action seems rather harsh, it may be a weak alternative in many situations. Even in military organizations where absolute authority and right to command have traditionally been a basis for issuing orders, there is a growing recognition that formal authority and commands are not the only ways to guide people.

FIGURE 2–5 Organizational hierarchies.

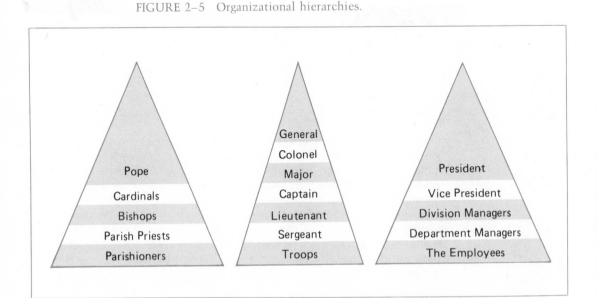

Informal authority is a concept often used along with formal authority in describing leadership. The idea is that the right to direct resources is given by followers. Instead of having a formally designated position, an "authority figure" emerges from the group or is given authority by subordinates. This dimension of authority is explored in some depth in Chapter 3 in the discussion on leadership.

Line and Staff

A distinction can be made between two types of formal authority. The traditional distinction between "line" and "staff" refers not only to differences in formal authority, but differences in types of work as well. *Line authority* is usually described as the right of a manager to demand accountability from subordinates for their performance. It includes the right to command subordinates. The *line* is generally considered to be the operating branch of the organization or that portion directly concerned with producing the product or service. *Staff authority* commonly refers to an advisory or supportive relationship. The line part of a university is the faculty, and the athletic and business functions are staff in nature.

In Figure 2–6, the president, the vice-president of operations, and the division plant managers make up the line organization while the others are staff units. Traditionally, staff gives advice, but line managers decide whether or not they will accept the advice offered by staff people.

Typically, line officials consult staff people for their expertise when a decision is to be made. The real authority or influence of a staff department emerges from that department's ability to make worthwhile and significant contributions to solving the problems facing line people. A staff department that can provide useful advice or service to the line departments may soon do more than just advise. For example, a staff legal department may actually begin to make decisions on legal matters for a company president.

How are line and staff authority different?

Personnel's Role in Organizations

Personnel management is often considered a staff function. As a functional part of the organization, personnel activities are localized into one department. In Figure 2–6, note that personnel is a separate specialized department. However, the authors of this text feel that personnel management is a set of activities which cannot be neatly segmented into one department.

The personnel department has normally been considered a staff department, but the distinction is becoming more clouded. In some organi-

FIGURE 2–6   Line and staff authority on an organizational chart.

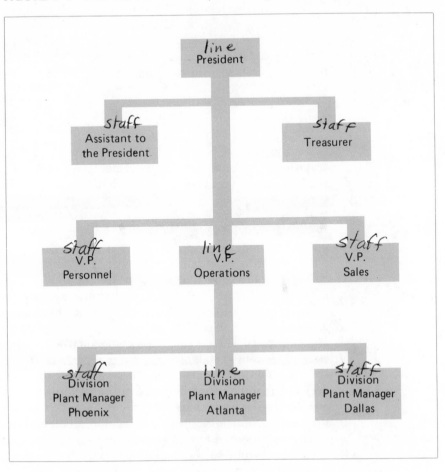

zations certain duties, often considered line in nature, have been delegated to the personnel department. For example, hiring management trainees to work in the line organization could be considered a line activity because the success of hiring directly affects future operations. However, hiring is very often done by the personnel department. This delegation of some line authority to a staff department is neither unusual nor a problem as long as both sides agree on who is to do what, as emphasized in the first chapter. However, line managers and personnel specialists do not always agree on exactly what the role of the personnel specialists should be.

In one study, a group of personnel executives and a group of line managers from different organizations were asked to rank the importance of a list of activities that the personnel department could perform in their organizations.[4] The results are interesting. As Figure 2–7 shows, there is considerable disagreement between the personnel executives and line

FIGURE 2–7   Ranking of personnel's roles

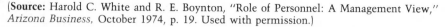

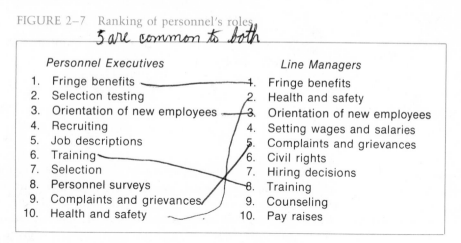

5 are common to both

Personnel Executives	Line Managers
1. Fringe benefits	1. Fringe benefits
2. Selection testing	2. Health and safety
3. Orientation of new employees	3. Orientation of new employees
4. Recruiting	4. Setting wages and salaries
5. Job descriptions	5. Complaints and grievances
6. Training	6. Civil rights
7. Selection	7. Hiring decisions
8. Personnel surveys	8. Training
9. Complaints and grievances	9. Counseling
10. Health and safety	10. Pay raises

(**Source:** Harold C. White and R. E. Boynton, "Role of Personnel: A Management View," *Arizona Business,* October 1974, p. 19. Used with permission.)

managers on the involvement of the personnel department in certain activities. Of the most important activities ranked by personnel executives, only five are included in the top ten ranked by line managers. These are complaints and grievances, fringe benefits, health and safety, orientation, and training. Setting wages and salaries, civil rights, hiring decisions, counseling, and pay raises were viewed by line managers as important for the personnel department to handle, but the personnel executives ranked these considerably lower.

From this study, it is clear that the "proper" role of personnel has not been agreed upon. Further, it is inappropriate to say that all management people want the personnel unit to perform a given activity. The division of personnel activities obviously depends upon which specific activities are included in the personnel specialists' domain. As pointed out in the first chapter, the degree of each activity performed by specialists varies from company to company. A study such as the one reported here can be done easily in any organization to determine what personnel specialists and other managers think the ideal division of duties should be. To compound the difficulty in identifying "the proper role" of personnel, consider the wide variety of organizational settings in which personnel activities occur.

Where does personnel "fit" in the organization?

PERSONNEL IN VARIED ORGANIZATIONAL ENVIRONMENTS

Personnel activities are managed in a wide range of organizations facing widely varied environments. Personnel management in three environments have grown in importance: (1) *public organizations,* (2) *interna-*

tional organizations, and (3) *matrix organizations*. These three were selected because they illustrate the expanding nature of personnel in organizations today. Growth in each of these areas creates special problems and challenges that need to be considered when viewing personnel management.

Personnel in Public Organizations

Even though a slightly different environment exists in the public sector, personnel activities must be managed if effective utilization of human resources is to occur. Building on the U.S. Civil Service System, established in the 1880s to reduce patronage and favoritism in the selection of governmental employees, many state and local governmental bodies have established "merit systems" and formal personnel policies and procedures. The head of the U.S. Civil Service System commented that such a system "is trying to create and maintain a personnel management system while simultaneously protecting employees from abuses in the system."[5]

Increasingly in the late 1970s, complaints are being voiced about governmental personnel systems at all levels. The rules and regulations developed to protect governmental employees are being criticized for preventing flexibility in the management of public organizations. However, as a personnel manager for Los Angeles indicated, "Public personnel management is experiencing the same stress and strain that is being felt in other sectors of our society."[6]

Some of the challenges facing public organizations focus on personnel activities. Specifically, concerns to be dealt with include: (1) quality of working life, (2) executive development, (3) new systems for determining pay, (4) attracting and rewarding experienced managers, (5) controlling employee retirement costs, (6) assuring equal employment opportunity for all, and (7) improving the collective bargaining process in the public sector.[7]

Those personnel specialists who will be dealing with those challenges are not significantly different from private personnel directors. A study of the characteristics of public personnel directors in Iowa found great similarities with those in the private sector. The public sector directors tended to have more education but less experience than their private counterparts.[8]

Personnel professionals in public organizations must be able to translate their expertise into creative solutions to problems faced by public agencies. Likewise, other managers in public organizations need to recognize the importance of effective personnel administration on the success of their agencies. The manager of a group of welfare claims clerks might use the expertise of personnel specialists to increase effectiveness in the claims office and thereby provide better service to welfare claimants and taxpayers alike.

Personnel in International Environments

More personnel specialists and operating managers in the 1980s may manage in many countries outside of the United States. The growth of the American-based multinational corporation (MNC) typifies the importance of viewing an organization as a system affected by environmental factors such as culture, language, climate, politics, and social upheavals. The importance of international awareness is illustrated when one considers that a firm such as Gillette obtains a large percentage of its sales and profits overseas.

The character of personnel activities varies significantly according to the location of the company. Some countries, such as Zambia and Japan, expect top management positions to be filled by executives from those countries. Other countries have requirements on the percentage of jobs which may be filled by foreigners. U.S. citizens who transfer to Saudi Arabia, for example, must adjust to cultural and religious codes on the role of women, the prohibition of liquor, and many other factors.

One study of multinational staffing policies revealed that a variety of other problems exist. Some of the personnel problems identified include: (1) blocking of promotions by reserving certain slots for host-country nationals, (2) anxiety caused by transfers and adjusting to a different setting, (3) using inappropriate decision making styles which do not fit cultural norms.[9]

To illustrate how some personnel activities are complicated in the international area, consider the information labeled in Figure 2–8 below. A study of 33 multinational corporations revealed that the basis for selecting American employees for overseas assignments "will vary from culture to culture, from job to job, and from location to location, even within the same country."[10] Women almost never are transferred overseas because of cultural values. In the interview process spouses and

FIGURE 2–8   Foreign service orientation programs by number of U.S. expatriates employed.

Total No. Companies Reporting	No. of U.S. Expatriates Low	High	Companies with Formal Orientation Programs	Companies with Pretransfer Visits Abroad	Companies Using Outside Consultants	Companies Requiring Language Training
11	101	1400	9	2	6	4
11	35	100	3	6	3	6
11	11	34	3	2	2	6
33			15	10	11	16

(Source: Burton W. Teague, "Transplanting Executives in Foreign Soil," *The Conference Board Record*, September 1976, pp. 42–45.)

children are often interviewed also to determine if a manager's family can adjust to a foreign environment.

Compensation can be a significant problem also, especially if overseas living costs are significantly higher than in the United States. For example, the cost of living in Tokyo is much above comparable costs in most U.S. cities. A decision must be made as to how to adjust a person's salary to compensate. Also, should a firm reduce the pay of someone who is transferred from overseas to the United States or Canada?

Tax laws may be an important factor. A 1976 amendment to the U.S. Tax Code has an important impact on the tax bill for U.S. citizens working overseas. Prior to 1977, U.S. citizens employed in foreign countries could exclude up to $25,000 of income from U.S. taxes and reduce their U.S. tax bill by deducting all foreign income taxes. Beginning in 1977 only $15,000 of income can be excluded, and foreign taxes may not be deducted from U.S. taxes due. Further, if a firm reimburses an employee for housing or schools, that payment is considered an income. The result of this change has had a significant impact on the number of U.S. citizens abroad.[11]

Orientation programs and language training may be offered and required by multinational firms. Many times spouses and older children will participate in these programs.

An additional problem is the promotion and transfer of foreign citizens to positions in the United States. Special training to ease the adjustment of foreign managers and their families may be required. The acceptance of a foreign boss by a U.S. worker is another concern.

The above information suggests personnel activities must be changed to deal with the demands of an international organization. As more and more firms engage in cross-national trade, managing personnel activities in an intercultural environment will be of increasing importance.

Personnel in Matrix Organizations

A new, nontraditional form of organization, the *matrix organization*, offers a different environment for personnel management. In a matrix organization two organization structures exist at the same time—a conventional functional organization and a "project team" oriented organization. The result of the overlay of the project teams on the conventional structure is a grid or "matrix." The project teams are created and dissolved as the situation demands. People may join a project team for a certain project, retain their position in the conventional organization, and return full time to it when the project is completed. A project manager is in charge of the team which draws expertise from wherever he/she finds it in the organization.

Starting in the defense and aerospace industries, the matrix organization form has spread to many other areas. Industrial firms using a matrix format in some or all areas of operation include Dow Corning, TRW Systems, General Electric, Equitable Life Insurance, Shell Oil, and Citicorp—a large New York bank holding company.[12] Nonindustrial users include CPA firms, hospitals, real estate development companies, law firms, and various governmental agencies.[13]

Figure 2–9 illustrates how two management groups can be established

FIGURE 2–9 Matrix organization.

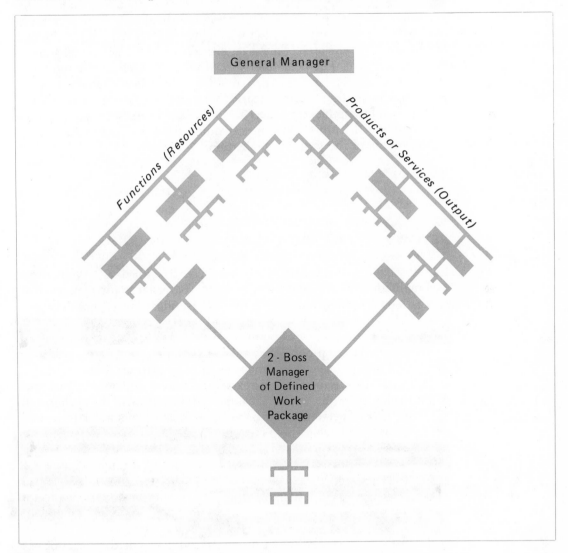

(Source: Stanley M. Davis and Paul R. Lawrence, *Matrix*. (Reading, Mass.: Addison-Wesley Publishing, 1977).)

in a matrix organization.[14] The resources side of the diamond represents the typical functional approach. (Specialized departments in personnel, marketing production, and finance, exist.) The right side of the diamond represents various special groups or consumers. The bottom of the diamond is the project manager who is responsible for compiling all needed resources from the left side to work on a distinct product, project, or service for markets identified on the right.

The ultimate result of such a format is that a functional personnel specialist may report to two bosses—the director of the personnel function and the product manager. The personnel specialist is responsible for coordination of all personnel activities performed on the project. As is evident, the potential for conflict is heightened, especially if the director of personnel and the project manager disagree on how a personnel activity is to be managed. The personnel specialist may be left in the middle of such a conflict. Recognition that conflict is possible makes it especially important to manage the organizational interface between the functional manager and the project manager so that needed personnel activities are performed on the project, but in a manner that considers the personnel requirements of the entire organization.

Can you discuss personnel in several organizational environments?

REVIEW AND PREVIEW

In this chapter, the organization has been described as a vehicle for accomplishing cooperative human efforts. Basic ideas for managing organizations have evolved and many of these ideas are still widely used today. Currently the most useful way to view each organization is as an open system. From this viewpoint the emphasis is placed on the need for including the environment, technology, structure, people, and tasks to determine how to design and manage an organization.

One important issue for this text is the role of personnel. Questions about the nature of the work to be done and the nature of the authority to be given to the personnel unit are often raised. Personnel is usually described as a staff department, but there is little agreement between line managers and personnel managers as to exactly what activities should be directed by the personnel department. To avoid this confusion, personnel management should be viewed as an interface between the personnel unit and the other parts of an organization. Therefore, personnel management is a group of activities which must be done, and should be done by the organizational unit which can best do them.

Because the management of human resources is at the heart of personnel, the basics of human behavior in an organizational context must be considered. Every manager needs some basic understanding about why people behave as they do. Motivation, leadership, group behavior, and communications are the basics of human behavior discussed in the next chapter.

Review Questions

1. What is an organization? Why must organizations be defined as open systems?
2. Identify the four organizational subsystems. What is the concern of each subsystem?
3. What is authority? What are the concepts of line and staff? How do these ideas relate to personnel management?
4. Why should personnel be seen as an organizational interface? How does this view help understand personnel's role in varied organizational environments?

OPENING CASE FOLLOW-UP

The importance of viewing an organization as an open system is highlighted in the case of Frances Marvin. External factors are a major concern of MPF. Expansion to Mexico would place new demands on Frances and her management team because the firm would be dealing with a new culture and a two plant situation at the same time.

The organization structure would face realignment and new reporting relationships would be required. The problems of transferring key people to an international operation must be considered. Likewise, the need to recruit and select additional managers in a short period of time must be considered. In sum, Frances faces personnel decisions that could "make or break" the company.

Case: Credit Service Company

Harold Stanley started Credit Service Company about three years ago. The company is a data processing service bureau that primarily handles charge account billings, charge card production, and credit record processing. The firm started small but has now grown to have 75 employees. Harold has done all of the recruiting and selection since the firm began. Most of the personnel activities had been handled on a very informal and haphazard basis by Mr. Stanley or the supervisors. Because of the time pressures and the many other demands on him, Harold hired Sam Ford, a recent college graduate, as the firm's first personnel manager.

Sam was determined to set up a true personnel department. Since the firm has grown rapidly, Sam could see that the firm would probably have to add 75 to 100 more employees over the next two years to keep up with the projected sales increase. Within a short period of time Sam had redesigned the application blank and had established a personnel file for each employee. He discovered that the firm had many women employees but no female supervisors. Also, there was a noticeable lack of any employees from racial minorities. Therefore, Sam developed a detailed plan to head off potential equal employment problems. He also developed a revised selection procedure in which he did most of the selection interviewing.

Mr. Stanley voiced support for Sam's selection efforts. However, he was very adamant that he wanted to be able to have the final say over any new employee hired. Also, Mr. Stanley voiced strong feelings about the government telling him who he could hire or not hire. As he said, "I'll hire whoever I damn well please." Sam was quite concerned by this reaction, since it looked as if he was not going to be given the flexibility he needed to do what he felt should be done.

QUESTIONS

1. Discuss why it is important to look at Credit Service Company as an open system.
2. Identify the authority and structural problems that exist.
3. If you were Sam, how would you proceed in trying to implement your plans?

Notes

1. Adapted from a conceptual framework in John A. Seiler, *Systems Analysis in Organizational Behavior* (Homewood, Ill.: Dorsey Press–Richard D. Irwin, 1967).

2. Harold J. Leavitt, *Managerial Psychology*, 3rd Ed. (Chicago: University of Chicago Press, 1972), p. 262.

3. David F. Gillespie and Dennis S. Mileti, "Technology and the Study of Organizations: An Overview and Appraisal," *The Academy of Management Review*, **2** (January 1977), p. 8.

4. H. C. White and R. E. Boynton, "Role of Personnel: A Management View," *Arizona Business* (October 1974), p. 19.

5. "Interview with Alan Campbell, Chairman, U.S. Civil Service Commission," *U.S. News and World Report*, October 3, 1977, p. 28.

6. Muriel M. Morse, "We've Come a Long Way," *Public Personnel Management* (July-August 1976), p. 221.

7. Elmer B. Staats, "Personnel Management: The Starting Place," *Public Personnel Management* (November-December 1976), pp. 434–441.

8. Myron D. Fottler and Norman A. Townsend, "Characteristics of Public and Private Personnel Directors," *Public Personnel Management* (July-August 1977), pp. 250–258.

9. Yoram Zeira and Ehud Harari, "Genuine Multinational Staffing Policy: Expectations and Realities," *Academy of Management Journal*, 20 (June 1977), pp. 327–333.

10. Burton W. Teague, "Transplanting Executives in Foreign Soil," *The Conference Board Record* (September 1976), pp. 42–45.

11. Robert E. Billings and Felix B. Probandt, "Double Tax Jeopardy for Americans Working Abroad," *The Personnel Administrator* (September 1977), pp. 31–38.

12. "How to Stop the Buck Short of the Top," *Business Week*, January 16, 1978, pp. 82–83.

13. Stanley M. Davis and Paul R. Lawrence, *Matrix* (Reading, Mass.: Addison-Wesley Publishing, 1977).

14. *Ibid.*, pp. 21–24.

chapter 3

The Human Resource and Personnel Management

When you have read this chapter, you should be able to:

1. Define motivation and discuss several problems involved in defining and learning about motivation.

2. Identify and discuss four ideas about why people behave as they do.

3. Identify and compare the three major leadership approaches.

4. Define what a work group is and discuss at least four characteristics of groups.

5. List three barriers to successful communication.

Please, C'mon and Follow

About three months ago Leonard Steinberg accepted a position with a medium-sized firm in a town of about 45,000 in the South. Leonard is an Army veteran with four years service in the artillery branch. Even though he received several promotions, he decided to leave the Army and go to school. Leonard completed a degree in general business at Metro Community College in Atlanta, Georgia. Through an uncle who is a banker, Leonard learned of a management position with Wallace's Department Store. His position was as assistant to Mr. Wallace, the 41-year-old son of the founder, who is president.

Because of his interests, Leonard was assigned to the appliance department. This department has had continuing problems, both with sales and service matters. Leonard's enthusiasm soon resulted in his spending long hours, even on Sundays, trying to resolve the administrative problems in the appliance department.

The four salesmen in the appliance department are 50- to 55-, years-old and have grown up with the business. Two of the salesmen are cousins, and one of them is a brother-in-law to one of the others. Because they are all "local boys," and because of the family ties, the salesmen are a very tight-knit group.

When Leonard joined the firm Mr. Wallace told him, "Those four fellows are good employees, but I think they need some leadership to get them revved up and motivated again. They are getting too set in their ways. Your education can be valuable to us as we try to improve our operations."

The men reacted to Leonard by being very reserved and aloof. Whenever he would go out on the sales floor, the salesmen would ignore him. Leonard hoped he could soon win their confidence. However, last Saturday Leonard stepped out of his office for a moment. When he returned, a salesman was in his office, supposedly looking for a new sales book. What happened then is under question. The two versions told to Mr. Wallace went as follows: Leonard feels that the salesman deliberately spilled a cup of coffee all over the desk and the papers on it. The salesman said it was an accident, that he apologized, and that Leonard should not be so touchy. Mr. Wallace is contemplating what to do now.

Many different perspectives are available for studying people at work, ranging from the academician's research on people and their work problems to the practitioner's "practical" approach to solving such problems. Although the difference between these two approaches can be great, advocates of each agree it is important that all managers understand human behavior.

The purpose of this chapter is not to provide the reader with a detailed examination of human behavior—that is best left for a course on organizational behavior. Rather, some of the key considerations in viewing human resources from a behavioral vantage point are highlighted.

Some managers still feel behavioral science concepts and studies are useless because they cannot grasp their relevance. This simply is not true. A tremendous number of scientific studies of human behavior are related to the management of employees. From this research comes a continuing flow of ideas, new approaches to old problems, and new ways to manage people in organizations. The concepts and methodologies of research studies must be interpreted for many practicing managers before being applied to personnel management.

Interpreting and using research insights on human behavior is essential for effective human resource management. The areas of human behavior emphasized here are the concepts of *motivation, leadership, group behavior*, and *communication*.

MOTIVATION

Motivation is concerned with the "whys" rather than the "hows" or "whats" of human behavior. Why did the salesman spill coffee on Leonard's desk? Why did the salesmen shun their new manager? The primary focus of motivation is to explain why people do what they do. Motivation attempts to account for the "drives" or "wants" inside an individual rather than describing the individual's actions or behaviors.

What Is Motivation?

MOTIVATION is derived from the word *motive* and is an emotion or desire operating on a person's will and causing that person to act.

This definition emphasizes that motivation is an action device. People usually act for one reason: to obtain a goal. Thus, motivation is a goal-directed drive, and as such, it seldom occurs in a void. The words "need," "want," "desire," and "drive" are all semantically similar to "motive."

Importance of Motivation

Most managers will agree with the statement that: "The success of any organization is determined by the efforts of the people in it." And, managers often say that problems relating to people's behaviors are the most perplexing. Questions such as the following are often asked: "How do you get people to do what you want them to do?"; "How can one be sure that people will do their work without a supervisor constantly watching them?" Because human resources are a crucial determinant of how well an organization performs, the effective motivation of people to acceptable behavior and performance is necessary.

Approaches to Understanding Motivation

It is often difficult to determine why employees behave as they do simply by observing their behavior. People's actions cannot always be directly related to their conscious or subconscious thoughts. Nor are these actions always related to obvious daily occurrences. For example, if Frank Palmesano has an argument with his supervisor and fails to report to work the next day, it may appear that his behavior is a result of the confrontation. However, that behavior may be motivated by a combination of factors including overwork, family problems, or some other problems.

Multiple causes. Different people may have different reasons for behaving in the very same manner. For example, one manager may join a service club because it is a good place to make business contacts; another may join because of the social environment; still another joins because of the interesting programs and speakers at the club. Thus, three different "whys" can underlie the same behavior, which further complicates inferring motivation from behavior.

Multiple behaviors. In addition, the same motive may result in different behaviors. For example, if Jan Welch wants a promotion, she may work at performing her job exceptionally well. But Bill Proust, who also wants a promotion, might take a different approach. He may try to "apple polish" the boss to get the promotion. Another manager, who also wants the promotion very badly, may be afraid to do anything at all for fear he will fail. The motivation for these three behaviors is the same, but it cannot be determined simply by viewing the behaviors of the three managers.

Motivation information. A basic source for information on motivation is practical experience. A manager who has had experience dealing with people will probably be able to make better personnel management decisions than a manager with little or no experience.

Motivation information also comes to managers from behavioral research. Managers can then use this information to better understand, predict, and guide their employees. The research and literature on work motivation can be placed on a continuum, as illustrated in Figure 3–1.

FIGURE 3–1   A continuum of types of motivation information.

```
Completely                                                    "Recipe"
"Theoretical" ├──────────────────────────────────────────┤ Orientation
Orientation
```

"Theoretical" orientation.   **At** the far left of the continuum is the theoretical orientation taken by some academic researchers. Much of the material written by these scholars concerns advancing the behavioral sciences. This literature is sometimes criticized as: (1) having lost sight of the problems confronting managers in the real world, (2) concentrating only on demonstrating particular theories and points of view, and (3) looking only for a place to develop sophisticated measurement techniques rather than helping solve problems. Certainly a common legitimate complaint about this literature is the complex vocabulary used to present the basic concepts of motivation. Social science jargon can be a formidable or insurmountable barrier for lay individuals.

"Recipe" orientation.   **The** other extreme of the continuum describes the approach used by a group of writers who write only from "experience." This group includes writers who expound cookbook solutions to almost any motivation problem a manager may face. They offer "simplistic solutions for complex problems," suggesting that a recipe can direct managers to "cook up" a motivated employee, just as a recipe provides directions for baking a chocolate cake.

Motivation as a subject.   **The** coverage of the topic here will attempt to stay away from these extremes, but it is important to understand that the subject matter is somewhat complex. Approaches to understanding motivation differ because individual theorists have attempted to develop their own views of motivation. They approach the problem from different starting points, with different ideas in mind, and from different backgrounds. Different viewpoints include Herzberg's theory of work motivation or Maslow's approach to motivation or Porter and Lawler's model of motivation, among others. This variety of views does not mean that only one approach is correct. It does mean that each has made a different contribution to the understanding of human behavior. The perspective taken in this text is to provide a practical view of the important approaches to motivation.

What is motivation, and how can it be studied?

Many managerial views of motivation are based upon assumptions about what goals people are expected to achieve as employees. For example, if a

FIGURE 3–2   Managerial model of motivation.

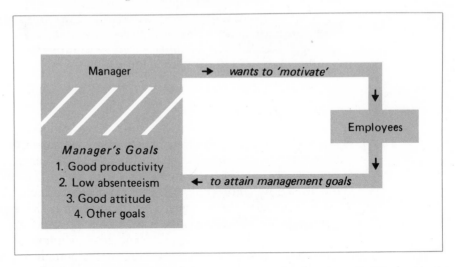

sales manager says he wants to "motivate" his employees, he is really saying he wants his employees to select the goals that *he* wants them to seek—goals related to what he considers proper for persons selling in his division. His employees are undoubtedly motivated but perhaps not toward doing what he would have them do. Figure 3–2 illustrates such a manager's model of motivation. However this view is too restrictive a view of motivation as will be revealed.

MOTIVATION AND VIEWS OF HUMAN NATURE

The study of motivation over the last century has been focused on answering the question, *What is the basic goal of man?* Managers have operated with their own preconceived ideas of basic human goals. Over time, four major assumptions about human nature and the mainsprings of motivation have emerged.[1] These assumptions which have been translated into managerial philosophies and approaches to employee motivation are varied.

One of the most long-lived approaches is based on the assumption that people are rational-economic beings. That is, people behave logically, and economic and monetary needs are the basis of this logical behavior. A second identifiable approach to human goals and motivations is based on an assumption that people are social beings, who reap great satisfaction from being with other people and whose predominant need is to belong to and be accepted by a group. A third approach is based on the assumption that humans are growing, striving beings. Their basic motives are directed at self-improvement and personal growth. A final assumption is that each person is different. This approach incorporates the previous three sets of assumptions into one useful framework. The practical implications of this final approach can be summarized by the expression, "different strokes for different folks."

Rational-Economic View

This idea basically suggests that humans reasonably, logically, and rationally make decisions that will result in the most economic gain for themselves. Therefore, employees are motivated by the opportunity to make as much money as possible and will act rationally in such a manner as to maximize their wages. The assumption is that *money* is the most important motivator of all people. This universalistic view of people assumes that everyone is alike and that everyone wants to maximize personal economic rewards. Further development of this view suggests that all managers should operate according to the same general set of principles, regardless of differences in their organizations, situations, or people. This rational-economic approach means that important behavioral and emotional factors are often ignored or unrealistically assumed away.

This explanation of human motivation is weak because a great deal of behavior does not reasonably follow from the rational-economic assumption made about human nature. For example, if employees are primarily interested in maximizing their economic return, why do some of them restrict piece-rate production and others refuse to take overtime? Obviously, the rational-economic man assumptions have some limitations. It is impossible to categorize human behavior so neatly as to suggest that *all people* are solely motivated by economic considerations.

The rational-economic view of employees in organizations was severely shaken by a set of prolonged research efforts. The famous Hawthorne studies showed clearly the fallacy of viewing all employee behavior as being rational and economic in nature.

Social View

A series of wide-ranging research studies were conducted between 1927 and 1932 at the Western Electric Company plant in Hawthorne, Illinois. A team of social scientists began the study originally to determine the effect that lighting in the work area had on employee productivity. The illumination experiments showed that as the researchers progressively increased the levels of light productivity progressively increased as well. However, when the process was reversed, the results stunned the researchers—as illumination intensity decreased, the output of the workers increased. In fact, as the researchers turned the lights down, productivity kept climbing until the lighting levels in the work areas were the intensity of a full moon. Productivity continued to increase until the workers could no longer see to perform the job.

After further investigation, the researchers discovered that the individual workers were part of a strong informal group that had "pulled together" to increase productivity and to protect each other. This finding led to the idea that workers derived social satisfaction through the interaction with others in the work group.

These experiments provided a great stimulus for more research in the field of "human relations" and contributed to the growing realization that more knowledge about human nature was essential. A major finding of later Hawthorne studies was that humans are not strictly motivated by money. Workers who could have been feeding their paychecks by turning out more pieces of work were found to be restricting production because of social pressures from the work group. These studies confirmed the impact of the informal work group on local organization plans and operations. The Hawthorne studies also emphasized that an organization is a *social system,* not just a collection of individuals acting as individuals would act alone.

These and other research results led many management thinkers to believe that humans are basically social in nature and that the human desire to be associated with others is possibly the strongest human characteristic. The implication was that management had to be aware of this social orientation and take advantage of it.

This social-man view of human nature suggested that all people can be motivated to perform if a manager appeals to their social needs. A predominant emphasis in the management literature became "happiness and harmony in the group leads to productivity," or "a happy worker is a productive worker." Unfortunately, proponents of this view went too far in trying to explain motivation with their one variable, as earlier proponents of money as a motivator had done.

The social view of human nature brought about the *"Human Relations Approach."* Humans were viewed as a bundle of attitudes, sentiments, and emotions. Managers were told that to be effective they should use cunning and manipulation to convince workers of their importance to the company. Employee participation in the decision-making process (as long as they could not hurt anything) was supposed to lead to a feeling of harmony, happiness, loyalty, and satisfaction.

The work of the researchers in the Hawthorne studies did provide valuable insights and progress in understanding people at work. Unfortunately, those who overgeneralized the results made a mistake similar to the one made earlier by the followers of the rational-economic approach. They adopted the social view as if it was universally true in every situation and for every person. Certainly people do have a social aspect to their nature, and for some persons social factors are very important.

However, not everyone is motivated by harmony and cooperation, and many found the insincerity of the human relations approach to be repulsive.

Self-Actualizing View

During the late 1950s and early 1960s the ideas of another group of management thinkers, many of whom were trained in the behavioral sciences became very popular. They assumed that people are *striving* beings attempting to reach *"self-actualization."* This concept means that a person desires to reach his or her full potential. This view of human nature, the self-actualizing philosophy, is illustrated by the ideas of Douglas McGregor, Abraham Maslow, and Frederick Herzberg.

Douglas McGregor.   The concepts behind the self-actualization view were perhaps best expressed by Douglas McGregor, who presented two opposite sets of assumptions which he believed were basic to most management approaches. One set was labeled Theory X and the other Theory Y. Figure 3–3 summarizes these theories. A key point in McGregor's Theory Y is that work is in and of itself a motivator. McGregor felt that managers typically held one of these sets of assumptions about human nature and managed in keeping with those assumptions. However, McGregor argued that people are really more like Theory Y than like Theory X.

Abraham Maslow.   A clinical psychologist, Abraham Maslow, developed a theory of human motivation which continues to receive a great

FIGURE 3–3   A summary of Theory X and Theory Y (McGregor).

Theory X	Theory Y
People dislike work and will try to avoid it.	People do not inherently dislike work.
People have to be coerced and threatened with punishment if the organization's goals are to be met.	People do not like rigid control and threats.
Most workers like direction and will avoid responsibility.	Under proper conditions, people do not avoid responsibility.
People want security above all in their work.	People want security but also have other needs such as self-actualization and esteem.

(Source: Douglas McGregor, *The Human Side of Enterprise* (New York: McGraw-Hill, 1960), pp 33–45.)

deal of exposure in the management literature.[2] Maslow classified human needs into five categories. He suggested that there is a fairly definite order to human needs, and until the more basic needs are adequately fulfilled, a person will not strive to meet higher needs. Maslow's well-known hierarchy includes (1) physiological needs, (2) safety and security needs, (3) belongingness and love needs, (4) self-esteem needs, and (5) self-actualization needs.

An assumption often made by those using Maslow's hierarchy is that workers in modern industrialized society have basically satisfied their physiological, safety, and belongingness needs. Therefore, they will be motivated by the need for self-esteem and the esteem of others and self-actualization. Consequently, items to satisfy these needs should be present at work: the job itself should be internally meaningful and motivating.

Frederick Herzberg.   In the late 1950s Frederick Herzberg and his research associates conducted interviews with 200 engineers and accountants who worked in different companies in the Pittsburg area. The result of this research was a theory that, like Maslow's, has been very widely discussed in the management literature.[3]

Herzberg's Motivation/Hygiene theory assumes that one group of factors, *motivators,* accounts for high levels of motivation to work. Another different group of factors cause discontent with work. These factors are labeled *hygiene,* or maintenance factors. The motivators are *achievement, recognition,* the *work itself, responsibility,* and *advancement.* The hygiene factors are *company policy and administration, supervision, salary, interpersonal relations,* and *working conditions.*

The implication of this research for management and personnel is that the hygienic or maintenance factors provide a base which must be carefully considered if dissatisfaction is to be avoided. But, even if all of these maintenance needs are taken care of, the people will still not necessarily be motivated to work harder. Only those factors called motivators cause more effort to be exerted and more productivity to be attained.

Herzberg's work has been the subject of much controversy, which revolves around his research method and later attempts to replicate his findings. The controversy still continues.

Critique of the organizational humanists.   The above group of writers and those who have built upon their work have been called *organizational humanists* because of their emphasis on humanization of all organizational work environments. Their basic approach is that the people want to achieve and strive to complete tasks, so that they do not necessarily have to be coerced into working. The self-actualizing assumptions, like the social assumptions, have some basis in behavioral science research. Advocates of this philosophy have held that failure to adhere to the assumptions of self-actualization has resulted in workers with no feelings of loyalty to a company and in job dissatisfaction. Some success has been noted by practicing managers and others who try to humanize work situations. Efforts to redesign work are discussed in some detail in Chapter 6. However, not all situations are appropriate for self-actualization efforts.

This approach to the basic nature of people has been criticized by some as unreasonably idealistic. A very pragmatic manager might say, "If you are going to get work done in an organized fashion, you simply don't turn people loose to self-actualize; a certain amount of structure is required to get work done."

Another criticism of this approach has been voiced by labor union leaders. These critics believe the self-actualizing approach overemphasizes the job as the place of need satisfaction. It can be argued that a great deal of an individual's need satisfaction takes place off the job. Obviously not all people are alike, and to suggest that these assumptions are proper in all situations is very likely wrong.

The self-actualizing school of thought, with its sometimes moralistic requests to improve the job and let the individual achieve self-actualization, has given way to the recognition that everyone is somewhat different and that job situations vary. To comprehend motivation and human behavior, one must understand the interactions between individual characteristics and characteristics of the situation. The fourth approach to motivation and human behavior recognizes that people are "complex."

Complex View

The complex view basically suggests that each person is different and that a variety of items may be motivating, depending upon the *needs* of the individual, the *situation* the individual is in, and what the individual *expects* in the way of rewards for the work done. Complex-man theorists such as Victor Vroom, Lyman Porter, and E. E. Lawler do not attempt to fit people into one category but accept human differences.

Victor Vroom. Vroom noted that people act to obtain goals.[1] But whether or not they will act at all depends on whether or not they believe their behavior will help them achieve their goal. In choosing a path to a goal, people establish preferences among various acts based upon their prediction of the outcome of each act. For example, will hard work lead to more money in the pay envelope? Some people will conclude that it does, and others will conclude that it does not, depending upon past experiences with hard work and more money.

Another critical element is how much the person wants the outcome. If Lisa Harmon does not really want a promotion, offering her a promotion that requires relocation to another city will not be highly valuable to her. To put it another way, a person's motivation depends on: (1) his or her *expectation* that a particular behavior will result in a desired outcome or goal, and (2) the *value* the person assigns to that outcome. Numerous other researchers have added to Vroom's model.

Lyman Porter and E. E. Lawler. Porter and Lawler contend that the above relationship is expanded by including *perceived equity* as a variable influencing job behavior. Perception is the way an individual views the job. Figure 3–4 contains a simplified Porter and Lawler model.

Assume that a male department store clerk is motivated to expend effort on his job by selling men's wear. From his job he receives two types of rewards, *intrinsic* (internal) and *extrinsic* (external). To this salesclerk, intrinsic rewards could include a feeling of accomplishment, a feeling of recognition, or other motivators (Herzberg's terminology). Extrinsic rewards might be such items as pay, benefits, good working conditions, and other hygiene factors labeled by Herzberg. The salesclerk compares his performance to both types of rewards he receives. This comparison is made from his perception of his performance and his rewards. He then reaches some level of satisfaction or dissatisfaction. Once this level is reached, it is difficult to determine what he will do. If he is dissatisfied, he might put forth less effort next time, or he might work harder to get the rewards he wants, or he might just accept his dissatisfaction. If he is highly satisfied, it does not mean he will work harder. He may emphasize quality, or he may say, "I got what I wanted."

The essence of the Porter and Lawler view of motivation is the important role of perception. They also show that performance leads to satisfac-

FIGURE 3–4   Porter and Lawler motivation model.

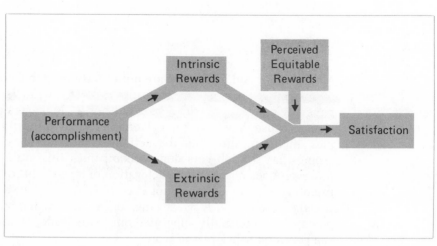

(Source: Edward E. Lawler, III, and Lyman W. Porter, "The Effect of Performance on Job Satisfaction," *Industrial Relations* 7 (October 1966). Used with permission.)

tion instead of satisfaction leading to performance. Porter and Lawler recognize that whether or not a highly satisfied employee works hard depends upon the individual's nature. They recognize that people are complex in their work motivations.

Importance of complex man. The complex-man approach to motivation is important in that it gets away from the simplistic assumptions of the three other views. Work motivation really is very complex. It depends on both the individual and the environment in which the individual works.

The important thrust of this view is that a manager must attempt to match individual needs and expectations to the types of rewards available in the job setting. Thus, the manager should try to determine the rewards the individual expects and put the individual in a job that provides those types of rewards. If one employee wants a self-actualizing job, placing him in a job that offers only monetary and safety rewards is likely to result in less motivation. Likewise, giving another employee a job designed for personal achievement when he wants money and security is likely to be ineffective.

What are four views about why people behave as they do?

In sum, the current state of knowledge about motivation emphasizes that motivation really does "depend upon" the individual and the individual's job situation. Managers who must direct or lead these "complex" people must have a basic understanding of leadership and its relationship to motivation.

LEADERSHIP

Management and leadership are not exactly the same concepts. *Management* implies the existence of formal authority, while *leadership* may not have any connection with formal authority. Managers are in their positions because they have been given the formal authority to perform their jobs, including directing the actions of others. The responsibility for seeing that the job gets done accompanies this authority. Leadership, however, does not require a delegation of formal authority from "above" in an organization. It does not even have to occur in a formal organizational environment. A street gang, for example, will have a leader, though perhaps not a formally appointed one. This leader is not a "manager" in the common sense of the word.

The distinction between leadership and management is not always clear. Employees obey or follow managers partially because they must. If employees consistently refused to cooperate, they typically would not be employed very long. People may obey or follow leaders for entirely different reasons. A group may follow a leader because the individual is physically attractive or knowledgeable, or for any number of other reasons.

The manager does not always have to be a leader to be effective, but some key ideas about leadership can be useful to the manager. The successful manager's concern with leadership focuses on obtaining the very best performance from employees. Some employees do only the minimum number of tasks required of them. But most managers prefer effective and creative employees who are willing to put extra effort into doing a job.

Successful managers have a good understanding of the basics of leadership. For example, Judy Harbeck, a new accounting supervisor, may rely on command rather than persuasion with Fred Abbott, a 60-year-old employee. If Judy does not understand the difference between being a manager (having a position) and being a leader (having followers), she may find that after a while command may not work with Fred and a different kind of relationship is needed.

Certain kinds of leadership skills can be learned and are an important part of many management training programs. Successful leadership also depends upon an individual's personality. Changing a person's leadership style may be very difficult, and placing the individual in a more compatible situation may be more effective.

Leadership Approaches

Many different approaches have been taken to understand leadership. For centuries leadership has been studied with varying degrees of rigor.

Trait approaches.   Many early studies on leadership were done by psychologists who examined personality traits of leaders. Leaders were thought to be dominant extroverts who possessed the traits of self-confidence, empathy, and intelligence.

This approach is closely connected with the "Great Man" theory of leadership. The great man approach assumed that a better understanding of leadership could be gained by studying the personalities of and behaviors of famous leaders. The implication is that if you study these people, "you too can become a great leader." Such study certainly can be interesting, but what worked for Queen Victoria, George Washington, or Benito Juarez years ago may not necessarily be applicable in today's world or in a different set of circumstances. Although numerous famous leaders had these traits, many other individuals with the same traits failed to become leaders.

"Style" approaches.   During the last few decades several attempts to classify leadership into two basic dimensions have been made. Largely based on the Ohio State Leadership Studies which began over 25 years

ago, these studies have significantly affected our knowledge of leadership. Through the use of sophisticated statistical techniques two basic dimensions of leader behavior were isolated: initiating structure and consideration.

Initiating structure refers to efforts on the part of the leader to get the job done. It may be scheduling, maintaining, and communicating standards of performance; emphasizing that deadlines be met; and assigning group members to particular tasks—in other words, a concern with productivity, costs, and getting the work done. It has also been called "production-oriented" style.

Consideration refers to behavior indicating warmth, trust, friendship, and mutual respect between the leader and the group members. Behaviors which show consideration include explaining why decisions were made, consulting group members before making decisions, listening to group members' problems, doing personal favors for group members, and performing other such actions. Leaders high on consideration have been called "people-oriented" leaders.

Managers who score high on *initiating structure* may be very effective and successful on performance measures such as productivity, profit, and efficiency. They are commonly rated very well by their superiors. Managers who are high on *consideration* tend to have high morale in their work group, lower employee turnover, and lower grievance rates than those who are low on consideration.

The general evidence that accompanies this "style" approach to leadership is that an effective leader is high on both initiating structure and on consideration. They are concerned with their people and concerned with getting the job done.

Initiating structure and consideration are important as behavioral patterns because they produce different follower behaviors and expectations.[5] However, viewing leadership only as initiating structure and consideration presents a problem because there is little evidence showing how successful a leader with either a "people" or "production" orientation, or both, will be in different situations.

Situational approaches.   Situational differences, such as the size and climate of the organization, the nature of tasks, and how well the leader gets along with the followers, all may make a difference in the effectiveness of a given leadership style. Consequently, the situational approach to the study of leadership evolved.

The question of which leadership style yields the best results or is appropriate is really determined by the conditions under which the leader is operating. Production-oriented leadership may be more effective under some conditions and people-oriented leadership under others. These issues are still being researched, but some general guides are available.

Fred Fiedler: Since the 1950s Fiedler and his associates have been researching leadership, studying nurses, supermarket grocery departments, steel crews, consumer sales cooperatives, church groups, athletic teams, factories, aviation cadets, and others. The main conclusion of Fiedler's situational approach is that the effectiveness of the leader depends upon both the leadership style and the favorableness of the situation.

The situation is measured by the three major dimensions of the task situation shown in Figure 3–5. The leader's situation may be favorable (good leader-member relations, a structured task, and strong position power). It may be intermediate in favorability, or the situation may be unfavorable (poor leader-member relations, unstructured task, and weak position power).

Figure 3–6 shows the favorability of the situation on the bottom part of the illustration and the appropriate leadership style on the upper part. Eight possible situations combining the three task situation variables are numbers one through eight.

Fiedler concludes that in either very favorable situations (1,2,3 in

FIGURE 3–5   Leadership task situation.

Task Situation	Description	Example
1. Leader-member relations	Leader is or is not *personally attractive* to members of the group and inspires loyalty and confidence	General McArthur personally inspired the confidence and loyalty of his troops A "bully" people dislike or fear would not be personally attractive
2. Task structure	The task can or cannot be easily described by a *written set of guidelines*	Product research is an unstructured task and hard to describe, while answering a telephone switchboard can be described in a set of written rules
3. Position power	*Formal rewards* and *punishments* are or are not available in the leadership position	A drill sergeant in the marines has much formal reward and punishment power President of a volunteer organization has little formal reward and punishment power

FIGURE 3–6 Situational leadership approach.

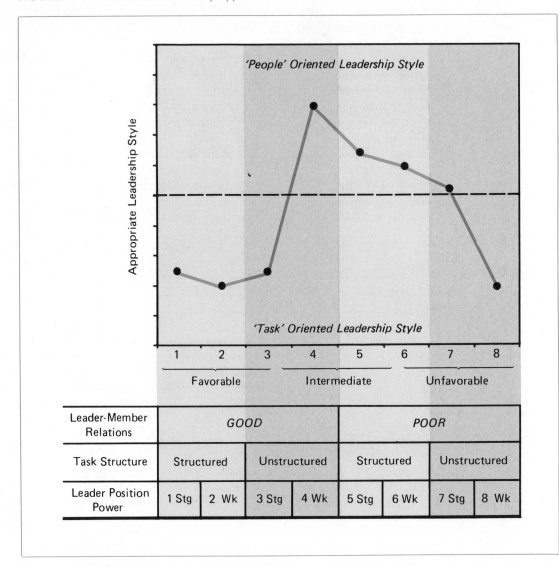

(Source: Fred E. Fiedler, "Engineer the Job to Fit the Manager," *Harvard Business Review*, September–October 1965, p. 119. Used with permission.)

Figure 3–6) or very unfavorable situations (8 in 3–6) production-oriented leadership works best. In other situations where poor leader-member relations, weak position power, or unstructured tasks combine to make the situation moderately unfavorable, such as 4, 5, 6 and 7, the people-oriented leader is more effective.[6]

An authoritarian or task-oriented leader is effective when fully accepted by the followers, strong formal authority is exerted, and the work is highly structured. An example here is a Marine drill instructor—he holds a great deal of power, is fully accepted by his followers, and the work is highly structured.

The task-oriented leader is also effective in a very bad situation (see situation 8). Unfavorable situations may require a person with a production or task-orientation to provide order in a confusing situation.

The people-oriented leadership style is more appropriate in an intermediate situation where the work is not structured or the power position of the leader with the followers is not as strong. The chairperson of a college department may have to be quite participative in order to direct the faculty in the department effectively, since formal position power is usually weak. The authoritarian would be less effective in this situation.

Fiedler's work has resulted in many studies, some of which have reached essentially the same conclusions as Fiedler, while others criticize his research methods. Even with the complexities encountered in Fiedler's work, perhaps more involved models and ideas are necessary to understand the phenomena of leadership. In any event, the recognition that situational factors are important in determining the effectiveness of leadership styles is a long step down the road from trying to specify the qualities of "great men" and the traits they possess.

Path-Goal Approach.   Another researcher, Robert House, has tried to identify those situations in which a leader's consideration or initiating structure behaviors affect employee performance or satisfaction.[7] His approach is based upon the path-goal motivation ideas of Vroom and Porter and Lawler mentioned earlier. House argues that a leader can affect (1) intrinsic rewards of work, (2) intrinsic rewards associated with achievement, (3) extrinsic rewards associated with achievement, (4) the clarity of the "path" an employee will follow to achievement, (5) and the probability that achievement will be rewarded.

This theory predicts that a considerate leader is important if the work itself is boring and uninteresting. "If you have a bad job you don't need a bad boss too." When the job itself is stimulating, the importance of consideration is less.

Initiating structure by the leader is important when the job is unstructured or ambiguous or when a crisis occurs. If the job already is well structured, a high degree of structure from the leader is unnecessary and irritating.

This approach to the situational nature of leadership represents another attempt to identify what leadership style is most appropriate in a given situation. As more research on the path-goal approach and similar theories is done, a better grasp on improving leadership effectiveness will become available.

Can you discuss the three major leadership approaches?

Leadership Effectiveness

Leadership effectiveness is determined by many factors. As already explained, some of these factors are leader-member relations, structure of the task, the position and personal power of the leader, and the way the leader chooses to affect the paths subordinates take to reach their goals. The kind of people who are recruited into the organization, the overall policies and strategies of the organization, the rules the manager has to work with, and the overall climate of the organization can have an impact on leadership effectiveness too. The effectiveness of managers at any organizational level clearly depends upon a good analysis of the factors in a given situation.

Managers as diagnosticians. The effective manager is a diagnostician who can analyze a situation and react to it appropriately. The diagnosis may require the manager to make a decision on his or her own or to use a participative approach. The manager must determine when each approach is appropriate. For example, subordinate participation in the decision may not work well if the manager needs the decision immediately, or is the only one who knows anything about the problem. If the employees are not used to participating, they may not want to do so. And, if the manager has a definite answer already in mind, participation is a sham and unnecessary. Likewise, a fairly authoritarian approach may be inappropriate when employees identify with the organization, have a high degree of expertise, or when strong employee commitment to a decision is needed. To the extent that good diagnoses of the situation are made, the manager has a greater possibility of being both an effective leader and an effective manager.

Matching styles and jobs. One means of increasing leader effectiveness is to match managers to situations compatible with their leadership styles. It is much easier to move a manager to a job which fits his or her leadership inclinations than it is to try to change the individual's way of leading.

Recognizing that certain kinds of behaviors are inappropriate in certain situations, it follows that some individuals may be incapable of providing the proper behavior in every situation. When a manager is improperly placed, the appropriate leadership style may require a set of behaviors he or she simply cannot provide. In such a case it is better for both the manager and the organization if the manager is moved into a more appropriate situation.

An important part of effective leadership is a basic understanding of how individuals behave as members of groups. Group forces can generally affect management operations, as the Hawthorne studies, mentioned earlier, revealed. The impact of work groups on productivity and operations demands that group behavior be discussed.

GROUP BEHAVIOR

Groups of employees can make a manager's job easy or impossible. Managers must understand the behavior and characteristics of groups to effectively direct progress toward organizational goals.

> A WORK GROUP is a collection of individuals brought together to perform organizational work.

Work groups frequently have varied and overlapping social arrangements. For example, a work group of 20 people in a government agency office may have several subgroups, which may develop because of such items as social considerations, car pools, and physical location. Figure 3–7 shows the overlap that often occurs in the membership of groups at work. Regardless of the type of work situation, a work group shares certain basic characteristics in common with groups in many other settings.

What is a work group?

Group Characteristics

Informal groups frequently develop common "codes of behaviors" to help attain group goals. During the growth, development, and maturity of a group, a "collective mind" develops which guides members' attitudes and

FIGURE 3–7   Overlap in group memberships.

	Office Group	Car Pool	Eat Lunch Together	Families are Friends
Bill	▲	▲		
Ann	▲	▲	▲	
Sam	▲		▲	▲
Juan	▲	▲		
Rita	▲		▲	▲
Charles	▲	▲		▲

actions as a group. This group understanding, called a *norm*, takes the form of agreement on issues, certain points of view about important matters, and accepted forms of behavior.

Norms.   Norms may develop in any group as a group's "code of behavior" for many reasons.

> NORMS are expected standards of behavior, usually unwritten and often unspoken, that are generally understood by all members of the group.

They deal with such behaviors as which other groups to associate with, how other groups are to be viewed, and what appropriate behaviors or expressions are within the group. For example, the employees in the detective division of a police department may have a group norm that implies that officers on parking patrol are to be viewed as inferior. As the Hawthorne studies revealed, norms can even evolve on acceptable productivity rates, and group "quotas" may be different from the formal quotas posted by management.

Cohesiveness.   Groups differ on "cohesiveness" or closeness among members. A highly cohesive group is one in which the members place a high value on group membership and are very attached to the group. Members of highly cohesive groups tend to accept group goals more than members of less cohesive groups. Group sanctions tend to be much more effective in a cohesive group. For example, if an X-ray technician is a member of the closely knit or cohesive X-ray department, negative comments about his attire from other group members will carry more weight than if he were unconcerned about his membership in the department.

Status.   As a group develops, each member's position and power in it tends to become organized into a status system.

> STATUS is the relative social ranking an individual has in a group or organization.

This status system becomes the structure of the group. Even in work groups, status usually results in a "pecking order" comprised of an informal leader and perhaps second- and third-level members.

A well-known study in the restaurant industry illustrates the development of a status structure within a work group.[8] In the kitchen of Mammoth Restaurant a researcher observed that a status level was identified with each work station. The most prestigious and important workplace was the stove where all the cooking was done. People who held stove positions were the most highly paid and skilled and had the highest status. Toward the bottom of the status hierarchy were the chicken and vegetable preparation jobs. At the very bottom were the fish preparation jobs. The influence of status also was seen in the way different vegetable jobs were assigned to different employees. Higher status individuals held jobs preparing decorative or luxury vegetables such as parsley, chives, and celery. Very low status accompanied a job preparing potatoes. The jobs preparing onions were considered the most undesirable because of the odor. The lowest status employees held nonpreparation jobs. Similar status distinctions are made in almost all work groups.

Size.   The size of a group tends to affect individual performance in the group. For example, at one university the department of management has only six faculty members; at another, the department of management has 25. Decisions about course assignments and curriculum will probably be easier in the smaller department.

The relationship between size and performance is not completely clear, but size certainly affects the speed with which decisions can be made in a group. Also, as the number of members in a group increases, role definitions must be clearer because face-to-face communication is reduced. Generally, it is safe to say management becomes more difficult as group size increases.

Group composition.   The success of a group is partially determined by the individual characteristics of group members. Age, sex, ethnic background, marital status, experience, and educational levels are important considerations. If the individual characteristics of a group's members are very similar, higher individual member satisfaction will usually result than in a group with diverse members. In homogeneous groups members tend to be more friendly and have higher group spirit. However, groups whose members have quite different characteristics (heterogeneous groups) tend to be more productive.

Groups composed of diverse individuals are likely to be superior in arriving at inventive solutions and new ideas because many different approaches to problems are presented by different people. For instance, when the product line supervisor for a ski-wear firm needed some new ideas for next year's product line, she called in people with very different backgrounds to brainstorm the problem: someone from engineering, sales, design, and public relations. They did not always agree on an idea, but they provided quite a variety of new ideas on the product line.

What are four pertinent characteristics of groups?

Group Effectiveness

In work organizations, very few goals can be achieved without the help of other individuals. To some extent, attaining organizational goals then

FIGURE 3–8   Characteristics of an effective group.

1. The atmosphere tends to be informal, comfortable, relaxed.
2. There is a lot of discussion in which virtually everyone participates.
3. The task or objective of the group is well understood and accepted by the members.
4. The members listen to each other.
5. There is disagreement. Disagreement is not suppressed or overridden by premature group action.
6. Most decisions are reached by a kind of consensus in which it is clear that everyone is in general agreement.
7. Criticism is frequent, frank, and relatively comfortable; there is little personal attack.
8. People are free in expressing their feelings as well as their ideas.
9. When action is taken, clear assignments are made and accepted.
10. The leader of the group does not dominate it, nor does the group defer unduly to him.
11. The group is self-conscious about its own operations.

(Source: Douglas McGregor, *Human Side of Enterprise* (New York: McGraw-Hill, 1960), chapter 16.)

becomes a group project. Douglas McGregor described effective groups based on the behaviors taking place within the group decision-making process. Figure 3–8 contains a summary of McGregor's characteristics of an effective group.

As Figure 3–8 indicates, many variables are involved in a group's effectiveness. Practicing managers must be aware of these variables because developing and maintaining group effectiveness is an important part of managerial jobs.

COMMUNICATION

Communication is a behavioral process that affects motivation, leadership, and group effectiveness. Interpersonal communication occurs both formally and informally in organizations in written, spoken, and other forms.

The basic communications process is represented in Figure 3–9. Before a message can be conveyed, formally or informally, it is *encoded* or converted to symbolic form (made into words, for example); then it is passed by way of a channel (or medium) to the receiver who decodes (or

FIGURE 3–9   The basic communication process.

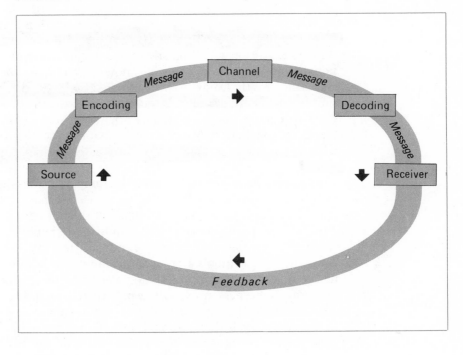

retranslates) it. The desired result is the transfer of reasonably accurate meaning from one person to another. The process is subject to many failures through imprecision.

Communication Barriers

Precision in communication comes about when people are aware of *semantic, technical,* and *perceptual* barriers. The *semantic* barrier is a barrier of words. Communication can be difficult because words or symbols have different meanings. The word "fire" can mean either a flame or to discharge an employee.

Technical problems can prevent a message from conveying the intended meaning. If you were in a room talking with friends and a rock band was playing loudly, you might not accurately hear what was said. A message can be interrupted by noise before it reaches the receiver. Noise and physical barriers can be technical problems in oral communication.

Perceptual problems occur because people have different mental frameworks. If Mary attempts to tell Paul about a dog, Paul conjures a visual image of a dog. Mary may be talking about a chihuahua, while Paul may be thinking about a German shepherd.

Informal Personnel Communication

An important part of organizational communication is through informal channels. These channels are referred to as the *grapevine.* Interweaving throughout an organization, the grapevine is a useful part of organizational communication. A well-known expert on the organizational grapevine, Keith Davis, says that effective supervisors and managers should use the grapevine as a supplement to formal channels.[9] The absence of a grapevine in a company might be evidence that employees are too scared to talk or they care so little about the company that they do not want to talk about it. Grapevines are usually a sign of a healthy organization.

Managers should be aware of current grapevine messages and listen for major distortions. Activity in the grapevine depends on how important a topic is and the presence (or absence) of official communication on it.

Both formal and informal communication should be matched to the receiver. The message should be transmitted over appropriate media using the right symbols at a level meaningful to both the sender and the receiver. Personnel communication also must match the message to the purpose. If the personnel unit wants to tell managers about a change which will affect their relations with union stewards, they send a memo to the managers. If the personnel unit did not care whether or not managers received the message, they could post it on the bulletin board in the cafeteria.

What are three barriers to successful communication?

REVIEW AND PREVIEW

This chapter has been concerned with basic considerations necessary to understand the human resource. Four major views of basic human nature—*rational-economic, social, self-actualizing,* and *complex*—have evolved over time and still exist. The complex view appears to recognize the current realities of people in organizations.

Leadership is an important part of managing people in organizations. The trait approach and leadership style approach are two past approaches to studying leadership. Contemporary situational theorists, such as Fiedler and House, emphasize that effective managers must be diagnosticians. They must be able to determine which leadership style is appropriate in a given situation and attempt to match leadership styles and situations as much as possible.

Also, the importance of group behavior has been reviewed. Because work groups are present throughout modern organizations, today's managers must have knowledge of some basic group characteristics: norms, cohesiveness, status, size, and composition. These factors must be recognized if work groups are to be managed effectively.

Finally, communication is important to any manager or personnel specialist. Because communications is an information transfer process, a manager must be concerned about barriers that can occur. The grapevine as an informal communication network may also affect a manager, especially in dealing with groups in the organization.

The next section of this text builds upon an understanding of human behavior and turns specifically to external concerns that affect *staffing* in an organization. To emphasize the importance of human behavior as the various personnel activities are examined, behavioral aspects of each activity will also be highlighted.

Review Questions

1. What is motivation: Why is it so difficult to identify the causes of behavior?
2. What are the four sets of views about basic human nature? Which one do you see as most compatible with your own values?
3. What is leadership? What are the three general approaches that have been used in studying leadership?
4. "An effective leader must be a good diagnostician." Discuss.
5. What is a work group and why would awareness of group characteristics help a manager?
6. Discuss how communication barriers and informal communication problems can be interrelated.

OPENING CASE FOLLOW-UP

The obvious differences between Leonard and the other appliance salesmen should have been considered more carefully by Mr. Wallace. The salesmen are an extremely cohesive group that has developed norms and relationship patterns over a long period of time.

As this case illustrates, placing someone in a position does not necessarily result in leadership. The young manager may be trying to lead, but the salesmen are not necessarily following. The assistant's willingness to attribute malice to the coffee spill indicates the tension that exists.

Equating motivation with "revved up" is fine, but there is an implied view that Leonard can do something to get an improved performance from the salesmen. Consideration for actually what may be the "why" of the salesman's behavior may lead to a set of actions that utilizes the strong group forces and interpersonal satisfactions present. Providing a group incentive or some other set of rewards may be feasible. Also, the president needs to realize that the older salesmen see the young man as an outsider who is a threat to their safe and secure world. A better awareness of behavioral forces may enable the president to reduce the tensions and get better results from the appliance department.

Case:
Shifting Stan

Stan Wharton had been a member of the loading dock crew for 15 years. His performance had always been above average, but he had never wanted to move to another job although the opportunities had been offered to him. Last year, Stan got married for the first time. He has shown some interesting behavior changes that have his supervisor puzzled.

Stan no longer seems to be part of the work group as he once was. In fact, for many years he was the informal leader and the member to whom the favor of the group seemed most important. Now he doesn't even eat lunch with them. He leaves the plant at lunch to go home to his new child and wife. His work is still good, however.

Stan has just asked to be considered for the next supervisory slot available, which was a great surprise after 15 years of refusing to change jobs. His supervisor isn't sure whether to recommend him or not based upon his seeming distance from the work group.

QUESTIONS

1. Would you recommend Stan for promotion? Why or why not?
2. How does an understanding of motivation and motivation ideas help in attempting to explain the changes in Stan's behavior?

Notes

1. The authors acknowledge the influence and contributions of Edgar Schein, *Organizational Psychology*, 2d ed. (Englewood Cliffs, N.J.: Prentice-Hall, 1970), in framing and structuring the various assumptions and approaches to motivation.

2. A. H. Maslow, *Motivation and Personality* (New York: Harper & Row, 1954), chapter 5.

3. F. Herzberg, B. Mausner, and B. Snyderman, *The Motivation To Work* (New York: John Wiley & Sons, 1959).

4. Victor H. Vroom, *Work and Motivation* (New York: John Wiley & Sons, 1964).

5. Ralph M. Stogdill, *Handbook of Leadership* (New York: Free Press, 1974), p. 141.

6. Fred E. Fiedler, "Engineer the Job to Fit the Manager," *Harvard Business Review* (September-October 1965), p. 119.

7. Robert House, "Path Goal Theory of Leader Effectiveness," *Administrative Science Quarterly*, 16, (1971), pp. 321–338.

8. William F. Whyte, *Human Relations in the Restaurant Industry* (New York: McGraw-Hill, 1948).

9. Keith Davis, "The Care and Cultivation of the Corporate Grapevine," *Dun's Review* (July 1973), pp. 44–47.

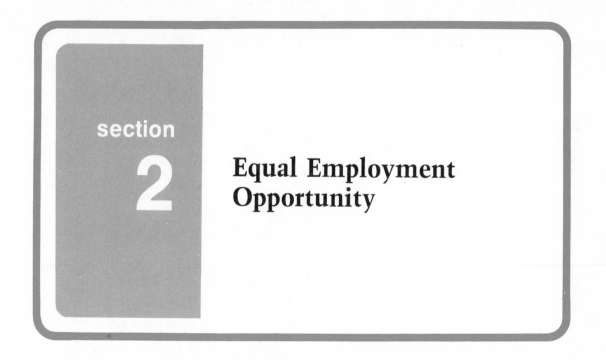

section

2

Equal Employment Opportunity

Before considering the individual activities and interfaces in personnel management, there is one area of which the reader must be aware. Equal Employment Opportunity (EEO) permeates all facets of an organization's operations. *penetrates*

Chapter 4 examines the legal constraints presented by EEO in the staffing process of an organization. Title VII of the Civil Rights Act of 1964 and landmark court cases have provided the general guidelines in this area.

Chapter 5 looks at issues associated with implementing EEO in an individual organization. Sex discrimination, handicapped, and seniority issues are a few concerns viewed. Also, the charge processing of the Equal Employment Opportunity Commission and the issues of Affirmative Action programs are examined.

*

chapter 4	# Equal Employment and Staffing

When you have read this chapter, you should be able to:

1. Explain the importance of staffing and give four reasons why staffing is often coordinated into a specialized unit in organizations.

2. Identify the nature of Title VII of the Civil Rights Act of 1964 and who the act covers.

3. Name and briefly explain the importance of four landmark court cases on equal employment.

4. Define the concepts of validity and reliability, and explain three types of validity.

Keep on Truckin'?

Tim Rowe owns a small trucking firm that specializes in local and metro-area delivery in a large city in the United States. In addition to 12 drivers, the firm employs a sales representative, a secretary-receptionist, and three clerks performing bookkeeping and general office duties.

All employment activities are handled by Tim who has always hired employees on the basis of three qualifications:

1) they must have a high school diploma;

2) they must pass a short paper-and-pencil test which is given to all applicants; and

3) they must have a valid driver's license if applying for the position of driver.

The short test is interesting, as it was devised by Tim from sample questions found on a GED (General Education Degree) Equivalency Test. The test consists of 33 vocabulary and mathematical questions, each worth 3 points. Tim likes to use the test to make sure anyone he hires has adequate basic education skills. Anyone scoring below 70 is automatically rejected.

Last month two drivers quit, so Tim advertised in the local paper for two new drivers. Ten people applied for the openings, but Tim rejected four applicants because they were not high school graduates. Three others were rejected because of test scores below 70. The two white males hired scored the highest on the test, had high school degrees, and also had valid driver's licenses.

This week Tim was notified that two equal employment complaints had been filed against him and his firm. One complainant, a female, alleges that the test does not measure a person's ability to drive and is not a valid predictor of job success. The other complainant, a minority male, alleges that the high school diploma requirement is not related to ability to do the job and unfairly discriminates against minorities. Tim is trying to decide how to respond to these complaints.

An important part of personnel management is providing the organization with a staff of employees to do its work. The components of staffing and some external constraints that affect those components are depicted in Figure 4–1.

As that figure indicates, staffing is composed of three distinct general activities—work analysis, recruiting, and selection. Work analysis is concerned with analyzing and defining jobs so that a clear picture is obtained of job duties and the qualifications needed for individuals to perform those duties satisfactorily. Recruiting focuses on generating an adequate number of qualified applicants for managers to review. Selection is the stage at which individuals are actually screened and either rejected or hired. Effective staffing also requires continual monitoring of each of these activities to insure that they are updated and changed to reflect future demands and situations.

Each of the staffing components is affected by a wide range of external environmental constraints. Some of the most important of these constraints are identified in the outer portion of Figure 4–1. The absence or presence of labor unions, good economic conditions, and current political forces and changes all must be considered when staffing activities are performed. In addition, the actions of competing employers, the appearance of social changes, and the state and composition of labor markets could all impact each of the staffing components.

The opening case provides a good example of another external environmental constraint, governmental legislation. The trucking firm manager faces two challenges to part of his staffing activities as a result of equal employment opportunity (EEO) legislation. Because of the importance of EEO requirements mandated by federal, state, and local governments, most of this chapter and all of the next one focus on the impact of this external environmental constraint. Before examining equal employment requirements, the nature of effective staffing is highlighted.

EFFECTIVE STAFFING

Objectives of an effective and legal staffing program are:

1. To maintain an adequate supply of appropriate applicants;
2. To select those applicants best qualified for employment in the organization;
3. To place applicants in the jobs for which they are best suited;
4. To verify selection and placement by a follow-up of employees to see how well they fit the jobs they are performing;
5. To do the above efficiently and in a manner which promotes good public relations;
6. To perform these functions within the constraints of the law and social expectations.

These objectives may not seem difficult to achieve. However, many

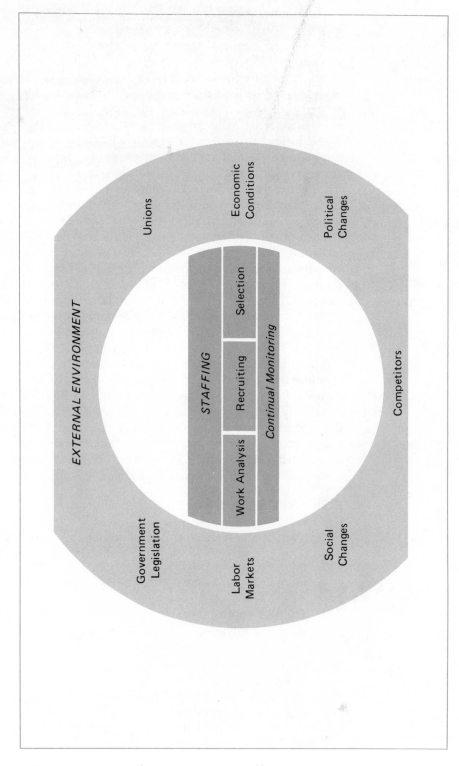

FIGURE 4–1   External Constraints and Staffing.

problems are involved which may not be evident at first. For example, in maintaining a good supply of applicants, an organization must deal with a variety of changes, both economic and social, over which it has little (if any) control. The organization must draw from essentially the same labor market that supplies all employers—private, public, and military. Significant changes in wages, working conditions, and demand in other sectors of the labor market can radically change the availability of job applicants. When a large new employer comes into a community, all organizations drawing employees from that market are affected.

Also, an organization must keep accurate records of its labor requirements in order to take steps to fill them. Recruiting methods should be planned to stimulate an increase of applicants when needed. The organization also needs to know where possible sources of labor are, including the approximate number and quality of potential workers from each source.

Sound selection and placement is important for both the employer and the applicant. How well an employee is matched to a job affects the amount and quality of the employee's work. This matching also directly affects training and operating costs. Workers who are unable to produce the amount and quality of work expected can cost an organization a great deal of money, time, and trouble.

Proper placement is also important to the individual applying for a job. The wrong choice of a vocation or improper job placement can result in wasted time when the employee could be getting useful experience in a more suitable field. Poor placement can result in an unhappy individual or dismissal if the employee cannot do the job.

Effective staffing also requires constant monitoring of the match between person and job. It is not just a one time effort ending with initial placement.

Can you explain the importance of staffing activities?

The days are past when a manager could handle hiring people in any manner that seemed convenient. Within the last 20 years both federal and state governments have become more involved because of social demands that organizations be more responsible in their staffing processes. Government pressure, however, is only one of several external staffing constraints.

Specific External Forces in Staffing

Government is one of the external forces which must be considered in staffing. Historically, certain minority groups and females have been discriminated against in staffing. As a result, government stepped in to see that discrimination did not continue. Staffing is no longer a simple process; it must be handled by someone knowledgeable about numerous legal requirements. Most operating managers usually do not have time to become involved with the intricacies of all the regulations. Consequently, many employers have equal employment specialists in their personnel units.

The *public* is another very important external factor. Public opinion in recruiting and hiring practices cannot be ignored. Recruiting qualified people may be very difficult if the public's opinion of an organization is that it is a poor place to work, that it treats employees unfairly, or that it hires only certain "types" of people.

Competitors are a third important external force in staffing. Failure to consider the competitive labor market and to offer pay scales and other benefits competitive with organizations in the same general industry and geographical location can be a mistake. Underpaying or "undercompeting" may result in a much lower quality work force.

In some instances *unions* can control or influence recruiting and staffing needs. An organization with a strong union may experience a reduction in its flexibility in deciding who will be hired and where he or she will be placed. Unions can also work to an employer's advantage through cooperative staffing programs. Examples are to be found in the building, trade, and printing industries. Such cooperativeness has not been the case in manufacturing. Union shops have typically given management a free hand in hiring while insisting on strong seniority provisions for promotion.

With all of these external forces bearing on the staffing activities in organizations, managers cannot afford to leave the process to chance. Managers must first be *aware* of the external forces relevant to their organization and how these affect them. Next, they must plan both immediate and future manpower needs. Then they must maintain an active and effective recruitment and selection program. Because the most important external force is government, the remainder of this chapter and the next examine in detail governmental constraints on staffing, especially EEO and Affirmative Action requirements.

EQUAL EMPLOYMENT: GOVERNMENTAL RESTRAINTS

The purpose of this section is to describe important government influences on staffing. Because the topic is so extensive, it is not possible to treat it in a totally comprehensive manner. This discussion is intended to provide a basic understanding and specific coverage of some of the most important areas.

Equal Employment Opportunity and Civil Rights

Discrimination against many minority groups is now clearly prohibited by law. The keystone of the structure of antidiscrimination legislation is the Civil Rights Act of 1964.

Section 703A, Title VII of the 1964 act states that:

> It shall be an unlawful employment practice for an employer (1) to fail or refuse to hire or to discharge any individual or otherwise to discriminate against any individual with respect to his compensation, terms, conditions, or privileges of employment because of such individual's race, color, religion, sex, or national origin; or (2) to limit, segregate or classify his employees in any way which would deprive or tend to deprive any individual of employment opportunities or otherwise inadvertantly affect his status as an employee because of such individual's race, color, religion, sex, or national origin.[1]

Section 704B provides that it is unlawful for an employer to "print or cause to be printed or published any notice or advertisement relating to employment by such employer . . . indicating any preference, limitation, specification, or discrimination based on race, color, religion, sex, or national origin." The only exception to this occurs when religion or sex, is a *Bonafide Occupational Qualification* (BFOQ), that is, reasonably necessary to the normal operations of the organization. Only then is it a lawful employment practice to advertise for and hire employees of a particular religion, race, or sex. For example, it may be legal to require a waiter or waitress in an Oriental restaurant to be an Oriental. However, the cook probably would not need to be Oriental because he/she is not seen by the public. It should be noted, however, that the definition of a BFOQ has been increasingly narrowed as a result of court rulings over the years. The next chapter has some examples of BFOQ situations.

The power to investigate illegal practices falls upon the *Equal Employment Opportunity Commission* (EEOC) created by the Civil Rights Act. The operation of the commission is discussed in detail later.

Under the Civil Rights Act employers are required to post an "officially approved notice" in a prominent place where employees can see it. This notice should state that the employer is an equal opportunity employer and does not discriminate. Employment records must be maintained as required by the EEOC and "employer information reports" must be filed with the federal government. Further, any personnel or employment record made or kept by the employer must be maintained for review by the EEOC. Such records include application forms and records concerning hiring, promotion, demotion, transfer, layoff, termination, rates of pay or other terms of compensation, and selection for training and apprenticeship. Even those application forms or test papers completed by unsuccessful applicants must be maintained. The length of time varies 3yrs. depending on the business of the employer, but generally the period is three years. (See Chapter 17, "Personnel Records and Research," for a discussion).

Who Is Covered?

Title VII as amended by the Equal Employment Opportunity Act of 1972 covers:

1. All private employers of 15 or more persons
2. All educational institutions, public and private
3. State and local governments
4. Public and private employment agencies
5. Labor unions with 15 or more members
6. Joint (labor-management) committees for apprenticeship and training[2]

Any organization meeting one of these criteria is subject to rules and regulations of the EEOC, set up by Congress to administer the act. Individuals who feel they have been discriminated against may file a complaint with the EEOC.

The powers of the EEOC are not to be taken lightly. Where the courts have upheld the EEOC's finding of discrimination they have ruled that remedies include back pay and remedial "affirmative action". Some examples include:[3]

Anaconda Aluminum Company—$190,000 in back wages to 276 women.

Virginia Electric Power Company—$250,000 to black workers and elimination of the use of high school diploma and aptitude tests that were not job related.

Lorillard Corporation—$500,000 in back pay to black employees and establishment of plant wide seniority.

Household Finance Corporation—$125,000 to white-collar female employees who were denied promotion because of sex.

AT&T—approximately $15 million to thousands of employees who suffered from discriminatory employment practices; plus an estimated $50 million in yearly payments for promotion and wage adjustments.

The net effect of such settlements are significant enough to impress upon management that the staffing policies and practices of the organization must be fair, defensible, and properly implemented.

Who is affected by Title VII of the Civil Rights Act, and how are they affected?

What Is Discrimination?

Generally, when courts have found that there is discrimination, they have found that what is important is the *effect* of employment policies and procedures *regardless of their intent*. Any practice however harmless in intent which has an *"adverse impact"* on members of a "protected class" is considered discrimination. Further, a percentage of women or minority workers in *any job classification* which is not in relation to their representation in the general population or workforce constitutes strong evidence of discriminatory practices and adverse impact.

A company which has only 3 percent minority employees when the minority workforce in the area is 25 percent will be hard pressed to show that their hiring is nondiscriminatory regardless of their intentions. The burden of proof is on the company to demonstrate that the statistics are not the result of discrimination, even if unintentional. This definition of discrimination has come about as a result of some very important "landmark" court cases in years past.

Landmark Court Cases

In March 1971, the Supreme Court's decision in the case of *Griggs* v. *Duke Power Company* put some teeth into the Civil Rights Act.[4] As a result, companies must be able to *prove* that their selection procedures do not tend to discriminate.

Griggs v. Duke Power. The Griggs case dealt with a promotion and transfer policy which required both a high school diploma and a satisfactory score on two professionally developed aptitude tests. An amendment to the Civil Rights Act allows employers to use professionally developed ability tests, provided the tests are not designed to discriminate because of race, color, religion, sex, or national origin. Prior to the Griggs case, the central issue had been whether or not the employer's *intent* was to discriminate, and not whether the test actually *did discriminate* against minority groups.

However, the Supreme Court ruled that Title VII of the Civil Rights Act prohibits not only overt discrimination but also practices which are fair in form but discriminatory in operation. For example, a word of mouth recruiting system may be discriminatory if the employees mainly pass the word to white males. The court also stated that if *an employment practice cannot be shown to be related to job performance, the practice is prohibited.* This decision established two major points: (1) it is not enough to show a lack of discriminatory intent if the selection tool discriminates against one group more than another; (2) it is the employer's responsibility to prove that any employment requirement is directly job-related.

U.S. v. Georgia Power.   In a second landmark case, the *United States* v. *Georgia Power Company,* the requirements of a high school diploma and aptitude test scores were important issues.[5] The central concern in the case was whether the requirements really were related to successful performance on the job. The Court found that the aptitude test in question was legal because it met the EEOC guidelines reasonably well and it measured performance. However, the *diploma requirement* in the case was found to be unlawful because *any requirement must measure the person for the job and not the person "in abstract."* It was felt that in this case, the qualification of a high school diploma did not measure the ability of the individual to do the job.

Albemarle Paper v. Moody.   In the Supreme Court case *Albemarle Paper* v. *Moody* in June 1975, the Court *reaffirmed* the idea that *any "test"* used for selecting or promoting employees must be a valid predictor or performance measure for a particular job.[6] The term "test" includes such items as *performance appraisals* used for promotion decisions. (The impact on performance appraisals is discussed in Chapter 12.) The Court also found that if it can be shown that any selection test has an *adverse impact* (evidenced by hiring, promotion, etc., that does not result in a pattern similar to minority representation in the population), the burden of proof for showing that test is valid falls upon the *employer.* Thus, if some tests appear to have an adverse impact on blacks, for example, the employer must be prepared to demonstrate that the selection/promotion instruments measure what they are supposed to measure. Also, employment tests must be sound predictors of a person's future job success.

Washington v. Davis.   A 1976 Supreme Court decision in a case involving the hiring of police officers in Washington, D.C., represents a slight shift in emphasis. In this case the issue was a reading comprehension and aptitude test given to all applicants for police officer positions. The test contained actual material that the applicants would have to learn during a training program. Also, the city could show a good relationship between success in the training program and success as a police officer. The problem with the test was that a much higher percentage of women and blacks failed this aptitude test.

The court ruled that the city of Washington, D.C., did not discriminate unfairly because the test was very definitely job-related.[7] The implication of this case was that if a test is clearly related to the job and tasks performed, it is not illegal just because a greater percentage of minorities or females do not pass it. The crucial issue is that a test must be specifically job-related, and not solely judged on its adverse impact.

Bakke v. U. of California.   The existence of "reverse discrimination" was the major issue in this 1978 case. *Reverse discrimination* exists when a more qualified individual is denied an opportunity because of guarantees given to minority (protected class) individuals who may be less qualified.

In this case Bakke, a white male, applied to the University of California at Davis Medical School and was denied admission. The university had set aside sixteen places in each beginning class for ethnic minority persons. Bakke was denied admission even though he had scored higher on the admissions criteria than minorities who were admitted. Thus, Bakke felt he suffered "discrimination in reverse" and sued for admission.

The Supreme Court reached a somewhat nebulous decision by ruling 5-4 that Bakke should be admitted but that admission plans that consider race as a factor are not illegal. The nine justices wrote six different opinions, with the swing decision being written by Justice Powell, who said: "Equal protection cannot mean one thing when applied to one individual and something else when applied to a person of another color." However, Powell also ruled that preserving racial diversity was a legitimate goal of the university. But, having a specific number of reserved slots was illegal. Powell stated that "race or ethnic background may be deemed a 'plus' in a particular applicant's file, yet it does not insulate the individual from comparison with all other candidates for the available seats."

Some experts labelled the Bakke decision as a "non-decision" because it did not clearly answer the question of the existence of reverse discrimination in affirmative action plans. Also, the Bakke decision did not say how much ethnic background can be used as a "plus". Finally, the case dealt with a rather narrow situation that was somewhat different from that existing in employment situations.

The ultimate effect of the Bakke decision was to set up further court tests in order to clarify the legal status of reverse discrimination concerns. Other cases grounded in private industry, such as *Weber v. Kaiser Aluminum* in which a white male was denied admission to a company training program because of an affirmative action plan, will reach the court for its judgement. Undoubtedly, the issue of reverse discrimination represents a significant continuing legal concern in personnel.

Each case regarding discrimination is considered on its own merit, and while precedents such as these certainly do apply, they are not guarantees that an employer will or will not be charged and found guilty of discrimination. Employers must be aware of precedents and the intent and interpretation of the law itself by the EEOC and other enforcement agencies.

Can you identify and discuss four important cases on EEO?

VALIDITY AND EQUAL EMPLOYMENT

At the heart of all EEO requirements on testing is the concept of validity.

✗   VALIDITY means that a "test" actually measures what it says it measures.

For a general intelligence test to be valid, it must actually measure intelligence, not just a person's vocabulary. Therefore, an employment test that is valid must measure the person's ability to perform the job for which he/she is being hired.

The idea that personnel staffing practices must be valid includes such instruments as job descriptions, application blanks, interviews, employment tests, promotion tests, and performance appraisal practices. Hence, validity touches many of the common sources used to make employment and promotion decisions.

Using a modern view of personnel management, the governmental legislation and court decisions mentioned earlier are forcing employers to make changes that should have been made earlier. Using an invalid instrument to select, place, or promote an employee is not good management practice, as well as now being illegal. Management should be concerned with using valid instruments from the standpoint of the efficiency of operations. Many organizations however, were content to use instruments that had not been demonstrated to be valid. In one sense, the current requirements have done management a favor in that they are now forced to do what they probably should have been doing previously.

Test Validity and Reliability

A test is useful only if it is *valid* and *reliable.*

RELIABILITY refers to the consistency with which a test measures an item.

For a test to be reliable, an individual's score should be about the same every time that individual takes it, excluding practice effects. Unless a test measures a trait consistently (or reliably), it is of little value in predicting job performance. Consequently, the reliability of a test must be established before it is used.

A test is said to be valid for selection purposes if there is a significant relationship between performance on the test and performance on the job. The better a test can distinguish between satisfactory and unsatisfactory performance of the job, the greater its validity. Applicants' scores on valid tests can be used to predict their probable job performance. Acceptable reliability coefficients are quite high—a correlation of .80 or better. On the other hand, acceptable validity coefficients are considerably lower because of intervening variables, perhaps as low as .30 for "practical significance."

Tests of any kind attempt to predict performance on the job. The test is the *predictor,* and the job behavior is called the *criterion variable.* Careful job analysis determines exactly which behaviors are needed for each particular task. Predictors are validated against behaviors. If they accurately predict behavior, they are useful in selection and legally acceptable.

What are the definitions of *validity* and *reliability?*

If a charge of discrimination is brought against a company, the company must be able to demonstrate that its tests are valid. In Section 1607.4 of the EEOC guidelines the required evidence of validity is: (1) where technically feasible, a test must be validated for each minority group who will be taking it; (2) evidence of a test's validity should consist of empirical data demonstrating the test is predictive of or significantly correlated with important elements of work behavior.

General aptitude and psychological tests, such as those dealing with mental abilities, are becoming increasingly difficult to validate, because a test must measure the person for the job and not the person in abstract (*Griggs* v. *Duke Power*). Current EEOC guidelines recognize four types of validity which may be used.

Types of Validity

The four basic types of validity are: (1) Predictive validity, (2) Concurrent validity, (3) Content validity, and (4) Construct validity. Each type is discussed in terms of its relationship to employment.

Predictive validity. This method of validating employment practices is the one which the EEOC has most strongly advocated. Predictive validity is calculated by giving a test and then comparing the test results with the job performance of those tested. Figure 4–2 depicts predictive validity.

To illustrate how a predictive validity study might be designed, consider the following. A retail chain, Eastern Discount, wants to establish predictive validity for a pencil-and-paper arithmetic test it plans to use to hire cashiers. Obviously, it wants a test that will do the very best job of separating those who will do well from those who will not. Eastern Discount first hires 30 people and gives them all the pencil-and-paper test. Sometime later (perhaps six months) the scores on the test are compared with the 30 employees' success on the job. The test items that correlate highly with success on the job are considered valid predictors of performance and may be used to hire future employees.

FIGURE 4–2   Predictive validity.

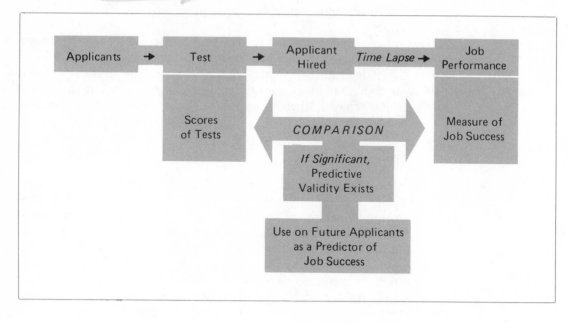

There are several problems with using predictive validity, however, even though it is considered sound in a statistical sense. For example, a relatively large number of people have to be hired at once, and the test scores cannot be considered. Obviously the firm may hire both good and bad employees initially. Because of these and other problems, another type of validity is often used—concurrent validity.

Concurrent validity.   Concurrent essentially means "at the same time." Figure 4–3 shows how concurrent validity is determined.

Using concurrent validity, current employees instead of those newly hired are used to validate the test. The test is given to current employees and then the scores are correlated with their performance ratings. A high correlation suggests that the test is able to differentiate between the better and the poorer employees.

A major potential drawback with concurrent validity is that the *extremely* poor employees are no longer with the firm to be tested and the firm does not really have a representative range of people to test. Another problem is that the learning that might have taken place on the job has influenced the test score, and applicants taking the test without the benefit of the job experience might score low on the test, but might be able to do the job.

Content validity.   This type of validity uses a logical and less statistical approach. In content validity a person would perform a test which is an

FIGURE 4–3  Concurrent validity.

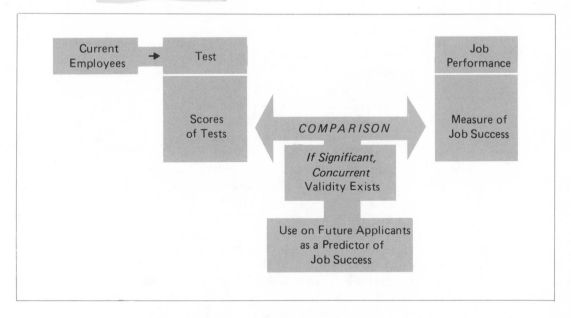

actual sample of the work done on the job. Thus, an arithmetic test for a cashier would contain some of the calculations that a cashier would have to make on the job. Content validity is especially useful if the workforce is not large enough to accommodate better statistical designs.

Construct validity. This type of validity is somewhat more difficult to deal with than the others. In psychology a *construct* is an idea or characteristic inferred from research. In a sense, it is a figment of scientific imagination, something that cannot be seen but is assumed to be there. Most tests are designed to measure something; that something is typically a hypothetical construct, such as Intelligence Quotient (IQ), which attempts to measure a person's basic intelligence. Construct validity is more likely to run into difficulties with measuring the person in abstract than the other three validities.

Validity–Current Directions

Of the four types of validity, two stand out as being the most useful and preferred in personnel staffing activities: *predictive* and *content*. In the past, predictive validity has been preferred by EEOC because it is presumed to give the strongest tie to job performance. However, because predictive validity requires (1) a fairly large number of people and (2) a time gap between the test and the performance, content validity is increasingly being used.

Growth of content validity.   Content validity is a solid alternative because its basic requirement is a good analysis of what tasks one performs in a job. By knowing exactly what is done, a test can be derived using an actual work sample.

In a metropolitan U.S. city, to establish a test for firefighter applicants, a personnel specialist analyzed and rated the tasks of current firefighters. Then a test was devised at a training center that reflected a realistic sample of a firefighter's job. Instead of having applicants lift weights to test strength, all applicants were required to drag a 75-pound hose up three flights of stairs in a four-minute time period. This test represented the average amount of time that firefighters actually have in a real fire.

Many practitioners and specialists alike see content validity as a way to validate staffing requirements using a common sense approach. In the *Washington* v. *Davis* case discussed earlier, the Supreme Court also appeared to give support to the content validity approach because the training course test represented actual training materials used by police officers. The importance of a content validity approach will also be highlighted in Chapter 6 on analyzing jobs and work.

Can you explain predictive, concurrent, and content validity?

Choosing a "Test."   The kind of predictor variable or test selected should depend upon what is being predicted. Aptitude tests predict certain items well; histories predict different characteristics; and proficiency tests predict still other factors. For example, in clerical selection, proficiency is predicted best by clerical ability tests on samples of work. Turnover is best predicted by personal history data in combination with skill tests. Sales performance is predicted best by personal history data. Trainability and proficiency of computer programmers have been predicted successfully by quantitative and symbolic reasoning abilities tests.[9]

Many people claim that when properly used and administered, formal paper-and-pencil tests can be of a great benefit in the selection process. Considerable evidence supports this. However, because of EEOC pressure, many employers are reducing the use of tests or omitting their usage altogether. General personality and psychological tests have been especially affected. The problems of validation and making the validation job-related are quite time-consuming and not worth the cost to some employers.

A study of 2,500 companies by Prentice-Hall, Inc., and the American Society for Personnel Administration found that 36.5 percent of the companies sampled do not test at all. Of those still using tests, three of

FIGURE 4–4   Incidence of testing for hiring and promotion (by size of employer).

	Fewer than 100 Em-ployees	100 to 499 Em-ployees	500 to 999 Em-ployees	1,000 to 4,999 Em-ployees	5,000 to 9,000 Em-ployees	10,000 to 25,000 Em-ployees	More than 25,000 Em-ployees	All Re-spondents
Test for Hiring	30.4%	43.4%	46.8%	55.4%	62.7%	54.9%	57.1%	49.1%
Test for Promotion	17.9	17.3	24.0	29.3	27.4	32.7	32.4	24.0
Not Test	61.0	49.2	45.1	40.3	32.9	38.4	39.6	36.5

(Source: Reprinted with permission from *Personnel Management: Policies and Practices* Report #22, 4-2-75, published by Prentice-Hall, Inc., Englewood Cliffs, N.J. 07632. © 1975 by Prentice Hall, Inc.)

four have reduced their use, and nearly 14 percent indicated that they would soon stop.[10] Figure 4–4 shows the use of testing for hiring and promotion by size of employers revealed in the study.

REVIEW AND PREVIEW

This chapter is primarily concerned with the effects of legal constraints on staffing. Forces such as the general public, competitors, and unions are major external forces; however, governmental influence is the most immediate concern for most personnel decisions. Racial, religious, or sexual discrimination is firmly prohibited by law. A manager involved with the staffing activities of an organization must be familiar with these external constraints.

There have been a number of large and well-publicized cases in which employers were found guilty of discrimination in their personnel practices. A number of landmark court cases have helped define what really is considered discrimination. These cases have emphasized the importance of reliability and validity of selection instruments or "tests."

In the next chapter the issues associated with implementing Equal Employment laws in an organization are considered. Affirmative Action, as well as a number of other areas, such as sex discrimination, handicapped employees, and age discrimination, are discussed.

Review Questions

1. Discuss the following comment: "Staffing is too important to leave to chance. Therefore, a specialized unit must coordinate staffing activities."
2. What is equal employment opportunity and how is it enforced?

3. Identify the impact of each of the following court cases:
   a. *Griggs* v. *Duke Power*
   b. *U.S.* v. *Georgia Power*
   c. *Albemarle Paper* v. *Moody*
   d. *Washington D.C.* v. *Davis*
   e. *Bakke* v. *U. of California*

4. Explain what validity is and differentiate among content, concurrent, and predictive validity.

OPENING CASE FOLLOW-UP

Tim Rowe is on shaky ground with his selection procedure. He will be hard pressed to demonstrate that his selection instrument (pencil-and-paper test) has any validity because it is a safe bet he has never formally analyzed its validity.

Second, in light of the Griggs case, unless a high school diploma can be shown to be related to job performance of a truck driver, it is not a legal criterion for selection. Tim might be better off to try and settle these complaints than to fight them through the courts. Of the three requirements only the driver's license "test" appears to be job-related.

ACD Corporation

Over the years ACD Corporation has used personnel tests for promotion, selection, and placement. The company has had a policy that tests will be fair to all regardless of race, sex, creed, or color. Sally White is going to audit ACD's selection testing program. What should Sally look for to ensure that ACD's policy (and the law) is being observed?

Notes

1. Civil Rights Act, 1964, Title VII, Section 703A.

2. *Affirmative Action and Equal Employment*, U.S. Equal Employment Opportunity Commission, Washington, D.C., 1974, p. 12–13.

3. *Ibid.* pp. 8–10.

4. *Griggs* v. *Duke Power Co.*, 401 U.S. 424 (1971).

5. 474 F. 2d 906 (1973).

6. *Albermarle Paper Co.* v. *Moody*, 74–389 (1975).

7. *Washington, Mayor of Washington, D.C.* v. *Davis*, 74–1492 (1976).

8. *Bakke* v. *U. of California* (1978).

9. R. M. Guion, *Personnel Testing* (New York: McGraw-Hill, 1965), p. 454.

10. Prentice-Hall/ASPA Survey, "Employee Testing and Selection Procedures: Where Are They Headed?" in *Personnel Management Policies and Practices* (Englewood Cliffs, N.J.: Prentice-Hall, 1975).

chapter 5

Implementing
Equal Employment

When you have read this chapter, you should be able to:

1. Explain the importance of good record keeping to EEO compliance.

2. Discuss the EEOC charge handling process.

3. Define Affirmative Action and identify its relationship to EEO practice.

4. Give examples of six different potential areas for discrimination charges.

Discrimination?

Ms. Ruth Wilson, a black female, was employed as an operator of a check reader-sorter machine in a bank. After two years on the job, Ms. Wilson was discharged for being habitually absent and tardy. She filed an official charge of discrimination with the District Office of the Equal Employment Opportunity Commission (EEOC). She listed the following allegations.

1. Although the bank had terminated her employment because of excessive absenteeism, a Caucasian employee in her department, who had as many absences as she, was not terminated or reprimanded by the department manager.

2. A Caucasian worker in the department was allowed to leave the building during working hours, whereas she was not allowed to leave the building during working hours.

3. A Caucasian employee was given "lighter" duty than she because management assigned lighter blocks of work to the Caucasian employee for processing.

4. She was restricted by the assistant department manager from having conversation with her co-workers. When she discussed this problem with the department manager, he did not seem to understand the problem and failed to correct it.

The bank made the following responses to the allegations.

1. No employee in the entire bank had a combined absence-tardiness record as poor as that of Ms. Wilson. Written documentation was furnished demonstrating that Ms. Wilson had been counseled on 54 separate occasions in a two-year period concerning excessive absenteeism and tardiness.

2. Bank policy prohibits employees from leaving the building during working hours except under unusual circumstances and then only with management permission. The department manager stated that he administers this policy in a completely fair manner without regard to race or color.

3. All blocks of work in the department are assigned on a random basis without regard to race or color. Employees in training programs normally have lighter work loads until the training period has been completed.

4. A grievance procedure is outlined in the Employee Handbook. If an employee is not satisfied after talking with his department manager, he is encouraged to talk with the personnel officer or another officer of the bank.

Question: Is this discrimination on an illegal basis?

The previous chapter dealt with the relationship between an organization staffing process and external constraints on that process, especially Equal Employment considerations. But *exactly* how does the system for handling complaints work? What *exactly* does the EEOC expect from an employer in complying with the somewhat general guidelines in Title VII? And, what actions on the part of employers have led to findings of discrimination? These and other questions will be examined in this chapter as the EEOC charge processing system, Affirmative Action, and EEO and management practices are considered.

First, perhaps a point from political science should be made clearer. The Civil Rights Act was passed by Congress to set up the mechanism for bringing about equality in hiring and job opportunity. As is often the case, the law contains ambiguous provisions which gives great leeway to the agencies who enforce the law. In addition, interpretations of these ambiguous provisions in laws change as the membership of the agencies change. Title VII language and EEOC rulings may sometimes cause confusion since they may seem to be in conflict at times. However, the power that agencies have in interpreting the law explains the potential for such a situation to occur.

EEO SURVEYS AND RECORDS

To aid enforcement of the equal employment opportunity (EEO) laws, the federal government through the Equal Employment Opportunity Commission (EEOC) has required an employer to survey its workforce and maintain records on the distribution of minority individuals in the workforce.

Since racial data are not permitted on application blanks or other preemployment records, the EEOC allows a "visual" survey or a separate "applicant information form" that is not used in the selection process. The fact that minority group identification is not present on company records is not considered a valid excuse for failure to provide the data required.

The employment data is filed with the federal government on an EEO-1 form. (See Figure 5–1.) This form requires employment data by job category. Other communications and internal reports may include:

1. Applicant flow data
2. Training information by minority group
3. Promotion and transfer data
4. Equal pay survey
5. Termination data
6. Survey of college graduate employees

In general, all employers subject to Title VII with 100 or more employees and all employers who hold government contracts or subcontracts over $10,000 are required to file these reports annually.

Keeping good records, whether required by the government or not, is simply good personnel practice. Complete records, including individual records, are necessary for responding when a charge of discrimination has been made. If proper documentation is lacking, it may lead to an employee being given back a job which he performed poorly. More will be said about records in Chapter 17, "Personnel Records and Research."

Why is good record keeping a part EEO compliance?

EEOC Charge Processing

When a charge is received by the EEOC it is processed as shown in Figure 5–2. Notice that there are a number of decision stages and points. The three stages represent increasingly more involved actions in which a complaintant and an employer continue to disagree. The rapid charge processing system was introduced in 1977 to try to eliminate the extremely long delays that had occurred in the past to investigate discrimination complaints.

The issues and the nature of charges filed with EEOC are shown in Figure 5–3. Racial discrimination charges form the basis for the greatest number of complaints, followed by sex discrimination complaints. Also, several charges relate to discriminatory discharge. The Ruth Wilson case at the opening of the chapter was a complaint based on discharge. That case was selected to illustrate the most common basis for discrimination charges.

AFFIRMATIVE ACTION

Beginning with President Franklin D. Roosevelt and continuing through the passage of the Civil Rights Act of 1964, numerous executive orders and actions have been issued that require employers holding federal government contracts to be nondiscriminatory. During the late 1960s, the Office of Federal Contract Compliance (OFCC) in the Labor Department was established with the responsibility of enforcing nondiscrimination in government contracts. Under Executive Order 11246, the Secretary of Labor was given the power to (1) publish the names of noncomplying contractors or unions, (2) recommend suits by the Justice Department to compel compliance, (3) recommend action by the EEOC or the Justice Department to file suit in federal district court, and (4) cancel the contract of a noncomplying contractor or blacklist a noncomplying employer from future government contracts.

FIGURE 5–1

Standard Form 100
(Rev. 12-76)
Approved GAO B-180541 (R0077)
Expires 12-31-78

EQUAL EMPLOYMENT OPPORTUNITY
EMPLOYER INFORMATION REPORT EEO-1

Joint Reporting Committee

- Equal Employment Opportunity Commission
- Office of Federal Contract Compliance Programs

Section A — TYPE OF REPORT
Refer to instructions for number and types of reports to be filed.

1. Indicate by marking in the appropriate box the type of reporting unit for which this copy of the form is submitted (MARK ONLY ONE BOX).

(1) ☐ Single-establishment Employer Report

Multi-establishment Employer:
(2) ☐ Consolidated Report
(3) ☐ Headquarters Unit Report
(4) ☐ Individual Establishment Report (submit one for each establishment with 25 or more employees)
(5) ☐ Special Report

2. Total number of reports being filed by this Company (Answer on Consolidated Report only) _____

Section B — COMPANY IDENTIFICATION *(To be answered by all employers)*

OFFICE USE ONLY

1. Parent Company

a. Name of parent company (owns or controls establishment in item 2) omit if same as label

| Name of receiving office | | | Address (Number and street) | | a. |

| City or town | County | State | ZIP code | b. Employer Identification No. | b. |

2. Establishment for which this report is filed. (Omit if same as label)

a. Name of establishment

| Address (Number and street) | City or town | County | State | ZIP code | c. |

b. Employer Identification No. _____ (If same as label, skip.)

d.

3. Parent company affiliation (Multi-establishment Employers: Answer on Consolidated Report only)

a. Name of parent—affiliated company   b. Employer Identification No.

| Address (Number and street) | City or town | County | State | ZIP code |

Section C — EMPLOYERS WHO ARE REQUIRED TO FILE *(To be answered by all employers)*

☐ Yes ☐ No 1. Does the entire company have at least 100 employees in the payroll period for which you are reporting?

☐ Yes ☐ No 2. Is your company affiliated through common ownership and/or centralized management with other entities in an enterprise with a total employment of 100 or more?

☐ Yes ☐ No 3. Does the company or any of its establishments (a) have 50 or more employees AND (b) is not exempt as provided by 41 CFR 60-1.5, AND either (1) is a prime government contractor or first-tier subcontractor, and has a contract, subcontract, or purchase order amounting to $50,000 or more, or (2) serves as a depository of Government funds in any amount or is a financial institution which is an issuing and paying agent for U.S. Savings Bonds and Savings Notes?

NOTE: If the answer is yes to ANY of these questions, complete the entire form; otherwise skip to Section G.

Section D — EMPLOYMENT DATA

Employment at this establishment--Report all permanent, temporary, or part-time employees including apprentices and on-the-job trainees unless specifically excluded as set forth in the instructions. Enter the appropriate figures on all lines and in all columns. Blank spaces will be considered as zeros.

JOB CATEGORIES	NUMBER OF EMPLOYEES										
	OVERALL TOTALS (SUM OF COL B THRU K)	MALE					FEMALE				
		WHITE (NOT OF HISPANIC ORIGIN)	BLACK (NOT OF HISPANIC ORIGIN)	HISPANIC	ASIAN OR PACIFIC ISLANDER	AMERICAN INDIAN OR ALASKAN NATIVE	WHITE (NOT OF HISPANIC ORIGIN)	BLACK (NOT OF HISPANIC ORIGIN)	HISPANIC	ASIAN OR PACIFIC ISLANDER	AMERICAN INDIAN OR ALASKAN NATIVE
	A	B	C	D	E	F	G	H	I	J	K
Officials and Managers											
Professionals											
Technicians											
Sales Workers											
Office and Clerical											
Craft Workers (Skilled)											
Operatives (Semi-Skilled)											
Laborers (Unskilled)											
Service Workers											
TOTAL											
Total employment reported in previous EEO-1 report											

(The trainees below should also be included in the figures for the appropriate occupational categories above)

Formal On-the-job trainees	White collar											
	Production											

1. NOTE: On consolidated report, skip questions 2-5 and Section E.
2. How was information as to race or ethnic group in Section D obtained?
   1 ☐ Visual Survey   3 ☐ Other — Specify ....
   2 ☐ Employment Record   ....
3. Dates of payroll period used –

4. Pay period of last report submitted for this establishment

5. Does this establishment employ apprentices?
   This year? 1 ☐ Yes 2 ☐ No
   Last year? 1 ☐ Yes 2 ☐ No

Section E — ESTABLISHMENT INFORMATION

1. Is the location of the establishment the same as that reported last year?
   1 ☐ Yes 2 ☐ No 3 ☐ Did not report last year 4 ☐ Reported on combined basis

2. Is the major business activity at this establishment the same as that reported last year?
   1 ☐ Yes 2 ☐ No 3 ☐ No report last year 4 ☐ Reported on combined basis

OFFICE USE ONLY

3. What is the major activity of this establishment? (Be specific, i.e., manufacturing steel castings, retail grocer, wholesale plumbing supplies, title insurance, etc. Include the specific type of product or type of service provided, as well as the principal business or industrial activity.)

e.

Section F — REMARKS

Use this item to give any identification data appearing on last report which differs from that given above, explain major changes in composition or reporting units, and other pertinent information.

Section G — CERTIFICATION (See Instructions G)

Check one
1. ☐ All reports are accurate and were prepared in accordance with the instructions (check on consolidated only)
2. ☐ This report is accurate and was prepared in accordance with the instructions.

Name of Certifying Official	Title	Signature		Date
Name of person to contact regarding this report (Type or print)	Address (Number and street)			
Title	City and State	ZIP code	Telephone Area Code / Number / Extension	

All reports and information obtained from individual reports will be kept confidential as required by Section 709 (e) of Title VII

FIGURE 5–2   Rapid charge processing system.

TIME LAPSE	EEOC ACTION	PROBLEM RESOLUTION
	STEP 1: **INTAKE INVESTIGATION**	
Immediate Action	CP Initial Inquiry • Mail • Telephone • Drop in	If Non-Jurisdictional, Refer to Appropriate Agency
Immediate Action Subject to CP Availability	If EEOC Matter Require In-Depth Interview at EEOC Office or via Telephone • Obtain Full Story and Names of Witnesses and Comparitive Data • Prepare Detailed Charge • Post-Charge Counseling RE: EEOC Process and to Promote Settlement Interest	If Non-Jurisdictional or not valid Title VII claim refer to appropriate Agency
2-3 Days	Docketing, Deferral to 706 Agency where Appropriate or Request for 706 Waiver under Work-Sharing Arrangement; Assignment to Investigator.	
2-3 Days	Charge Served on R with Notice of Fact-Finding Conference, Interrogatory and Invitation to Settle on 'No Fault Basis'	If R Responds to Settlement Overture, Negotiate Settlement and Close
	STEP II: **FACT FINDING CONFERENCE--** **INVESTIGATION/SETTLEMENT**	
Held within One Month from Date of Charge	Fact-Finding Conference Held if No Pre-Conference Settlement • Sort Out Disputed and Non-Disputed Facts • Clarify Issues • Identify Additional Documentation Needed • Continue Settlement Efforts	If Settlement Succeeds, Execute Settlement Agreement and Close
	(Continued on opposite page)	

100

TIME LAPSE	EEOC ACTION	PROBLEM RESOLUTION
	STEP III: **POST-CONFERENCE ACTIONS**	
Completed within Three to Four Months from Date of Charge	If Continued Settlement Efforts Fail and Case has Merit and/or Investigation is Incomplete • Prepare Investigative Report • Identify Areas of Further Inquiry	*Close* Charge has No Merit: No Cause Further *Settlement* Effort Succeeds CP Fails to Cooperate: *AD. CL*
	Refer for Extended Investigation	CP Requests *Rt. to Sue* CP Requests *Withdrawal*

(Source: U.S. Equal Employment Opportunity Commission, *Mission*, 5 (1977), p. 13.)

Nature of Affirmative Action

Under an affirmative action plan, an employer will specify targets and steps that will be taken to guarantee equal employment opportunities for minority group personnel.

> AFFIRMATIVE ACTION generally refers to efforts by organizations to identify and analyze problem areas in their minority employment as well as to identify goals to overcome those problems.

Affirmative action programs often include specific timetables and goals for hiring of minority members where there are deficiencies.

Affirmative action basically means *results*. This effort requires continuing commitment by an employer to improve its equal employment opportunity posture, rather than make merely a one-time effort to comply with certain standards. As an example in the AT&T settlement, affirmative actions included:

1. Hiring and promotion targets for women and minorities in each job classification. These targets are to be reviewed by OFCC regularly.
2. Goals for employing males in previously female jobs.
3. Assessment of all female college graduates hired since 1965 to determine interest and potential for higher level jobs.[1]

FIGURE 5–3   Distribution of actionable charges

All United States (Type Respondent) Private Employers	Race	Religion	Sex	Natl. Origin	Color	Unspec. & Other	No Basis
Issues							
Hiring	4,324	179	2,821	970	167	167	38
Discharge	11,887	543	4,977	2,387	411	414	264
Layoff	1,900	40	989	572	51	64	32
Recall	419	8	211	70	14	10	6
Wages	3,278	110	3,629	891	102	96	61
Promotion	3,758	89	2,275	855	126	82	62
Demotion	678	19	387	132	18	16	20
Seniority	1,920	23	1,182	310	24	49	19
Job Classification	1,714	27	1,600	441	32	33	15
Training & Apprenticeship	1,300	25	667	368	30	30	10
Exclusion	185	3	284	24	23	7	2
Representation By Union	265	8	69	38	26	6	8
Segregated Locals	6		1		1		
Referral	66	1	32	13	19	7	2
Qualification & Testing	733	25	656	187	46	30	13
Advertising	30	9	59	16			
Benefits	1,047	52	2,105	243	39	56	25
Segregated Facilities	95	2	22	8			
Intimidations & Reprisals	2,421	128	956	531	132	81	141
Reprisal (704 Only)	827	41	408	148	13	132	18
Terms & Conditions	7,903	358	5,077	1,578	295	249	141
Unspecified	1,496	70	892	334	32	240	15
Blank or Invalid Issue	296	6	110	162	3	5	57
Tenure	12			1		1	
TOTAL	46,560	1,766	29,409	10,279	1,604	1,775	949

(Source: U.S. Equal Employment Opportunity Commission, Office of Public Affairs, *EEOC: Tenth Annual Report*, (Washington, D.C.: U.S. Government Printing Office, Supt. of Documents, 1976), p. 63.)

Development of an Affirmative Action Plan

The EEOC has suggested eight specific steps for developing an affirmative action program that will be effective. See Figure 5–4 for an example of these basic steps.

What is the relationship of affirmative action to EEO?

FIGURE 5–4   Basic steps to develop an effective affirmative action program.

1. Issue written EEO policy and Affirmative Action Commitment.
2. Appoint a top official with responsibility and authority to direct and implement the program.
3. Publicize the policy internally and externally.
4. Survey present minority and female employment by department and job classification.
5. Develop *goals* and *timetables* to improve utilization of minorities, males and females in each area where underutilization has been identified.
6. Develop and implement specific programs to achieve goals.
7. Establish internal audit and reporting systems to monitor progress.
8. Develop supportive in-house and community programs.

EQUAL EMPLOYMENT AND MANAGEMENT PRACTICES

A wide variety of managerial practices have been affected by equal employment and affirmative action regulations. To provide a broad picture of the current impact of equal employment, the following overview of selected management practices indicates some which have been upheld and some which have been found to be illegal. It is difficult to draw general conclusions from court decisions because the court approaches each factual situation with a straightforward legal analysis of *that particular situation,* rather than trying to establish ideological patterns. However, this analysis will highlight some recent court decisions in the discrimination area.

Sex Discrimination

Title VII of the Civil Rights Act prohibits discrimination in employment on the basis of sex. However, as with racial discrimination, it has taken a series of court decisions and EEOC rulings to determine exactly how broad that prohibition really is. For example, the EEOC established that hiring policies excluding women from jobs because of pregnancy violate the Civil Rights Act, and benefits from health or insurance plans for sickness or temporary disability must be extended to women employees disabled by pregnancy, miscarriage, abortion, or childbirth, or recovery from any of these.

Firing employees because absences exceeded allowed leave time may be unlawful if this practice has a disproportionate impact on one sex. This ruling means that an employer allowing employees six days leave a year may be in violation of the law if a woman is fired who missed three weeks of work because of pregnancy.[2]

Maternity leaves and pregnancy benefits.   Closely related, the Supreme Court held that an employer's refusal to permit female employees returning to work following a pregnancy leave to retain their accumulated seniority is a violation of Title VII. But not awarding sick pay for absence of pregnant employees is *not* discriminatory.[3]

A significant decision for employers involved approximately 100,000 female employees of the General Electric Company. The female employees had filed suit and claimed that the company discriminated when it did not give disability pay for pregnancy related absences. However, the Supreme Court ruled that the employer does not have to provide disability insurance to cover pregnancy related costs.[4]

Bonafide occupational qualifications and sex discrimination.   Some of the difficulties encountered in enforcing the abolition of sex discrimination center around the Bonafide Occupational Qualification (BFOQ) mentioned in the Civil Rights Act. What constitutes a BFOQ is subject to different interpretations in various courts across the country. Employment can be reasonably restricted to one sex on the basis of "authenticity." An example of this authenticity is women actresses portraying women characters. Also BFOQ's exist on the basis of "community standards of morality" or "propriety," such as male restroom attendants in men's restrooms.

A BFOQ was found to exist in the following case:

A college girl whose major is statistics, marketing, and survey work decided she wanted to spend the summer working for a poll-taking firm. She planned her course of action carefully, writing the government bureaus to learn where concentrated centers of surveying activity might be. She picked several large metropolitan areas where polls were taken and watched newspapers from these areas for employment ads. When one appeared she wrote and requested a job. She received no answer. Because summer was near she traveled to that city to visit the company. She was told that the two areas that were being studied required work and travel in rough neighborhoods. The company had a policy of not hiring females for such assignments.

The girl knew that the Civil Rights Law prohibited discrimination because of sex. She decided she would attack this company's decision through the EEOC which agreed to investigate. The company in question reiterated its position and said that it had two territories left open, both in slum neighborhoods. The surveyors had to travel on foot a good part of the time they were in the area, and interviews were sometimes held at night. In fact, one of their regular workers had been beaten by a gang of youths and was recuperating at home. The worker, a woman, had quit, saying the area made her too nervous. The company therefore felt it had a right to specify the sex of employees for these areas. It was looking for a man, one who was both diplomatic and able to take care of himself. Because of the dangers involved, interviewers for these areas were being paid time and a half.

The girl student countered that during the day a woman alone in a house would be more receptive to another woman. She expressed confidence that she could handle any situation that developed. The commission said it felt there were no legal grounds for further action. It based its decision on the dangerous conditions which prevailed in the surveying area and concluded that hiring a man for the position made good sense and was not necessarily wrongful discrimination.[5]

Restrictive state laws.   Many states have laws to "protect" women by requiring that they be restricted to a certain number of working hours a week or by specifying the maximum weight a woman is allowed to lift (25 pounds in several states). The EEOC has disputed these laws, and in many cases they have been ruled invalid in court because they conflict with federal law and are not reasonable grounds for denying jobs to women.

Equal pay.   An amendment to the Fair Labor Standards Act enacted in 1963 forbids employers to pay lower wage rates to employees of one sex than to the other sex for equal work performed under similar working conditions. This Equal Pay Act, administered by the Wage and Hour Division, U.S. Department of Labor, applies only to employees subject to the minimum wage provisions of the Fair Labor Standards Act. An exception to this law is a difference in pay based on some factor other than sex.

To illustrate, a county hospital violated the Equal Pay Act by paying female aides and male orderlies substantially different salaries for the same work. The hospital could not show that the higher paid orderly positions required substantially greater effort, greater skill, or assumption of greater responsibility.[6] In another case, three females employed by the Fargo Police Department as "car markers" showed that, because their salaries were 50 percent lower than their male predecessors, there was a violation of the Equal Pay Act. Even though the males were trained as patrol officers, they seldom, if ever, performed any duty other than car marker.[7]

However, the courts have not always ruled for a female complainant. In one case Ms. Katy, a teaching assistant, brought suit. Although Katy was hired as a teaching assistant, she voluntarily assumed extra duties in the form of unsupervised teaching and counseling. She then sued under the Equal Pay Act claiming she was entitled to a teacher's salary. The Court found no violation of the act because the school district was under no obligation to pay Katy for work for which she volunteered and was not required to do.[8]

In summary, the critical aspect of differences in pay is that the *jobs must be substantially different.* Tasks performed only intermittently or infrequently do not make jobs different enough to justify significantly different wages. This point is best clarified by the decision in a case involving male and female managers working for a major national retailer. A wage difference between male and female managers was not justified merely because two of the male managers did "extra duties." Other managers did "extra duties" at about the same rate, which was infrequent and sporadic. Different wages may not be paid male and female managers who are performing essentially the same job.[9]

The Handicapped and Discrimination

It is estimated that there are more than 20 million disabled Americans.[10] These people have special discrimination problems in that often they are not considered for jobs for which they are qualified.

In 1973, Congress passed the Vocational Rehabilitation Act, and in 1974 it passed twelve amendments officially titled The Rehabilitation Act of 1974. These acts constitute the basis for federal intervention into employment of the handicapped.

Generally, the net effect of the law and subsequent executive orders is as follows:

1. Federal contractors and subcontractors with more than $2,500 contract must take affirmative action to hire qualified handicapped people.
2. Contractors have an obligation to inform all employees and unions about their affirmative action plans and to survey their internal labor forces to locate qualified handicapped.
3. The Architectural Barriers Act of 1968 attempts to ensure that buildings financed with public money are accessible to the handicapped.

Many companies have recognized the advantages associated with hiring the handicapped without any pressure from the law or courts. McDonnell Douglas Corporation and Inland Steel were leaders in the area before the laws were enacted.[11]

Seniority and Discrimination

The U.S. Supreme Court has ruled that seniority systems are not invalid just because they perpetuate the effects of past discrimination. The decision involved alleged discrimination by a trucking company against blacks and Spanish-surnamed persons who sought employment as line drivers. Those who were hired were given lower-paying and less-desirable jobs as servicemen or city drivers and, when they sought to transfer to line jobs, they could not carry over their seniority. The Court concluded that the seniority system was entirely bonafide, applying equally to all races and ethnic groups. To the extent it locked employees into non–line-driver jobs, it did so for all.[12]

Discrimination in Job Assignments

Title VII was violated when an employer (1) established job categories designated "male" or "either" and refused to consider women under any circumstances for jobs designated as male jobs, (2) established weight limitations that had the effect of continuing male and female job classifications that previously existed, and (3) subsequently adopted a policy of designating jobs as either "heavy" or "light" and failed to consider women for jobs designated as "heavy" unless women specifically requested such jobs. Since the employer had historically classified its employees on the basis of sex (in violation of Title VII), it could not rely on word of mouth notice of job vacancies.[13] Another case involved a major airline; since airline purser and stewardess jobs are essentially equal in duties and responsibilities, Title VII was violated when the airline blocked the entry of women into the purser category.[14]

A qualified woman who unsuccessfully applied for a position of resident trainee mortician established sex discrimination by showing that (1) the funeral home shortly thereafter hired a man for that position; (2) licensed embalmers and morticians, both nationally and locally, were, in overwhelming preponderance, male; (3) the funeral home had never employed a woman as a licensed embalmer, licensed mortician, or resident trainee mortician; and (4) the funeral home did not employ both men and women to do the same work in any of its job categories.[15]

Employment Uses of Conviction and Arrest Records

Generally, courts have held that conviction records may be used if the offense could be considered job-related in nature. For example, a bank could use an applicant's conviction for forgery as a valid basis for rejection. However, some decisions have held that only convictions which could be seen as job-related occurring within the most recent five years are allowed. Consequently, employers often have a phrase added to an inquiry about conviction, such as, "Indication of a conviction will not be an absolute bar to employment."

Arrest records have been generally viewed with suspicion by courts. Statistics indicate that in some geographic areas a greater number of minorities are arrested than nonminorities. Consequently, using arrests, not convictions, may have an adverse impact on some groups protected by Title VII.[16]

Discrimination because of Grooming and Appearance

A variety of appearance features have been examined for discriminatory impact. Some of the common areas that have been ruled on are hair length, beards, and dress codes. Employer grooming codes which require different hair lengths for male and female employees bear such negligible relation to the purposes of Title VII that it cannot be concluded that they violate the act.[17] Regarding beards, an employer that maintained a rule forbidding employees at its produce warehouse to wear beards did not violate Title VII's ban on sex discrimination when it discharged a warehouse employee for refusing to shave off his beard.[18] Likewise, regarding dress codes, an employer did not violate Title VII's ban on sex discrimination when it discharged a male employee for refusing to wear a tie. There was no merit found in his contention that it enforced unequally separate dress and grooming codes for male employees and female employees.[19]

Discriminatory Use of Height-Weight Restrictions

The state of Alabama violated Title VII in setting height and weight restrictions for correctional counselors. The restrictions (5 feet, 2 inches and 120 pounds) would exclude 41.13 percent of the female population of the country but less than 1 percent of the men. The Supreme Court found that the state's attempt to justify the requirements as essential for job-related strength failed for want of evidence. The Court suggested that if strength were the quality sought, the state could have adopted a strength requirement.[20]

Age Discrimination

The Age Discrimination in Employment Act of 1967, which was amended in 1978, makes it illegal for an employer to discriminate in compensation, terms, conditions, or privileges of employment because of the employee's age.

> It is unlawful (1) to fail or refuse to hire or to discharge or otherwise discriminate against any individual, applicant, or employee 40 to 70 years old as to compensation, terms, conditions, or privileges of employment because of age, or because he has opposed an unlawful employment practice or taken part in asserting his rights against an employer who has unlawfully so discriminated, (2) to limit, segregate, or classify employees so as to deprive any employee 40 to 70 years old of employment opportunities or adversely affect his status as an employee because of his age, (3) to use printed or published notices or advertisements indicating any preference, limitation, specification, or discrimination based upon age, (4) to reduce the salary rate of any employee in order to comply with the act.[21]

The act does not apply if age is a Bonafide Occupational Qualification. Nor do the prohibitions against age discrimination apply when an individual is disciplined or discharged for good cause, such as poor job performance. The employer must post an official government-approved notice accessible to all employees and maintain records required by the Secretary of Labor.

For many years racial and sex discrimination cases overshadowed age discrimination cases. However, in May 1975, Standard Oil of California agreed to a $2 million settlement for 160 older workers laid off during a reduction-in-force beginning in 1970. In June 1974, the U.S. Labor Department filed a $20 million suit on behalf of 300 older employees laid off when the B & O Railroad merged with the C & O Railroad.[22] With the passage of the 1978 Age Discrimination Act, the potential for more age discrimination cases has increased significantly.

Child Labor

Child labor laws, found in Section XII of the Fair Labor Standards Act, sets the minimum age for most employment at 16 years. For "hazardous" occupations, 18 years is the minimum.

Examples of operations considered hazardous or detrimental to health are:

1. Driving a motor vehicle at any time in connection with the transportation or delivery of goods or riding on a motor vehicle
2. Operating or assisting in the operating of an elevator, crane, derrick, hoist, or highlift truck
3. Operating or assisting in the operating of feeding of power-driven wood-working machines
4. Work which involves riding in a freight elevator

The importance of child labor provisions are heightened because an estimated 2.8 million students aged 16 and older were expected to enter the labor force in 1978 looking for temporary work. Such an inflow means that managers must be certain of the law and the age of the applicant.[23]

Younger workers are also prohibited from most jobs in mining, roofing, demolition, logging, sawmills, and other such industries. The law is quite strict for 14- and 15-year-olds, who may essentially hold only clerical, office, and retail food service jobs, pump gas, or do errand and delivery work. They can work only between 7 A.M. and 9 P.M. from June 1 to Labor Day and are restricted to an eight-hour day and a 40-hour week. The restrictions are even stronger in the winter. These provisions do not apply to newspaper delivery, theater performances, children working for their parents in non-hazardous occupations. In farming there are no restrictions on workers 16 years and older.

Many organizations require *age certificates* for employees because the Fair Labor Standards Act places the responsibility on the employer to ascertain an individual's age. Asking for an age certificate helps an employer avoid unknowingly hiring someone who is too young to perform a hazardous job. These certificates may be issued by a representative of a state labor department, education department, or by a local school official. In various states these certificates may be referred to as age certificates, employment certificates, work permits, or working papers.

Can you identify and discuss six bases of possible discrimination?

GUIDELINES FOR EQUAL EMPLOYMENT INQUIRIES

The variety of areas in which discrimination may occur is quite broad, as the discussion has indicated. To narrow the focus, Figure 5–5 contains guidelines for lawful and unlawful preemployment inquiries. Although many different questions are often asked in interviews and on application blanks, all of them may not be permitted under existing equal employment regulations. This list, developed by an equal employment enforcement agency, illustrates the care that managers must take to avoid the appearance as well as the actual act of discrimination.

It should be clearly understood that this guide is not a complete list of questions. Employers can obtain all needed information about applicants as long as the information cannot be used for discriminatory purposes. As additional court decisions are made, employers should keep informed of changes that occur.

Once an employer tells an applicant he or she is hired (the "point of hire"), earlier prohibited inquiries may be made. *After* hiring, medical examination forms, group insurance, and other enrollment cards containing inquiries relating directly or indirectly to race, color, religion, or national origin may be filled out. Photographs or other evidence of race or religion and national origin may be requested *after* hire for legal and necessary purposes, but not before. However, such data may need to be maintained in a separate personnel records system in order to avoid its use when making promotion decisions.

REVIEW AND PREVIEW

This chapter has dealt with some of the implementation issues surrounding EEO. The importance of surveying the workforce and keeping good records was noted. Affirmative Action programs and EEOC charge processing were explained. Finally, a number of areas of management practice affected by EEO were described.

The number of court cases mentioned indicate that managers must stay current in this field, since it is changing rapidly. Areas such as equal pay, maternity, and seniority policies have been affected by court decisions recently.

FIGURE 5–5   Guidance to lawful and unlawful preemployment inquiries

Subject of Inquiry:	It is not discriminatory to inquire about:	It may be discriminatory to inquire about:
1. Name	a. Whether applicant had ever worked under a different name	a. The original name of an applicant whose name had been legally changed. b. The ethnic association of applicant's name
2. Birthplace & Residence	a. Applicant's place of residence, length of applicant's residence in Nebraska and/or city where employer is located.	a. Birthplace of applicant b. Birthplace of applicant's parents c. Birth certificate, naturalization or baptismal certificate
3. Race or Color	a. General distinguishing characteristics such as scars, etc.	a. Applicant's race or color of applicant's skin
4. National Origin & Ancestry		a. Applicant's lineage, ancestry, national origin, descendants, parentage or nationality b. Nationality of applicant's parents or spouse
5. Sex & Family Composition		a. Sex of applicant b. Dependents of applicant c. Marital status
6. Creed or Religion		a. Applicant's religious affiliation b. Church, parish or religious holidays observed
7. Citizenship	a. Whether the applicant is in the country on a visa, which permits him to work or is a citizen	a. Whether applicant is a citizen of a country other than the United States.
8. Language	a. Language applicant speaks and/or writes fluently	a. Applicant's mother tongue, language commonly used by applicant at home
9. References	a. Names of persons willing or proved professional and/or character references for applicant	a. Name of applicant's pastor or religious leader
10. Relatives	a. Names of relatives already employed by the Company b. Name and address of person or relative to be notified in an emergency	a. Name and/or address of any relative of applicant
11. Organizations	a. Applicant's membership in any union, professional service or trade organization	a. All clubs, social fraternities, societies, lodges, or organizations to which the applicant belongs where the name or character of the organization indicates the race, creed, color, or religion, national origin, sex or ancestry of its members
12. Arrest Record & Convictions		a. Number and kinds of arrests and convictions unless related to job performance.
13. Photographs		a. Photographs with application or before hiring b. Resume with photo of applicant.
14. Height & Weight		a. Any inquiry into height and weight of applicant, except where it is a bona fide occupational requirement
15. Physical Limitations	a. Whether applicant has the ability to perform job related functions	a. Whether an applicant is handicapped, or the nature or severity of a handicap
16. Education	a. Training an applicant has received if related to the job applied for	a. Educational attainment of an applicant unless there is validation that having certain educational backgrounds (i.e., high school diploma or college degree) is necessary to perform the functions of the job or position applied for
17. Financial Status		a. An applicant's debts or assets b. Garnishments

(Source: Used with permission of Omaha, Nebraska, Human Relations Department.)

111

The next section builds upon this general understanding of equal employment and turns specifically to activities involved in staffing the organization and its jobs. Chapter 6 looks at the process of analyzing jobs and work, a critical prelude to recruiting and selecting employees.

Review Questions

1. Discuss: "How can I report race to the EEOC when I cannot ask it on my application blank?"
2. What is affirmative action?
3. Evaluate the following statement by the president of a small company. "I can hire or promote whomever I please, as long as I get someone who can do the job."
4. Why do some employers require age certificates?

OPENING CASE FOLLOW-UP

After reviewing the charge of discrimination and the evidence furnished by the bank, the EEOC District Director rendered the following determination of the case.

The Charging Party, a Black female, alleged the Respondent employer (Bank) has engaged in unlawful employment practices in violation of Title VII of the Civil Rights Act of 1964, as amended by the Equal Employment Opportunity Act of 1972, by discriminating against her in the terms and conditions of employment and discharging her because of her race (Negro).

The Respondent denied the allegations and maintains the Charging Party was discharged because of absenteeism and tardiness and she was treated no differently than other employees in the subject department.

With respect to the Charging Party's terms and conditions issue, the Charging Party specifically alleged she was not allowed to leave the building during working hours; she was not allowed to have conversation with co-workers; management was strict in reporting her attendance; and management favored a Caucasian employee over her with respect to working procedures. The evidence gathered in the investigation demonstrated the Charging Party was treated no differently than similar place Caucasians in her terms and conditions of employment as alleged. Therefore we conclude, there is no reasonable cause to believe the Respondent is in violation of Title VII of the 1964 Civil Rights Act.

The Charging Party alleged she was discharged because of her race (Negro). The evidence gathered in the investigation revealed from the analyzation of attendance records and time cards the Charging Party was absent and tardy more than any other employee in the subject department. The Respondent's records also show Caucasians have been discharged for the same reason as stated for the Charging Party. Accordingly, we conclude, there is no reasonable cause to believe the Respondent is in violation of Title VII as alleged.

This determination concludes the Commission's processing of the subject charge. Should the Charging Party wish to pursue this matter further, she may do so by filing a private action in Federal District Court within 90 days of her receipt of this letter and by taking the other procedural steps set out in the enclosed NOTICE OF RIGHT TO SUE.

Case: Bob Wilson Versus the Feds

Bob Wilson works for International Paper Suppliers, a small paper wholesaler in a large city in the North-central United States. Bob is the general manager and usually does most of the hiring. Selection is not an overwhelming burden since International Paper Suppliers has only 45 employees, and Bob generally hasn't had to hire more than four or five people a year.

Three weeks ago Bob rejected three applicants and hired a fourth for the position of route drive with the company. One of the four applicants was Emilio Gonzales, a Chicano man about 35-years-old. Bob didn't feel that Emilio would feel "comfortable" with the rest of the work group. Bob had no personal biases, but he knew that some of the other drivers did have strong prejudices. Also, Emilio would have been the only Chicano in the company, so he was rejected.

This morning in the mail Bob received a notification from the Equal Employment Opportunity Commission that Emilio Gonzales filed a complaint with the commission against International Paper Suppliers alleging that they are discriminatory in their hiring practices. Bob doesn't know very much about the EEOC or what his responsibilities are regarding their operation, but he does know that this is a problem he doesn't need during this busy time of the year.

QUESTIONS

1. What do you think of Bob's concern for how well Emilio will fit into the group? What weight will that carry with the EEOC?
2. What actions will Bob likely face as a result of this incident?

Notes

1. *Affirmative Action and Equal Employment* (U.S. Equal Employment Opportunity Commission, 1974), p. 10.

2. "EEOC Declares Illegal Employer Policies that Discriminate on the Basis of Pregnancy," *Wall Street Journal*, April 3, 1972, p. 2.

3. *Nashville Gas Co.* v. *Salty*, 46 LW 4026, (1977).

4. *Gilbert* v. *General Electric Co.*, US 12CCH, *Employment Practices Decisions* 11,240, U.S. Supreme Court, 1976.

5. *Dynamic Management Series, 106*, p. 9. Used with permission of Bureau of Business Practice, Waterford, Connecticut.

6. *Brennan* v. *Owensboro-Daviess County Hospital*, 523 F.2d 1013 (6th Cir. 1975).

7. *Peltier* v. *City of Fargo*, 533 F. 2d 374 (8th Civ 1976).

8. *Katy* v. *School District of Clayton*, 411 F. Supp. 1140 (E.D. Mo. 1976).

9. *Brennan* v. *Sears, Roebuck and Co.* 410 F. Supp. 84 (ND Iowa 1976).

10. "Handicapped Workers," *Fair Employment Practices Series* (BNA, May 1977), p. 443–551.

11. Gopal C. Pati, "Countdown on Hiring the Handicapped," *Personnel Journal,* 57(March 1978), p. 149.

12. *International Brotherhood of Teamsters* v. *U.S.,* 45 L.W. 4506, 1977.

13. *Nance* v. *Union Carbide Corp.,* 13 FEP Cases 211/39 F. Supp. 436 (W.N.C. 1975).

14. FEP Cases 1068, _____ F.2d _____ (D.C. Cir. 1976).

15. *Sharp* v. *Brown and Co. Funeral Home,* _____ F. Supp. _____ (E. Mich. 1977).

16. *1977 Guidebook to Fair Employment Practices* (Chicago: Commerce Clearing House, Inc., 1977), p. 44.

17. For example, see Baker v. Taft Broadcasting Co. 14 FEP Cases 697, _____ F. 2d _____ (6th Cir. 1977); *Drura* v. *Delta Airlines,* 13 FEP Cases 1167, _____ F. Supp. _____ (E. Mich. 1976); *Allen* v. *United Parcel Service,* 14 FEP Cases 888, _____ F. Supp. _____ (N. Ca. 1977).

18. *Kearney* v. *Safeway Stores,* 14 FEP Cases 55, _____ F. Supp. _____ (W. Wash. 1975).

19. *Fountain* v. *Safeway,* 15 FEP Cases 96, 555 F.2d 753 (9th Cir. 1977).

20. *Dothard* v. *Rawlinson,* 45 LW 4888.

21. *Employment Act of 1967, as amended in 1978.*

22. "The Courts Reinterpret Old-Age Discrimination," *Business Week,* February 24, 1975, p. 91.

23. "Warning issued on Teen Workers" *Rocky Mountain News,* June 12, 1977, p. 24.

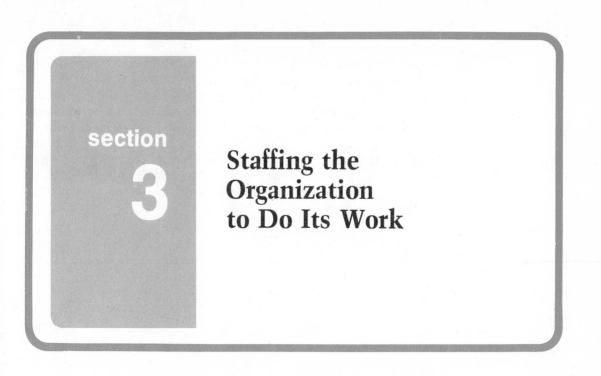

section 3

Staffing the Organization to Do Its Work

Staffing involves three distinct processes: work analysis, recruiting, and selection.

STAFFING		
Work Analysis	Recruiting	Selection

The first phase of staffing any organization is understanding the components of jobs. When a person is hired, both management and the individual must have a clear understanding of the job the new employee will perform. A job is an organizational unit of work, and Chapter 6 examines job design and effects on people. The second part of the chapter looks at the specific personnel activities related to the systematic analysis of jobs.

Chapter 7 examines the planning for and development of an appro-

117

priate group of persons to be considered for possible employment. Man-power planning, a longer-range form of determining the need for human resources, is one focus in recruiting. A short-range focus is also discussed.

Once a pool of applicants has been accumulated, the actual selection of persons for employment takes place. The selection can be made using a variety of data sources as a basis for selection decisions. Application blanks, interviews, tests, physical examinations, references and assessment centers are all data sources which may be used. Finally, the method of offering employment to a person is examined. Chapter 8 presents the information on selection.

chapter 6

Analyzing Jobs and Work

When you have read this chapter, you should be able to:

1. Define what a job is and three components of a job.

2. Explain the difference between job simplification and job enlargement.

3. Define job analysis and indicate three uses of job analysis information.

4. Discuss the impact of behavioral and legal concerns on the job analysis process.

5. List and briefly discuss four common methods of conducting a job analysis.

6. Identify the three parts of a typical job description and the relationship of a job description to a job specification.

The Reluctant Receptionist

Superior Products Company has recently hired a new personnel assistant, Virginia Nanfito. Virginia just received a college degree. Frederick Mills, the personnel director, was extremely pleased to find someone who had some familiarity with basic management concepts since he was the entire personnel department, except for a clerk-typist. During the interview Frederick emphasized that he planned to have Virginia function as his assistant and that she would be doing some interviewing and be responsible for maintaining employee records. Because Superior has had about 300 employees, Frederick had been too busy to prepare anything resembling a job description except for some scrawled notes on the back of an envelope.

Everything went fine for the first week for Virginia. On Monday of the second week, Frederick called Virginia into his office and explained that there was another minor duty that he had not mentioned to her. Frederick said, "In order to get approval to hire you from the president, I had to agree that who ever was hired would be the relief receptionist from 11:30 to 12:30 every day. The switchboard is usually quite busy and we wanted to be sure someone who is capable would be the backup." Virginia was not very happy about this assignment being sprung on her, but she agreed to try it for a while.

Within two weeks she was beginning to dread having to work the switchboard an hour everyday. Also, she discovered that she was expected to be the relief if the receptionist was sick or unable to work. On Wednesday and Thursday of the third week the regular receptionist was sick and Virginia filled in for her. On that Friday, Virginia told Frederick she was quitting in two weeks. When asked why, Virginia replied, "You misrepresented the job to me. You never said anything about my receptionist duties. If you had, I probably would not have taken the job."

The focus of personnel management is effective work performance by the organization's employees. Before people can be recruited and hired for jobs, managers should have a thorough understanding of jobs and the responsibilities that go with them. This understanding includes the design of a job and how it fits with other jobs. As the opening case indicated, the lack of a clear and accurate job preview led to Virginia Nanfito quitting her job. This chapter is primarily concerned with the processes of dividing the total work of an organization into the work to be performed in individual jobs, and the identification of qualifications needed by employees to perform those jobs satisfactorily.

WHAT IS A JOB?

Every job is composed of *tasks, duties,* and *responsibilities.*

> A JOB is an organizational unit of work.

Although the terms "position" and "job" are often used interchangeably, there is a slight difference in emphasis. A *position* is a collection of tasks, duties, and responsibilities performed by one person. A job may include more than one position which is very similar to another. Thus, if there are two persons operating postage meters in a mail room, there are two positions (one for each person) but just one job (postage meter operator).

A United States Civil Service Commission manual notes that a task is composed of motions and "is a distinct identifiable work activity," whereas "a duty is composed of a number of tasks and is a larger work segment performed by an individual."[1] Because both tasks and duties describe activities, it is not always easy or necessary to distinguish between the two. If one of the employment supervisor's duties might be to "interview applicants," one task which is a portion of that duty would be "asking questions."

Responsibilities are obligations to perform accepted tasks and duties. When a person becomes a manager, he or she also accepts responsibilities for the performance of the work unit. Closely related to responsibility is authority. As noted in Chapter 2, *authority is the right to direct resources.* An authority relationship statement for a sales manager might be: "Has authority to place advertisements costing less than $500." Thus, the extent of the authority that goes with that job is identified.

Nature of Job Design

Identifying the components of a given job is an integral part of job design.

> JOB DESIGN refers to conscious efforts to organize tasks, duties, and responsibilities into a unit of work to achieve a certain objective.

Designing jobs encompasses many considerations, and many different techniques are available to the manager. It has been equated with job enrichment, a technique developed by Frederick Herzberg, but, as the following discussion of considerations and techniques will demonstrate, job design is much broader than job enrichment alone.

Job design must consider (1) the *content* of the job, (2) the *methods* or technology used, and (3) their combined *effects* on the people doing the job, (4) the relationships with other people at work that are likely to develop through interpersonal contact.

What is the definition of a *job* and what are its components?

JOB DESIGN CONSIDERATIONS AND TECHNIQUES

When designing jobs, there are several considerations. There are also a number of different techniques that can be used in designing or redesigning jobs. The following is not intended to be an exhaustive treatment of all possibilities but rather to acquaint the reader with some of the issues.

Specialization/Simplification

The *specialization* idea suggests that greater efficiency and productivity result from having a job with only a very limited number of tasks. The people holding specialized jobs can learn them more easily and perform them more efficiently. They can become a "specialist" in a simplified job.

Job simplification is an extension of scientific management and the division of labor framework discussed in earlier chapters. This approach emphasizes the industrial engineering techniques of motion-and-time study and work sampling. *Motion-and-time study* is a precise observation and clocking of the actions performed in a job to determine the most efficient way to get it done. *Work sampling,* a somewhat different approach, does not require observing each detailed action throughout an entire work cycle. A manager can determine the content of a typical workday through statistical sampling of certain actions rather than timing all actions. Work sampling is particularly useful for clerical jobs.

Specialization and simplification are very powerful concepts for improving productivity. Without the application of specialization to manufacturing, the cost of televisions, automobiles, appliances, and many other products would be so high that very few people could afford them. However, there are costs associated with using these techniques as well.

In recent years there have been problems noted regarding extensive specialization and simplification of jobs. Critics say that it has gone too far, to the extent of deliberately ignoring or inadequately considering the human element. By creating extremely specialized jobs, managers may find some employees who react negatively to them. Boredom, lower quality, absenteeism, turnover, and increased coordination costs may accompany too much specialization.

Another major problem is coordinating all the various highly specialized parts of the organization. Specialists may have difficulty seeing the "big picture," and may define the organization and its objectives in terms of their own small speciality.

Job Enlargement/Job Enrichment

Attempts to alleviate some of the problems encountered with excessive job simplification fall under the general heading of job enlargement.

> JOB ENLARGEMENT is the concept of broadening the scope and/or depth of a job.

Some authors contend that job enlargement means only increases in job scope and that increases in both job scope and job depth are different and should be called job enrichment. Nevertheless, the above definition of enlargement (as encompassing scope and/or depth) reflects a general view.

Job depth is the amount of planning and control responsibility in a job. An assembly line worker is very restricted in choosing what is done and when it is done and would therefore have very little depth in the job. *Job scope refers to the number and variety of tasks performed by the job holder.* The vice-president of purchasing would have a wide job scope whereas the purchasing file clerk would have a much narrower job scope.[2] Enlarging job scope means that more operations are added to a job. More tasks of a similar nature are added, or the employee is allowed to rotate to a different unit of work on a similar level. This latter technique, known as job rotation, can be a way to break up an otherwise routine job.

Job rotation is the process of shifting a person from job to job. For example, one week on the auto assembly line, John Williams attaches doors to the rest of the body assembly. The next week he attaches bumpers. The third week he puts in seat assemblies and then rotates back to doors again the following week. Job rotation need not be done on a weekly basis. John could have spent one-third of a day on each job or one entire day, instead of a week, on each job. It has been argued, however that rotation does nothing to get at the *real root* of the boredom with routine problems. Rotating a person from one boring job to another may help some in the short run, but they are still perceived to be boring jobs.

Enlarging *job depth refers to increasing the influence and self-control employees have over their jobs.* Methods include giving an employee more planning and control responsibilities over the task to be done. Simply adding more tasks does not enlarge job depth. The essence of enlarged job depth is to design jobs to provide

. . . a greater variety of work content, require a higher level of knowledge and skills, giving the worker more autonomy and responsibility for planning, directing, and controlling his job and provide opportunities for personal growth and meaningful work experience.[3]

Supporters of the idea that more job depth is a positive step contend that higher productivity, lower absenteeism, and higher motivation will result because of the additional challenge and responsibility. They say that work will be more meaningful and satisfying and therefore employees will be more productive.

However, not all employees want their job enlarged in scope or depth. It depends on the employees' motivations and expectations and the rewards the employees want. For example, when a towel rack manufacturer attempted to enlarge some jobs by giving workers the latitude to assemble, package, and label five-piece towel racks, the experiment was unsuccessful. The workforce was primarily older, long-service employees who felt secure with the routine to which they had become accustomed. They were successful in resisting the change in job design, even though some of the younger workers would have agreed to the change.

Professionalization

Some jobs can be designed such that "professionals" are used to do the work. This "professionalization" presents some interesting advantages and disadvantages. Lawyers, accountants, physicians, as well as master plumbers, electricians, and medical technicians come equipped with the necessary knowledge to do certain kinds of work as a result of their training. Consequently, they often require less direct supervision in getting that work done.

However, using professionals may present some problems as well. They tend to relate to their profession rather than to the employer. Also, they may have different expectations about treatment and pay. Still, when the situation is right, designing a job so that professionals can be used can offer some real advantages.

Performance Feedback

There is increasing evidence that a job that can provide the worker with feedback on how he or she *is* performing relative to how he or she *ought to be* performing has some advantages.[4] In many situations these opportunities for feedback on performance can be designed right into the job.

For example, a job may be designed so that the worker keeps records on the number of units he or she produces daily and a record of rejects or quality errors. This recording and reporting is built right into the job duties and not added in afterward. Such feedback on performance relative to expected standards has been shown to improve productivity in several instances. More on this approach is discussed in Chapter 9 regarding *behavior modification.*

Social Ecology: The Physical Setting of Work

Designing jobs properly requires that the layout of the work or the setting in which a job must be done is considered. The way the work space surrounding a job is utilized can influence the worker's performance of the job itself. Several different job-setting factors have been identified, including size of work area, kinds of materials used, sensory conditions, distance between work areas, and interference from noise and traffic flow.[5]

Group versus Individual Jobs

Typically a job is thought of as being something one person does. However, where it is appropriate, jobs may be designed for groups. The use of groups or "work teams" has been found to increase satisfaction with the job and decrease turnover.

The Volvo plant at Kalmar, Sweden, has made very successful use of work teams in building automobiles. A work team has responsibility for a complete component of a car, such as the engine or the body. The team can become expert on a whole subassembly of a car, and members can influence work procedures and work rates.[6]

Job Design Summarized

For such innovations as those discussed above to be successful, they must be a part of the original design of jobs or a part of a rather complete redesign. Further, such considerations as pay (individual incentives versus group incentives) and time requirements (shift, eight-hour day, flexitime, four-day work week) are best built into the job design. Some of these issues will be given more detailed treatment in later chapters.

Job design involves the consideration of specialization and simplification, job rotation, professionalism, and enlargement of scope and depth relative to the organization, the personal desires and motivations of the employees, and many other situational factors. Job design is crucial and requires perceptive understanding and analysis of employees and organizational work. One way to begin to understand organizational work is a formal program of job analysis, which examines the tasks, duties, and responsibilities contained in an individual unit of work.

What is the difference between job simplification and job enrichment?

JOB ANALYSIS

Job analysis is the most basic personnel activity because it focuses on what people are expected to do.

> JOB ANALYSIS is a systematic investigation of the tasks, duties, and responsibilities of a job, and the necessary knowledge, skills, and abilities someone needs to perform the job adequately.

For example, if a supervisor tells an employee, "You are a grocery clerk," that clerk may not know what behaviors are expected, because there are many different tasks and duties a grocery clerk could do. But when an individual is hired for a job with specific duties and responsibilities, the manager can then expect certain work to be done.

End Products of Job Analysis

Job analysis identifies the components of a job which can be communicated to employees so they know exactly what to do. Figure 6–1 shows that job analysis serves as the basis from which job descriptions, i.e. job specifications, and job evaluations are prepared.

Job description. A JOB DESCRIPTION *is a summary of the tasks, duties, and responsibilities in a job.* Basically, the job description indicates what is done, why it is done, where it is done, and briefly, how it is done. *Performance standards* should flow directly from a job description, telling what the job accomplishes and the satisfactory performance expected in each area of the job description. The logic here is very clear. If employees know what is expected and what is good or poor performance, then they have a much better chance of performing acceptably. Unfortunately, performance standards, while beneficial, are often omitted from most job descriptions.

Job specification. A JOB SPECIFICATION *lists the various knowledge, skills, and abilities an individual needs to do the job satisfactorily.* The job description describes the job; the job specification describes the person needed for the job. The major use of job specifications is to guide in the recruiting and selecting of people to fill jobs. An example of a job specification for a clerk-typist might be: "Types 50-words per minute

FIGURE 6–1   Job analysis: most basic personnel activity.

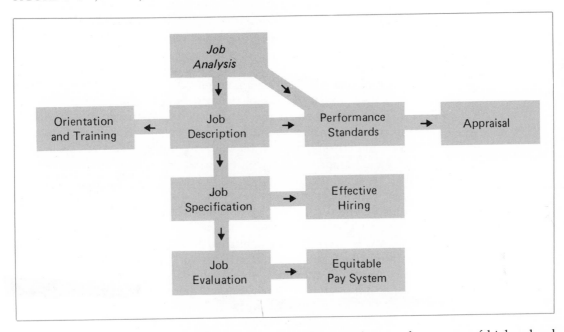

more than two errors, successful completion of one year of high school English, or passing of an English proficiency test.''

Job evaluation.   **A JOB EVALUATION** *uses the other parts of job analysis information to determine the worth of a job in relation to other jobs so that an equitable and meaningful wage and salary system can be established.* Because job evaluation is such an integral component in the compensation of human resources, a detailed discussion is postponed until Chapter 13.

What is job analysis?

Uses of a Job Analysis

Good personnel management requires both the employee and the manager to have a clear understanding of the duties and responsibilities to be performed on a job. Job analysis facilitates this understanding by focusing on a unit of work and its relationship to other units of work by identifying what composes a job. Job analysis has several key uses.

Employee selection.   Selecting a qualified person to fill a job requires knowing clearly the work to be done and the qualifications needed for someone to adequately perform the work. Without a clear and precise understanding of what a job entails, a manager cannot effectively select someone to do the job. If a retail store manager has not clearly identified what a clerk is to do, it is difficult to know, for example, if the person hired must be able to lift mail boxes, run a cash register, or keep the books.

Recruitment.   Closely related to selection is the use of job analysis for planning how and where to obtain employees for openings anticipated in the future. An understanding of the types of skills needed and types of jobs that may be open in the future enables managers to have better continuity and planning in staffing their organization. For example, in Witlow Corporation, a recent job analysis showed that the "Accountant II" job which traditionally required a college-trained person could be handled by someone with high school bookkeeping. As a result, the company can select from more available candidates and may save a considerable amount of money in salary costs.

Compensation.   While the established and unwritten assumption is that people are to be compensated for their work, more difficult jobs should pay individuals more for doing them. Job analysis information is used in a job evaluation to give more weight, and therefore more pay, to jobs with more tasks, duties, and responsibilities.

Training and orientation.   By providing a definition of what comprises a job through job analysis, the supervisor can easily explain to a new employee the boundaries of the employee's unit of work. It is difficult for an employee to perform well if there is confusion about what the job is and what is supposed to be done. The Virginia Nanfito case at the beginning of the chapter illustrates the problems caused by a poor job analysis.

Performance appraisal.   By comparing what an individual employee is supposed to be doing (based on job analysis) to what an individual has actually done, the value of the individual's performance and competency can be determined. The ultimate objective for any organization is to pay people for performance. To do this fairly, a comparison of what individuals should do, as identified by performance standards, with what they have actually done is necessary.

What are three uses of job analysis information?

Work Activities as an Interface

The twin activities of job design and job analysis together form the work interface. The activities involved in designing and analyzing jobs require

FIGURE 6–2   Work interface.

Personnel Unit	Managers
Monitors and researches effects of job design on turnover, absenteeism, and attitudes	Design jobs with assistance from specialists
	Supervise performance of jobs as designed and make adjustments as needed
	Monitor productivity and its relationship to job design
Prepares and coordinates job analysis procedures	Complete or assist in completing job analysis
Prepares job descriptions and job specifications	Review and maintain continuing accuracy of job descriptions and job specifications
Periodically reviews and assists managers in maintaining current job descriptions and job specifications	
	Develop performance standards with assistance from specialists

cooperation and coordination by personnel specialists and operating managers. Use of the interface concept, which is the theme of this book, puts the focus on who can best perform various aspects of job design and job analysis.

Figure 6–2 is a typical work interface that can be found in organizations having a specialized personnel unit. In small organizations managers have to perform all of the work interface activities. In Figure 6-2, notice that the managers are the main individuals with the responsibility for developing work procedures, performance standards, and designing and supervising the performance of work or jobs. The personnel unit attempts to determine the effects of job design and to suggest changes when research discovers job design is having negative effects. The analysis of jobs is coordinated by the personnel unit, which also provides special assistance in actually writing job descriptions and job specifications. Managers provide or assist in providing job analysis information.

Throughout the book, illustrations of various interfaces between the personnel unit and other managers will appear. Figure 6–2 shows the first of these, the work interface. The various interfaces are not intended to suggest what the "proper" division of responsibilities should be, but only what the division actually is in some organizations for illustration purposes.

BEHAVIORAL AND LEGAL ASPECTS OF JOB ANALYSIS

When systematically analyzing jobs, managers must be aware of two general concerns. One concern is the reactions of other managers and employees to such an intensive look at their jobs. The other concern is the impact of governmental constraints, especially equal employment, on job analysis and its outcomes. First, the impact of human behavior on the job analysis process must be considered.

Behavioral Side of Job Analysis

A detailed examination of jobs, while necessary from a managerial point of view, can also be a demanding and threatening experience for both managers and employees. Yet, the reactions of employees and managers can be critical to the ultimate success of any analysis of jobs and work.

The administrative use of job analysis can encounter conflict with the desires and fears of employees, managers, and unions. For example, in one shoe manufacturing firm, Paul Goetz had worked very hard in the packing department for many years. Everyone knew Paul worked hard, but no one really knew what he did. Because he was a hard worker no one ever really questioned it. When a new manager came to the packaging department, he felt a job analysis was in order. Paul violently resisted any attempt to analyze his job and refused to cooperate with the analyst. Paul was sure he would be put back to packing shoes eight-hours a day instead of working on many different projects as he was presently doing.

Employee fears.   One fear that some employees have is that clearly analyzing, specifying, and defining their jobs will put a *straitjacket* on them. Just as the shoe packer, they feel creativity and flexibility may be limited by formalizing the duties, responsibilities, and qualifications needed for a job. But, it *does not* necessarily follow that analyzing a job will limit job depth.

Another concern that some employees have is a fear about the *purpose* of a detailed investigation of their jobs. The attitude that "As long as someone doesn't know precisely what I am supposed to be doing, then I am safe" may generate attempts to hide the uniqueness of a job. The employee's concern is that somebody must feel they did something wrong if such a searching look is to be taken of their jobs. Consequently, explanation of the job analysis process and why it is being done should be the part of any job analysis.

Resistance to change.   As an organization changes to meet changing conditions, jobs also change and the job descriptions should reflect this. Consequently, there is a continual need to update and revise job descriptions and job specifications to make them more meaningful.

As would be expected, people become used to working within defined boundaries of responsibilities. When an attempt is made to change those "job fences," fear, resistance, and insecurity are generated. Suggesting it is time to revise job descriptions provokes anxiety because the employees' safe and secure job world is threatened. Their jobs may be changed and they may have to take on new and difficult responsibilities.

Because resistance in this situation is a natural reaction, effective managers should expect it and be prepared to deal with it. Perhaps the most effective way to handle this problem is to involve the individual in the revision process. Allowing Diane Morris, a purchasing analyst, to help reexamine her job and play a vital role in writing up the new job description and job specification can help overcome a certain amount of this fear and anxiety. However, this uneasiness may not completely diminish until the individual becomes accustomed to working under the new set-up. Because jobs change, supervisors and managers should expect to continually strive to overcome resistance as changes in jobs and work occur.

In addition, as work is changed and becomes more complex, especially at managerial and administrative levels, it is more difficult to precisely analyze and determine exactly what constitutes the job. For example, trying to write a job description for the president of a corporation is very difficult because of the general and often varied actions required. Likewise, clearly identifying the tasks, duties, and responsibilities for a head nurse or for a university dean is difficult because of the wide scope, flexibility, and complexity of the activities in which they engage.

Overemphasis on current employee.   A good analysis and the resulting job descriptions and specifications do not describe only what the individual currently holding the job does and that individual's qualifications. That person may have unique capabilities and the ability to expand the scope of the job to assume more responsibilities. The company would have difficulty finding someone exactly like that individual if he or she left. Therefore, the job description and job specification should indicate duties, responsibilities, and *key* qualifications needed and should not merely be a description of the person currently filling the job.

Managerial "straitjacket."   Through the information developed in a job analysis, the job description is supposed to capture the scope of a job. However, some individual employees may use job descriptions in order to limit managers' flexibility, thus putting a "straitjacket" on a manager. Consequently, some nonunion employers refuse to show job descriptions to their employees. This refusal makes it difficult for an employee to say, "I don't have to do that because it is not in my job description." In some organizations with a unionized workforce, very restrictive job descriptions may be encouraged or even demanded by union representatives as a mechanism to keep employees from having to accept additional work assignments.

A good example of using job descriptions to restrict work occurred when the air traffic controllers followed "the book" and caused havoc with airplane departures and landings at major airports such as O'Hare International Airport in Chicago. The attitude, "It is not in my job description," can become very burdensome for a management involved in changing an organization, its technology, and jobs in response to changing economic or social conditions.

Legal Aspects of Job Analysis

In addition to behavioral concerns, managers must also be aware of the importance of the legal impact of job analysis. The equal employment discussion in the previous chapter continually made reference to the need for "job-relatedness" in staffing activities. A job analysis provides the basis for job relatedness through the development of job descriptions and job specifications.

Federal employment agency enforcement guidelines clearly indicate that a sound and comprehensive job analysis is required for selection criteria to be validated. Without a systematic investigation of a job, an employer may be utilizing requirements that may not be specifically job-related. For example, if a trucking firm requires a high school diploma for a dispatcher, that firm must be able to indicate how such an education requirement matches up to the tasks, duties, and responsibilities of a dispatcher. The only way the firm might be able to justify that requirement would be to identify that the knowledge, skills, and abilities needed by the dispatcher could only be obtained through formal education.

In summary, it is extremely difficult for an employer to have a legal staffing system without performing a sound job analysis. Consequently, job analysis truly is the most basic personnel activity, primarily because it focuses on the jobs employees perform.

Why must managers be aware of the behavioral and legal aspects of job analysis?

METHODS OF ANALYZING JOBS

Job analysis does not have to be a complicated process. However, the systematic investigation of jobs should be done in a practical, logical manner. The process of collecting and using information about a job is aimed at determining what work is done, how it is done, why it is done, and what skills and abilities are needed to do it.

Gathering information about jobs can be done in several ways. Four common methods used are: (1) functional job analysis, (2) observation, (3) interviewing, and (4) questionnaires. Some combination of these approaches may be used depending upon the situation and the organization.

Functional Job Analysis (FJA)

Functional job analysis attempts to analyze jobs by building standardized task statements and job descriptions which can be used in a variety of organizations.[7] A functional definition of what is done in a job can be generated by examining the fundamental components of *data, people,* and *things.* One of the tools that can be used in FJA is the *Dictionary of Occupational Titles* (DOT), a standardized data source.

Dictionary of Occupational Titles (DOT).[8]   The DOT describes a wide variety of jobs. Specifically, over 20,000 jobs are classified and described using standard occupational categories (SOC). The DOT classifies and numbers jobs in a nine-digit code. Using this method a manager would look up a general analysis contained in the DOT, and then FJA can be used to sharpen the standardized DOT information. The job descriptions in Figure 6–3 are contained in the current DOT.

Using the identification code from the Director of Athletics, (090.117–022), a brief explanation can be given of how the DOT is used. The first three digits (090) indicate the occupational code, title, and industry designations. The next three digits (117) represent the degree to which a director of athletics *typically* has responsibility and judgment over *data, things*, and *people*. The lower the number of each item, the greater the responsibility and judgment involved. Further detail on these middle digits is provided in Figure 6–4. The final three digits are used to indicate the alphabetical order of titles within the occupational group having the same degree of responsibility and judgment.

The value of the DOT is in the wide range of jobs described. A manager or personnel specialist confronted with preparing a large number of jobs can use the DOT as a starting point. Then the job descriptions contained in the DOT can be modified as needed to fit the particular organizational

090.117-022   DIRECTOR, ATHLETIC (education)

Plans, administers, and directs intercollegiate athletic activities in college or university. Interprets and participates in formulating extramural athletic policies. Employs and discharges coaching staff and other department employees on own initiative or at direction of board in charge of athletics. Directs preparation and dissemination of publicity to promote athetic events. Plans and coordinates activities of coaching staff. Prepares budget and authorizes department expenditures. Plans and schedules sports events, and oversees ticket sales activities. Certifies reports of income produced from ticket sales. May direct programs for students of physical education.

151.047-010   DANCER (amuse. & rec.)

Dances alone, with partner, or in group to entertain audience: Performs classical, modern, or acrobatic dances, coordinating body movements to musical accompaniment. Rehearses dance movements developed by CHOREOGRAPHER (amuse. & rec.) May choreograph own dance. May sing and provide other forms of entertainment. May specialize in particular style of dancing and be designated according to specialty as ACROBATIC DANCER (amuse. & rec.); BALLET DANCER (amuse. & rec.); BALLROOM DANCER (amuse. & rec.); BELLY DANCER (amuse. & rec.); CHORUS DANCER (amuse. & rec.); INTERPRETATIVE DANCER (amuse & rec.); STRIP-TEASE DANCER (amuse. & rec.); TAP DANCER (amuse. & rec.).

160.162-010   ACCOUNTANT, TAX (profess. & kin.)

Prepares Federal, state, or local tax returns of individual, business establishment, or other organization: Examines accounts and records and computes tax returns according to prescribed rates, laws, and regulations. Advises management regarding effects of business, internal programs and activities, and other transactions upon taxes and represents principal before various governmental taxing bodies. May devise and install tax record systems. May specialize in particular phase of tax accounting, such as income, property, real estate, or Social Security taxes.

166.117-018   MANAGER, PERSONNEL. (profess. & kin.)

Plans and carries out policies relating to all phases of personnel activity. Recruits, interviews, and selects employees to fill vacant positions. Plans and conducts new employee orientation to foster positive attitude toward company goals. Keeps record of insurance coverage, pension plan, and personnel transactions, such as hires, promotions, transfers, and terminations. Investigates accidents and prepares reports for insurance carrier. Conducts wage survey within labor market to determine competitive wage rate. Prepares budget of personnel operations. Meets with shop stewards and supervisors to resolve grievances. Writes separation notices for employees separating with cause and conducts exit interviews to determine reasons behind separations. Prepares reports and recommends procedures to reduce absenteeism and turnover. Contracts with outside suppliers to provide employee services, such as canteen, transportation, or relocation service. May keep records of hired employee characteristics for govermental reporting purposes. May negotiate collective bargaining agreement with BUSINESS REPRESENTATIVE LABOR UNION (profess. & kin.)

709.684-026   BIRD-CAGE ASSEMBLER (wirework)

Fabricates wire birdcages, using handtools and drill press: Cuts wire to specified length, using wirecutter. Positions metal plate in *jig*, and drills holes around circumference of plate, using drill press. Fits ends of wires into holes in plate, and fastens upper ends of wire together to form cage.

Source: U.S., Department of Labor, *Dictionary of Occupational Titles*, 4th ed. (Washington, D.C.: United States Government Printing Office, 1977).

FIGURE 6–4   Work functions from *Dictionary of Occupational Titles.*

DATA *(4th Digit)*	PEOPLE *(5th Digit)*	THINGS *(6th Digit)*
0 Synthesizing	0 Mentoring	0 Setting Up
1 Coordinating	1 Negotiating	1 Precision Working
2 Analyzing	2 Instructing	2 Operating-Controlling
3 Compiling	3 Supervising	3 Driving-Operating
4 Computing	4 Diverting	4 Manipulating
5 Copying	5 Persuading	5 Tending
6 Comparing	6 Speaking-Signalling	6 Feeding-Offbearing
	7 Serving	7 Handling
	8 Taking Instructions- Helping	

(Source: U.S. Department of Labor, *Dictionary of Occupational Titles*, 4th ed. (Washington, D.C. United States Government Printing Office, 1977).)

situation. The importance of the DOT is demonstrated by the fact that job descriptions based on the DOT are considered satisfactory by federal employment enforcement agencies.

FJA is advocated as being easy to learn and use because statistical percentages can be assigned to each of the three dimensions (things, data, people) following the preparation of a task statement. A detailed explanation of the procedures in the FJA is not appropriate here, but it is relevant to note the use of DOT and FJA can be helpful to managers who are *not* personnel specialists. FJA can be used in developing occupational "career ladders" by identifying jobs requiring progressively more skill or responsibilities. This identification can clarify promotion and career progress. Also, because FJA is standardized, statistical data can be developed for personnel decision-making areas such as test validation.[9]

Observation

The observation method requires the manager to begin without any standardized information sources such as the DOT. The manager watches and observes the individual performing the job and takes notes to describe the tasks and duties performed.

Use of the observation method is limited because many jobs do not have complete and easily observed job cycles. For example, to analyze the job of a pharmaceutical sales person would demand that the observer follow the sales person around for several days. Furthermore, many managers may not be skilled enough to know what to observe and how to analyze what they do see. Thus, observation may be more useful in repetitive type jobs and in conjunction with other methods. Managers using other methods may watch the performance of parts of a job to gain a general familiarity with the job components and the conditions in which it is performed. This observation will help them better apply some of the other job analysis methods.

Interviewing

The interview method requires that the manager or personnel specialist visit each job site and talk with the employee performing each job. Usually a structured interview form is used to record the information. Frequently the employee and the employee's supervisor must be interviewed to obtain complete understanding of the job. During the job analysis interview the manager or personnel specialist must make judgments about the information to be included and its degree of importance.

The interview method can be quite time consuming. If Jones Computing Service has 30 different jobs, and the job analysis interviewer spends at least 10–15 minutes on each interview, the time involved for just interviewing and obtaining the analysis information will be extensive. The time problem will be compounded if the interviewer talks with two or three employees doing the same job. Furthermore, professional and managerial jobs are more complicated to analyze and usually require a longer interview.

For these reasons, combining the interview with one of the other methods is suggested. For example, if Mary Bowen has observed an employee perform a job, she then can check her observation data by also interviewing the employee. Likewise, the interview as a follow-up means is frequently used in conjunction with the questionnaire method.

Questionnaire

The questionnaire is a widely used method of analyzing jobs and work. A survey instrument is developed and given to employees and managers to complete. Figure 6–5 shows a sample questionnaire which has been condensed. As used, this questionnaire is six pages long, with ample space provided for respondent answers under each of the headings. At least one employee per job should complete the questionnaire, which is then returned to the supervisor or manager for review before being used for the preparation of job descriptions.[10]

The major advantage of the questionnaire method is that information on a larger number of jobs can be collected in a relatively short period of time. However, some follow-up observation and discussion is necessary to clarify inadequately completed questionnaires and interpretation problems. The questionnaire method assumes that the employees can accurately analyze and communicate information about their jobs. For these reasons, the questionnaire method is usually combined with interviews and observations to clarify and verify the questionnaire information.

Position Analysis Questionnaire. A specialized questionnaire method is the *Position Analysis Questionnaire* (PAQ), a structured instrument for job analysis. Each job is analyzed in terms of the 194 job "elements" contained in the PAQ. A manager using the PAQ checks either applicable elements or the appropriate place on a six-point rating scale. The PAQ attempts to identify the occupant behaviors involved in jobs. The nature of the PAQ job elements makes it possible for almost any type of position or job to be analyzed. It is easily quantified and can be used to conduct validity studies on tests. The PAQ can be easily translated into a job evaluation system to insure internal pay fairness, which considers the varying demands of jobs.[11]

Can you list four job analysis methods and describe each?

JOB DESCRIPTIONS AND JOB SPECIFICATIONS

The job description is the product of job analysis. It is complied and prepared to concisely summarize the job analysis information for each job. Job descriptions should be accurate, readable, understandable, and usable. Figure 6–6 shows a job description for a benefits manager at a hospital.

Job Description Components

The typical job description, such as the one in Figure 6–6 contains three major parts.[12] The first part is the *identification section*. In this part the employee's job title, department, and the reporting relationship are presented. Additional information such as the date of analysis, a job number, the number of employees holding the job, and the current pay scale of the job occupants can also be included.

The second part, the *general summary*, is a concise summarization of the general responsibilities and components that make that job different from others. One personnel specialist has said about the general summary statement: "In 25 words or less describe the essence of the job." In the example the listing of major accountabilities serves as the general summary.

The third part of the typical job description, the *specific duties* sec-

FIGURE 6–5 Employee position questionnaire.

Position Title _____
Name _____ Date Issued _____
Division _____ Dept. _____ Section _____
Name of Immediate Supervisor _____ His Title _____

1. GENERAL RESPONSIBILITIES: Indicate your position's basic function in one or two sentences. This statement should be a general summary of your position's responsibilities.

   _____
   _____

2. DESCRIPTION OF DUTIES: Describe, on the next page, all the duties of your position as fully as you think is necessary to give a complete picture of your position to someone who does not know what you do. Please list and describe *all* the duties of your position no matter how routine they seem or how seldom you do them. Number each duty, starting with those you consider most important and finish with those of a more routine or unimportant nature.

   If more space is needed, attach a separate sheet or sheets.

   In the column marked "No. Times Per _____," indicate the estimated number of times you perform each duty on a *daily, weekly, monthly,* or *yearly* basis.

   In the column marked "Approx. No. of Hours," indicate the estimated number of hours consumed in performing each duty in the period of time (day, week, month or year) indicated in the previous column.

No.	Description of Duties	No. Times Per _____	Approx. No. of Hours

3. MACHINES AND EQUIPMENT USED: List types used and indicate average percentage of time used *Daily* or *Weekly* or *Monthly*.

Type	%	Per	Type	%	Per
___	___	___	___	___	___
___	___	___	___	___	___

4. SUPERVISION—RECEIVED: List the number of each duty or task from Section 2 opposite the statement below which most nearly describes the extent to which the work is supervised.

   Direct and close supervision. Frequent and short assignments. Detailed instructions. Frequent and regular checks for progress.

   Routine supervision. Follow established work routines. Periodic checks for performance. Question off-standard conditions.

General supervision. Perform routine assignments alone. Follow established standard practices. Refer questionable off-standard conditions to supervisor.

Specific direction. Plan and arrange own work. Accomplish assigned objectives. Use a wide range of procedures. Refer only unusual off-standard conditions to superior.

General direction. Work from company policies and general objectives. Rarely refer to superior, only for clarification and interpretation of company policy.

Administrative direction. Work from overall policies, goals and budgetary limits. Virtually self-supervising with direct accountability for final results.

SUPERVISION—GIVEN:

A. List the position title(s) over which you have direct supervision and indicate under each title, the number of people so supervised:

_____

B. If your position involves functional (staff) supervision over programs, functions or positions other than those of your immediate subordinates, please indicate the specific programs, functions or positions over which such supervision is exercised and the nature of this staff supervision.

Program, Function or Position   Nature of Staff Supervision

_____

6. REGULAR CONTACTS: Please indicate the positions within or outside the company with which your position requires you to have regular contact. Specify the purpose, nature and frequency of such contacts. Do not include contacts with direct superiors or subordinates.

Position or Persons Contacted	Subject of Contact	Frequency in Normal Duties

7. WORKING CONDITIONS: Check appropriate squares and list any unusual conditions in your working environment:

☐ Usual Office Conditions   Unusual Conditions: _____

☐ Shop Conditions   _____

☐ Part Shop and Part   _____

   Office Conditions

☐ Outside Travel   If so, how often? _____

8. ADDITIONAL REMARKS: Indicate any other information or comments which you feel would be helpful in conveying a clear picture of your position.

_____

Date: _____ Your Signature: _____

Date: _____ Supervisor's Signature: _____

(Source: *Wage and Salary Administration: A Guide to Current Policies and Practices* (Chicago: The Dartnell Corporation, 1969). Used with permission.)

FIGURE 6–6   Sample job description

Date: March, 1978	Job Title: Benefits Manager	
Div. Administration	Dept: Personnel	Sect:
Reports to: Personnel Director		
Supervises: N/A		
Education: College degree in Personnel or Business Administration preferred but not essential		
Experience: Considerable experience with employee group insurance programs preferred		

Used with permission.

Major Accountabilities

1. Insures ERISA compliance and reporting for all pension and welfare benefits, keeping a current knowledge of IRS and DOL regulations.
2. Coordinates employee benefits and services.
3. Counsels employees regarding benefit problems.
4. Manages the office in the absence of the Personnel Director.

Duties and Responsibilities

1. Maintains ERISA reporting calendars for TSA, Retirement Plan, LTD and Life Insurance, Health Insurance.
2. Prepares and files appropriate reports to IRS, DOL, and employees, including gathering and verifying information from all insurance companies and/or other sources.
3. Maintains ERISA records for Retirement Plan. Correlates and insures accuracy of records with Trustee, Actuary, and legal counsel.
4. Calculates retirement benefits and processes forms, including Vested Terminations, Early, Normal, and Late Retirement, including Joint and Survivor and Lump sum cash-out benefits.
5. Counsels employees regarding benefits at the time of transfer in status, termination and retirement. Monitors pay period benefits reports insuring accuracy.
6. Processes garnishments on employees.
7. Approves requests for Educational Assistance and makes payments and receives reimbursements to the Hospital.
8. Administers absence control program, monitoring excused and unexcused absences, records and insures proper disciplinary action is being executed according to established policy and procedures. Maintains records and distributes reports on absenteeism to Department Heads and Personnel Director.
9. Manages salary security program, including processing of claims insuring proper reporting to insurance companies and employee understanding of life and LTD benefits and procedures.
10. Manages health insurance program including counseling employees regarding benefits and claim procedures, pays billings and insures proper payroll input for deductions.
11. Administers TSA program, including conducting annual reopenings with broker, counseling employees regarding benefits and maintains records insuring correct salaries, deductions and billing procedures.
12. Receives and processes unemployment compensation claims and verifies and pays quarterly billings.
13. Ensures accurate and timely payment of terminal benefits.
14. Conducts and analyzes benefits surveys in order to maintain pay competitiveness with area hospitals.
15. Recommends changes in benefit policy and practices.
16. Performs other duties as assigned.

tion, contains clear and precise statements on the major tasks, duties, and responsibilities performed. The most time-consuming aspect of writing job descriptions is this listing of specific duties.

Writing Job Descriptions

In writing job descriptions it is important to use precise action verbs which accurately describe the employee's tasks, duties, and responsibilities. For example, avoiding the use of vague words such as "does" or "handles" is important. Also, the specific duties should be grouped and arranged in some sensible pattern. If a job requires an accounting supervisor to prepare several reports and to perform other functions, those statements relating to the preparation of reports should be grouped together.

A guide to writing a job description statement for a social welfare job is shown in Figure 6–7. The manager preparing the job description should use precise and clear language but should not fall into the trap of writing a motion analysis. The statement, "Walks to filing cabinet, opens drawer, pulls folders out, and inserts material in correct folders," is a motion statement. The specific duty statement, "Files correspondence and memoranda to maintain accurate customer policy records," is sufficiently descriptive without being overly detailed.

FIGURE 6–7   Writing a job description of a social welfare job.

Performs What Action? (verb)	To Whom or What? (object of verb)	To Produce What? (expected output)	Using What Tools, Equipment, Work Aids, Processes?
Asks Questions/ listens Records answers	To/of applicant On eligibility form	In order to determine eligibility	Eligibility form Eligibility criteria in manual Interviewing techniques

This task statement can be more readable in this way: "Asks client questions, listens and records answers on standard eligibility form, using knowledge of interviewing techniques and eligibility criteria in order to gather information from which client's eligibility for food stamps can be determined."

(Source: *Job Analysis: Developing and Documenting Data, A Guide for State and Local Governments*, U.S. Civil Service Comm., BIPP 152–35, December 1973, p. 6.)

It is not the intent of this section to provide a detailed guide to writing job descriptions, but only to highlight some of the key ideas a manager should remember in writing or revising job descriptions.[13] Some job descriptions contain other sections about materials or machines used, working conditions, or special tools used. This information often is included in the specific duty statements or in a comments section. Also, the final statement in many job descriptions is often the "miscellaneous clause." This statement is included to cover the abnormal and unusual situations that comprise a very small part of an employee's job. Having such a statement is an attempt to prevent an employee from saying, "It's not covered in my job description."

One of the challenging aspects of writing job descriptions involves describing executive and upper management level jobs. Because of the wide range of duties and responsibilities, those jobs often are described in more general terms than jobs at lower levels in the organization.

What are the three components of a job description and how do you write them?

Job Specification

The job specification, a logical outgrowth of a job description, attempts to describe the key qualifications someone needs to perform the job satisfactorily. Specific factors identified often can be grouped into three categories: *Knowledge, Skills,* and *Abilities* (KSA's). Within these categories factors include education, experience, work skill requirements, personal requirements, mental and physical requirements, and working conditions and hazards. A job specification for a remote visual display terminal operator might include such items as a required education level, a certain number of months of experience, typing ability of 60 wpm, high degree of visual concentration, and ability to work under time pressure.

A job specification can be written by talking with the current holder of the job about the qualifications needed to perform the job satisfactorily. But caution should be exercised so that the characteristics of the current job occupant are not used as the sole basis for the job specification statements. Checking the job requirements of other organizations and businesses with similar jobs is another means to obtain information for preparing job specifications.

Critical KSA's.   In writing any job specification, it is important to list only those KSA's essential for satisfactory job performance. Only directly job-related items which are nondiscriminatory should be included. For example, a high school diploma should not be required for a job unless the manager can demonstrate that an individual with less education cannot perform the job as well. Because of that concern, some specification statements read: "high school diploma, or equivalent acceptable experience." In some technical jobs the exact educational skills can be indicated: "Must have thorough knowledge of PL-l and COBOL computer languages."

A process for developing relevant KSA's has evolved very recently in the public sector. Using a content validity approach that focuses only on critical job-related criteria, this process uses a group of experts in a job, including employees holding the job, to identify clear, recognizable, and ratable KSA's. These KSA's then become the basis for selecting employees using only job-related KSA's.[14]

Why are a job description and a job specification closely linked?

Using Job Descriptions and Job Specifications

Once the job descriptions and specifications are prepared, the manager should provide feedback to the current job holders, especially those who assisted in the job analysis. One feedback technique is to give employees a copy of their own job descriptions and specifications for review. Giving the current employees the opportunity to make corrections, ask for clarification, and discuss their job duties with the appropriate manager or supervisor is one way to enhance manager-employee communications. Questions about how work is done, why it is done that way, and how it can be changed are topics that arise. When employees are represented by a union, it is essential that union representatives be included in reviewing the job descriptions and specifications. Otherwise, the possibility for future conflict is heightened.

Performance standards. An important use of the prepared job descriptions and specifications is to generate performance standards for each of the job responsibility statements. Because performance standards list what is satisfactory performance in each area of the job description, the employee has a clear identification of what is expected on the job.

The development of clear and realistic performance standards can intercept some problems which often arise when employees' performances are appraised. The mutual generation of performance standards serves as the basic foundation for the development of a Management by Objectives system, discussed in detail in Chapter 12.

A good job specification is useful in selecting human resources for the firm because it provides a specific set of qualifications for an individual to be hired for a specific job. Clarifying what type of person is to be recruited and selected definitely helps a manager, supervisor, or personnel specialist. Likewise, the well-written job description can be used to give applicants an initial statement of what they will be doing if they are hired. Thus, the type of job, job requirements, and job expectations can be identified more effectively to prospective or new employees.

As is evident, job descriptions and job specifications are valuable tools for managers and employees in any organization. The development and use of job descriptions and job specifications is a time-consuming process, but one necessary for effective organizational staffing and operation to occur.

REVIEW AND PREVIEW

The major thrust of any organization is to move toward goals or objectives. Progress toward these goals is made by performing the work of the organization in a logical and coordinated fashion. To do so, the work of the organization must be divided into jobs. When properly designed, the jobs have the dimensions of scope and depth and form an integrated unit of work. The expectations and rewards desired by the individuals performing the jobs should be considered when jobs are designed. A successful matching of individual expectations and the organization's need for performance is important.

Once jobs are designed they must be analyzed, keeping both behavioral and legal concerns in mind. The job analysis process generates information used in the development and utilization of job descriptions, job specifications, and job evaluation. The job description delineates the key tasks, duties, and responsibilities of a job; the job specification translates those job requirements into the human knowledge, skills, and abilities needed to perform the described job satisfactorily.

There are several uses that can be made of the job description and job specification information obtained by analyzing jobs and work. One of the most beneficial of these uses is in recruiting and selecting the people to fill the analyzed jobs. The next chapter examines recruiting activities, and Chapter 8 explores the nature of personnel selection.

Review Questions

1. What do you do when you design a job? What are some key concerns you must consider?
2. Distinguish the relationship or lack of it between job simplification, and job rotation. What is a criticism of each?
3. Clearly define and discuss the relationship between job analysis, job descriptions, and job specifications.
4. "Job Analysis is the most basic personnel activity." Discuss.

5. How do human behavior and governmental considerations affect the job analysis process?
6. In two sentences each, describe the four common methods of analyzing jobs.
7. Construct a form for a sample job description. Why is a job description necessary before developing a job specification?

OPENING CASE FOLLOW-UP

The importance of job descriptions and job specifications is highlighted in this case. Lack of a prepared job description has led to the firm's losing an employee after only a short time. The personnel director did misrepresent the job, and now the firm loses the opportunity to recover the costs associated with Virginia's recruiting, selection, and training.

By seeing a job description, an applicant can gain a more accurate picture of the expectations associated with a job. Preparation of a job description would also provide the basis for developing a clear job specification that the personnel manager could use in recruiting, selecting, and training a personnel assistant.

Hopefully, the personnel director will have learned from this experience. If he has, he will develop a well-written job description and identify the relevant KSA's needed by this personnel clerk-receptionist.

Case: College Bookstore

In a large college bookstore the number of new textbooks to be received, priced, and shelved at the start of a new term can be extensive. There are basically five different operations involved in getting books from the receiving dock to the retail shelves. They are: (1) transporting the boxes from the receiving dock to the pricing area, (2) unboxing and sorting the books in each shipment, (3) checking a shipment against the purchase order, (4) placing a price tag on each book, and (5) shelving books in appropriate course locations. Because of the volume of books involved at the beginning of each term, student helpers are usually hired for about two weeks before each term to process the incoming books. These temporary employees usually work six-to-eight hours a day on the textbook receiving process.

QUESTIONS

1. How does job design apply to this case?
2. a. How many jobs would you have under a job simplification approach?
   b. Why might job rotation be considered?
   c. Why might a job enlargement strategy be considered?
   d. How would job analysis, job descriptions, and job specifications be useful to the textbook department manager?

NOTES

1. *Job Analysis: Developing and Documenting Data, A Guide for State and Local Governments,* U.S. Civil Service Commission, BIPP 152-35, December 1973, p. 1.

2. Allen Filley and Robert J. House, *Managerial Process and Organizational Behavior* (Glenview, Ill.: Scott, Foresman, 1976), p. 340.

3. Robert M. Monczka and William E. Reif, "A Contingency Approach to Job Enrichment Design," *Human Resource Management* (Winter 1973), p. 10.

4. See, for example, Fred Luthans and Robert Kreitner, *Organizational Behavior Modification* (Glenview, Ill.: Scott, Foresman, 1975).

5. For more information see Fred I. Steele, *Physical Settings and Organizational Development* (Reading, Mass.: Addison-Wesley Publishing, 1973).

6. Richard E. Walton, "Successful Strategies for Diffusing Work Innovations," *Journal of Contemporary Business* (Spring 1977), pp. 7–9.

7. A concise but detailed explanation of FJA is contained in *ASPA Handbook of Personnel and Industrial Relations: Volume I, Staffing Policies and Strategies,* Dale Yoder and Herbert G. Heneman, Jr., eds. (Washington, D.C.: The Bureau of National Affairs, 1974), pp. 4-58 through 4-63.

8. U.S., Department of Labor, *Dictionary of Occupational Titles*, 4th ed. (Washington, D.C.: United States Government Printing Office, 1977).

9. Sidney A. Fine, "Functional Job Analysis: An Approach to a Technology for Manpower Planning," *Personnel Journal*, 53 (November 1974), pp. 813–818.

10. Adapted from *Wage and Salary Administration: A Guide to Current Policies and Practices* (Chicago: The Dartnell Corporation, 1969). Used with permission.

11. For information on the job elements and the refinement of the PAQ, see Ernest J. McCormick, Paul R. Jeanneret, and Robert C. Mecham, "A Study of Job Characteristics and Job Dimensions as Based on the Position Analysis Questionnaire (PAQ)," *Journal of Applied Psychology*, 56 (August 1972), pp. 347–368.

12. David W. Belcher, *Compensation Administration*, 3d ed. (Englewood Cliffs, N. J.: Prentice-Hall, 1974), p. 130.

13. For a detailed guide on preparing and writing job descriptions see *Job Analysis*, U.S. Civil Service Commission, or Herbert G. Zollitsch and Adolph Langsner, *Wage and Salary Administration*, 2d ed. (Cincinnati: Southwestern Publishing, 1970).

14. For detailed information, see Robert Otteman and J. Brad Chapman, "A Viable Strategy for Validation: Content Validity," *The Personnel Administrator* (November 1977), pp. 17–22.

chapter 7

Recruiting Human Resources

When you have read this chapter, you should be able to:

1. Define manpower planning and explain the nature of the manpower planning process.

2. Discuss several controllable and uncontrollable variables that affect the forecasts of supply and demand of manpower.

3. Identify and briefly explain at least three internal sources of employees.

4. Name and briefly discuss at least four external recruiting sources.

5. List three advantages and disadvantages of internal and external recruiting.

Northwest State College

Northwest State College (a disguised name) is a four-year regional state college and has an enrollment of about 3,500 students. Its business department has a faculty of seven full-time instructors, and other part-time instructors are used as needed. Currently about 900 students are majoring in business. The college is located in a medium-sized northern community of about 70,000. Most of the faculty recruiting is done by one person, the department head, who makes the initial contact with prospective faculty members at various professional meetings held during the school year. If the department head cannot attend a meeting, recruiting is done by an instructor from the business department.

Projections are that enrollment at Northwest State will increase about 25 percent in the next five years. Most of the increase is expected in the business area. The ideal faculty size would be about 16 full-time instructors to handle the load and to eliminate the need for part-time instructors. Most of the full-time instructors currently in the Department of Business Administration hold MA's or MBA's from various northern colleges. The salary scales and fringe benefits are considered to be slightly lower than the compensation available at similar colleges in the region. In addition to any increase in faculty members needed due to enrollment, three replacements are needed for this fall in the business area to replace individuals who have gone elsewhere.

Northwest State has a recruiting policy that requires final approval of candidates by the department head, the vice-president for academic affairs, and the president of the college. In addition, the school has a policy requiring that at least two candidates be invited to the campus before any candidate can be hired so that adequate screening can take place. Often the result is a waiting period of two months between initial contact, application, and campus interview for most applicants. Some other small colleges in the area pay full travel expenses for potential candidates, while the majority of the others pay at least half. Northwest State does not pay any travel expenses if the candidate is *not* hired. Only if the candidate is offered a position and accepts is full reimbursement for travel expenses given. Usually the payment comes about two months following the campus interview.

In the past Northwest State has not been very successful in filling empty positions. The president is concerned and wants to evaluate the recruiting program so that a better one can be designed.

FIGURE 7–1   Recruiting portion of staffing interface.

Personnel Unit	Managers
Collects data from managers to prepare manpower plans	Determine qualifications and anticipate needs
Assists in career planning and training to accomplish planned goals	Identify and monitor career plans of employees
Plans, coordinates and evaluates recruiting efforts	Assist in recruiting effort

An organization can develop an effective work force *only* if it first determines the skills and number of people it will need, and then can find and hire them. Such actions require: (1) *manpower planning* to determine the needs, and (2) a knowledge of appropriate *recruiting sources* and *methods.*

In most large organizations the manpower planning and recruiting functions are coordinated through a personnel department. It is the responsibility of this department to maintain, analyze, and coordinate manpower plans with other departments as part of a perpetual recruiting effort.

Often other managers help in the recruiting effort by determining the skills and qualifications needed in individuals who will fill vacancies in either area. Figure 7–1 shows a typical interface between the personnel department and managers regarding recruiting. In smaller organizations and even in some divisions of large organizations, it is possible for several different managers to work on recruiting.

NATURE OF RECRUITING

The objective of the recruiting process is to provide a sufficiently large group of candidates so that qualified employees can be selected.

> RECRUITING is the process of generating a pool of qualified applicants for organizational positions.

If the recruitment process does not provide an adequate group of candidates for selection, good employees may not be hired. If the number of available candidates equals the number of people to be hired, there *is no selection*—the choice has already been made. The organization must either leave some jobs unfilled or take all of the candidates.

In addition to *general* recruiting, an organization must engage in *specialized* recruiting. Such recruiting efforts are directed at the particular type of individual the organization wants to hire. For example, recruiting college-educated, electronics engineering employees is a more specialized process than recruiting drafting clerks.

While extensive recruiting efforts are usually associated with tight labor markets and a high organizational need for employees, recruiting efforts should not be limited to such difficult periods. Even during periods of reduced hiring, long-range manpower plans should include contacts with outside recruiting sources to maintain visibility, and maintenance of employee recruiting channels within the organization is important. These activities are essential so that the recruiting activity can be stepped up on short notice when needed.

Important activities for proper recruiting include:

1. Determining and categorizing long-range and short-range needs by job title.
2. Staying informed of conditions in the employment market,
3. Developing effective recruiting material,
4. Recording the number and quality of applicants from each recruiting source, and
5. Following up on applicants to evaluate the effectiveness of the recruiting effort.

When a vacancy occurs which must be filled, generally, internal sources of qualified applicants are considered first. Employees can be promoted or transferred into the position, or sometimes an individual may be demoted into the vacant position. A good manpower planning program maintains information on present employees for internal transfers. In the normal course of events employees resign, retire, die, or are fired. Without proper planning, unforeseen vacancies can hamper the organization's operation, especially if a new employee is not promptly found and trained.

MANPOWER PLANNING

As with other areas of operations, planning is important in personnel activities. Manpower planning is tied in with generally accepted planning efforts in financing, marketing, and production.

MANPOWER PLANNING consists of estimating the number, type, and sources of employees required for an organization to meet its overall objectives.

Process of Manpower Planning

The general process of manpower planning is illustrated in Figure 7–2. Notice that the first stage of manpower planning is an examination of *organizational objectives and plans.* If a retail chain plans to double its number of stores from 100 to 200 in a three-year period, that firm must also identify how many, and what types of, new employees will be needed to staff these new stores. Thus, its *gross manpower requirements* must be identified.

FIGURE 7–2   Manpower planning and programming process.

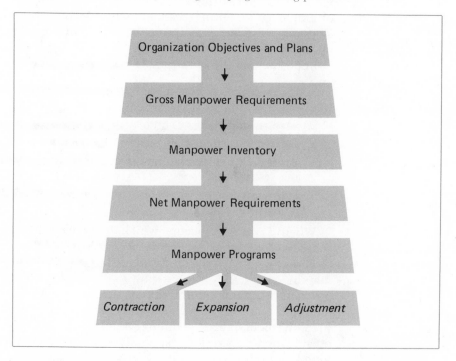

(Source: Bruce P. Coleman, "An Integrated System for Manpower Planning," *Business Horizons,* October 1970, p. 91. Reproduced with permission.)

Following this identification of how many employees will be needed, the firm would then need to "inventory" its existing employee work force. This *manpower inventory* identifies the skills and capabilities of current employees so that the firm can build on its existing reservoir of workers.

Net manpower requirements can be identified by comparing the number of people and the skills that will be needed to what the firm anticipates is available in its current workforce. Using this data as a base, the firm then must develop *manpower programs* to expand, contract, and/or adjust the composition of its workforce.

Why Plan?

Manpower planning must be viewed *over time* because it allocates human resources to jobs over long periods, not only for the next month, or even the next year. Manpower planning concerns the *current* level of skills in an organization and expected vacancies due to retirements, promotions, transfers, sick leaves, discharges, or other reasons. Also, through this type of planning, expansions or reductions in operations and projected technological changes can be analyzed. On the basis of such analysis, plans can be made for shifting employees internally, laying off or otherwise cutting back manpower, or for training present employees, as well as for recruiting and hiring new people.

What is manpower planning and generally how is it done?

Benefits of planning.   Some of the potential benefits of an *effective* manpower planning system are:

1. Reduced personnel costs, because of management's ability to anticipate shortages and/or surpluses of manpower and correct these imbalances before they become unmanageable and expensive;
2. A better basis for planning employee development that is designed to make optimum use of workers' attitudes within the organization;
3. Improvement in the overall business planning process;
4. More opportunities for including women and minority groups in future growth plans and identifying the specific development or training programs needed today to make specific skills available tomorrow;
5. A greater awareness of the importance of sound manpower management throughout all levels of the organization;
6. A tool to evaluate the effect of alternative manpower actions and policies[1]

Manpower problem signals.   When organizational and technological changes occur in an organization, good manpower planning can ease the impact. A study on the impact of such changes upon the human resources in an organization found that, while manpower planning problems differed somewhat for each firm, the most common sources of human resource problems were new technology, severe labor, and outside pressures. It was found that difficulties arise when a company incorporates new technologies that require a new level of knowledge to perform the same job.[2] For example, a company may purchase a new machine to expedite a particular job. The employee who must operate it may need extensive training to learn to use the machine, that is, if the employee has the aptitude to learn such a technical procedure. Often when machines replace human effort, the employee involved must be given more duties, time off, or another job.

Problems also arise when labor shortages are severe, especially shortages of people with specialized talents such as welders or computer programmers. Also, when the average age of a company's labor force is increasing, sometimes it becomes difficult to motivate older people to work under a new, highly automated system. Outside pressures, such as equal employment legislation, may cause problems with managers and employees. Proper manpower planning can forecast these changes long before plans for dealing with the problems need to be implemented.

Nature of Forecasting

Forecasting is an attempt to predict future changes in manpower. It is not an easy undertaking, since it has some "crystal-ball gazing" aspects to it. Although some rather advanced forecasting techniques have been developed, it is far from being an exact science. Forecasts generally take historical data and project them into the future. This method is adequate, but the manager must keep in mind that the historical data are based on trends that *may be changing*.

Forecasting periods. Manpower forecasting should be done over three planning periods: *short-range, intermediate*, and *long-range*.[3] The most commonly used planning period is short-range, usually over a period of six months to one year. This level of planning is almost a routine matter in many organizations. It is common because very few assumptions about the future are necessary. These short-run forecasts indicate an organization's best estimates of immediate personnel needs. Intermediate and long-range forecasting is a much more difficult process. Intermediate plans usually project one to five years into the future and long range plans extend beyond five years.

Forecasting Internal Demand and Supply

Manpower planning attempts to match the organization's forecasted *demand* for manpower with the anticipated *supply* of available manpower. To identify the demand required, two basic approaches can be used: (1) calculating the demand for people on an organization-wide basis, using the *average demand* for the entire organization over a period of time; (2) considering individual "units" in the organization rather than the entire organization. For example, a forecast that Apex Corporation needs 75 new employees next year might mean less than a forecast that Apex Corporation needs 25 new people in sales, 25 in production, 10 in accounting, 5 in personnel, and 10 in the warehouse. This unit breakdown obviously allows for more consideration of specific necessary skills than the aggregate method.

Auditing internal manpower sources. Managers for some time have recognized the need for periodic financial audits. Auditors' reports are generally used to pinpoint areas of potential problems, such as excessive cost overruns, inadequate reporting techniques, or fraud. The same technique can be used to check the use of personnel in an organization and to determine future demand for manpower.

One of the first steps in conducting a manpower audit is a performance appraisal for each individual in a department that identifies each person according to the quality of his or her work. This information is then combined by work group to pinpoint the level of performance in a work unit. For example, combining the performance ratings of the eleven people in one company's management group shows that the company has a high percentage of very qualified managers; nine of the eleven are rated good or excellent overall.

Charts giving an overview of the department's manpower situation may be plotted for each department in an organization. When overall data are charted, the accumulated information can show where there are few internal candidates for future positions. Likewise, the manpower audit can indicate where there is a reservoir of trained people that the employer can tap as it meets future conditions.

A part of internal auditing must consider some factors over which there is little control. Some employees will die, quit the firm, retire, or otherwise reduce the current employee force. Likewise, new employees will be hired. Thus, internal planning must utilize forecasts about these factors when an internal audit is conducted.

Manpower Supply Factors

Except for some qualified individuals already in the organization, most new employees must be obtained from outside the organization. A great many factors can affect the supply of labor available to an employer and the economy in general.

Economic conditions. General business cycles of recessions and boom times can make labor readily available or dry up a good source of recruits. There is a considerable difference between finding qualified applicants in a 2 percent unemployment market and in a six percent unemployment market. In the 2 percent unemployment market, very few qualified applicants are likely to be available for any kind of position. Those that *are* available may be basically unemployable because they are uneducated, unskilled, or unwilling to work. As the unemployment rates rises, the number of qualified candidates available rises.

FIGURE 7–3   Occupational distribution by sex

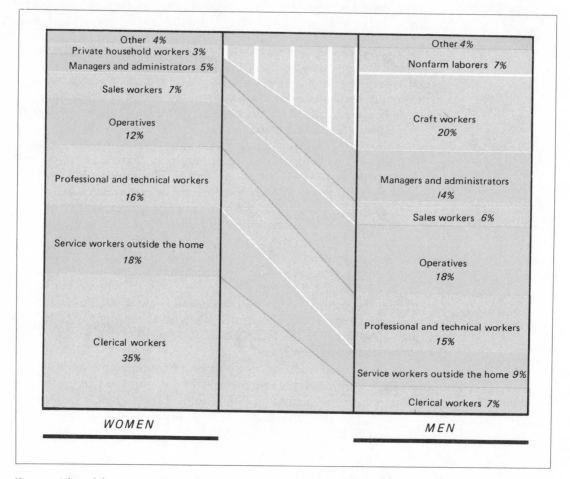

(Source: Adapted from U.S. Department of Labor, Women's Bureau Employment Standards Administration, *World Workers Today*. (Washington, D.C.: Government Printing Office, 1976).)

Government policies. Government pressure on organizations to hire more minority group members has increased the difficulties involved in finding qualified minority group members for many high-skill positions. The effect of affirmative action pressures to hire minorities and women for certain jobs has led to a real shortage of such potential employees in those areas. Figure 7–3 shows the occupational differences between men and women. Consequently, internal development of females and minorities must be considered by many employers. It is clear from Figure 7–3 that finding a woman craft worker or manager/administrator with experience is going to be much more difficult than finding a man for either job.

Job mobility and workforce participation. **Another important, documented** trend affecting the supply of labor is job mobility. While people changed jobs more regularly during the 1960s than in the past, they are changing jobs less frequently in the 1970s than they did in the last decade. This mobility may not be reflected in the unemployment figures, because many people look for job changes while still on their present job.

A company also cannot control *people's decisions to leave or enter the job market.* A significant factor in the available work force is caused by more women entering and reentering the job market. It is estimated that well over 60 percent of all women in the United States will be in the labor force by 1990. Figure 7–4 indicates this increase graphically.

Geographical and competitive conditions. The demand for manpower from other employers in a geographical region also affects the labor

FIGURE 7–4   Civilian labor force participation rates of women, by age, 1970, 1980, and 1990.

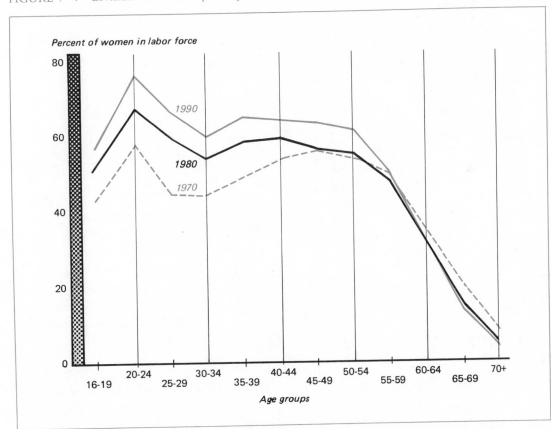

(Source: "New Labor Force Projections to 1990," *Monthly Labor Review*, December 1976.)

supply. If, for example, a large military facility is closing or moving to another geographical location, a large supply of very good civilian labor may be available for a while. On the other hand, the opening of a new plant may decrease the supply of labor in a given market for some time.

Another factor affecting the supply of manpower is the net migration in a particular geographic region. For some time after World War II the population of cities grew rapidly and provided a ready source of labor. Now there is exodus from some cities, drying up some of the skilled labor supply.

Managing Labor Supply Factors

Figure 7–5 illustrates the interrelationship in the labor supply of variables that an organization *can control* and the variables that are *uncontrollable*. Uncontrollable variables in the labor markets, include *retire-*

FIGURE 7–5   External supply of manpower

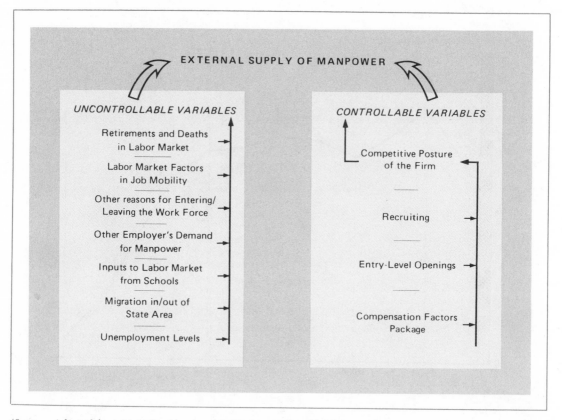

(Source: Adapted from N. S. Deckhard and K. W. Lessey, "A Model for Understanding Management Manpower, Forecasting, and Planning," *Personnel Journal*, 54 (March 1975), p. 171. Reprinted with permission *Personnel Journal*. Copyright March 1975.)

ment and deaths since they reduce the overall number of people available to work. Another variable is *job mobility*, which largely depends on the economy. In a high unemployment market, people are less apt to leave a job without having another job available. They might be looking, but probably will not leave a sure thing without some sort of security. The effects of *other employer's demands* for manpower on a given organization have been previously discussed in the chapter.

Input to the labor market from schools is an uncontrollable variable which changes somewhat with time. For example, those born during the "postwar baby boom" graduated and reached the job market in the mid-1960s. There is a reduction in the number of young people graduating from school during the 1970s corresponding to a reduced birthrate in the 1950s.

Variables that *can* be controlled are the *kind of recruiting efforts* made by the firm and the *number of entry-level job openings.* A vigorous recruiting effort will turn up a larger supply of available candidates than will little effort. Both of these variables affect the overall *competitive posture* of the company. *Compensation package factors* affect competitive posture, too. Employers offering a *competitive compensation package* have less difficulty securing a supply of manpower than those employers who are not competitive.

In summary, manpower planning is vital. The extent to which an organization attempts to plan and control its need for human resources will determine the extent to which the firm either *shapes* its participation in the labor market or *is shaped by* the labor market situation.

Can you list six factors that must be considered in making manpower forecasts?

RECRUITING SOURCES

The major thrust of recruiting efforts is often shorter term in nature. Building upon manpower plans, employers must translate manpower plans into action. They must also fill openings when unexpected vacancies occur.

Recruiting can occur using a wide variety of sources for applicants. For ease of discussion, these sources are grouped into four categories: (1) *internal sources,* (2) *external institutional sources,* (3) *media sources,* (4) *competitive sources.*

Internal Sources

There are numerous internal recruiting sources: present employees, friends of employees, former employees, and former applicants. Also, promotions, demotions, and transfers can provide additional people for a given organizational unit, if not for the entire organization. Using internal manpower sources has some advantages over external sources. First, it may allow management to observe an employee over a period of time and evaluate that person's potential and specific job behaviors. These factors cannot be as easily observed off the job. For an organization to promote its own employees to fill job openings may be motivating. On the other hand, employees may have little motivation to do a good job or to do more than just what the job requires if management's policy is to promote externally.

If the skill level needed does not exist in the present workforce, employees may be trained in the new skill. For example, one organization, unable to hire computer programmers, decided to train its own programmers on a pilot project basis. It selected 44 manufacturing employees and put them in a 23-week full-time programming class. The overall success of this program was evaluated and it was found that 74 percent of the employees so trained were satisfied with their new jobs. Only 5 percent were really dissatisfied. As to meeting the requirements of the new job, 93 percent of the managers for whom the programmers went to work rated their retrained employees as meeting or bettering the requirements.[4] Such programs can be costly and time-consuming. However, internal retraining can be considered if the necessary skills are not available in the organization's work force.

Job posting and bidding.   One procedure for moving employees into other jobs within the organization is a *job posting and bidding* system. Employees can be notified of all job vacancies by posting notices, circulating publications, or inviting employees to apply for jobs. In a unionized organization, job posting and bidding can be quite formal and usually is spelled out in the labor agreement. Such action gives each employee an opportunity to move to better positions within the organization. Without some sort of job posting and bidding, it is difficult to find out what jobs are open elsewhere in the organization.

A survey of employee promotion policies and practices revealed that the most common method of notifying current employees of openings is by posting notices on bulletin boards. However, professional job openings were posted on bulletin boards much less frequently than clerical and blue-collar openings. The results of that survey are shown in Figure 7–6.

Job posting and bidding systems can become *ineffective* if handled improperly. Jobs should be posted *before* any external recruiting is done. A reasonable period of time must be allowed for present employees to check notices of available jobs before considering external applicants. When employees' bids are turned down, they should be informed of the reasons.

Many other potential problems must be worked out. What happens if there are no qualified candidates on the payroll to fill new openings? Is it

FIGURE 7–6 Publicizing job vacancies in house.

	% of Companies*					
	By industry			By Size		All Companies
	Mfg.	*Nonmfg.*	*Nonbus.*	*Large*	*Small*	
For office/clerical jobs:						
Job vacancies are—						
Posted on bulletin boards	51	65	94	66	63	64
Circulated in memos to supervisors	12	9	17	14	11	12
Reported in employee publications	4	11	20	11	8	10
Publicized by other methods	17	9	17	21	10	15
Not publicized	27	20	3	14	25	20
For plant/service jobs:						
Job vacancies are—						
Posted on bulletin boards	80	67	100	78	86	82
Circulated in memos to supervisors	11	11	16	12	13	12
Reported in employee publications	4	7	19	10	6	8
Publicized by other methods	13	7	6	13	7	10
Not publicized	8	19	0	7	9	8
For professional/technical jobs:						
Job vacancies are—						
Posted on bulletin boards	32	41	91	49	46	48
Circulated in memos to supervisors	17	23	21	26	15	20
Reported in employee publications	4	12	21	12	8	10
Publicized by other methods	15	12	6	16	9	12
Not publicized	40	30	6	23	35	30

* Unless noted otherwise, in the tables throughout this report, figures are percentages of companies providing data for each employee group. All but one of the responding companies reported information for the office/clerical group, 83 percent reported for plant/service employees, and 95 percent for professional/technical employees.

(Source: *Employee Promotion & Transfer Policies*, PPF Survey No. 120, (Washington, D.C.: The Bureau of National Affairs) January 1978, p. 2.)

necessary for an employee to inform his supervisor that he is bidding for another job? How much lead time should an employee be required to give? When should job notices not be posted? These questions must be adequately anticipated. In any event, a mechanism such as job posting and bidding helps an employer tap the talents of current employees.

Recruiting through current employees. A good source of people to fill vacancies can be reached through the organization's current staff. Employees can develop good prospects among their families and friends by acquainting them with the advantages of a job with the company, furnishing cards of introduction, and encouraging them to apply. This source is usually one of the most effective methods of recruiting because many qualified people are reached at a very low cost to the company. In an organization with a large number of employees, this approach can provide quite a large pool of potential organization members. Most employees know from their own experience about the requirements of the job and what sort of person the company is looking for. Often employees have friends or acquaintances who meet these requirements. A word of caution is appropriate here. If the organization has an *underrepresentation* of a particular minority group, word of mouth referral might be considered a violation of Title VII of the Civil Rights Act.[5]

There are two principal plans for employee recruiting. One plan is the *campaign method,* usually a concentrated drive for a short period of time. It is used principally when large numbers of new people are required quickly. For example, when a large resort motel needed several dishwashers and busboys, the manager asked current employees if they knew of anyone to fill these places. Several of those suggested were hired the next day. The second and preferable plan is a *continuing program* which anticipates the need for qualified individuals. This plan may generate fewer applicants than the first, but the continuing program brings far better results.

A good arrangement is to have each first-level supervisor contact his or her own work group about possible recruits because they know the employees best, and contacts on recruiting are very natural. A continuing program needs to provide incentives to help maintain the enthusiasm necessary for good results. One incentive is knowing that management and supervisors support the recruiting effort and that all employees are invited to participate. One firm gives a $25 savings bond to each employee recommending someone who is eventually hired.

Former employees. Former employees are also an internal source of applicants. Some retired employees may be willing to come back to work on a part-time basis or may recommend someone who would be interested in working for the company. Sometimes people who have left the company to raise a family or finish a college degree are willing to come back to work. Individuals who left for other jobs might be willing to come back for a higher rate of pay. An advantage with this group of former employees is that their performance is *known.*

Previous applicants. Another source of applicants is the organization's applicant files. Although not truly an internal source, those who have previously applied for jobs can be recontacted by mail, a quick and inexpensive way to fill an unexpected opening. Although "walk-ins" are likely to be more suitable for filling unskilled and semi-skilled jobs, some professional openings can be filled by applicants for previous jobs. One firm that needed two cost accountants immediately contacted qualified previous applicants and was able to hire two individuals who were disenchanted with their current jobs.

Can you identify three internal recruiting sources?

External Institutional Sources

Assuming these internal sources do not produce an acceptable candidate, several types of external sources are available. These include schools, colleges and universities, employment agencies, temporary help firms, and labor unions.

School recruiting. High schools and junior colleges may be a good source of new employees for many organizations. A successful recruiting program with these institutions is the result of careful analysis, thorough training and planning, and continuing contact on an individual school basis.

Major considerations for such a recruiting program are as follows:

1. School counselors and other faculty members concerned with job opportunities and business careers for their students should be contacted regularly.
2. Good relations should be maintained with faculty and officials at all times, even when there is little or no need for new employees.
3. Recruiting programs can serve these schools in ways other than the placement of students. For instance, the organization might supply educational films, provide speakers, or arrange for demonstrations and exhibits.
4. It should be recognized that numerous organizations compete for their share of the capable graduates. Continuing contact and good relations provide an organization a better opportunity to secure the best graduates.
5. The extent and scope of this recruiting program will depend on needs. However, a long-range view of recruiting is more desirable to avoid a campaign approach if possible.
6. Some larger schools have a centralized guidance placement office. Contact can be established and maintained with the supervisors of these offices, as they are in a good position to help plan and conduct recruiting activities.

School counselors are generally interested in the employer's policies and working conditions and will usually cooperate with an organization that treats its employees fairly. Promotional brochures to acquaint students with starting jobs and career opportunities can be distributed to high school counselors, librarians, or principals to help school relations. Participation in career days and giving tours of the company to school groups also aid in maintaining good contact with school sources.

College and university recruiting. At the four-year college or university level the recruitment of graduating students is a large-scale operation for many companies. Most colleges and universities maintain placement offices where employers and applicants can meet. However, college recruiting presents some interesting and unique problems. One survey suggested that almost every company surveyed in recent years will admit to losing somewhere around 30 percent of its college hires within the first three to five years of employment. In a sample of *graduate* management students, over 50 percent left their first company within three years after graduation and a considerable number moved two or three times.[6]

There is a great deal of competition for the top students in a college and *much less* competition for those farther down the ladder. One study pinpointed attributes that recruiters seem to value most highly in college graduates: *ambition, motivation, specialized courses,* (such as engineering or accounting), *grades,* and the *student's ability to express himself/herself.* The only jobs that seemed to consistently stress other qualities were sales jobs, where *grades* were deemphasized, and *interpersonal relations abilities, appearance, leadership,* and *impressing the interviewer favorably* seemed to be more important.[7]

College recruiting can be very expensive. Therefore an organization should consider very carefully if the positions it is trying to fill with college graduates *really* require a college degree. A great many positions do not; yet many employers insist upon filling them with college graduates. The result may be a disgruntled employee who must be paid more and who is likely to leave if the job is not sufficiently challenging.

Employment agencies. Every state in the United States has a *state* employment agency. These agencies operate branch offices in many cities throughout the state. Such agencies can provide a potential source for recruiting applicants.

Also, *private* employment agencies are found in most cities. For a fee collected from either the employee or the employer, these agencies will do some of the preliminary screening for an organization and put the organization in touch with applicants. These agencies differ considerably in terms of their level of service, costs, policies, and the types of applicants that they provide. An employer can determine from the Better Business Bureau, National Employment Association, or Chamber of Commerce which agencies are reputable. Employers can reduce the range of possible problems with these sources by giving an employment service a *good definition* of the position to be filled, including such details as job title, skills needed, experience and education required, and pay ranges available.

Temporary help. Perhaps the most easily accessible and immediate source of certain types of help is the temporary help agency. These agencies supply secretarial, clerical, or semi-skilled labor on a day-rate basis. As Figure 7–7 indicates, temporary employees are used for a variety of reasons. The use of temporary help might make sense for an organization if the work it does is subject to seasonal or other fluctuations. Hiring

FIGURE 7–7   How Temporary Employees Are Used.

	Percentage of Companies*				
	Large Cos.	Small Cos.	Mfg.	Non-Mfg.	All Cos.
a. *Temporary–Company Payroll*					
To replace employees on leave	70%	51%	63%	57%	60%
To assist with special projects	66	67	59	73	66
To augment workforce during peak seasons	64	63	57	69	63
To fill vacancies until permanent employee hired	2	0	2	0	1
	Percentage of companies**				
b. *Temporary–Outside Agency*					
To replace employees on leave	79%	56%	69%	63%	66%
To assist with special projects	74	79	87	69	77
To augment workforce during peak seasons	58	58	54	61	58
To fill vacancies until permanent employee hired	5	2	3	4	3

* Percentages are proportions of companies that employ temporary—company payroll workers
** Percentages are proportions of companies that employ temporary—outside agency workers

(Source: "Part-Time and Temporary Employees," ASPA-BNA Survey 25, *Bulletin to Management*, December 5, 1974, p. 5. (Washington, D.C.: The Bureau of National Affairs).)

temporary help may be more efficient than hiring to meet peak employment needs. In the latter case, the employer either has to find something to keep employees busy during less active periods or resort to layoffs.

Labor unions. Labor unions are a source of certain types of labor. In some industries, such as construction, unions have traditionally supplied workers to employers. A labor pool is generally available through a union, and workers can be dispatched to particular jobs to meet the needs of employers.

Media Sources

Media sources are widely used and familiar to many people looking for a job: newspapers, magazines, television, radio, and billboards. Almost all newspapers carry help-wanted sections and these frequently are a source of applicants for many organizations. Newspapers are useful because there is usually a two- or three-day lead time to place the ad. For positions which must be filled quickly, newspapers may be a good source. However, with newspaper advertising there can be a great deal of waste circulation and often applicants are only marginally suitable, primarily because employers do not describe their jobs and the relevant needed qualifications well. Many employers have found it is usually not economically advisable to schedule newspaper ads on days *other* than Sunday.

Media ads can also be helpful. To illustrate, at a window manufacturing company an affirmative action program suggested by the EEOC required the company to advertise all positions in the local newspaper as "public announcements." Therefore, the company used the newspaper as their main media source.

A representative of Hughes Aircraft Corporation has reported some interesting findings regarding newspaper and magazine advertising for applicants.[8] He suggests that conditions of the labor market exert quite an influence on ads. For example, during a recession a 4-inch, one-column classified ad for electronics technicians experienced with radar, and fire control systems produced 437 replies. At a time of labor shortages, this same ad expanded to two columns brought just two responses.

Consequently, it is suggested that *records* be kept of the success of ads. For instance, during the 1950s, over 75 percent of the engineers Hughes Aircraft employed came from outside California, primarily from the Northeast. But by the mid-1960s, the majority of the engineers were recruited from southern California. During that decade, Hughes gradually phased out newspaper ads in the major cities throughout the country because only New York City and San Francisco produced enough responses to pay for the ad cost.

Other media sources include general magazines, television and radio, or billboards. These sources might be less suitable for frequent use, but may be useful for one-time campaigns aimed at providing specially skilled workers quickly. A major appliance manufacturer might use a billboard at its major plant to advertise its openings for welders. Radio ads have been tried by some employers but success has been spotty.

Trade and Competitive Sources

Other sources for recruiting are trade associations, trade publications and competitors. Trade associations usually publish a newsletter or magazine containing job ads. Such publications may be a good source for specialized professionals needed within an industry. Also, by placing ads in specialized publications or by listing at professional meetings, openings for professional personnel can be publicized.

In addition, an employer may meet possible applicants currently employed with a competitor at trade associations and industry meetings. Some employers directly contact individuals working for a competitor. Employees recruited from these sources spend less time in training because they already know the industry.

What are four general external sources for applicants?

INTERNAL vs. EXTERNAL SOURCES

There are pros and cons associated with both promotion from within (internal) as a source of employees and resorting to hiring outside the organization (external) to fill openings. Figure 7–8 summarizes some of the most commonly cited advantages and disadvantages of each source.

Generally speaking, promoting from within is thought to be a positive force in rewarding good work. However, it has the major disadvantage of perpetuating old ways of operating if followed exclusively. Recruiting externally for professionals such as lawyers and CPAs may be cheaper than training them. It also infuses the organization with new ideas that are needed from time to time. But recruiting from outside the organiza-

FIGURE 7–8   Internal versus external sources.

INTERNAL

Advantages	Disadvantages
1. Morale of promotee	1. Inbreeding
2. Better assessment of abilities	2. Possible morale problems of those not promoted
3. Lower cost for some jobs	3. "Political" infighting for promotions
4. Motivator for good performance	4. Need strong management development program
5. Causes a succession of promotions	
6. Have to hire only at entry level	

EXTERNAL

Advantages	Disadvantages
1. "New blood", new perspectives	1. May not select someone who will "fit"
2. Cheaper than training a professional	2. May cause morale problems for those internal candidates
3. No group of political supporters in organization already	3. Longer "adjustment" or orientation time
4. May bring competitors secrets, new insights	

tion for any but entry-level positions has the problem of "adjustment" time for the new persons. A serious drawback to external recruiting is the impact of selecting an outsider instead of promoting a current employee.

Most organizations combine the two methods. In organizations that exist in rapidly changing environments and competitive conditions, a heavier emphasis on external sources might be necessary. However, for those organizations existing in environments that change slowly, a heavier emphasis on promotion from within likely would be more suitable.

What are three advantages and disadvantages of internal and external recruiting?

REVIEW AND PREVIEW

The importance of recruiting has been emphasized. Manpower planning is basically an attempt to determine an employer's short, intermediate, and long-term demand for people and to predict the availability of the supply of manpower. By attempting to match these elements, an organization can determine potential problems and move to take care of those problems.

Four general groups of recruiting sources exist: (1) internal sources, (2) external institutional sources, (3) media sources, and (4) trade and competitive sources. A basic decision that must be made is whether to look within the organization or to use external sources for new employees, or to use some combination of each. The particular source to be used should be determined according to the number of positions open, the qualifications needed of applicants, and other environmental factors.

The selection process requires a *large number* of applicants. If there are only as many people applying for jobs as there are jobs, there *is no* selection process. Therefore, recruiting activities aim at providing an adequate number of qualified applicants. Once an adequate number of applicants has been generated, a manager and/or personnel unit must make decisions about which applicant(s) to hire. The manager making a selection decision can use a number of information sources about applicants, including application blanks, tests, interviews, background information, and physical examinations. These and other aspects of selection are covered next in Chapter 8.

Review Questions

1. Recruiting has a time-frame. Discuss.
2. What is manpower planning? Why is it important? What information would you need to develop a manpower plan?

3. Suppose you had to locate a new sales representative and you wanted to recruit within your organization. How would you proceed?

4. You need a computer programmer. What external sources would you use and why?

5. You are vice-president of administration in an insurance company and need to hire a controller. Discuss what considerations you would have in deciding to go outside versus promoting someone from inside your firm.

OPENING CASE FOLLOW-UP

The Northwest State College case demonstrates the need for a well-coordinated recruiting program to meet staffing needs. It also shows a very common problem with many recruiting programs, that of unnecessary red tape and counterproductive requirements. It is likely that this same set of recruiting requirements has been in existence for some years. When Northwest was smaller, some of these procedures might have been useful. However, as often occurs, the recruiting procedures have not been modified or examined in light of different circumstances that currently exist. Recruiting programs must be continually examined and revised to coincide with the current market conditions if an organization is to be successful in hiring the people it needs.

Finally, the case demonstrates the necessity for being competitive in recruiting procedures. Lack of competitiveness is seen in such problems as the long wait between initial contact and visits to the potential employer and a poor travel expenses repayment policy. In the actual situation, Northwest was able to hire only mediocre candidates. The result was a deterioration in the academic reputation of the college, which led to reduced student enrollments. Finally, the policy was changed significantly. Only time will tell if past damage can be overcome.

Case: Eppex Corporation

Eppex Corporation is a medium-sized manufacturing firm. It has not been among the vanguard of those firms to adopt modern personnel management techniques. There is no formal manpower planning, and replacement charts have not been developed even though there are some 75 middle- and upper-level management persons.

Last week a tragedy occurred. Seven of the managers at the third management level were flying from Chicago to San Francisco in the company plane when it crashed. Unfortunately, all of the persons aboard were killed.

The president has asked the personnel department and the fourth-level managers involved to recommend replacements for the seven third-level managers by this Friday so work can continue. That means screening some 35 candidates to make the recommendations.

QUESTIONS

1. What could have been done to help minimize the impact of this tragedy on the selection decision?
2. Is promotion from within an advantage or disadvantage in this case?

Notes

1. E. H. Burack and T. J. McNichols, *Human Resources Planning, Technology, Policy Change* (Kent, Ohio: The Comparative Administration Research Institute, 1973), p. 128.
2. Ibid.
3. James W. Walker, "Forecasting Manpower Needs," in *Manpower Planning and Programming*, E. H. Burack and H. W. Walker, eds. (Boston: Allyn & Bacon, 1972), p. 94.
4. D. Sirota and A. D. Wolfson, "Can Employees be Re-trained, Relocated?" *The Personnel Administrator* (January–February 1973), pp. 33–35.
5. William Brown III, "The Equal Employment Opportunity Act of 1972," in *Contemporary Problems in Personnel*, rev. ed., W. C. Hamner and F. L. Schmidt, eds. (Chicago: St. Clair Press, 1977), p. 146.
6. L. Stessin, "Developing Young Managers: Immediacy Sets the Tone," *Personnel* (November–December 1971), p. 32.
7. R. A. Stone, L. R. Drake, and H. R. Kaplan, "Variables Affecting Organizations in College Recruiting," *The Personnel Administrator* (September–October 1973), p. 47.
8. R. A. Martin, "Employment Advertising: Hard Sales, Soft Sale, or What?" *Personnel* (May–June 1971), pp. 33–40.

chapter 8

Selecting
Human Resources

When you have read this chapter, you should be able to:

1. Identify at least four reasons for having a unit specializing in selection.

2. Diagram a typical selection process in sequential order.

3. Discuss the reception and application blank phases of the selection process.

4. Identify several key ideas to remember when using selection tests.

5. Contrast the initial screening interview and the in-depth selection interview.

6. Construct a guide to interviewing based upon the interviewing suggestions in the chapter.

7. Describe the need for background investigations and privacy considerations which arise in the investigation of applicants.

8. Tell why medical examinations are a useful part of the selection process.

The Super Management Trainee

Kathy Campbell had been employment office manager for just ten weeks. She had spent the first weeks acquainting herself with office procedures and trying to get a feel for the needs of the employment office. The employment office handles the recruiting and screening for a large corporation employing about 10,000 persons. It screens about 10,000 people a year and hires 10–15 percent of those screened.

Kathy noticed a position requisition for a management trainee for one of the offices on the south side of the city. This requisition had been on file for six weeks and had remained unfilled. Kathy took it upon herself to fill the requisition as soon as possible. Two days later, a very likely looking candidate for the position was referred to her from testing.

The individual who had been referred to Kathy was Bruce Williams, an aggressive young man of age 22. He had not finished college but had come within one semester of graduating. When questioned, Bruce revealed that he had quit school to support his terminally ill mother after his father had died of cancer. Bruce was an impressive young man and his firm handshake, pleasant smile, and quick wit impressed Kathy immediately. His scores on the aptitude test were not as high as Kathy would have liked, but she felt that personal qualities exhibited by Bruce overcame these difficulties. Kathy felt it was very obvious that this individual was the kind of person who would make a good manager and saw no need to contact Bruce's former employers. Kathy sent Bruce to the manager of the office where the position was located. Shortly thereafter, Kathy received a phone call from the manager indicating that he shared her high opinion of this young man and Bruce was hired.

Three weeks later Kathy got a telephone call from the manager. The manager most angrily suggested that Kathy ought to be a bit more careful in the kinds of candidates chosen to be considered as management trainee prospects. Bruce had been discovered stealing from the company and had been fired last week.

Kathy was mystified and amazed that she could have misjudged someone so badly. She decided to check with Bruce's former employers and found that the reasons Bruce had given in the interview for leaving were not the reasons why he had left at all. She also found out that Bruce's father and mother were alive and well. Kathy spent a rather melancholy day reflecting on the difficulty of selecting good employees.

When a person applies for a job, that individual brings many expectations, desires, and emotions to the employment situation. Selection is a very important concern of personnel management because its objective is to match that person to a job.

> SELECTION is the process of picking individuals who have the necessary and relevant qualifications to fill jobs in the organization.

As the opening case illustrates, many perils exist in the process of selecting employees.

NATURE OF SELECTION ACTIVITIES

Legal and effective selection is based on job analysis. As discussed in Chapter 6, job analysis is the systematic investigation of a job and qualifications people need to perform the job satisfactorily. Usually selection begins when a manager or supervisor sends a request to the employment office, if one exists, that a person is needed to fill a certain vacancy. Job descriptions, a part of job analysis, are contained in the request to identify the vacancy. A job specification may accompany the request to describe what kind of person is wanted to fill the vacancy. The employment specialists then use the job description and the job specification to begin the recruiting process. The pool of applicants generated by recruiting activities must be reduced and one person selected to fill the job.

Selection Interface

Figure 8–1 shows the selection portion of the staffing interface. In different organizations these activities are done to a greater or lesser degree by the two organizational entities. Some organizations maintain the traditional practice that the personnel unit initially screens the candidates, and the appropriate managers or supervisors make the final selection.

Until recently, the basic hiring process was performed in a rather unplanned manner in many organizations. In some companies each department screened and hired its own employees. Many managers insisted upon selecting their own people because they were sure no one else could choose employees for them as well as they could. This attitude still prevails in many organizations and may create a difficult relationship between managers and the personnel unit.

This practice has been reexamined in some larger organizations because of the need to maintain equitable, nondiscriminatory hiring practices. To consider an example, in the San Francisco Bay Mercantile

FIGURE 8–1   Selection portion of staffing interface.

Personnel Unit	Managers
Provides employment process and facilities	Request employees with certain qualifications to fill jobs
Evaluates success of selection process	Provide information to allow evaluation of selection process
Applies selection criteria	Help develop and perhaps apply selection criteria

Company (disguised name) the personnel office screened applicants and sent them to the individual job foreman to be hired or not. William J. Smythe, the foreman in charge of dock operations and delivery, made it a point to insist that no "minority" person could work for him. He would reject all applicants the employment office sent unless they were white, Anglo-Saxon, and Protestant. One day the employment office was notified by the EEOC that a Mr. Fernando Martinez had filed a complaint against the company because Mr. Smythe had rejected him for employment. A subsequent EEOC hearing found Mr. Smythe's behavior to be blatantly discriminatory and Mr. Martinez was ordered hired, and he was given back pay to the date the discrimination occurred.

Multiple government regulations on hiring practices have removed the possibility of managers doing their own hiring in many organizations. However, careful relations between the department doing the hiring and other parts of the organization are still needed. Many organizations have established a specialized part of the personnel unit to handle employment.

The Employment Office

Staffing activities, including work analysis, recruiting, and selection, may be centralized into a specialized organizational unit that is part of a personnel department. This specialization depends to a large extent on the size of the organization. In smaller organizations, a full-time hiring specialist or unit may be impractical.

Some of the more important reasons for coordinating the employment function within such a unit, as much as is realistic, are:

1. It is easier for the applicant because there is only one place to apply for a job.
2. It facilitates contact with outside sources of applicants because issues pertaining to employment can be cleared through one central location.

3. It frees operating managers to concentrate on their operating responsibilities. This release is especially helpful during peak hiring periods.

4. It can provide for *better* selection because hiring is done by specialists trained in staffing techniques.

5. The applicant is more assured of consideration for a greater variety of jobs.

6. Hiring costs may be cut because duplication of effort is avoided.

7. With increased government regulations on the selection process, it is important that people who know about these rules handle a major part of the hiring process (this point will be expanded in this chapter).

What are some reasons for having a unit specializing in selection?

The employment section of the personnel unit is generally concerned with the following operations: (1) receiving applicants, (2) interviewing applicants, (3) testing applicants, (4) arranging for physical examinations, (5) checking references, (6) placing and assigning new employees, (7) follow-up of these employees, (8) termination interviewing, and (9) maintaining adequate records and reports. These activities are at the heart of the selection process.

SELECTION PROCESS

Certain steps are taken to process applicants for jobs in most organizations. Variations on this basic progression occur, depending upon organizational differences, including factors such as size of the organization, nature of the jobs to be filled, the number of people to be selected, and the pressure of outside forces such as EEO considerations.

The process shown in Figure 8–2 is a typical selection process and Pete Dickens is a typical applicant. He comes to the organization and is directed to the employment office where he is received by a receptionist. Some firms conduct a very brief interview to determine if an applicant is qualified before the applicant is given an application form. In Pete's case, the receptionist gave Pete an application form to complete. This completed application form serves as a basis for an initial screening interview, after which Pete may be told that he does not fit any positions the company has available.

If Pete is deemed to have the minimum necessary qualifications, he may go to an in-depth interview or to testing. If he is applying for a job which requires typing, he may be given a typing test before he has an in-depth interview. However, if he is applying for a job as a lab technician,

FIGURE 8–2 A typical selection process

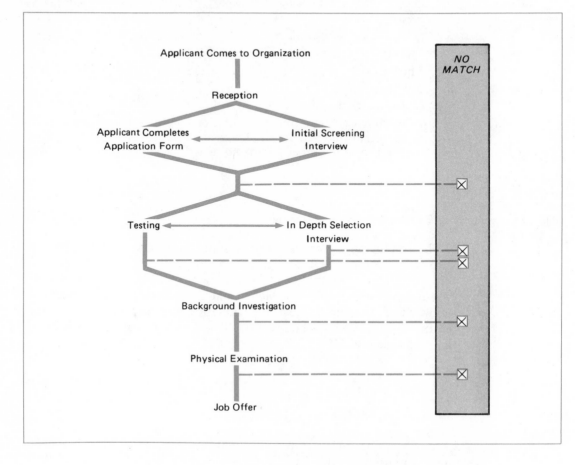

he will likely have the in-depth interview before any tests are given. If he does not meet the minimum validated test scores or is deemed unsuitable through the in-depth interview, he is rejected.

If everything is in order to this point, his references and background may be investigated. If favorable feedback is received, Pete may be asked to take a physical exam. Based upon the results of the physical exam, he is either given a job offer or rejected. Some firms would wait to give a physical until after he has accepted the job, especially if the job has no specific physical requirements.

This process takes place in a day or over a much longer period of time. If the applicant is processed in one day, checking references usually takes place after selection. If the process takes longer, checking references may be done before the selection decision is made. Often one or more phases of the process are omitted or the order is changed depending upon the job applied for, the size of the employer, and many other factors.

It is important that the selection process be seen as a series of data-gathering activities. The employer wants to generate as much *job-related* information as possible to aid in choosing an individual to fill a job.

One study showed an interesting ranking of the importance of some employee selection techniques. Figure 8–3 shows that the *interview* was listed by almost 64 percent of the respondents as being the most important single criterion used to select employees. *Previous experience* was most often selected as second in importance. *References* were selected by a large number as either third or fourth in importance. *Education* ranked either third or fourth in importance for most respondents, and a *credit check* was least important for 74 percent of the sample.

FIGURE 8–3   Priority ranking of employee selection criteria.

	Most Important	Second in Importance	Third Importance	Fourth in Importance	Least Importance
Interview	63.8%	21.0%	11.6%	3.4%	0.2
Previous Experience	32.3	51.2	13.0	2.3	0.3
References	2.2	16.1	38.2	39.9	9.6
Education	1.4	10.6	32.0	40.5	15.5
Credit Check	0.3	0.2	5.2	19.9	74.4

(Source: Reprinted with permission from *Personnel Management: Politices and Practices* Report #22, 4-2-75, published by Prentice-Hall, Inc., Englewood Cliffs, N.J. 07632. © 1975 by Prentice-Hall, Inc.)

The model in Figure 8–2 of the selection process represents the various data-gathering steps that can be used. The rest of the chapter examines each of these steps separately.

Can you diagram a typical selection process?

Reception

A person's first impression of the organization is made at this initial stage of selection. The importance of making a favorable impression at this time cannot be overemphasized. The person's attitudes about the organization and even the products or services it offers can be influenced at this encounter. Poorly handled selection can considerably damage the image other departments have worked hard to build. Discriminatory hiring practices, impolite interviewers, unnecessarily long waits, or inappropriate testing procedures can elicit very unfavorable impressions. There-fore, in addition to matching qualified people to jobs, the selection pro-cess has an important public relations impact.

Whoever meets the applicant initially should be tactful and able to offer assistance in a courteous, friendly manner. If few jobs are available, applicants can be so informed at this point. It should be made clear that the applicant is welcome to fill out an application blank, but employment possibilities must be presented honestly and clearly. If the applicant wants to apply regardless of the availability of jobs and appears to be qualified, he or she should be given an application blank.

Why is applicant reception important?

Initial Screening Interview

In some cases, before the applicant has filled out the application blank for an available job, it is usually appropriate to interview him or her briefly to determine if there is any advantage to be gained by either the applicant or the organization in pursuing contact. In other situations, the applicant will have completed an application form before the short interview. This brief interview is called an *initial screening interview*.

This interview helps to find out whether or not the applicant is likely to match any of the jobs available in the organization. Questions can be asked to determine if the applicant is likely to have the ability to perform the job, and whether or not the applicant represents a reasonable return on investment in training. Typical questions might concern job interest, location desired, salary expectations, and availability for work.

The structured interview, in which the interviewer is supplied with a list of questions that require short answers, is the most suitable method for screening. In more in-depth interviews the applicant is asked "open-ended" questions requiring elaboration. It should be noted that the screening interview is an evaluation of sorts. However, in the longer interview, much more information is available to evaluate and in-depth interviewing is more valuable.

The Application Form

Application forms are a very widely used selection device. Properly pre-pared, the application form serves three purposes: (1) it is a record of the applicant's desire to obtain a position; (2) it provides the interviewer with a profile of the applicant which can be used in the interview; (3) it is a basic personnel record for applicants who later become employees.

EEO considerations and application forms.   While application forms are not usually thought of as "tests," the data requested on application forms must conform to EEOC guidelines and be validated as a predictor of job-related behavior. All information requested on the application form must be a valid predictor of performance unless it qualifies as a *Bonafide Occupational Qualification* (see Chapter 4).

The EEOC defined the term "test" in their guidelines as follows:

> For the purpose of the guidelines in this part, the term "test" is defined as any pencil and paper or performance test used as a basis for any employment decision . . . . The term "test" includes all formal, scored, quantified, or standardized techniques of assessing job suitability, including specific educational or work history requirements, scored interviews, biographical information blanks, interviewers rating scales, scored application forms, etc.[1]

This broad definition of "test" includes three major types of performance predictors: (1) formal tests, (2) interviews, and (3) application forms.

Studies have demonstrated that application forms can be predictive of job success in certain companies. One study found that age, weight, marital status, age at marriage, number of children, class standing, activities in college, father's occupation, rank in military service, and ten-year goals taken together help to predict job success.[2] To adhere to EEOC guidelines, *all of these items must be validated for each job.* (But not each person.) However, also notice that many of those items listed above probably could not be asked because of EEO considerations.

One interesting point to consider is that an employer must collect data on the race and sex of those who apply for reporting to EEOC, but the application blank cannot contain those items. The solution picked by a growing number of employers is one in which an applicant provides EEOC reporting data. This separate form is then filed separately and is not used in any other personnel selection activities.

Weighted application blank. One way to make the application blank more precise is by developing a weighted application blank. A job analysis is used to determine ability, skills, and behavioral characteristics needed to do the job. The weighted application blank is an attempt to put a weight or numeric value on different responses to application blank items. The higher weights are associated with the more desired performance and lesser weights with undesirable performance.

The weights assigned to different items on an application blank must be updated periodically. For example, in one study it was found that over a five-year period only three variables on one organization's application blank retained their predictive ability. The researchers recommended that weights assigned application blank responses be reviewed at least every three to five years.[3]

There are several problems associated with weighted application blanks. One difficulty is the time and effort required to develop such a blank. For many small employers and for jobs that do not have numerous employees, the cost of developing the weights would be prohibitive. Also, the blank must be updated every few years to ensure that the factors

FIGURE 8–4   Verification of application information

| | % of Companies | | | | | |
| | By Industry | | | By Size | | |
	Mfg.	Nonmfg.	Nonbus.	Large	Small	All Companies
A. Type of information included on application forms—						
Previous employment record	100	100	100	100	100	100
Education record	99	100	100	99	100	99
Military service record	89	88	86	93	81	87
Personal references	60	71	65	56	72	64
Medical history	54	52	41	53	49	51
Police/arrest record	36	29	59	43	34	39
(Convictions only)	(8)	(19)	(8)	(12)	(10)	(11)
Credit record	9	25	5	14	11	13
Other verifiable items (see discussion)	9	19	19	19	8	14
B. Same application form used for all nonmanagement jobs	80	88	95	84	85	85
C. Have conducted validation studies of application blank items	11	12	22	13	13	13
D. Have used biographical inventories or weighted application blanks	3	4	8	6	2	4

(Source: *Selection Procedures and Personnel Records*, PPF Survey # 114 Washington, D.C.: The Bureau of National Affairs, September 1976, p. 3.)

previously identified are still valid predictors of job success. Finally, and probably most importantly, many of the items that earlier studies identified as predictors could not be asked because of EEO restrictions. For example, asking about family responsibilities (married, number of children) and age, is likely to cause the employer difficulty because of the need to show job-relatedness of those inquiries. In a survey of almost 200 firms, only 4 percent were using a weighted application blank.[4]

Using application forms.　　The results of a survey of employers on application forms is contained in Figure 8-4. Notice that 85 percent of the surveyed organizations used only one application blank. This practice may not be "targeting" the application form to specific occupational groups as much as is possible. A hospital might have one form for nurses and medical technicians, another for clerical and office employees, another for managers and supervisors, and one for support persons in housekeeping and food service areas.

Several studies indicate that the information received on application blanks may not be completely accurate. A sampling of 100 applications at Bulova Company showed that 24 percent of returned reference checks reflected discrepancies in either dates of employment, job title, past salary, or reason for leaving past position.[5] In another study an examination of the application blank responses provided by prospective applicants and the applicants' previous employers showed that there was substantial disagreement. In two categories, length of previous employment and previous salary earned, the two sources disagreed in 57 percent of the cases. The typical applicant *overestimated* both the duration of the prior employment and the previous salary. Further, there was substantial disagreement on the reason for leaving the previous job.[6]

In an attempt to correct the inaccuracies, many application forms carry a statement at the bottom of the form which the applicant is to sign, "I realize that falsification of this record is grounds for dismissal if I am hired." Whether or not this phrase reduces inaccurate information on the application blank is not known. Requesting the names of previous supervisors on the application blank may be extremely useful for future use in investigating the application, and is perhaps a better idea than having an applicant sign an "oath."

What are some important ideas to remember in using application forms?

If the applicant shows no obvious disqualifications, testing can be scheduled or the applicant can be given an in-depth interview. As mentioned earlier, the choice of using the interview or a test next would depend upon the nature of the job applied for, the cost of the test, and other related factors.

Testing

Tests may be divided into three basic groups: *aptitude tests, proficiency tests,* and *general psychological tests.* Aptitude tests are used to measure an applicant's ability to handle the work for which he or she is being considered. Included are tests of "general aptitude," such as mental ability, and "specific aptitude," such as finger dexterity. Proficiency tests measure certain knowledge or skills, such as typing or stenography. (History exams in school are proficiency tests.) General psychological tests attempt to measure personality characteristics.

Tests attempt to predict performance on the job. As pointed out in Chapter 4, the test is the *predictor*, and the job behavior is called the *criterion* variable. Careful job analysis determines the essential behaviors needed for each particular task. Then a test is constructed to measure the person's ability to perform the job behavior. If the test is validated using one of the approaches mentioned in Chapter 4, the test may be useful in selecting employees for that job.

General aptitude and psychological tests, such as those dealing with mental abilities, are difficult to validate because a test must measure the person for the job and not the person in abstract (see the *Griggs* v. *Duke Power* case, Chapter 4). However, proficiency tests can be more easily correlated with job performance and a high degree of validity can be established.

There are two psychological tests that are used in the selection process that are extremely controversial. They are a polygraph and graphology.

Polygraph.   The polygraph, more generally and incorrectly referred to as a "lie detector," is a mechanical device that measures the galvanic skin response, the heart and pulse rate, and the breathing rate of a person. Once a person is hooked up to the machine, an examiner asks questions and the person's physiological response is charted by the machine. The theory behind the polygraph is that if a person answers incorrectly, their body will "reveal" their falsification through the polygraph's recording mechanisms.

The use of the polygraph has grown rapidly in recent years. One survey revealed that one-fifth of the largest employers in the United States use polygraphs.[7] Also, polygraph operators estimate that the volume of tests given for business doubled in a five-year period in the late 1970s.[8]

Employers use polygraph both when selecting new employees and with current employees. A drug store chain uses it to try to control employee theft. A pharmaceutical manufacturer uses it to screen potential employees who may try to conceal personal drug problems. Another manufacturer uses the polygraph to reveal if an applicant is trying to conceal prior workmen's compensation claims.[9] Organizations involved in security and law enforcement also are heavy users of the polygraph.

Serious questions about the usage of polygraph in employment settings have been raised, especially concerning issues of constitutionality and invasion of privacy. As a result, one U.S. senator introduced legislation to severely restrict polygraph usage. However, that bill had not been passed at the time this book was prepared. Another criticism is the heavy reliance placed on the polygraph examiner who interprets the responses of a person. Less than half of all the states in the nation have licensing laws for polygraph examiners. Consequently, there has been little control exercised over the qualifications of examiners.[10] In spite of these criticisms and the difficulty of identifying the job-relatedness of some of the questions used in some polygraph examinations, the usage of polygraphs is likely to continue until or unless legislation restricting its usage is passed.

Graphology.   This test is similar to a polygraph in that it relies heavily on the person, in this case a graphologist, who analyzing the responses and attempts to discern personality characteristics as revealed in a person's handwriting. One graphologist claims to be able to identify over 100 personal traits from a handwriting sample.[11]

The problems with such a test are similar to those with the polygraph. Much depends upon the graphologist who interprets the results but may be relatively untrained. Also, as with many personality tests, an employer might have difficulty identifying the relationship between a series of personality traits and job performance.

Test usage.   The most important factor to consider when choosing and using a formal test is the validity of that test. As emphasized in the chapters on equal employment opportunity regulations, unless the test measures what it is supposed to measure (validity) on a consistent basis (reliability) it should not be used. Finally, individuals trained in testing and test interpretation should be involved in the establishment and maintenance of a testing system.

Given the above provisions, it is easy to see why many employers, especially small ones, have dropped tests or significantly reduced their usage. The result is that much more weight and emphasis is placed on the in-depth interview.

What should you remember when choosing and using tests in the selection process? *they should be valid & reliable*

In-Depth Selection Interview

Unlike the screening interview, in-depth selection interviews are designed to *probe* areas of interest to the interviewer to determine how well the applicant will work for the organization. The interview, like a pencil-

and-paper test and an application blank, is a type of predictor and must meet the standards of job-relatedness and nondiscrimination. Some court decisions and EEOC rulings have attacked the interviewing practices of some firms as being discriminatory. In one EEOC case involving Detroit Edison the court ruled that relying heavily on the subjective judgments of interviewers violated EEOC guidelines.[12]

The in-depth interview is designed to integrate all the information about the applicant gathered from the tests, the screening interview, application blanks, and perhaps reference checks, so that a selection decision can be made. There may be conflicting information at this point, so the interviewer needs to obtain as much pertinent information about the applicant as possible during the limited interview time and then appraise this information against job standards. One writer feels that the safest and fairest type of interview to use is a structured interview,[13] one of several types of interviews.

Types of interviews.   There are three basic types of interviews. They range from the relative consistency of a *structured interview* to the wide-ranging *nondirective interview* and *stress interview*.

The *structured interview,* as mentioned in the discussion of the screening interview, is conducted using a set of standardized questions that are asked of all applicants. The purpose of a structured interview is to generate data on applicants that can be compared. If an interviewer asks Mary Mazzaro one question and does not ask the same question of Steve Smith, the interviewer has no similar basis for evaluating each of the applicants.

This type of interview also allows an interviewer to prepare questions in advance that are job-related and to then complete a standardized interviewee evaluation form. Completion of such a form provides some documentation if anyone, including an EEO enforcement body, should question why one applicant was selected over another.

Even though a series of patterned questions are asked, the structured interview does not have to be rigid. The predetermined questions should be asked in a logical manner, but the interviewer should avoid reading the questions and rigidly continuing down the list of questions. The applicant should be allowed adequate opportunity to clearly explain the answers given. Also, the interviewer should probe until an adequate understanding of the applicant in each area has been gained.

The *nondirective interview* is heavily used in psychological counseling but is also widely used in selection. The interviewer asks general questions designed to have the applicant discuss himself or herself. The interviewer then picks up on an idea in the applicant's response to one question to phrase the next question. For example, if the applicant says, "One aspect of my last job that I enjoyed was my supervisor," the interviewer might ask, "What type of supervisor do you most enjoy working with?"

Difficulties with a nondirective interview include maintaining its job-relatedness and obtaining comparable data on each applicant. A manager may indicate a preference for the nondirective interview as a way to hide a lack of preparation for the interview. Also, by not having the same data from each applicant, a manager may hire one applicant instead of another because of "general attractiveness" of the applicant. Although not just physical appearance, the general attractiveness is often a result of an interviewer's subjective perceptions and biases, which may not have a direct relationship to a person's ability to perform the job. While these biases can enter into a structured interview also, they are not as well restricted in the nondirective interview.

The problems with using a nondirective interview are summarized by one writer as follows:

> Previous research has clearly shown that unstructured interviews are more likely to be unreliable. There are two reasons for this. Systematic biases and selective perception can affect different interviewers in different ways . . . [and] entirely different topics may be covered by one interviewer than by another; hence content varies.[14]

The stress interview is a special type of interview. It is designed to create anxiety and pressure on the applicant to see how the applicant responds. In the stress interview the interviewer assumes an extremely aggressive and insulting posture. Those who utilize this approach often justify its use when interviewing individuals who will encounter high degrees of stress on the job, such as a consumer complaint clerk in a department store or an air traffic controller.

The stress interview does not appear to be widely used. The typical applicant is already somewhat anxious in any interview. The stress interview can easily generate a very poor image of an interviewer and an employer, thus creating resistance by applicants who might be offered a job.

Can you compare and contrast the screening and in-depth interviews?

Interviewing Suggestions

Many people think the ability to interview is an innate talent. This contention is difficult to support. Just because someone is personable and likes to talk is no guarantee that the person will be a good interviewer. Interviewing skills are developed through training.

Planning the interview. Effective interviews do not just happen; they are planned. Pre-interview planning is essential to a well-conducted in-depth selection interview. A useful planning tool to determine unexplained gaps in an individual's past work or school record is *plotting a chronology.*

A *chronology* is simply an accounting of activities during a period of time. For example, when Bill Ellis applies for a job as a management trainee, the in-depth interviewer asks Bill, with the help of his application blank, to recall his past work experience. Questions such as the following can be asked:

"How did you get that job?"

"Where else did you apply?"

"Why did you choose that particular job?"

"What were the qualifications for the job?"

"What were your duties specifically?"

"What did you like and what did you dislike about the job?"

"What kind of training did you receive?"

"Describe the supervision you received."

"What promotions and raises did you receive?"

"Why did you leave the last job?"

"Why don't you return to that job?"

All the jobs that Bill has had for the last five years are arranged into a time-frame which allows the interviewer to see any gaps in the chronology. By questioning Bill about the dates of his employment, the interviewer determines that two years ago there was a four-month period during which Bill did not work, nor was he going to school. Careful questioning about this fact that had not appeared on the application blank revealed that Bill had been involved in an automobile accident and had suffered a back injury. He had not noted this fact on the application blank.

Questioning.   Many questions an interviewer asks assume the past is the best predictor of the future, and it usually is. An interviewer is less likely to have difficulty when questioning the applicant's demonstrated past performance. For example, at the racetrack there are many ways to pick a horse. You can guess a winner, you can ask someone, you can stick a pin in your program, or you can study the track record of the horses. Unless you are very lucky, you are likely to lose the least amount of money in the long run by using the last method. While the applicant who has had seven jobs in the last two years *may* settle down and stay on this job, the chances are much greater that this will not occur.

Some types of questions provide more meaningful answers than do others. Good interviewing technique is dependent upon the use of open-ended questions directed toward some particular object. An open-ended question is one which cannot be answered "yes" or "no." *Who, what, when, why, tell me, how, which* are all beginnings for questions that will produce longer and more informative answers. "What was your attendance record on your last job?" is a better question than "Did you have a good attendance record on your last job?" The latter question can be answered simply, "Yes."

The interviewer should talk no more than 15 to 20 percent of the time in the in-depth interview. If the interviewer talks more than that, the interviewer is being interviewed. The purpose of the interview is to have the interviewee provide information, and the interviewee is the one who should be doing the talking.

Certain kinds of questions should be avoided:

1. Questions which rarely produce a true answer. For example, "How did you get along with your co-workers?" This question is almost inevitably going to be answered, "Just fine."
2. Leading questions. A leading question is one in which the answer is obvious from the way the question was asked. For example, "You do like to talk to people, don't you?" Answer: "Of course."
3. Illegal questions. Questions which involve race, creed, sex, national origin, and so on, are obviously illegal and are just as inappropriate in the interview as they are on the application blank.
4. Obvious questions. An obvious question is one for which the interviewer already has the answer, and the applicant knows it. Questions already answered on the application blank should be probed, not reasked. If an interviewer asks, "What high school did you attend?", Joyce Smith is likely to answer, "As I put on my application blank, South High School in Caveton." Instead, ask questions that probe that information: "What were your favorite subjects at South High, and why?"

Listening responses.   The good interviewer avoids listening responses such as nodding, pausing, casual remarks, echoing, and mirroring. Listening responses are an essential part of everday, normal conversation. While they are necessary to maintain rapport, they do provide feedback to the applicant. Applicants may try to please the interviewer and look to the interviewer's listening responses for cues. Even though the listening response may be subtle, it does provide information to the applicant.

While the total absence of listening responses can create stress, listening responses may be overly supportive and foster cultural noise as well. For example, one interviewer used the casual remark, "That's nice," constantly. After every statement the applicant made, the interviewer would comment, "That's nice," while trying to think of the next question. This habit had a tendency to encourage the interviewee to talk about things that were really not pertinent to the interview and the job at hand. As a result, the interviews took much longer than necessary.

Snap judgments.   Ideally the interviewer should collect *all* the information possible on an applicant before forming a judgment. Reserving judgment is much easier to recommend than to do. It is very difficult not to form an early impression. Too often interviewers form an early impression and spend the balance of the interview looking for evidence to support it. Research studies show that unfavorable information about an applicant is the biggest factor in decisions about overall suitability. Unfavorable information is given roughly twice the weight of the favorable information received. It has been found that a single negative characteristic may bar an individual from being an accepted candidate, but no number of positive characteristics will guarantee a candidate's acceptance.[15]

Halo effect.　Interviewers should strictly try to avoid the "Halo Effect," which occurs when an interviewer allows some very prominent characteristic to overshadow other evidence. The halo effect would be present if an interviewer let a candidate's college alma mater overshadow other aspects and lead the interviewer to hire the applicant because "all State University grads are good employees."

Biases.　An interviewer must be able to face up to personal biases. An indication that personal bias has influenced a selection decision is the selection of an applicant who falls below standards or the rejection of an applicant who meets standards. An interviewer should be able to honestly write down the reasons for selecting a particular applicant. The solution to the problem of bias lies not in claiming that a person has no biases, but in demonstrating that they can be controlled.

Control.　Another very important part of the interview is control. If the interviewer does not control the situation, the applicant usually will. Control involves knowing in advance what information must be collected, systematically collecting it, and stopping when everything needed is collected.

The interviewer can lose control by the type of question he or she asks. Lou Markley, an interviewer might ask, "Can you tell me about your part-time jobs?" The applicant might take off on a 30-minute discussion. Control of the interview is lost if the interviewer cannot break in. Letting the applicant know what is to be accomplished during the interview and how it is to be accomplished helps establish control because the applicant understands his or her role in the interview.

Cultural noise.　The interviewer must learn to recognize and handle "cultural noise." Applicants want a job; to get it they know they have to get by the interviewer. They may feel that if they divulge any of the "wrong things" about themselves, they may not get the job. Consequently, applicants may be reticent to tell the interviewer all about themselves. Instead they may try to give the interviewer responses which are *socially* acceptable but not very revealing. These types of responses are _cultural noise_—responses the applicant believes are socially accept-able rather than facts.

An interviewer can handle cultural noise by not encouraging it. Any support of cultural noise by the interviewer is a cue to the applicant to continue those answers. Instead, the applicant can be made aware that the interviewer is not being taken in. An interviewer can say, "The fact that you were the best flag handler in your Scout troop is interesting, but tell me about your performance on your last job."

There are certain question areas that an interviewer may minimize. These can be referred to as the "EGAD" factors. These are questions about the applicant's _e_xpectations, _g_oals, _a_spirations, and _d_esires. While the answer to an EGAD question _may_ produce a meaningful answer, usually the applicant will respond with cultural noise. For example, in answer to the question, "What are your aspirations?", the college gradu-ate will often tell you that he or she wants to become a vice-president. The person settles for vice-president instead of president because the applicant does not want to appear egotistical. Yet, it is considered "cul-turally acceptable" in our society to demonstrate a certain amount of ambition, and the vice-presidential level appears to be appropriate.

The applicant is not likely to be able to answer an EGAD question realistically. Consequently, the answer an interviewer will receive is likely to be the applicant's idea of what the interviewer wants to hear. Many times the answer is straight from the organization's advertise-ments and recruiting brochures. For example, "I am looking for a job that provides a challenge and an opportunity for advancement."

The answer to an EGAD question is not likely to be very predictive. The attainment of a B+ average in school is a fact, is verifiable, and is likely to be more predictive than hearing the applicant talk.

Review and Assessment of Interview Techniques

The following is a summary of procedures for the in-depth selection interview. These techniques are appropriate for most interviews; how-ever, for highly skilled positions or professional or managerial positions, different techniques may be more appropriate.

Interview summary.   The interviewer should set the stage for the inter-view by letting the applicant know what is going to happen and what is expected of him or her. For example, the interviewer might suggest: "The purpose of this interview is to determine whether there is a match between your interests and qualifications and what we have to offer. To do this, I'd like to briefly review your history from 1977 to the present, paying particular attention to your school and work activities; and then I'd like to come back and have you cover some of the areas in greater detail."

After the stage has been set, the interviewer can review the chronology presented in the application form. For example, "You worked for Orbus Company from January 1976 to September 1978 as a clerk"; "What did you do between September and November 1978?"

The interviewer can then probe important areas. Questions might include: "Let's discuss your job at Orbus Company." "What were your responsibilities?" "How did you get the job?" "What were several reasons you had for leaving?"

The applicant's questions also must be answered and the job situation should be explained. Whether hired or not, the applicant should feel that he or she has been given fair consideration and treatment.

And finally, the interviewer closes the interview. One question has proved very useful for closing an interview: "Is there anything else about you I should know before we close this interview?" Many times interviewees will use this opportunity to bring out something that may have been bothering them through the course of the interview. It also indicates that this is the *last* question before the interview closes.

The turndown.   A large percentage of applicants are not hired. The manner in which they are turned down can have a personal effect on the individual and on that person's impression of the organization. Most people can perform successfully in *some kind* of job in *some* organization—it is simply a question of finding a match. The best interest of the applicant is served if the applicant is *not* placed in an unsuitable position. The interviewer does well to direct attention to this fact.

A standard turndown phrase can be quite beneficial if properly developed. One company uses the turndown phrase, "In my judgment, we do not have a match between your qualifications and the needs of the job for which you have applied so as to use your qualifications to their best advantage."

It is generally good practice *not* to give reasons beyond a turndown phrase for not hiring someone. Considerable experience in this area has indicated that giving reasons for not hiring encourages argument or comparison of the applicant with a present employee. Reasons may be misquoted by the applicant when talking with other individuals, resulting in many other problems. In addition, such reasons may be taken as advice or counseling on the part of the interviewer. Vocational advice or counseling is inappropriate at this point. Interviewers should be trained to recognize qualifications for their own particular organization, but these qualifications may not hold for other occupations or organizations. Also, the applicant should not be encouraged to hope for a job with the company if there is no future possibility that he or she would even be hired.

Such phrases as, "Try back again in six months," or "We'll keep your application in our files and call you if something comes open," when untrue are unjustifiable. Utmost care must be taken not to hold out hope where none exists. It simply is not fair to the applicant, although it might be more comfortable for the interviewer.

Written record of the interview.   During or immediately after the interview, the actual decision is made whether or not to further consider the applicant. It is important that the interviewer make notes regarding interview data so that the information can be reevaluated later if necessary.

A written evaluation of interview data gives an overall view of findings, provides a check for consistency, and points up items that need further investigation. More important, the interviewer must use the information to support a final decision. Requiring written records forces the interviewer to justify the decision.

How do you prepare a guide for interviewing an applicant?

What interviewers look for.   One study determined that there *was* a core of information looked for by interviewers in the seven occupations investigated. One cluster is similar to a "personal relations" variable, and the second cluster seems to represent the "attributes of a good citizen." Included were trustworthiness, dependability, conscientiousness, responsibility, and stability.[16]

In another study, interviewers rated résumés which portrayed applicants with *average* grades, *excellent* work experience, and *appropriate* interests lower than résumés which portrayed people with *poor* work experience, *inappropriate* interests, but *high* scholastic standing. The information about scholastic standing in this study was so overwhelmingly important that the latter résumés received good evaluations.[17] Certain items are obviously more important to interviewers; but to the extent that these are not based on valid reasons, their use must be guarded.

Assessment of interviews.   Despite its widespread use, the interview is probably one of the *weakest* tools for predicting an applicant's job performance. First, no one is sure that much of the information covered in an interview is predictive of performance on the job. Second, of the information that is predictive, much of it cannot be measured reliably in an interview. Why, then, bother? The interview does provide *some* information which cannot be obtained in other ways, such as communicative ability and attitudes.

The results of a study on selection interviews is contained in Figure 8–5. Notice that over half (56 percent) of the respondents indicated that the interview was the most important selection procedure. Also, the value of the interface idea is employed under heading *A* by pointing out

FIGURE 8–5 Interviewing job applicants.

	% of Companies					
	By Industry			By Size		All Companies
		Small			Mfg.	
A. *Job applicants are given—*						
An initial interview in the employment office	93	92	73	91	87	89
An interview by the prospective immediate supervisor	88	83	89	86	88	87
An in-depth interview by a personnel representative	76	73	51	74	69	71
An interview by the department or division head	19	10	24	14	22	18
Other	6	6	8	7	6	7
B. *Interviewing Techniques—*						
Interviewers receive special training	61	63	57	71	51	61
A standard format is used	24	21	36	23	28	26
A written interview form is used	17	21	24	20	18	19
Interview procedures have been validated	0	2	8	2	2	2
C. *Interviews are considered—*						
The most important aspect of the selection procedure	64	50	41	56	56	56
To have equal weight with results of tests and other selection techniques	29	42	43	34	36	35
Merely a final check to verify data from other selection procedures	8	6	11	8	8	8
(No response)	(0)	(2)	(5)	(2)	(0)	(1)
D. *Person who makes final decision to hire—*						
Immediate supervisor	51	62	38	54	49	52
Department or division head	29	35	65	42	32	37
Personnel officer	21	21	11	17	22	19

(Source: *Selection Procedures and Personnel Records*, PPF Survey #114, Washington, D.C.: The Bureau of National Affairs, September, 1976, p. 11.)

that both personnel specialists and operating managers are generally involved in selection interviewing.

Background Investigation

Background investigation, as noted earlier, may take place either before or after the evaluation (in-depth) interview. Checking a person's background is a highly recommended activity, considering that a good deal of the information accumulated on the application blank and in the interview may be incorrect. Background checks may require investing a little time and money, but they are generally well worth the effort.

Types of references. Background references can be put in several categories: school references, prior work references, credit check references, or personal references. Often personal references are of little value and probably should not even be required. No applicant is going to ask somebody to write a recommendation who is going to give a negative response. Therefore, personal references from relatives, ministers, or family friends are likely to be a weak source of selection information.

Problems in investigating applicants' backgrounds arise because managers must contact people in other organizations they may not know. Often people are hesitant to give a negative reference, *especially in written form,* for a former employee. Some employers have a policy to give only the essential information such as dates of employment, title of the last job, and maybe salary. Although this information can be used to verify the applicant's statements, it has very little other use.

Impact of privacy legislation. A variety of federal and state laws designed to protect the privacy of personal information has been passed. The major law is the Federal Privacy Act of 1974, which applies primarily to governmental agencies and units. However, bills to extend the provisions of the privacy act to other employers have been regularly introduced. Employers should become aware of the impact pending privacy legislation could have on their employment practices, especially background investigations.

One provision in proposed laws is _selective exclusion._ This provision would allow an applicant to identify the areas that could be investigated. All other areas not identified would be _excluded_ from investigation. David Diness is an applicant who said, "You may check on my length of employment, my job titles, and rate of pay at BAP Company." All other areas such as job performance, absenteeism rate, and job accident rates could not be investigated by a potential employer of David. The impace of selective exclusion would drastically affect current employment practices.

Another proposed privacy provision would require signed written release from a person such as David before information could be given to someone else. Also, either a copy of the information would be given to the individual, or the right of David to inspect his personnel file would be established. Another person or employer who gave information that could not be documented and which prevented David from obtaining a potential job could be sued. Other provisions that would affect personnel files and records are discussed in Chapter 17.

It must be emphasized that many of these provisions were not law at the time this book was prepared. Figure 8–6 provides guidelines for reference information.

Contacting references.   In spite of the potential limitation imposed by privacy concerns, many employers do contact references. A study found that 77 percent of the employers responding used some combination of a letter and a telephone call as the main means of verifying background information.[18]

FIGURE 8–6   Guidelines for reference information

When asking for information:

1. Request job-related information only.
2. Obtain written release from job candidates prior to checking references.
3. Stay away from subjective areas.
4. Continue to use reference checks.
5. Evaluate who provides any subjective reference material received.

When responding to reference requests:

1. Do not blacklist former employees.
2. Fully document all released information.
3. Make no subjective statements.
4. Obtain written consent from employees prior to providing reference data.
5. Use a telephone "callback" procedure when verifying application blank data.
6. Do not offer reference data over the telephone.
7. Release only the following general types of information:
   Dates of employment
   Job titles during employment and time in each position
   Promotions and demotions
   Attendance record and salary
   Reason for termination (no details, just reason)
8. Do not answer the rehire question ("Would you rehire this person?")

(Source: Developed from information in John D. Rice, "Privacy Legislation: Its Effect on Pre-employment Reference Checking," *The Personnel Administrator*, (February 1978), pp. 46–51.)

Successful contact can sometimes be made by telephone. In many ways telephone contacts are superior to written ones because the former employer is more likely to provide information over the phone that would not be provided in a permanent written form. Some suggestions for checking references by phone are:

First, place the telephone call to the applicant's former supervisor rather than to the personnel office.

Second, it is important that checks should never be made with an applicant's present employer unless the applicant agrees that it is acceptable.

Third, identify who is calling immediately. Emphasize that you are verifying information given by a former employee who is applying for a position. It acts as an opening wedge to obtain additional information.

If it is necessary to use a letter to obtain reference information, the reference could be asked to determine to what extent the former employee could meet specific job requirements. These requirements should be based on job analysis and very clearly defined so that the reference can react to them.

How do privacy considerations affect background investigations?

Medical Examination

A medical examination may be given to all applicants who otherwise meet the hiring requirements. Often this examination is one of the last steps in the employment process. A medical examination is usually given in a company medical office or by a physician approved and paid by the organization. The purpose for a medical examination is to obtain information on the health status of the applicant being considered for employment. Medical information is useful in:

1. Assigning workers to jobs for which they are physically and emotionally fitted and are capable of performing in a sustained and effective manner.
2. Providing data about an individual as a basis for future health guidance.
3. Safeguarding the health of present employees through the detection of contagious diseases.
4. Protecting applicants who have had health defects from undertaking work that could be detrimental to themselves or might otherwise endanger the employer's property.
5. Protecting the employer from workmen's compensation claims that are not valid because the injuries or illnesses were present when the employee was hired.

Physical standards for jobs should be realistic, justifiable, and geared to the job requirements. Many very good potential employees can be rejected inappropriately by unnecessarily rigid medical standards. Physically handicapped workers can perform quite adequately in many jobs. These individuals, if they have the ability, can be among the best workers the organization can have. However, in many places, they are rejected because of their handicap, rather than being carefully screened and placed in a job where their handicap will not matter. In summary, handicapped workers can provide an untapped source of potential if placed in jobs compatible with their handicaps.

Some firms use a preemployment health checklist that the applicant completes. Then, depending upon the responses given, a physical examination may be scheduled with a physician. With the cost of a very simple physical examination being $50 or more per person, it is easy to see the potential cost savings available by using a questionnaire. The director of corporate medicine for Boeing Company believes that the use of a health questionnaire should be seriously considered by most employers.[19]

ASSESSMENT CENTERS

An assessment center is not a place but is a selection and development means composed of a series of evaluative exercises and tests. In one assessment center candidates go through a comprehensive interview, pencil-and-paper test, individual and group simulation, and work exercises. The candidates' performance is then evaluated by a panel of trained raters.

A number of state and local governments use the assessment center when selecting department or division heads because of the potential charges of political favoritism that could be leveled using a typical selection process. One major city has used the assessment center to select a director of public works, the fire chief, the city engineer, and the employee relations administrator.

Assessment centers are discussed in more detail in conjunction with personnel development in Chapter 10. Our purpose in this brief section is to indicate that assessment centers can be used in selection.

REVIEW AND PREVIEW

Important activities in the selection process have been covered in this chapter. From the reception of an applicant, through the application and initial screening process, to testing, in-depth selection interview, background investigation, and the physical examination, the entire process must be handled by trained, knowledgeable individuals.

Selection, if properly done, ensures that high-quality people can be brought into the organization. The government, however, has severely limited what can be done in the selection process. This limitation has forced many employers to examine and improve their selection processes to focus on predicting performance.

During the selection process the employer must make a decision about who is hired. In the next chapter the importance of training the individuals who have been hired is discussed. Initial orientation to the work situation, as well as the general nature of training, is discussed in the next section.

Review Questions

1. You are starting a new retail store. What phases would you go through to select your employees?

2. Agree or disagree with the following statement: "A good application blank is fundamental to a good selection process."

3. Discuss the following statement: "We stopped giving tests altogether and rely exclusively on the interview for hiring."

4. Make two lists. On one list indicate what information you would want to obtain from the screening interview; on the other indicate what information you would want to obtain from the in-depth interview.

5. Develop a structured interview guide for a 20-minute interview with a secretarial applicant. Include specific questions you would ask.

6. How would you go about investigating a new college graduate's background? Why would this information be useful to you in making a selection decision?

7. List the advantages and disadvantages of having a complete medical examination given to all new employees.

OPENING CASE FOLLOW-UP

This case raises the very commonly found problem of evaluating humans. Many people feel that they are good judges of people and resort to the use of "hunch," "gut-feeling," or "intuition." Unfortunately, these bases do not always hold up under close scrutiny. Therefore, certain steps, including checks and balances, are built into an effective selection procedure. One of these important checks is a background investigation. Former employers provide good sources of information about potential employees. Therefore, careful adherence to the checks and balances designed into an effective selection program will result in minimizing the kinds of problems that Kathy encountered in this case.

Case: Selecting a Programmer

Mary Pendergrass has been data processing supervisor for two years. She is in the process of selecting a candidate for a programmer trainee position she has created. Her plan is to develop the trainee into a systems analyst within two years. Since this is a fast track, she needs a candidate whose aptitude and motivation are high.

Fourteen candidates applied for the job at the employment section of the Personnel Department. Six were females, eight were males. An employment specialist screened the candidates for Mary using a carefully prepared interview format, including questions to determine job-related skills. Six candidates, three female, three male, were referred on to Mary.

Mary then conducted a structured in-depth interview and further narrowed the selection down to one female and two males. Her boss, a company vice-president, agreed with her judgment after hearing Mary's explanation of the candidates. However, Mary's boss feels particularly unsure of the abilities of the female candidate. From the selection interview, past job experience, and education, there is no clear indication of the candidate's ability to perform the job. The vice-president is insistent that Mary test the candidate with a programmer aptitude instrument devised by a computer manufacturing firm. The test had been given four years ago, and some of the most successful current analysts had scored high on it.

Mary went to the Personnel Department and asked them to administer the test to the "questionable" candidate. The personnel manager informed her that the company policy had been to do no testing of any kind during the last two years. Mary explained the request had come from a vice-president and asked that she be given a decision on her request by Friday.

QUESTIONS

1. Identify and evaluate the stages of the selection process reflected in the case.

2. If you were Mary, what would you do?

Notes

1. *Federal Register,* November 24, 1976, p. 51984.

2. C. C. Kessler and G. J. Gibbs, "Getting the Most from Application Blanks and References," *Personnel* (January–February 1975), p. 55.

3. P. F. Wernimont, "Re-evaluation of a Weighted Application Blank for Office Personnel," *Journal of Applied Psychology,* 46 (1962), p. 417.

4. *Selection Procedures and Personnel Records,* PPF Survey #114 (Washington, D.C.: The Bureau of National Affairs, September 1976), p. 3.

5. Robert Hershey, "The Application Form," *Personnel* (January-February 1971), p. 38.

6. I. L. Goldstein, "The Application Blank: How Honest Are the Responses?" *Journal of Applied Psychology* 55 (1971), p. 491.

7. John A. Belt and Peter B. Holden, "Polygraph Usage Among Major U.S. Corporations," *Personnel Journal,* 57 (February 1978), pp. 80–86.

8. "Business Buys the Lie Detector," *Business Week,* February 6, 1978, pp. 100–104.

9. *Ibid.*

10. "Pro and Con—Outlaw Lie-Detector Tests?" *U.S. News and World Report,* January 30, 1978, pp. 45–46.

11. Jitendra M. Sharma and Harsh Vardhan, "Graphology: What Handwriting Can Tell You About an Applicant," *Personnel* (March-April 1975), pp. 57–63.

12. F. 2d, *9CCH Employment Practices Decisions,* ¶9997 (6th Circuit, 1975).

13. Robert D. Gatewood and James Ledvinka, "Selection Interviewing and EEO: Mandate for Objectivity," *The Personnel Administrator* (May 1976), pp. 15–18.

14. James G. Goodale, "Tailoring the Selection Interview to the Job," *Personnel Journal,* 55 (February 1976), p. 64.

15. T. W. Dobmeyer and M. D. Dunette, "Relative Importance of Three Content Dimensions in Overall Suitability Ratings of Job Applicant Resumes," *Journal of Applied Psychology* 54 (1970), p. 69.

16. M. D. Hackel and A. J. Shuh, "Job Applicant Attributes Judged Important across Seven Diverse Occupations," *Personnel Psychology* 24 (1971), p. 50.

17. Dobmeyer and Dunette, "Content Dimensions of Resumes," p. 70.

18. George Beason and John A. Belt, "Verifying Applicant's Backgrounds," *Personnel Journal,* 55 (July 1977), pp. 345–348.

19. Sherman M. Williamson, "Eighteen Years' Experience Without Pre-Employment Examinations," *Journal of Occupational Medicine,* 13 (October 1971), pp. 465–467.

section 4

Training and Development of the Human Resource

In any organization people must receive some training to perform jobs, and to advance to better jobs. Training programs provide employees with the opportunity to learn new skills and ideas so that the organization develops its internal talent for the future.

Training and orientation are the topics of Chapter 9. Orientation is the first organizational training an employee receives. Before a person can perform well on the job, he or she must be properly introduced, or oriented, to the organization.

Part of Chapter 10 deals with some on-the-job and off-the-job methods to develop employees. Development is a broad and longer-range type of training. By developing employees, especially managers, an organization prepares itself for the future. Another part of this chapter focuses specifically on the importance of career planning for employees.

Organizations and the managers guiding them also must learn to adapt to change. Chapter 11 takes an even broader look at training and highlights the need for changing and developing managers and the entire organization. Managers and organizations must learn to change and grow in a shifting social, political, and cultural environment.

Anticipating and planning for change is necessary if organizations are to remain viable and healthy in the future. The last part of Chapter 11

201

focuses on organizational change and development and the demands and dimensions which force organizations to change, learn, and develop. Organizational Development (OD), a strategy for improving the current and future functioning of organizations, is described in Chapter 11, the last one in this section.

chapter 9

Orientation and Training

When you have read this chapter, you should be able to:

1. Explain the general purposes of the orientation process and the five aspects of an effective orientation system.

2. Define training and discuss at least five learning concepts that relate to training.

3. Discuss the three major phases of a training system in an organization.

4. Identify three ways to determine training needs.

5. Identify and discuss at least four training methods.

6. List and give an example of the four levels of evaluating training.

The New Payroll Clerk

Judy Kemp, a 39-year-old wife and mother, has just completed her first day on a new job at Key Data Processing Co. (KDP). Although she has been out of the workforce while raising a family, she recently was hired as a payroll clerk, based primarily on three years experience she had 15 years ago. Quite naturally, she approached a job with more anxiety than the average person taking a new job.

Upon arriving home, Jim, her 15-year-old son, asked, "How did it go today?" Judy replied, "Oh, okay I guess, although I'm not really sure." She continued describing her day to her son and related that upon arriving at work, she went to the personnel department. The personnel assistant said, "Are you starting today? Have a seat while I get some forms for you to fill out." After spending 30 minutes having various hospitalization, retirement, and other benefits explained, Judy was thoroughly confused, but had completed all the relevant forms. The personnel assistant then told her to go to the accounting department.

After taking two wrong turns, Judy entered the accounting department and asked one of the clerks where Mrs. Schultz, the supervisor, was. "Oh, she's in a meeting and will be back in about an hour. Can I help you?" Upon learning that Judy was a new employee, Bill Harman, the clerk, introduced Judy to the other six people in the department. Bill got Judy some coffee and began telling her "the true story" about KDP, including the fact that two supervisors had quit in other departments and how to "get along with Fran (the supervisor)".

About 10:15, Fran Schultz returned from her meeting, saw Judy and said, "Oh I'm sorry, I forgot you were starting today. Why don't you observe what Bill is doing while I return some calls." At 10:45 Fran called Judy into her office and spent 45 minutes reviewing work rules and the job responsibilities of payroll clerks. Then Fran left for lunch after asking one of the other clerks to "let Judy tag along with you for lunch."

After returning from lunch, Fran showed Judy the forms, where her desk was, and gave her some time cards which needed the hours computed. Judy spent most of the rest of the day completing the time cards, except for a break in mid-afternoon. At 4:10 Fran checked back with Judy, noted a few errors, and explained that she would have more time to spend with Judy tomorrow. Judy then punched out at 4:30 and went home.

Judy's son Jim, with the candor of a 15-year-old, said, "Man, they sound disorganized." Later that evening Judy told her son that she was having doubts about taking a job at KDP.

In order to be an asset to the organization, new employees need to know organizational policies and procedures. Also, new employees need training in how to perform their jobs. But learning does not stop after this initial introduction. Working in an organization is a continuous learning process, and learning is at the heart of training and development activities.

Orientation as a type of learning means supplying initial information about the company that new employees need and want. After this introduction employees must learn about their jobs. As they continue to learn about their work, their fellow employees, and the organization, they develop and grow as employees. Effective learning is at the heart of orientation and training.

ORIENTATION

In orientation, an attempt is made to "install" a new employee so that he or she is sufficiently acquainted with the company to feel comfortable and learn the job. This does not mean that orientation should be a mechanical process. It demonstrates the importance of a sensitive awareness to employees' anxieties, uncertainties, and needs.

> ORIENTATION is the planned introduction of employees to their jobs, their co-workers, and the organization.

Purposes of Orientation

The orientation process has several important purposes. One is to help new employees learn about their new work environment. A good orientation program will create a favorable impression of the organization and its work. Just as a favorable initial impression of an individual helps you to form a good relationship, so a good initial impression of a company, co-worker, or supervisor can help a new employee adjust. As the Judy Kemp episode describes, a new employee such as Judy has received a limited amount of information about KDP Company during the interview and selection process. Unfortunately, the first few hours and days of actually being a KDP employee may set the tone for her work in the future. She may decide she does not want to stay. One study concludes that the effectiveness of an orientation approach has a lasting effect on absenteeism and turnover.[1] The lack of a good orientation program may be responsible for a high turnover rate among employees during their first months on the job.

Another purpose of orientation is to ease the employee's entry into the work group. Meeting new people can create anxiety and concern, even in social situations such as a party. Similarly, new employees are concerned about meeting the people in their work unit. Some worries might be, "How will I get along with the people I will work with?"; "Will people be friendly?". As pointed out in Chapter 3 on group behavior, one of the characteristics of work groups is group norms or codes of behavior. New employees must be "instructed," or "socialized"; that is, they must be introduced to what the group expects of them. The expectations of a group of employees may not always parallel the management's formal orientation. As the opening case indicates, this informal orientation to groups will take place eventually. However, if a manager does not have a well-planned formal orientation, the new employee may be oriented only by the group.

An effective orientation program will reduce the adjustment problems of new employees by creating a sense of security, confidence, and belonging. So another purpose is to sustain or build up a new employee's self-confidence. Research at Texas Instruments indicated that new female assemblers were afraid they would not be able to perform well and did not want to appear awkward and uncoordinated in front of the experienced employees.[2] Orientation can aid in minimizing such problems.

Why is orientation important?

Orientation as an Interface

Orientation requires cooperation between individuals in the personnel unit and other managers and supervisors. In a very small firm without a personnel department, such as a machine shop, the new employee's supervisor or manager has the total orientation responsibility. In large organizations with personnel departments, managers, supervisors, and the personnel department should work as a team in employee orientation.

Certain types of information can probably be presented best by the immediate supervisor, while providing other orientation information is the task of the personnel specialist. A supervisor may not know all the details about the organization's health insurance or benefit options, but he or she can usually present information on safety rules, allowing the personnel department to explain insurance and benefits.

Figure 9–1 illustrates a common orientation interface in which managers work effectively with personnel specialists in orienting a new employee. Together they must develop a planned, comprehensive, and effective orientation program to communicate what the employee needs to learn. Figure 9–2 provides the results of one study of orientation pro-

FIGURE 9–1   Orientation interface.

Personnel Unit	Managers
Places employee on payroll	Prepare co-workers for new employee
Designs formal orientation program	
Explains benefits and company organization	Introduce new employee to co-workers
Develops orientation checklist	Provide overview of job setting and work rules
Evaluates orientation activities	

grams. As these data clearly indicate, both the personnel unit specialists and operating managers have responsibilities in a formal orientation program.

ESTABLISHING AN EFFECTIVE ORIENTATION SYSTEM

Unfortunately, orientation is often rather haphazardly conducted. Assume that Judy Kemp of KDP is a typical case. When she reported to the personnel office, certain basic information about KDP, including company rules, policies, and procedures, were presented. Individuals in the personnel unit worked with Judy to complete all the required forms for her to receive her pay and benefits and then gave her KDP's employee handbook. All of these activities occurred in two to three hours, and eventually the accounting manager gave Judy a brief tour of the work area and some basic job training so she was ready to go to work. In spite of all this introduction, Judy may still not have received or understood all of the information needed to make her comfortable in this new environment.

A more systematic approach to orientation requires attention to attitudes, behaviors, and information new employees need. The general ideas mentioned next highlight some ideas that are components of an effective orientation system.

Prepare for New Employees

New employees must initially feel that they belong and are important. Therefore, both the supervisor and the personnel unit should be prepared to receive the employee. It is very uncomfortable for a new employee to arrive at work and have a manager say, "Oh, I didn't realize you were

FIGURE 9–2 Responsibility for formal orientation program.

| | % of Companies with Formal Programs | | | | | |
| | By Industry | | | By Size | | All |
	Mfg.	Nonmfg.	Nonbus.	Large	Small	Companies
Person Responsible for Coordinating Program:						
Personnel Director	100	85	86	87	100	91
Training & Development Director	19	28	27	30	12	25
Line Manager	19	7	0	11	9	10
Participants in The Program Include:						
Personnel Department Representative	54	60	81	53	82	62
Company Officers Division Heads	21	26	31	26	23	25
Training, Education & Development Personnel	21	30	4	23	17	21
Immediate Supervisors &/or Employee's Department Head	28	21	0	22	14	20
Safety Supervisor	19	6	13	15	5	12

Note: Percentages add to more than 100 because of multiple responses

(Source: "ASPA-BNA Survey 32: Employee Orientation Programs," *Bulletin to Management*. August 28, 1977, p. 6. (Washington, D.C.: Bureau of National Affairs).) Used with permission.

coming to work today" or "Who are you?" This depersonalization obviously does not create an atmosphere of acceptance and trust initially.

Furthermore, co-workers need to be aware that a new employee is arriving. This awareness is especially important if the new employee will be assuming certain duties which might threaten a current employee's job status and security. The manager or supervisor should prepare the current employees by discussing the new worker and the purpose for hiring that person.

Determine Information New Employees Want to Know

The overriding question guiding the establishment of an orientation system is, "What does the new employee need to know now?" Often new employees receive a large amount of information they do not immediately need, but they fail to get vital information needed during the first day of a new job.

In a large organization, it is especially important that managers and personnel specialists try to coordinate the information to new employees. Such coordination is a further indication of the importance of the interface idea. In a small organization the manager or supervisor determines what is to be explained.

Some organizations systematize this process by developing an orientation checklist. Figure 9–3 indicates the items to be covered by the personnel department representative and the new employee's supervisor. Using a checklist, the manager and the personnel representative can be sure all necessary items have been covered. However, the presentation should not resemble a military briefing. The important concern is that the new employee understand the items covered. Much of the information on retirement, withholding, and insurance will be forgotten in the confusion of the first day anyway. Attempts to reduce this overload will result in better retention later.

Present Three Types of Information

There are three general types of information usually included in the orientation process. The first type of information concerns the normal workday and the employee's job.

Normal workday. The immediate supervisor or manager is probably better prepared to outline a normal day for the employee. The manager/supervisor should devote some time during the first morning solely to covering daily routine information with the new employee. This information would include the following: introducing the new employee to

FIGURE 9–3 Orientation Checklist

Name of Employee _____
Starting Date _____
Department _____

Name of Employee _____
Starting Date _____
Department _____
Position _____

PERSONNEL DEPARTMENT

Prior to Orientation

_____ Complete Form A and give or mail
       to new employee
_____ Complete Form B
_____ Attach Form B to Orientation
       Checklist–Supervisor & give to the
       supervisor

Employee's First Day

*Organization and Personnel Policies
    and Procedures*

_____ History of XYZ Inc.
_____ Organization Chart
_____ Service to Community—Purpose of
       the Co.
_____ Employee Classifications

Insurance Benefits

_____ Group Health
_____ Disability
_____ Life
_____ Workmen's Compensation

Other Benefits

_____ Holidays
_____ Vacation
_____ Jury and Election Duty
_____ Death in the Family
_____ Health Services
       _____ Professional Discounts
       _____ Appointments
End of Orientation—First Day
_____ Make Appointment for Second Day
_____ Introduce Employee to Supervisor

Other Items

_____ Job Posting
_____ Bulletin Board—Location & Use
_____ Safety
_____ No Drinking
_____ Where to Get Supplies
_____ Employee's Records—Updating

At the end of the employee's first two
weeks, the supervisor will ask if the
employee has any questions on the
above items. After all questions have
been satisfied, the supervisors will sign
and date this form and return it to the
Personnel Department.

SIGNATURE _____

DATE _____

SUPERVISOR

Employee's First Day

_____ Introduction to Co-workers
_____ Tour of Department
_____ Tour of Co.

Location of

_____ Coat Closet
_____ Rest Room
_____ Telephone for Personal Use and
       Rules Concerning it

Working Hours

_____ Starting and Leaving
_____ Lunch
_____ Breaks
_____ Overtime
_____ Early Departures
_____ Time Clock

Pay Policy

_____ Pay Period
_____ Deposit System

Other Items

_____ Parking
_____ Dress

During Employee's First Two Weeks

Emergencies

_____ Medical
_____ Power Failure
_____ Fire

Employee's Second Day

_____ Pension Retirement Plan
_____ Sick Leave
_____ Maternity Leave
_____ Job Posting
_____ Confidentiality
_____ Complaints and Concerns
_____ Termination
_____ Equal Employment Opportunity

ORIENTATION CONDUCTED BY _____

(Used with permission.)

other employees, showing the employee the work area, letting the new employee know when and where to take coffee breaks and lunch, indicating what time work begins and ends, identifying where to park and where the restrooms are, and indicating whether the custom is to "brown bag it" or not.

Nature of organization. A second type of information is a general organizational orientation. This might be a brief review of the organization history, its structure, who the key executives are, what its purpose is, its products and/or services, how the employee's job fits into the big picture, and any other information of a general nature. If an annual report for a firm is prepared, giving an employee a prepared annual report is an effective aid in providing a general overview of an organization and its components.

Organizational policies, rules, and benefits. Another important type of information is the policies, work rules, and benefits employees have. Typically this information is presented by both the personnel unit and the supervisor. Employee policies about sick leave, tardiness, absenteeism, vacations, benefits, hospitalization, parking, and safety rules are important facts that the new employee should know.

Determine How to Present the Information

Managers and personnel representatives should determine the most appropriate way to present orientation information. For example, rather than giving it verbally, information on company sick leave and vacation policies may be presented better on the first day in an employee handbook. The manager or personnel representative can review this information a few days later to answer any of the employee's questions.

One of the common failings of many orientation programs is *information overload*. This occurs when so many facts are presented to new employees that they ignore important details or inaccurately remember much of the information. By providing a handbook, the employee can refer to information when needed.

Employees will retain more of the orientation material if it is presented in a manner which encourages them to learn. The proper materials, handbooks, and information leaflets must be available and should be reviewed periodically for updates and corrections. Some organizations have successfully used filmstrips, movies, slides, charts, and teaching machines. However, one caution is that the emphasis should be on the information presented, not just "entertaining" the new employee.[3]

Evaluation and Reorientation

A final point which needs emphasis is that a systematic orientation program should have an evaluation and follow-up. Too often, typical orientation efforts assume that once oriented, employees are familiar with everything they need to know about the organization forever.

A personnel department representative or a manager can evaluate the effectiveness of the orientation by follow-up interviews with new employees a few weeks or months after the orientation. Employee questionnaires can also be used. Some firms give new employees a written test on the company handbook two weeks after orientation. In the survey results shown in Figure 9–4, only 27 percent of all surveyed employers use a questionnaire.

FIGURE 9–4   Employee Evaluation of Orientation Program.

| | % of companies with formal orientation programs | | | | | |
| | By Industry | | | By Size | | |
	Mfg.	Nonmfg	Nonbus.	Large	Small	All Companies
Employees Are Asked to Fill Out Questionnaire:	14	28	45	30	20	27
At end of program	71	76	90	78	85	80
After a period of time	28	23	10	21	14	20
Asked to sign questionnaire	0	30	10	13	28	16
Employees Are Asked Their Opinions of Program	23	45	50	35	44	38
Employees Receive Second Orientation	30	28	22	25	35	28

* Percentages are of those companies using questionnaires

(Source: "ASPA-BNA Survey #32: Employee Orientation Programs," *Bulletin to Management,* August 25, 1978, p. 8. (Washington, D.C.: The Bureau of National Affairs). Used with permission.)

A reorientation program in which all employees are periodically given a refresher "introduction" should be a part of follow-up. In 28 percent of the firms in the survey capsuled in Figure 9–4, a second orientation is conducted. Reorientation is especially important if significant changes in organizational policies or structure have occurred. For example, if one company is purchased by another, a reorientation of employees of both firms may be necessary because of changes in operating relationships and policies caused by the merger. Orientation is a never-ending process of "introducing" both old and new employees to the current state of the organization.

Although orientation introduces or reintroduces the organization to employees, they also need information about their jobs and how to perform them. Orientation is one *special* type of training. The next section examines the general nature of training.

What are the components of an effective orientation system?

TRAINING

There are many types of training besides orientation: job skill, supervisory, sensitivity training, and management development are a few of these. Another type of training, Organization Development, helps people in the organization to change with the times and to anticipate future conditions.

Training Defined

Training can be defined either narrowly or broadly. In a limited sense, *training* is concerned with teaching *specific* and *immediately usable* skills. In a broad sense, *training* provides *general information* used to *develop* knowledge for future long-term applications. In a personnel management context, the narrow definition of training means that it explores job-related skills, while *development* often denotes the broad scope of training. To illustrate, Kathy Morris receives skill training on a new word-processing machine. Pat Williams receives developmental training from a management course on effective leadership. The hope is that over time Pat will develop into a better leader. However, this distinction between training and development can be an artificial one because both focus on learning.[4] Training in this text will be used to include both the job-related and developmental dimensions.

> TRAINING is defined as a learning process whereby people acquire skills, concepts, attitudes, or knowledge to aid in the achievement of goals.

Training as an Interface

Figure 9–5 shows training as an interface. Notice that skill training, developmental training, and Organization Development are all included. In the sample interface shown in Figure 9–5, the personnel unit serves as an expert source for training assistance and coordination. Also, the personnel unit typically has a longer range view of employee careers and the importance of developing the entire organization.

FIGURE 9–5   Training interface.

Personnel Unit	Managers
Prepares skill training materials	Provide technical information
Coordinates training efforts	Monitor training needs
Conducts or arranges for off-the-job training	Conduct the on-the-job training
Coordinates career plans and personnel development efforts	Continually discuss employees' future potential and monitor employees' growth
Provides input and expertise for Organizational Development	Participate in organizational change efforts

On the other hand, managers, who serve as on-the-job and day-to-day trainers, are likely to be the best sources for providing the technical information used in skill training and for determining when employees need training or retraining. Because of the close and continual interaction they have with their employees, managers find a major part of their jobs is to determine and discuss employees' career potentials and plans. Also, organizational development and change efforts will fail without active managerial participation and involvement.

If an organization is small, managers may have to cover the activities normally performed by personnel specialists in larger organizations. In small organizations, most of all types of training often is done by managers. However, regardless of the size of an organization, employee training is extremely important.

What is training?

Importance of Training

Training has current and future implications for an organization's success. It is a learning process, whether its focus is orientation, initial job-skill training, developing employee potential, or retraining employees because of changes in technology or job assignments.

The goal of all types of personnel training is short- and long-term improvement of employee performance. Training can contribute to higher production, fewer mistakes, possibly greater job satisfaction, lower turnover, and the ability to cope with organizational, social, and technological change. Effective training is an *investment* in the human resources of an organization with both immediate and long-range returns. Regardless of whether training is called *education* (to denote conceptual learning) or *job-related* (to denote skill learning), learning has to occur for training to be successful. A basic understanding of some psychological learning principles is necessary for managers to become effective trainers.

BEHAVIORAL ASPECTS OF TRAINING

Personnel training is a planned effort to foster learning in an organization. Learning is a psychological process which has been intensely researched for many years. Managers can use information from this research to make total training efforts more effective. It is beyond the scope of this text to extensively review learning concepts and supporting research. Instead, some of the major considerations guiding personnel training efforts will be presented.

Motivation, which is heavily influenced by values, attitudes, and perceptions, underlies all learning. People best learn information they think is beneficial, if it is presented *when* they want to learn it. For learning to take place, *intention* to learn, even if subconscious, increases *attention* to what is being said, done, and presented. Motivation to learn is expressed in such questions as "How important is my job to me?"; "How important is it that I learn that information?"; "Will learning this help me in any way?"; "What's in it for me?"

It should be emphasized that learning is a very complex psychological process which is not fully understood by practitioners or research psychologists. Often, trainers or supervisors present information and assume it has been learned. However, learning takes place only when information is received, understood, and internalized, and some change or conscious effort has been made to use the information. Managers should be aware of the basic learning considerations which follow.

Reinforcement

The notion of reinforcement is based upon the *"law of effect,"* which states that if a behavior is positively rewarded, it probably will be repeated. Providing positive rewards for certain behavior is called *positive reinforcement.* Learning theories that revolve around the idea of reinforcement state that people tend to repeat response patterns which give them some type of positive reward and to avoid repeating actions associated with negative consequences.

As discussed in Chapter 3, the rewards or reinforcements an individual receives can be either external or internal. For example, Jean Lane, R.N., receives an external reward in learning how to use a new electrocardio-gram machine; if she performs the proper operations, Jean will get a certificate of completion.

An internal reward appeals to the trainee's internal needs. Likewise, a machinist learned to use a new lathe in the machine shop. Although he made many mistakes at first, he was beginning to do well. One day he knew he had mastered it and was quite pleased with himself. This feeling of accomplishment is a type of internal reward.

Many training situations use both internal and external rewards. If a new salesclerk answers her supervisor's question correctly and is com-plimented for giving the correct answer, she may receive both an internal and an external reward.

Behavior Modification

A comprehensive approach to training based upon reinforcement has been developed. This approach is known as behavior modification. Built upon the theories of psychologist B. F. Skinner, behavior modification (called BMod) has received an increasing amount of popularity. BMod makes use of four means of changing behavior, labeled *intervention strategies*.[5]

Intervention strategies.   The four strategies used in BMod are *positive reinforcement, negative reinforcement, punishment,* and *extinction.*

Positive Reinforcement occurs when a person receives a desired re-ward. If an employee is on time every day during a week, that employee receives extra pay equivalent to one hour of normal work. That employee has received positive reinforcement of his or her good attendance by receiving a desired reward.

With negative reinforcement an individual works to avoid an unde-sirable reward. An employee who is at work on time every day does so to avoid criticism of a supervisor. Thus, the potential for criticism leads to the employee taking the desired action.

Punishment is much more direct. It is action taken to repel the person from the undesired action. A grocery manager punishes a stockboy for leaving the stockroom dirty by forcing him to stay after work to clean it up.

Behavior can also be modified through extinction. *Extinction refers to a situation in which no response is given the trainee*. Assume an em-ployee dresses in a new style to attract the attention of her superior. The supervisor just ignores the dress. There is no reinforcement, positive or negative, and no punishment is given. With no reinforcement of any kind and no clear confirmation, the likelihood of the employee extinguishing the new dress behavior is increased. The expectation is that behavior receiving no reinforcement will not be repeated.

Although behavior modification has reached fad proportions at times, some sincere applications have been made.[6] Providing employees with direct information about their productivity, quality, and accuracy is a form of behavior modification. BMod strongly emphasizes the use of positive reinforcement. "The theory behind the use of [positive reinforcement] is that people will behave in ways that they find most personally rewarding and that management can improve employees' behavior by providing the proper rewards."[7] It has been suggested that organizations can change by modifying the behavior patterns of all their people through reinforcement of the performance of various organizational units. The performance of these units is identified and measured, and positive reinforcement and feedback information are applied.[8]

Immediate Confirmation

Another learning concept closely related to reinforcement is immediate confirmation. This concept indicates that people learn best if reinforcement is given *as soon as possible* after the training response.

To illustrate, a corporate purchasing department has developed a new system for reporting inventory information. The new system is much more complex than the old and requires a new recording form which is longer and more difficult to fill out. However, it does give computerized information much more quickly, and errors in the recording process delay the total inventory report. The purchasing manager training inventory personnel might not have the trainees fill out the entire inventory form when teaching them the new recording procedure. Instead the manager might explain the total process, then break it into smaller segments, and have each trainee complete the form a section at a time. By checking each individual's form for errors as each section is completed, the purchasing manager can give immediate feedback or confirmation before the trainees fill out the next section. This immediate confirmation corrects errors which, if made throughout the whole form, might have established a pattern to be unlearned.

Spaced Practice

Psychological research reveals that for certain kinds of tasks, practice spaced over a period of hours or days results in greater learning than the same amount of practice in one long period. For example, training a cashier to operate a new machine could be alternated with having him do a task he already knows how to do. Thus, the training is distributed instead of being concentrated into one period. For this reason some firms spread their orientation of new employees over an entire week by having an hour or two daily devoted to orientation, instead of covering it all in one day.

Whole Learning

The concept of whole learning suggests it is better to give an overall view of what the trainee will be doing than to go immediately into the specifics. Job training instructions should be broken down into small elements after the employees have had an opportunity to see how the elements fit together. For example, in a plastics manufacturing operation it would be good to explain to trainees how the raw chemical material gets to them in the plant and what is done with the plastic moldings after they finish their part of the manufacturing process.

Another term for whole learning is Gestalt learning. In this type, the trainee receives a general impression of the entire concept to be learned before being overwhelmed with specifics. The information is explained as an entire logical happening, so that trainees can see how the various pieces fit together into the "big picture." After a supervisor goes over the entire operation, showing how all the parts fit together, he or she can break the information into its separate parts.

Active Practice

Active practice is more effective than learning by reading or passive listening. For example, serving a tennis ball demands attention and concentration; actual performance is necessary rather than just reading about it or hearing an explanation of how to do it. Once some basic instructions have been given, active practice should be built into any learning situation. Jill McDonald is being trained as a customer service representative. After being presented some basic selling and product details, Jill should be allowed to call on a customer to use the knowledge she has received. Mixing learning methods such as reading and listening with more active methods is effective.

Plateaus

During the learning process employees can reach a stage where they make little or no progress. At this point, the trainees should be encouraged and advised that these temporary plateaus are expected, common, and understandable. This encouragement is needed to prevent a feeling of despair or a desire to "give up."

Applicability of Training

Training should be as real as possible so that trainees can successfully transfer the new knowledge to their jobs. The training situation should be set up so that trainees can picture the types of situations they can expect on the job. For example, training managers to be better interviewers should involve role-playing applicants who can respond the same way that applicants would.

The learning concepts and training ideas discussed above can be used by managers, training specialists, and personnel representatives to make their efforts more effective. Whether the training is a formal course, an orientation course, on-the-job preparation, or a supervisory development seminar, building the above learning consideration into the effort can result in better performance of trainees.

Can you explain five learning concepts?

SYSTEMS APPROACH TO TRAINING

The success of any training depends upon learning occurring. Too often, unplanned, uncoordinated, and haphazard training efforts significantly reduce the positive learning effects which are expected. Training and learning takes place whether an organization has a coordinated training effort or not, especially through informal work groups. Employees learn from other employees, but without a sound system of training, effective learning from the organization's viewpoint may not occur.

Training in an organization can be thought of as an instructional process. Figure 9–6 depicts the components of such a system.[9] Notice there are three major phases in a training process: (1) *the assessment phase,* (2) *the implementation phase,* and (3) *the evaluation phase.*

In the *assessment phase,* the need for training is determined and the objectives of the training effort are specified. A simple example: an examination of the performance of clerks in a billing department indicates their typing abilities are weak and that they would profit by having typing instruction. Then the objective of increasing the clerks' typing speed to 60 words per minute without errors could be established. The number of words per minute without errors is set as the criterion against which training success is to be measured and represents the way the objective is made specific.

In the next phase, *implementation,* the clerks would be given a typing test, and the billing supervisor and a personnel training specialist would work together to determine how to train the clerks to increase their typing speed. A programmed instruction manual might be used in conjunction with a special typing class set up at the company. Then the training is actually conducted.

The *evaluation phase* is crucial and focuses on measuring how well the training accomplishes the desired objective. Monitoring of training serves

FIGURE 9–6   Model of training system

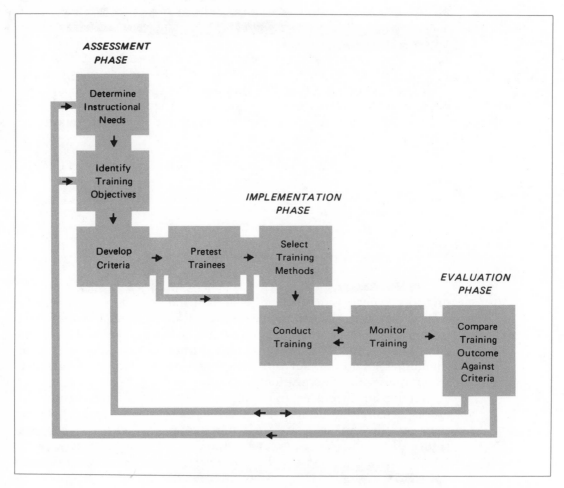

as a bridge between the implementation phase and the evaluation phase. This monitoring is concerned with assuring that the training class is being conducted in accordance with prior plans. Thus, the progress of these clerks is monitored during the training. Then, at the end of the training class the clerks would be retested and their typing abilities compared to the preset criterion of 60 words per minute without errors. This final measurement serves as feedback information which may be used in the future to assess other training needs and the setting of other training objectives. Also, this feedback allows the billing supervisor and training specialist to evaluate how well they identified the clerks' instructional needs and the soundness of the objective set.

This example illustrates the importance of having a systematic training process. Additional information about each phase is examined in the following sections of this chapter.

What are the three phases in a training System?

DETERMINATION OF TRAINING NEEDS AND OBJECTIVES

All types of training are designed to help the organization accomplish its objectives. Determining training needs is the diagnostic phase of setting training objectives. To consider an analogy, a physician must examine a patient before prescribing medication to deal with the patient's ailments. Likewise, by examining the symptoms of the "patient," whether an organization or an individual employee, a course of action can be planned to make the "patient" healthier or function better.

Training needs can be assessed in several ways. Figure 9–7 shows the methods used for assessing training needs which were reported in a survey of organizations of various sizes and types.

FIGURE 9–7   Methods for determining training needs.*

	All Companies	Larger Companies	Smaller Companies
Observation and analysis of job performance	49%	44%	53%
Management and staff conferences and recommendations	24	28	17
Analysis of job requirements	19	18	21
Consideration of current and projected changes	16	22	7
Surveys, reports, and inventories	10	8	14
Interviews	6	6	7
Other	15	12	21

* Percentages total more than 100 since some companies use more than one method.

(Source: Personnel Policies Forum, *Training Employees*, PPF Survey #88 (Washington, D.C.: Bureau of National Affairs, November 1969), p. 5. Used with permission.)

Pinpointing Needs: Job Performance

One way to assess training needs is through the performance appraisal process. If an employee's performance inadequacies are revealed in a formal review during appraisal, some type of training can often help the employee overcome the weakness. This type of training is designed to be corrective or remedial in nature. Also, employees receiving very favorable appraisals indicating they have a good future in the organization can receive developmental training to help prepare them for future organizational roles. A department supervisor in a bank received a good performance rating and was identified as having supervisory potential. The need for this supervisor to begin a management development program was assessed through the appraisal process. Consequently, a planned program for future career development as a manager was then begun.

Pinpointing Needs: Job Requirements

A second means of assessing training needs is to examine job descriptions and specifications. As Chapter 6 pointed out, a job description contains a capsule summary of the tasks, duties, and responsibilities of a job. A job specification highlights needed skills and abilities for people to perform a job well. Training programs can be developed from these sources of information to provide the skills and abilities necessary for employees to perform other organization jobs or to be retrained in skills needed for current jobs.

Pinpointing Needs: Organizational Analysis

Another way of diagnosing training needs is through organizational analysis. Organizational analysis considers the scope of an organization as a system. Both internal and external factors would need to be considered. For example, as a part of a five-year business plan, a manufacturer of mechanical cash registers identifies the need to shift to the production of computer-based electronic point of purchase equipment. As the organization implements its plans, current employees will need to be retrained so that they can do electronic instead of mechanical assembly work. The analysis of the firm's business strategies and objectives helps identify training needs before those needs become critical.

On a continuing basis, detailed analysis of personnel data can reveal training weaknesses. Departments or areas with high turnover, high absenteeism, low performance records, or other deficiencies can be pinpointed. After these problems are analyzed, some training objectives can be developed.

Pinpointing Needs: Survey

Training needs may be assessed through a survey of both managerial and nonmanagerial employees. A survey can provide some insight into what employees believe their problems are and what types of actions they recommend. Some surveys can be generalized to include more than one employer. A survey of first-level supervisors in state and local governments in North Carolina was useful in identifying that individualized training would be more useful than general programs because of widely varying needs identified by the supervisors themselves.[10]

A survey can be in the form of questionnaires or interviews with supervisors and employees on an individual or group basis. The purpose is to gather information on problems as the individuals involved perceive them. Surveys are discussed further in Chapter 17 as a part of personnel research.

How can training needs be identified?

Setting Training Objectives

Once training needs are determined, objectives should be set to begin meeting these needs. As Figure 9–8 suggests, training objectives can be of three types.[11] The first type of training objective is *regular* training, which

FIGURE 9–8   Types of training objectives.

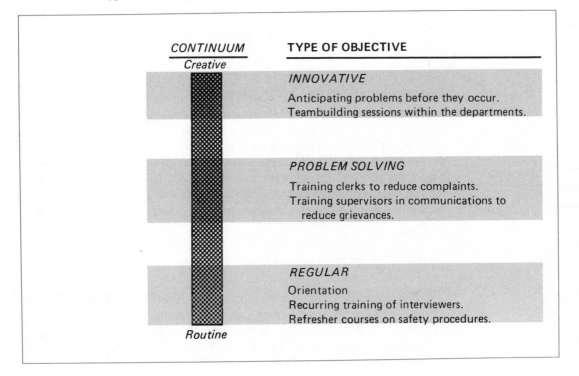

CONTINUUM	TYPE OF OBJECTIVE
Creative	
	INNOVATIVE
	Anticipating problems before they occur.
	Teambuilding sessions within the departments.
	PROBLEM SOLVING
	Training clerks to reduce complaints.
	Training supervisors in communications to reduce grievances.
	REGULAR
	Orientation
	Recurring training of interviewers.
	Refresher courses on safety procedures.
Routine	

is ongoing. Orientation is an example of regular training because it attempts to provide learning for all employees as they enter and work in the organization. The second type of training objective is *problem-solving*. Through problem-solving objectives the organization attempts to deal with its problems and with difficulties in individual performance. The emphasis is on solving a particular problem instead of presenting general information on problem areas. The final type of objective is *innovation* or *change-making*, which is primarily developmental in nature and has a longer effect and return.

As a part of identifying training objectives, managers and trainers should attempt to be "behaviorally specific." By specifying the behavioral objective to be attained in the training, specific criteria can be developed to evaluate how much the employee learned.[12] The effectiveness of the training effort can be measured against the behavioral objectives. In a military situation, for example, the training objective might be to teach new recruits how to clean their rifles. One training criterion could be that the recruits should be able to disassemble, clean, and reassemble the entire rifle in five minutes. Thus, the criterion for measuring how well the recruit has learned to clean the rifle is specified.

Behavioral objectives should also be set for developmental training, if possible. However, the objectives of developmental training are often more nebulous and more difficult to define because of the more general impact and longer-range effect. Attempting to define the behavioral objectives and specific criteria for supervisory training or sensitivity training is much more difficult than indicating the behavioral objectives of a skill-training program.

TRAINING METHODS AND MEDIA

Once needs and objectives have been determined, the actual training effort must be begun. Regardless of whether the training is job-related or developmental in nature, some particular training method must be chosen. Some methods involve the use of various visual aids to enhance the learning experience. The following overview of common training methods and techniques classifies methods into several major groups.

Job-Experiential Training

The most common type of training at all levels in an organization is on-the-job training. Whether or not the training is planned, people do learn from their job experiences, particularly if these experiences change over time. This type of training is usually done by the manager and other employees. A manager or supervisor training an employee must be able to teach, as well as show, the employee.

A special guided form of on-the-job training is Job Instructional Training (JIT). Developed during World War II, JIT is still used widely. The JIT method is a four-step instructional process involving *preparation, presentation, performance tryout,* and *follow-up.* [13]

Another job-experiential method of training is *job rotation,* where the employee performs one job for a period of time and then moves to another job for another period of time. The intent is to provide employees with a broad exposure to their job-related responsibilities. Job rotation as a personnel development method is discussed in more detail in Chapter 10.

Cooperative Job-Experiential Training

There are two widely used cooperative training means. One type of cooperative job-experiential training is an *internship.* Internship is a form of on-the-job training which usually combines job training with classroom instruction in trade schools, high schools, colleges, or universities. In a typical internship, students receive educational credit for on-the-job experience. For example, William Jefferson, a junior petroleum engineering student at a state university, goes to school one semester and works for an oil company the next semester. He gets nine hours of independent study credit for his work semester. William's objective is to acquire *knowledge and skill.* The internship also helps him earn his way through school. It gives him a chance to look at the oil company as a future employer, and the firm can decide whether or not they want to offer him a job when he graduates.

Apprentice training. Another form of cooperative training involving employers, trade unions, and government agencies is *apprentice training.* An apprentice program involves on-the-job experience by an employee under the guidance of a skilled and certified worker. Certain requirements for training, equipment, time length, and proficiency levels may be monitored by a unit of the U.S. Department of Labor. Apprentice training is most often used to train people for jobs in skilled crafts such as carpentry, plumbing, photoengraving, type-setting, and welding. Apprenticeships usually last from two to five years, depending upon the occupation. During this time the apprentice receives lower wages than the certified individuals.

Simulated Training

Another type of training is done off-the-job but attempts to reproduce or simulate on-the-job experiences. Such training allows an employee to train using equipment or in a job setting similiar to the actual work situation in a separate room. In this way a trainee can learn in a realistic manner but may avoid some on-the-job pressures during the initial learning process. Allowing Rose Hoffman to practice on a switchboard in a simulated setting before taking over as a telephone receptionist allows her to learn her job. Consequently, she is likely to make fewer mistakes in handling actual incoming calls. Airlines use simulators to train pilots and cabin attendants, and astronauts train in mock-up space capsules. One caution about simulated training is that it must be realistic. The equipment should be as similiar to the type the trainee will actually use as possible so the transfer of learning can be made easily.

Behaviorally Experienced Training

Some training efforts focus on emotional and behavioral learning. Employees can learn about behavior by *role playing,* in which individuals portray an identity in a certain situation. *Business games, cases,* incomplete cases called *incidents,* and short work assignments called *"inbaskets"* are behaviorally experienced learning methods. *Sensitivity training* or *laboratory training* is personal emotional learning. A more detailed examination of some of these behaviorally experienced methods appears in Chapter 10 because these methods are primarily developmental and designed for long-range impact.

Classroom and Conference Training

Training seminars, courses, and presentations can be used both in job-related and developmental training. Lectures and discussions are a major part of this training. The numerous management development courses offered by trade associations and educational institutions are examples of conference training.

Company-conducted short courses, lectures, and meetings are usually classroom training, while company sales meetings are a common type of conference training. This type of training frequently makes use of training techniques and media to enhance the learning experience. Films, tapes, cases, and other means may be used to stimulate the classroom and conference learning methods.

Training Media

Several aids in presenting training information are available to the trainer. Some of these aids, which can be used in many settings and with a variety of training methods, are *programmed instruction, computer-assisted instruction,* and *audio and video aids.*

Programmed instruction. Programmed instruction is a method of guided self-learning which provides trainees immediate confirmation and step-by-step learning. The total information to be learned is divided up into meaningful segments. Using either a teaching machine or a book, an employee is presented small segments of information which progressively increase in difficulty. Trainees respond to each segment of information by answering a question or responding on a machine. The trainee receives an answer or looks up the answer. Correct responses allow the trainee to proceed to other material. If an incorrect response is given, the trainee is guided back to previous material for review.

Examination of the effectiveness of programmed instruction revealed that it reduced training time on the average by one-third, but it did not appear to be more or less effective in increasing retention than conventional training.[14] The logical conclusion is that managers or trainers should not expect programmed instruction to do their training better, only faster. Therefore, programmed instruction should be seen as an aid, not as a training end in itself.

Computer-assisted instruction. Another media using sophisticated modern equipment, *computer-assisted instruction,* focuses on trainees learning by interacting with a computer, a method that offers a wide variety of exciting possible applications. For example, trainees learning about collective bargaining can play a bargaining game using the computer to generate moves and counter moves. This simulation gives the trainees some feel for the problems, difficulties, and strategies involved in union-management bargaining. As would be expected, the cost and programming knowledge required to use computer-assisted instruction in such a manner are factors which may limit its use.

Audio/Visual. Other technical training aids are audio and visual in nature and include audio and video tapes, films, and closed-circuit television. These means are especially useful if the same information must be conveyed to different groups at different times, such as information on new products for sales personnel in several states.

These various media and technical aids can be beneficial tools for managers and trainers. However, trainers must avoid becoming dazzled with the "machine gadgetry" and remember that the real emphasis is on learning and training. The effectiveness of the technologies and media need to be examined as a part of the evaluation of the training effort.

Can you list and explain four training methods?

EVALUATION OF TRAINING

To be justified, training must demonstrate an impact on the performance of the employees trained. By determining how well (or *if*) trainees have learned, a manager can make decisions about the training and its effectiveness. The evaluation phase compares the post-training results to the objectives expected by managers, trainers, and trainees. Too often, training is done without any thought of measuring and evaluating how well the objectives are accomplished. Because training is both time-consuming and costly, evaluation of training should be built into any effort. As described in Figure 9–9, training can be evaluated at four levels.

FIGURE 9–9   Levels of training evaluation.

1.	Reaction	How well did the trainees like the training?
2.	Learning	To what extent did the trainees learn the facts, principles, and approaches that were included in the training?
3.	Behavior	To what extent did their job behavior change because of the program?
4.	Results	What final results were achieved? (reduction in cost, reduction in turnover, improvement in production, etc.)

(Source: Ralph F. Catalnello and Donald L. Kirkpatrick, "Evaluating Training Programs— The State of the Art," *Training and Development Journal*, May 1968, pp. 2–3. Reproduced by special permission from the May, 1968 *Training and Development Journal*. Copyright 1968 by the American Society for Training and Development, Inc.)

Reaction-level evaluation can be measured by interviewing or by trainee questionnaires. The immediate reaction of trainees may measure how the people *liked* the training, rather than how it *benefited* them.

Learning-level evaluation measures how well trainees have learned facts, ideas, concepts, theories, and attitudes. Tests on the training material are commonly used for evaluating learning and can be given both before and after training to compare scores.

Evaluating training at the *behavior-level* attempts to measure the effect of training on job performance. This is more difficult to measure than learning. Interviews of trainees and their co-workers and observation of job performance are ways to evaluate training at the behavior level.

The *results-level* evaluation of training measures the effect of training on the achievement of organizational objectives. Because results such as productivity, turnover, quality, time, sales, and costs are more concrete, this type of evaluation can be done by comparing records before and after training. The difficulty with this measurement is the easy deduction that training caused the changes in results. This implication ignores the impact that other factors may have had. As an example, Joe Riveria, a department manager for a shoe manufacturer, goes through a supervisory training program. By comparing turnover in Joe's department before and after the training, some measure of results can be obtained. However, turnover is also dependent on the current economic situation, demand for shoes, and the quality of employees being hired. Therefore, when using results evaluation, Joe's manager should be aware of the complexity involved in determining the exact effect of his training.

Evaluation Methods

Figure 9–10 shows the methods of evaluating training reported by firms in a nationwide survey. Note that the behavioral methods of job performance and supervisory discussions and critiques are widely used.

FIGURE 9–10   Methods of evaluating training.*

	All Companies	Larger Companies	Smaller Companies
Job performance after training	49%	47%	57%
Supervisory discussion and written critiques	19	33	5
Trainee opinion questionnaires	18	18	18
Testing	15	16	14
Trainee discussion and written critiques	14	15	14
Observation	10	11	9
Other	22	22	19

* Percentages total more than 100 since some firms use a variety of evaluating techniques.

(Source: Personnel Policies Forum, *Training Employees*, PPF Survey #88 (Washington, D.C.: Bureau of National Affairs, November 1969), p. 5. Used with permission.)

Managers, trainers, and trainees can benefit by evaluating training. This evaluation can help to improve training efforts by providing feedback on how well training is meeting its desired objectives. The evaluation phase is both the end and the beginning of the systems approach to training.

What are the four levels of evaluating training?

REVIEW AND PREVIEW

A key part of personnel management is training. Training activities provide employees with information and encourage them to learn about the organization, their jobs, and their capabilities. This chapter has dealt with training as a personnel interface and has highlighted the importance of training as a planned activity. One type of training is orientation, which introduces a new employee into a work organization so that he or she adjusts quickly.

The main concern behind training is learning. Training can be narrow in scope, such as job-related training, or broad in scope, as in development, but it does not always equal learning. Familiarity with basic learning concepts can guide managers and trainers in planning and evaluating training efforts.

A systems approach to training incorporates these learning concepts into planned training efforts. The first phase of planned training is to assess needs and determine objectives. Then a training program can be formulated and conducted using various methods and media. After the training program is completed, its effectiveness should be evaluated. This evaluation, at levels of reaction, learning, behavior, and results, provides managers information to determine future training needs and to revise current efforts.

This chapter has examined training as a general personnel activity. The next chapter deals with the longer-range aspects of training—personnel development. Chapter 10 looks at personnel development in general and career development in particular.

Review Questions

1. Identify the importance of orientation and tell how you would orient a new management trainee.
2. Differentiate between training and development. Indicate how learning is a part of each.
3. What are the three major phases in a training system? Identify the processes within each phase.
4. You are training key-punch operators. What training methods would you use?
5. You want to evaluate the training received by the key-punch operators. Give examples of how to evaluate their training at four different levels.

OPENING CASE FOLLOW-UP

This case represents an all-too-common occurrence—unplanned and poorly handled orientation. The personnel assistant will be quite lucky if Judy remembers one-third of what was explained. In addition, the lack of an escort to the department further created the image of a cold and impersonal firm.

The lack of preparation by the supervisor is additional evidence of poor orientation. As the case illustrates, a new employee does get oriented, but often it is done by a co-worker.

The supervisor took effective action in allowing Judy to work on the time cards. Judy did accomplish something her first day. However, the uneasiness that Judy voiced at the end of the day will take some time and effort to be dissolved.

Case: Confused Claims Clerks

The claims department has been causing continual problems at the Mutual Aid Insurance Company (MAIC). Employees in the claims department review the adjuster's reports, check the policyholder's records, and then type up a claim report and a claims voucher. Using the claims voucher, the accounting department draws up the payment to the policyholder. Before the check is mailed, however, the claims department clerk must verify the check against the claims report and the claims voucher. If you are confused so far, you can understand why new clerks had problems.

In the past, turnover had been quite high in the claims department. During exit interviews the claims clerks often said that they were reprimanded for making mistakes, but they really did not know how to do the job well. Janet Hollenbeck, the assistant personnel manager, decided to check into the training the claims clerks received. Janet found that the claims supervisor had about 25 clerks to supervise. Consequently, she had very little time to spend training new claims clerks. The on-the-job training was really "sink or swim" in nature. A new clerk was shown the forms and was told "Ask someone if you have any problems, but don't make any mistakes." Janet has decided that the on-the-job training that is now done is the major cause for the mistakes and turnover.

QUESTIONS

1. What objectives could be set for the training of claims clerks?
2. What methods do you believe should be used in a new training program?
3. Present a capsule sketch of how you would evaluate the new training effort.

Notes

1. Hjalmar Rosen and John Turner, "Effectiveness of Two Orientation Approaches in Hard-Core Unemployed Turnover and Absenteeism," *Journal of Applied Psychology*, 55 (August 1971), pp. 296–301.

2. Earl R. Gomersall and M. Scott Myers, "Breakthrough in On-the-Job Training," *Harvard Business Review* (July-August 1966), pp. 62–72.

3. Murray Lubliner, "Employee Orientation," *Personnel Journal*, 57 (April 1978), p. 208.

4. Bernard M. Bass and James A. Vaughn, *Training in Industry: The Management of Learning* (Belmont, Calif.: Wadsworth Publishing, 1966), chapter 5.

5. Fred Luthans and Robert Kreitner, *Organizational Behavior Modifications* (Glenview, Ill.: Scot, Foresman, 1975).

6. See W. Clay Hamner and Ellen P. Hamner, "Behavior Modification on the Bottom Line," *Organizational Dynamics* (Spring 1976), pp. 2–21 for a discussion of some organizational applications and results.

7. See Edgar F. Huse, *Organizational Development and Change* (St. Paul, Minn.: West Publishing, 1975) p. 278.

8. Luthans and Kreitner, chapters 4, 8.

9. The model is an original one, but the authors acknowledge the stimulation provided by a model contained in Irwin L. Goldstein, *Training: Program Development and Evaluation,* (Monterey, Calif.: Brooks/Cole Publishing, 1974).

10. Thomas H. Jerdee and Richard P. Calhoon, "Training Needs of First-Level Supervisors," *The Personnel Administrator* (October 1976), pp. 23–24.

11. George S. Odiorne, *Training by Objectives* (New York: Macmillan, 1970), chapter 6.

12. For a more detailed discussion see Robert C. Gallegos and Joseph G. Phelon, "Using Behavioral Objectives in Industrial Training," *Training and Development Journal* (April 1975), pp. 42–48.

13. War Manpower Commission, *The Training within Industry Report* (Washington, D.C.: Bureau of Training, War Manpower Commission, 1945), p. 195.

14. Allen N. Nash, Jan P. Muczyk, and Frank L. Vettori, "The Relative Practical Effectiveness of Programmed Instruction," *Personnel Psychology*, 24 (1971), pp. 397–418.

| chapter 10 | # Personnel Development and Career Planning |

When you have read this chapter, you should be able to:

1. Define personnel development and identify two conditions for its success.

2. Describe the difference between organization-centered and individual-centered career planning.

3. List and describe at least five on-the-job and off-the-job personnel development methods.

4. Discuss specific benefits and problems associated with assessment centers.

The Outdoor Sales Manager

Bob Allen is vice-president of sales for Outdoor Equipment Incorporated. Outdoor Equipment Incorporated manufactures and sells to retail customers backpacks, sleeping bags, tents, and related outdoor camping equipment. Bob is very pleased with the performance of the regions for which he is responsible, with the exception of one. The Rocky Mountain region has been in a state of constant turmoil since Joe Harris took over as the region manager six months ago. Joe is a 49-year-old individual who has been with the company for 25 years. Because he had been an excellent salesman, he was promoted to management five years ago and did an adequate job as a regional sales manager in the Southeast region. OEI had no management training program per se and Joe had "picked up" the management knowledge he had by observing the people he worked for in the past.

Joe had generally been considered "a good old boy" by those people who had worked for him in the Southeast. His easy-going style of management fit in well with the older group of salesmen that worked for him there. Six months ago Joe became the regional manager in the Rocky Mountain area. He had applied for that particular job because of his strong personal interest in relocating in the Rocky Mountain area. Because his interests including hiking, hunting, fishing, and skiing, he and his family were extremely happy to move to the part of the country that coincided with their interests.

Joe was assigned three "young tigers" as his immediate subordinates in the region. Bob Allen's idea in assigning those young aggressive sales representatives to Joe was to provide a situation in which Joe could coach the young aggressive individuals since Joe had been such a good salesman himself at one time. Unfortunately Joe and his aggressive young sales reps have had nothing but trouble. Bob had hoped that time would iron out the troubles and that sales for the region would pick up, but they have continued to slump.

Yesterday Sherrill Jones, one of Joe's subordinates, called Bob Allen and suggested that he and another of the sales representatives would send Bob their resignations unless something was done immediately about Joe. Sherrill said that Joe seemed to be spending more time planning skiing trips or fishing weekends than trying to show the young sales reps the finer points of selling. In fact, Sherrill says that Joe has contributed nothing to the development of the three young sales representatives. Sherrill said, "Joe seems to have retired on the job. We could learn from him if he could only communicate some of his knowledge of selling." Bob Allen's immediate problem is how to handle the situation.

Ultimately an organization's effectiveness depends on the abilities of its people. Although general abilities are screened in the selection process, many employee skills must be developed over time, and human development certainly comes from many sources. People "develop" in the normal process of maturing. Development occurs from the experiences people encounter as they grow older. A *planned* system of developmental experiences for employees can help expand the overall level of abilities contained in an organization and increase its potential and flexibility.

Many effective organizations are guided by management teams that have developed through exposure to planned learning opportunities. Development methods and programs, career planning, and assessment of development needs are necessary for both managerial and nonmanagerial personnel. These efforts require thorough and careful planning to place competent employees at all levels where they are needed. An organization cannot "stockpile" good people for long by placing them in "make work" positions until they can be used. Trying to "store" employees like cans on a shelf results in the loss of valuable people. The material in this chapter is presented as a guide for developing all personnel; *management development* is emphasized in the next chapter.

PERSONNEL DEVELOPMENT—WHAT IS IT?

The purpose of personnel development is to enlarge an employee's *capacity* to successfully handle greater responsibilities and/or better handle current responsibilities.

> PERSONNEL DEVELOPMENT is composed of activities concerned with increasing the capabilities of employees for continuing growth in the organization.

An individual's development depends, to an extent, on his or her relationship with the manager. By concentrating on the individual employee's goals and potential, a manager can significantly affect an employee's development. Performance appraisals obviously play an important role in development. Through dicussions about an employee's past performance and current strengths, concrete proposals can be planned for future development. A performance appraisal can determine, for example, if employees are placed in jobs which exceed their abilities, or if they need additional training to improve performance (see Chapter 12). Then plans can be initiated to develop the required knowledge and skills.

Conditions for Successful Personnel Development

Personnel development is much more than just acquiring a specific skill, such as learning to type. For instance, progress can be made in developing (1) attitudes about the greater involvement of employees, (2) improved abilities to communicate, and (3) technical knowledge of a subject such as capital budgeting. Regardless of the objective, two conditions must be recognized for successful personnel development: *top management support* and the *interrelated nature of development.*

Top management support.   Top management support and belief in the importance of development efforts is necessary to give people the "room" they need to expand their capabilities. Top management must be willing to delegate some decision-making authority to lower-level positions in the organization to develop young managers. These efforts must be made even if some of them fail. For example, if top management is afraid or unwilling to relinquish control and authority to a younger manager for learning purposes, little management development is likely to result.

Those persons coordinating development programs either need to receive full support from top management or have sufficient freedom to carry out their programs on their own. If the developmental activities planned for an employee do not really affect that employee's rewards, the program will not be successful. Suppose a supervisor in a department store is sent to a supervisory development course. The store is not really supporting that supervisor's development efforts unless it provides opportunities for the supervisor to try out some of the new ideas acquired in the course. This usage may require some upper management concessions.

Upper management might allow younger employees to participate in important decisions to encourage development toward career advancement. Unfortunately, some top managers tend to be uninvolved in personnel development because they see it as a lower management activity. Nothing could be further from the truth. The active involvement of top management in the personnel development process is necessary to make it work.

Personnel developmental interrelationships.   Important relationships exist between personnel development efforts and selection, placement, compensation, and appraisal activities. Neglect of any of these important links can lead to problems with development efforts throughout the whole system. The ultimate result may be the organization's failure to effectively use its human resources.

One writer identifies the development process and its interrelationships with other personnel activities this way:

> In any organization it [personnel development] must be an on-going, continuing process that requires constant vigilance and scrutiny. Some technologies and occupations are more prone to be affected by obsolescence than others. A number of entry level people in the organization may not have the necessary prerequisite skills, some individuals may have studied for career changes and seek transfers, and some become dissatisfied and want to change jobs in the organization and require development. Also there will be cases of performance deficiencies that require correction and a host of other situations that call for personnel development activity. Testing, counseling, education, and training programs, internal transfers, skills inventories, special education programs, etc. are all important elements in this personnel development and employee relation lattice structure. They are all aimed at enhancing the utilization of existing human resources in the organization.[1]

The essence of the above idea is activated in many organizations through career planning and guidance.

What are two key conditions for successful personnel development?

CAREER PLANNING AND GUIDANCE

In the past, career guidance has been considered a service for high school or college students. However, as the employee work role becomes more complex, more employers are providing career counseling. Exxon Corporation is just one of many employers that use career planning for many of its managers.

Certain common career concerns are frequently expressed by employees in all organizations. These concerns include the following: "What do I really *want* to do?"; "What do I *know* how to do?"; "What career opportunities can I expect to be *available*?"; "Where do I want to *go*?"; "What do I *need* to do to get there?"; "How can I tell *how well* I am doing?"; "How do I get out of the box I am in?"[2] Usually, in-house career planning and guidance is limited to what the organization has to offer. These opportunities may not always include all possibilities in a particular field. A good presentation of what is available and what an employee can reasonably expect can generate more commitment from the employee.

Organization-Centered vs. Individual-Centered Career Planning

The nature of career planning can be somewhat confusing because two different types exist. Career planning can be either *organization-centered* or *individual-centered*.[3]

Organization career planning involves career paths which are the logical progression of people between jobs. These paths represent "ladders" that each individual can climb to advance in certain organization units. For example, one might enter the sales department as a sales counselor, then be promoted to account director, then sales manager, and finally vice-president of sales.

Individual career planning, on the other hand, focuses on individuals rather than jobs. People's goals and skills are the focus of analysis. Such analysis might include situations both within and outside the organization that can expand an employee's capabilities. It might even include movement to another organization. The points of focus for organization- and individual-oriented career planning are compared in Figure 10-1.

Manpower planning (Chapter 7) forms the basis for successful organizational career planning. Only by forecasting the demand for people needed in various jobs in the future and the current internal supply of people and their potentials can a career system be put together for the organization.

ORGANIZATIONAL CAREER PLANNING matches individual goals and potentials with the manpower needs of the organization.

If careful matching of organizational needs and personal goals takes place, human resources planning will consider both the organizational and individual perspectives. Unfortunately many organizations often compile recruiting and career ladders or both without considering information about how current employees fit into those plans.

FIGURE 10–1   Two main parts of career planning.

Organization Career Planning (OCP)	Individual Career Planning (ICP)
future needs	self-awareness: abilities and interests
career ladders	planning goals: life and work
assessment of individual potential	planning to achieve goals
connecting organizational need/opportunity with individual need/desire	alternatives, internal and external to organization
coordination and audit of career system	career ladders, internal and external to organization

(Source: Elmer Burak, "Why All the Confusion About Career Planning?" *Human Resources Management* (Summer 1977), p. 21. Graduate School of Business Administration, University of Michigan; Ann Arbor, MI 48109).

How Do People Choose Careers?

Recent studies indicate that four general characteristics of an individual help affect the career choices made.[4]

1. *Interests*: Persons tend to pursue careers that they perceive match their interests.
2. *Self-identity*: A career is an extension of a person's self image, as well as a molder of it.
3. *Personality*: This factor includes personal orientation (whether one is realistic, enterprising, artistic, etc.), personal needs (including affiliation, power, and achievement needs).
4. *Social background*: Socioeconomic status and the education and occupation level of a person's parents are some of the factors included here.

Less is known about exactly how people choose specific organizations. One factor is the opportunity for and availability of a job when the person is looking for work. The amount of information available about alternatives is an important factor as well. Beyond these issues people seem to pick organizations on the basis of a "fit" between the climate of that organization *as they perceive it* and their own personal characteristics.

Effective individual career planning.   Good career planning at the individual level first requires that a person accurately know himself/herself. One must face issues such as: How hard are you really willing to work? What kind of factors are important to you? What kind of trade-off between work and family or leisure are you willing to make? These questions and others must be dealt with honestly before personal goals and objectives can realistically be set. Professional counseling may be available to persons to help them make these decisions.

Supervisors and managers high in the organization can help a person determine what skills and talents are necessary for success at each organizational level. Other information on occupations or careers outside the employee's current employer often must be gathered by the employee. Once this material is gathered, decisions can be made.

Individual goal setting about the nature of a career is an important first step. Once goals have been set, planning for their achievement must be done. This planning consists of determining a series of actions that will lead to the goals. These steps may include a variety of training and development methods, such as those discussed in the next part of this chapter.

Career planning is still more an art than a science. However, the alternative to no career planning for both the organization and the individual is not a sound one either.

What is the difference between organizational-centered and individual-centered career planning?

PERSONNEL DEVELOPMENT METHODS

Many methods can be used to help personnel develop. The following discussion presents an overview of some widely used major methods. These methods are not limited in their use to either management or nonmanagement employees. They can be used to develop personnel at any level, depending on specific needs.

Development methods can be generally classified as *on-the-job* or *off-the-job*. On-the-job methods include coaching, conference leadership, and guidance, committee assignments, job rotation, and "assistant-to" positions. These efforts are normally set up within the organization's facilities and are directly related to an employee's job.

Off-the-job development methods can be arranged either inside the organization or at some external location. Methods commonly used here include classroom training, T-group or sensitivity training, university-type programs, psychological testing, human relations training, case studies, role playing, simulation or business games, sabbaticals, and assessment centers. Each of the on-the-job and off-the-job methods is briefly discussed next.

On-the-Job Methods

On-the-job methods generally are directly job-related, an advantage to the organization and the personnel involved. Some of the most common advantages are:[5]

1. Effective training can be *tailored to fit* each trainee's background, attitudes, needs, expectations, goals, and future assignments. Off-the-job training cannot usually be tailored as well to the exact measurements of each trainee.
2. The importance of *"learning by doing"* is well recognized in on-the-job training.
3. Some development programs can be very time-consuming and managers in training may be reluctant to leave the organization for the amount of time required. On-the-job training is *not as time-consuming.*
4. The employee's development is influenced to a large extent by his immediate supervisor. He is likely to go along with his *superior's expectations* in an on-the-job training situation.

5. When an organization relies mostly on off-the-job training, supervisors do not feel that their obligation to develop their subordinates is a primary one. They tend to neglect it. On-the-job training *focuses a supervisor's attention on subordinates' development.*

These five points emphasize that on-the-job methods focus on day-to-day learning. The major difficulty with on-the-job methods is that often too many unplanned activities are lumped under the heading of "development." It is imperative that the managers plan and coordinate development efforts so that desired learning actually occurs.

Coaching. The oldest on-the-job development technique is that of coaching, the daily instruction of subordinates by their immediate superior. It is a continuous process of learning by doing. For coaching to be effective, a healthy and honest relationship must exist between subordinates and their supervisors or managers. Management By Objectives (discussed in Chapter 12) is a focus for one type of this working relationship.

Some informal coaching is effective, but development may not always result. Managers and supervisors should have some training in the applications of coaching to be effective. A major insurance firm in the Midwest conducts formal training courses to improve managers' coaching skills.

Subordinates will benefit from coaching only if they consider it a positive development tool. At the heart of an effective coaching relationship are mutual goals and objectives, including a personal career plan for the subordinates. This plan must then be followed up by regular discussions between the employee and the manager. For example, Marion Brewer, a management trainee, and her boss regularly discuss certain critical job behaviors she has exhibited. During their last meeting, her boss discussed her good decision-making ability and pointed out her willingness to assist subordinates with their job problems. He then pointed out a situation where Marion had been soundly chewed out by a manager of equal rank from another department. Her supervisor emphasized that Marion needs to develop more self-confidence and an ability to stand up to opposition when she knows she is right.

Unfortunately, like many on-the-job methods, coaching is easy to implement without any planning at all. The opening case about Joe Harris indicates what can occur when little planning and no training in coaching occurs. Because someone has been good at a job or particular part of a job is no *guarantee* that they will be able to teach someone else to do it well. It is often too easy to neglect systematic guidance of the learner even if the "coach" knew which systematic experiences were best. Sometimes doing a full day's work gets priority over learning. Also, many skills have an intellectual component to them that might be better learned from a book or lecture before coaching occurs.

This discussion of the problems should not lead one to believe that coaching cannot work. It can, but it requires a knowledgable coach and some planning.

Conference leadership. Conference leadership is an on-the-job technique which has a limited but beneficial place in a personnel development program. Conference leadership usually requires that the trainee organize and chair problem-solving conferences. As an example, junior executives may be asked to plan and preside at meetings with other managers to solve problems, such as why the production department has been unable to meet a sales request on time. In so doing, the junior executives will learn more about sales and production problems, human nature, and how to organize a conference.

Committee assignments. Assignment of a promising employee to important committees can be a very broadening experience. Employees who participate in committees which make important decisions and plans may gain a real grasp of personalities, issues, and processes governing the way the organization functions. Assigning persons to a safety committee may give them the safety experience needed to become supervisors. Also, they may experience the problems involved with maintaining employee safety awareness. Hopefully, this committee experience will help employees emphasize safety to workers they would supervise. Caution should be exercised so that committee assignments do not become time-wasting nuisances.

Job rotation. Job rotation involves shifting employees from one position to another similar one. (See chapter 6.) For example a promising young manager may spend three months in the plant, three months in corporate planning, and three months in purchasing.

In some companies job rotation is unplanned; other companies have elaborate charts and schedules precisely planning the program for each employee. Managers should recognize that job rotation can be expensive because a substantial amount of managerial time is lost. The trainee must take time after each change of position to become reacquainted with different people and techniques in the new unit.

When properly handled, rotation encourages a deeper and more general view of the organization. The General Electric Co. uses job rotation during a 15-month sales manpower training program. Trainees in this program work in at least three areas. Included are such assignments as contractor sales, retail sales, credit, advertising, and product training.

Bringing outsiders into a department often provides new and different points of view to old problems. Rotation also allows trainees to determine which operations they are most interested in and where they fit best.

A disadvantage of job rotation is that it may discourage the trainee from taking a long-term perspective of the job. If a move is imminent, the employee may become more concerned with short-term problems.

Assistant-to positions.   The assistant-to position is a staff position immediately under a manager. Through this job, trainees can work with outstanding managers they may not otherwise meet. Some organizations have "junior boards of directors" or "management cabinets" to which trainees may be appointed. Assignments such as these are useful if trainees have the opportunity to deal with challenging or interesting assignments.

Can you list five on-the-job methods of personnel development?

Off-the-Job Techniques

Off-the-job development techniques can be effective because an individual has an opportunity to get away from the job and to concentrate solely on what is to be learned. Meeting other people who are concerned with somewhat different problems and different organizations may provide an employee with different perspectives on old problems. There are a variety of methods which may be used.

Classroom training.   Many off-the-job development programs include some classroom instruction. The advantage of classroom training is that it is widely accepted because most people are familiar with it. Classroom training can be conducted by specialists who are either employed by the organization or outside experts.

A disadvantage of classroom instruction is that lectures often produce passive listeners and lack of participation. Sometimes trainees have little opportunity to question, clarify, and discuss the lecture material.[6] Classroom effectiveness depends upon the size of the group, the ability of the instructor, and the subject matter.

T-group training.   T-group training has also been called sensitivity training, encounter group, and laboratory training. It is a technique for learning about one's self and others by observing and participating in a group situation. These small groups may meet for two or three hours or more daily for a period of a week or longer, usually off the job site. The leader attempts to keep a free format of activities and group relationships.

At first, group members tend to be frustrated and do not understand why they are "wasting" their time. They may be openly hostile toward the leader and each other. The leader tries to encourage "openness" in the expression of feelings and reactions to other people in the group. Some topics of discussion are motives and impressions of other people. The participants may gradually open up and show themselves for what they are.

T-group training is supposed to develop an awareness of human, group, and personal behavior. Even though people may be changed by the training, findings suggest that the sponsoring organization does not always benefit from the changes. One study found that "sensitivity training ranks low as an effective management development tool when compared to several other common approaches."[7]

Special programs. A widely used personnel development method is to send employees to university-sponsored courses or short courses. These programs are offered by many colleges and universities and professional associations such as the American Management Association. Trainees in these courses are exposed to a variety of problems and learning materials. However, a common complaint about these programs is that they do not deal specifically with the realities of an individual's workplace.

Some larger organizations have established training centers exclusively for their own employees. For example, the federal government, through the Civil Service, has created Executive Seminar Centers in Kingspoint, New York; Berkeley, California; and the Federal Executive Institute in Charlottesville, Virginia. The first two are aimed at developing middle managers while the latter is designed for top-level Civil Service employees. The aim of the center concept is to stimulate new ideas and discussions between speakers and participants, to expose participants to new ideas from other people, to recharge participants' administrative batteries, and to stimulate them intellectually.[8]

Some difficulties common to many developmental efforts are found in this federal training method. A high percentage of the participants simply are not ready for the courses they attend. Some attend at the wrong time in their careers, while others are near retirement. Many have not had the preliminary training in management the centers assume, and many do not have jobs requiring a broad perspective of the federal government. All of these items are indicative of a lack of career planning in most federal agencies.[9] However, the situation is not limited to the Federal Government. These same complaints are common in many other management development efforts.

Psychological testing. Psychological pencil-and-paper tests have been used for several years to determine an employee's developmental potential. Intelligence tests, verbal and mathematical reasoning tests, and personality tests are often used. Such testing can provide useful information to employees in understanding such aspects as motivation, reasoning difficulties, leadership styles, interpersonal response traits, and job preferences.

The biggest problem with good psychological testing lies in interpreting the results. An untrained manager, supervisor, or worker cannot accurately interpret test results. A professional reports scores to someone in the organization, but then the interpretation is left essentially to untrained novices who may attach their own meanings. It should also be recognized that some psychological tests are of limited validity and can be easily faked. Psychological testing appears appropriate only when closely supervised by a qualified professional throughout the testing and feedback process.

Human relations training.   Human relations training originated in the well-known Hawthorne studies. Originally the idea was to prepare supervisors to handle the "people" problems brought to them by their employees. This type of training focuses on the development of human skills a person needs to work well with others. Many human relations training programs are aimed at new or relatively inexperienced first-line supervisors and middle managers. Human relations programs typically deal with motivation, leadership, communication, and humanizing the workplace. Participation is emphasized and components of morale are carefully examined.

The major problem with such programs is the difficulty in measuring their effectiveness. The development of human skills is a longer-range goal. However, the tangible results associated with human relations training is hard to identify over the span of several years. Consequently, such programs are often measured using only the participant's reaction to them. As mentioned in the previous chapter, reaction-level measurement is the weakest form of evaluating the effectiveness of training.

Case study.   A case study is a classroom-oriented development technique which has been used widely in such well-known institutions as Harvard Business School. Cases provide a medium through which the trainee can study the application of management or behavioral concepts. The thrust is on application and analysis instead of mere memorization of concepts.

One common complaint about the case method is that the cases cannot be made sufficiently realistic to be useful. Also, cases may contain information inappropriate to the kinds of decisions that trainees would make in a real situation.

Role playing.   Role playing is a development technique which requires the trainee to assume a role in a given situation and act out behaviors associated with that role. Hopefully, participants gain an appreciation of the factors in a certain situation. Andrew McBride, a labor relations director, may be asked to play the role of the union vice-president in a negotiating situation to give him insight into the constraints and problems facing union bargaining representatives. Role playing is a useful tool in some situations, but a word of caution: trainees are often uncomfortable in role-playing situations and care must be taken to make role playing realistic but nonthreatening.

Simulation (business games). Several different business games are available commercially. These may be computer interactive games where individuals or teams draw up a set of marketing plans for an organization, such as trying to determine the amount of resources to be allocated toward advertising, product design, selling, and sales for effort. The participants make a decision and then the computer tells them how well they did in relation to competing individuals or teams. Other computer-based business games often have to do with labor/management negotiations. In one such simulation a player takes the role of either management or union and the computer takes the other role. The trainee and the computer bargain on such items as wages and benefits.

Simulation, when properly done, can be a useful management development tool. However, simulation receives the same criticism as role playing. Realism is sometimes lacking and the learning experience is diminished. Learning must be the focus, not just "playing the game."

Sabbaticals and leaves of absence. Sabbatical leaves are a very useful development tool. Sabbaticals have been popular for many years in the academic world, where professors take a leave to sharpen their skills and advance their education or research. Similar sorts of plans have been adopted in the business community. For example, Xerox Corporation gives some of its employees six months or more off with pay to work on "socially desirable" projects. Projects include training people in the ghettos or providing technical assistance to overseas countries.

Paid sabbaticals can be an expensive proposition, however. Also, the nature of the learning experience is not within the control of the organization and the exact nature of the developmental experience is left somewhat to chance.

One report indicated that leaves of absence (without pay) are growing more common, but that sabbaticals (with pay) are still rare in business. A survey by Hay Associates of 434 companies showed only 16 companies granting paid sabbaticals. However, 89 percent of those companies offered unpaid leaves of absence to employees, and younger employees are more likely to favor such policies than older employees.[10]

What are five off-the-job methods of personnel development?

Assessment Centers

Assessment centers can help identify areas in employees that need development. They also are useful for selecting certain categories of employees to fill certain jobs.

Essentially, an assessment center is a series of individual and group exercises in which a number of candidates participate. During these exercises, the participants are observed by several specially trained judges. For the most part these exercises are work samples of managerial situations that require the use of managerial skills and behaviors. The "center" is a set of activities rather than just a physical location.

The assessment center approach was originally developed during World War II for selecting OSS agents. One major company, American Telephone and Telegraph, has since made large-scale use of the concept. Candidates may participate in a wide variety of standardized exercises such as management games, leaderless discussion groups, and in-baskets over a several day period. Trained observers watch the candidates' behavior in detail and record impressions. Each assessor writes a report on each candidate which is given to the candidate's superior to use in selection and promotion decisions. The reports often identify guidelines for further development of the assessed employee.

Assessment centers are an excellent means for determining management potential. However, one problem is that some managers may use the assessment center as a way to avoid a difficult promotion decision. For example, suppose a plant supervisor has personally decided that a subordinate is not a qualified candidate for promotion. Rather than stick by the decision and tell the employee, the supervisor sends the employee to the assessment center in hopes that the report will show that the employee is not qualified for promotion. The problems will be worse if the employee receives a positive report. However, if the report is negative, the supervisor's views are validated. Using the assessment center in this way is not recommended. Two other problems are (1) making sure the exercises in the assessment center are valid predictors of management performance and (2) properly selecting and training the assessors.[11]

The validity of assessment centers for selection has been the subject of many studies. These studies have generally suggested that assessment centers predict management success much better than other methods.[12] However, some researchers have been concerned with the very high validity coefficients found in these studies. They question whether the use of salary growth and advancement to measure the success of assessment centers is appropriate. It can be argued that these items may not be related to competence, effectiveness, or superior performance.[13]

Finally, assessment centers are expensive. The actual cost varies from organization to organization, but it has been estimated that it costs at least $500 for each candidate to go through the center.[14] However, the cost of making a mistake with management selection is great too. One firm reported $19,000 worth of legal, salary, and benefit payments to terminate a department head.[15]

Can you discuss benefits and problems associated with assessment centers?

REVIEW AND PREVIEW

Personnel development takes a longer range and broader view of training than does job-skill training. While development may include some skill development, it is more specifically oriented toward a person's capacity to handle future responsibilities. Development activities can include persons at all levels of the organization. Regardless of the level of the people involved, upper management support is important because development requires integration with other organizational activities.

Career planning is one of several development methods mentioned in this chapter. It is a process for matching people and jobs. Career planning can be individual-oriented, organization-oriented, or both.

A wide range of development methods are available. Some of these methods can be conducted on-the-job. Other methods often require an employee to be off-the-job when participating in personnel development activities.

Assessment centers are a special off-the-job development technique. By simulating actual work situations, the assessment center has been fairly successful at predicting future job success of those assessed. But, they are expensive to initiate and operate and may not be measuring performance properly.

The next chapter considers a special kind of development—management development—and a related issue—Organizational Development. Many of the techniques discussed in this chapter are used in management development also. The next chapter will concentrate on special problems involved in developing managers and in preparing them and the organization for future changes.

Review Questions

1. What is personnel development and why is top management support so important?
2. Discuss whether you would prefer organization-centered or individual-centered career planning.
3. You are the head of a governmental agency. What two methods of on-the-job development would you use with a promising supervisor? What two off-the-job methods would you use? Why?

OPENING CASE FOLLOW-UP

Several important issues are involved in the case. One is that coaching is an excellent form of personnel development if it is done well. However, not everyone can automatically coach someone else, and Joe has had no training in coaching. Second, the company must share responsibility with Joe for his performance since they transferred him into the region. Also, there is a lack of a clear identification of what the sales reps need that Joe can provide.

Bob Allen should get Joe's perceptions of the job and problems that are involved as a starting place for a discussion with Joe regarding his behavior. Joe may not realize how his subordinates are reacting to his behavior. Also the kind of coaching behaviors that were appropriate in another region of the country may be inappropriate in another with a different group of sales representatives. An additional concern is the lack of developmental training Joe is doing with his subordinates. One of the original ideas behind putting Joe in that job was to provide sales training for some aggressive young individuals. This currently is not working and calls into question the use Joe can be to the company in the Rocky Mountain region.

There are three aspects of personnel development that this case illustrates. First, there is always a need to carefully select the individuals who will be doing any kind of training, whether it is coaching or more formal kinds of training. Second, some training for those individuals who are trainers should be done. Also, it is important to get the perceptions of the individuals involved in a situation when poor performance is a problem before making some changes.

Case: Development Obligation[1]

Harvey Halm is 40 years old and has been an employee with Obris Corporation for 15 years. Obris Corporation is an employer of about 2,500 in the eastern part of Pennsylvania. Harvey has been a very good employee and has participated in a number of company sponsored development experiences. He has enjoyed company-paid night school at the local college. He has participated in several in-house experiences designed to prepare him for a management job, and last year he went through the company assessment center. He passed with flying colors.

Last week Harvey was offered a first-level management job. Today he turned it down saying he was happy doing what he was doing and did not want the new job. His boss, Samuel Reitz, is flabbergasted. He feels the company has invested a good deal of time and effort preparing Harvey for this opportunity. Besides, Harvey is his best candidate for the job.

Samuel is considering suggesting to the president of the company that this expenditure for "development" be discontinued. He feels that situations such as this clearly indicate that the money is being wasted.

QUESTIONS

1. Should Harvey be viewed as ungrateful?
2. Is the development money spent on Harvey wasted?
3. What *should* a company expect from employees it has spent money on to "develop"?

Notes

1. Richard A. Morano, "A New Concept in Personnel Development and Employee Relations," *Personnel Journal,* 53 (August 1974), p. 608. Reprinted with permission of *Personnel Journal.* Copyright August 1974.

2. Jack Brewer, et al., "A New Dimension in Employee Development: A System For Career Planning and Guidance," *Personnel Journal,* 54 (April 1975), p. 229.

3. Elmer Burack, "Why All the Confusion About Career Planning?" *Human Resources Management* (Summer 1977), p. 21.

4. Douglas T. Hall, *Careers in Organizations* (Pacific Palisades, Calif.: Goodyear Publishing, 1976), pp. 11–13.

5. Adapted from Yoram Zeira, "Introduction of On-the-Job Management Development," *Personnel Journal,* 52 (December 1973), pp. 1050–1051. Reprinted with permission of *Personnel Journal.* Copyright December 1973.

6. Bernard M. Bass and James A. Vaughn, *Training in Industry: The Management of Learning* (Belmont, Calif.: Wadsworth Publishing, 1966), p. 94.

7. William J. Kearney and Desmond D. Martin, "Sensitivity Training: An Established Management Development Tool?" *Academy of Management Journal*, 17 (December 1974), p. 759.

8. John A. Rehfuss, "Executive Development: Executive Seminar Style," *Public Administration Review*, 30 (September-October 1970), pp. 553–559.

9. *Ibid.*

10. "Leaves of Absence," *Wall Street Journal*, December 20, 1977, p. 1.

11. Ann Howard, "An Assessment of Assessment Centers," *Academy of Management Journal*, 16 (October 1973), pp. 907–912.

12. R. J. Klimoski and W. J. Strickland, "Assessment Centers—Valid or Merely Prescient?" (Autumn 1977), p. 353.

13. *Ibid.*, p. 355–356.

14. D. P. Slevins, "The Assessment Center: Breakthrough in Management Appraisal and Development," *Personnel Journal*, 51 (April 1972), pp. 255–263.

15. E. Yager, "Assessment Centers: The Latest Fad?" *Training and Development Journal*, (January, 1976), pp. 41–44.

chapter 11

Management and Organization Development

When you have read this chapter, you should be able to:

1. Discuss the importance of viewing management development in an organizational context.

2. Identify at least three problems that occur in management development.

3. Identify key factors involved in the choice of a management development program.

4. Explain managerial modeling and the special nature of developing women managers.

5. Describe at least three limitations of management development activities.

6. Discuss four general forces for change in organizations.

7. Explain why resistance to change occurs and how it can be managed.

8. Define Organization Development (OD) and identify two general approaches to OD.

Developed Today, Gone Tomorrow?

A large midwestern firm maintains an organizational policy of promoting individual growth. By offering generous allowances for costs associated with tuition, books, and miscellaneous expenses, employees are supported in their efforts to gain a college or other institutional education. This program is also offered to persons whose individual goal it is to continue their education through a graduate program if the field of endeavor is one that could prove to be advantageous to the corporation.

The computer programming department has a high rate of participation in the educational supportive program. It is generally accepted that this high rate is due to the above-average aptitudes of the personnel in the department and to the high personal goals set by them. In addition, the department has its own in-house set of training courses and purchases "space" in various seminar classes. These programs are geared to making the employee specifically more valuable to the department. The managers in the programming department have been very proud of the development of their personnel and feel that the education (from all sources) has improved departmental performance.

Just recently, however, the system seemed to backfire in the programming department. Ezra Brooks, a very bright and aspiring young programmer for whom management had high hopes, quit. Ezra had found that the extensive intraorganization training, the invaluable work experience, and a newly awarded college diploma represented a fairly lucrative portfolio of credentials that he took to a large national accounting firm. Ezra had expressed a desire to stay, but he was told that there were no anticipated openings at managerial levels in the computer area.

Ezra's manager had a dilemma. Loss of Ezra meant a ten labor-month setback for the project he was working on. He also felt that the benefit of the extensive training Ezra had received at the company's expense was little utilized compared to what Ezra would have contributed had he remained with the company. However, the manager's greatest concern was that Ezra was the first in a group of several employees who would graduate from college in the near future. To the remaining group Ezra had shown that if the firm would not recognize his achievement and aspirations, other employment could be easily obtained. Ezra's manager was perplexed with the situation.

The rapid rate of change that exists in our society has some powerful implications for personnel management. As the products, competition, and environment in which organizations operate change, both the organization itself and the management group must be willing and able to adjust to changes.

This chapter will consider two major activities associated with the adjustment to change:

1. Management development—a specific subset of activities associated with personnel development;
2. Organization Development—an approach for helping the organization adjust to and originate change.

The Organization Development and management development interface is shown in Figure 11-1. As with other interfaces, it suggests that the personnel unit and operating managers share responsibilities for these activities.

FIGURE 11-1 Organization and management development interface.

Personnel Unit	Managers
Monitors societal changes affecting the organization's personnel	Must deal with major changes
Assists in evaluating turnover problems and their impact	Provide information on turnover problems
Provides assistance in planning for the effect of change on managers	Recognize and manage resistance to change in individuals
Develops and coordinates management development efforts	Participate in management development programs
Recognizes and plan for Organization Development needs	Participate in OD when appropriate

Adaptation to change includes the training and development interfaces in organizations. Everyone in the organization must "learn" how to change and "learn" ways to prepare for it. It is especially important for an organization to prepare its managers to guide the organization in the future. Preparing managers to handle future responsibilities and challenges is at the heart of management development activities.

FIGURE 11-2 Management development as part of the organizational system.

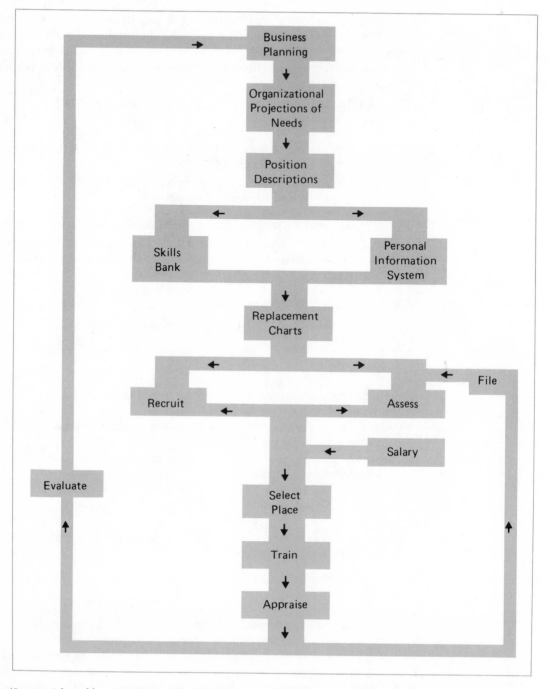

(Source: Adapted from J. D. Somerville, "A Systems Approach to Management Development," *Personnel Journal*, 53 (May 1974), p. 369. Reprinted with permission of *Personnel Journal*. Copyright May 1974.)

MANAGEMENT DEVELOPMENT AS AN ORGANIZATIONAL SUBSYSTEM

Management development can be viewed as part of a system such as that shown in Figure 11-2. That figure shows that as a result of business planning for the future, the organization can project its staffing needs for managers. Then position descriptions are made, which indicate the jobs that need to be done and the positions to be filled.

Top management uses two sources to determine the *raw material* on hand to fill positions: (1) a *skills bank,* which is basically a listing of skills available in the present work force, and (2) *personal information* such as age, education, performance appraisals, and past performance. This information is often developed as a part of manpower planning activities (see Chapter 7).

With information from the skills bank and personal information records, *replacement charts* are drawn, very similar to depth charts used by a football team. (Such charts show the back-up players at each position.) Replacement charts indicate where weaknesses exist. If some positions are without adequate back-up, then a decision or *assessment* must be made, either to develop someone to fill the position internally or to recruit outside. An individual must be selected, placed in the proper position, then trained, and receive a performance appraisal. This information then becomes feedback to the entire management development system. The success of manager development is evaluated and incorporated into future business plans, and the cycle continues.

Management Replacement Charts

The purpose of replacment charts is to insure that the right individual is available at the right time and has had sufficient experience to handle the job. In Figure 11-3 a replacement chart for the Rocky Mountain Manufacturing Company is shown.

Note that the chart specifies the kind of management development each individual needs to be promotable. Ms. Wilson needs exposure to manufacturing to be promotable to superintendent. Her job as office manager has not given her much exposure to the production side of the operation. Ms. Paul needs exposure to plant operations and personnel. Mr. French needs to learn how to handle young, aggressive managers. However, Mr. French's appraiser felt French would not be promotable to superintendent—even with additional training.

Why is management development considered an organizational subsystem?

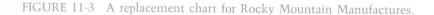

FIGURE 11-3   A replacement chart for Rocky Mountain Manufactures.

Mr. Jones, Superintendent

Age: 62
Education: High School
Performance Appraisal: Excellent
Next Position: Retirement

Mr. Smith, Plant Supervisor

Age: 46
Education: College graduate
Performance Appraisal: Average
Next Position: Promotable,
    could move to Superintendent

Ms. Wilson, Office Manager

Age: 40
Education: Junior College
Performance Appraisal: Excellent
Next Position: Needs exposure
    to manufacturing to be
    promotable to Superintendent

Mr. French, Plant Supervisor

Age: 55
Education: Junior College
Performance Appraisal: Adequate
Next Position: Perhaps a staff
    position — Has difficulty with
    young aggressive managers.
    Not promotable to
    Superintendent

Ms. Paul, Data Processing Supervisor
Age: 32
Education: MBA
Performance Appraisal: Excellent
Next Position: Plant Supervisor
    or staff position in personnel

Mr. Garcia, Personnel Manager
Age: 45
Education: High School
Performance Appraisal: Doing
    an above average job
Next Position: Promotable but
    prefers to stay in present job

Problems in Management Development

Management development efforts are subject to certain common mistakes and problems. Managers at all levels, especially top managers, make these same mistakes. Figure 11-4 contains a summary of major problems identified by one author.

An awareness of the ten management development problems in Figure 11-4 can help to guide the establishment and operation of development efforts. Notice that most of these problems are the result of inadequate planning and narrow thinking about the subject. Some problems are a result of seeing management development as a separate activity from

FIGURE 11-4   Ten serious mistakes in management development.

---

1 Placing the primary responsibility for trainee development on staff.
2 Lack of training in training for trainers.
3 Hasty or shallow needs analysis.
4 Substituting training for selection.
5 Limiting the planning of development activity to "courses."
6 Over-concern with personality.
7 Lumping together of training/development needs.
8 Preoccupation with mechanics.
9 On-again, off-again crash programs.
10 Lack of provision for practical application of the trainee.

(Source: J. W. Taylor, "Ten Serious Mistakes in Management-Training Development," *Personnel Journal*, 53 (May 1974), pp. 357–362. Reprinted with permission of *Personnel Journal*. Copyright May 1974.)

organizational operations. Such a view can result in "encapsulated" management development.

Encapsulated management development. **Failure** to consider how management development fits the organization can result in *encapsulated training.* This occurs when an individual learns new methods and ideas in a management development course and returns to a work unit which is still bound by old attitudes and methods. The reward system and the working conditions have not changed. Although the trainee has learned new ways to handle certain situations, these methods cannot be applied because of the *status quo* and the unchanged work situation. The new knowledge remains encapsulated in the classroom setting.

Encapsulated management development is an obvious waste of time and money because it is ineffective. Encapsulated training can be avoided by good *organizational needs diagnosis.* Research and diagnosis can lead to a tailored management development program.

What are several management development problems?

CHOOSING A MANAGEMENT DEVELOPMENT PROGRAM

The previous material indicates that many variables are involved in selecting the appropriate management development approach. The proper

FIGURE 11-5 A model for selecting personnel development techniques.

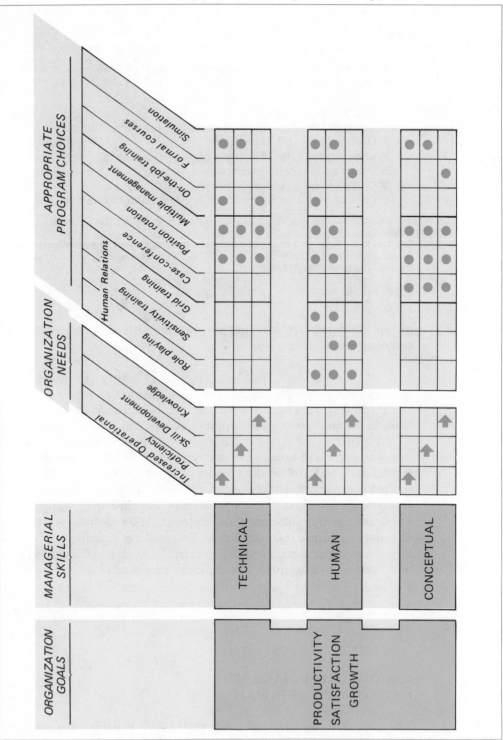

(*Source:* Adapted from Thomas J. Von DerEmbse, "Choosing a Management Development Program: A Decision Model," *Personnel Journal*, 52 (October 1973). Reprinted with permission *Personnel Journal*. Copyright October 1973.)

program depends on the organization's objectives, the managerial skills involved, and the organization's needs.

The model presented in Figure 11-5 is useful when choosing an appropriate management development technique.[1] Given the organizational objectives, managerial skills, and the organizational needs which can be developed from skills inventories, appropriate programs can be selected. Figure 11-5 shows the beginning point for such an operation is *organizational objectives*. Three basic objectives are common to all organizations: *productivity, satisfaction,* and *growth.* Next, to reach these objectives, managers need *skills* in three basic categories: *technical, conceptual,* and *human.*

There are several *levels* within each skill. Level I is increased operational proficiency (obtaining additional experience in areas where skills are already developed). Level II is skill development (acquiring the capacity to perform a particular skill). Level III is fundamental knowledge (developing the basic understanding of the field, getting acquainted with the language concepts and relationships involved).

Figure 11-5 shows, for example, that if a manager's technical skills need development and if the organization has a need for increased operational proficiency, the following development techniques might be appropriate: position rotation, multiple management, on-the-job training, and simulation. If the organization needs basic knowledge, the following techniques might be considered: case or conference methods, position rotation, multiple management, or formal course work.

Use of this model provides a framework for selecting development techniques. Analytical use of the model may help a decision-maker avoid "bandwagon" program choices and encourage the person to weigh carefully the various alternatives in terms of organizational needs, skill requirements, and overall goals.[2]

What key factors affect the choice of a management development program?

Two additional areas of special interest when dealing with management development are: (1) managerial modeling and (2) special problems of women managers. These areas will be examined to show the impact and importance of sound management development planning and implementation.

Managerial Modeling

There is an old truism in personnel management development that says managers tend to manage as they were managed. Another way of stating this idea is that much management is learned by modeling the behavior of other managers.

This revelation is not surprising because a great deal of human behavior is learned by modeling others. Children learn by modeling parents and older children; they are quite comfortable with the process by the time they grow up.

Modeling, a very powerful management development tool, has been used successfully in industry in several ways. Over 2,700 first line supervisors at General Electric have been trained in the use of modeling to help ease the hard-core unemployed into the work world.[3] As a supervisory development method, modeling has been used by firms such as Quaker Oats, Ford Motor, Xerox, Lukens Steel, Gulf Oil, and American Cyanamid.[4]

Modeling is a very natural way for managers to develop, since it will likely occur regardless of design, intent, or desire. Management development efforts can take advantage of the natural human behavior by matching young or developing managers with appropriate models and then reinforcing the desirable behaviors that are exhibited.

What is managerial modeling?

Management Development and the Woman Manager

Management development efforts for some groups may need a different orientation than for individuals in other groups. During the last several years, employers have experienced increasing pressure to promote women into management positions. Both legal and societal pressures have encouraged the movement of women out of traditional "women's" jobs and into the mainstream of managerial activity.

The biggest obstacle for a woman seeking advancement in management is the traditional attitudes of both men and women towards masculine and feminine roles. Further, studies have shown that women tend to have different self-concepts than men, and possibly a different orientation toward achievement as well.[5]

Development of women managers seems to require an understanding of their special needs, as well as the requirements of the business. Research on women managers leads to the following recommendations for management development programs:

1. Women need to raise their self-esteem as managers.
2. Women need to learn new behaviors for managing interpersonal conflict.
3. Women need to develop leadership and team-building skills.
4. Women need help with career planning.
5. Training for *women only* is desirable initially.[6]

Rather than resorting to special training for potential women managers, selecting those who are already qualified would be most efficient. However, the demand for qualified women managers sometimes precludes this solution, especially when there is an urgency to hire and promote qualified female managers under an Affirmative Action plan.

As the foregoing suggests, if special training for women is necessary, it is likely to be more attitudinal in nature than ability-oriented.[7] Research has shown that male managers tend to "plan ahead" for their careers, while women managers tend to express a high incidence of "Horatio Alger" thinking.[8] This factor and the popularity of assertiveness training with women managers suggest that the differences and special problems are more related to attitudes than to ability.

As with any social change, the initial introduction of women into management has been difficult for some organizations. Some male managers maintain that special training for women is "reverse discrimination." Most organizations, however, do not allow talented men to develop in a haphazard, laborious manner. They take positive steps to insure that a talented man has the opportunity to develop his managerial ability. The same treatment for talented women must be available also.

What is the focus of management development activities for women?

EXTENT AND LIMITATIONS OF MANAGEMENT DEVELOPMENT

More than 7,000 American managers enrolled in the general management division of the American Management Association were surveyed to obtain their thoughts and feelings about contemporary management training and development.[9] As summarized in Figure 11-6, results indicate that management development is a widespread activity.

Nearly four out of every five firms surveyed have some type of tuition refund program for employee self-study and self-development. Two-thirds of the managers indicated that their companies regularly send managers to professional management training organizations. Nearly 40 percent of the companies surveyed send managers to university-sponsored courses.

Another study found that for first level supervisors the most common training activities are: (1) coaching, (2) tuition aid for college, and (3) in-house training programs. Programs for middle managers include more outside programs.[10]

FIGURE 11-6　Extent to which respondent's organizations have management development.

Program	Have Such a Program	Do Not Have Such a Program
Well-defined in-house program	43%	57%
Well-established OD program	32%	68%
Formally used MBO	49%	51%
Tuition refund for self-development	79%	21%
Send managers to professional management training	66%	34%
Send managers to colleges or universities	39%	61%

(Source: Robert F. Pearse, *Manager to Manager: What Managers Think of Management Development* (New York: Amacom Division, American Management Association, 1974). Used with permission.)

Management Development Limitations

In viewing these and other results, one author concludes that managers are indicating that management development is currently limited by the following factors:

1. Small and middle-sized organizations do not have the time or the money to spend in developing complete management education programs.
2. Authoritarian and conservative top managements do not want much subordinate initiative or creativity, especially in large governmental bureaucracies. Individuality is a liability.
3. Top managements' investments in human resources development are more poorly handled than any other resource investment which the firm makes.
4. Without a philosophy of professional management, development expenditures are largely wasted. However, much of the waste is not recognized.
5. Unlike equipment, organizations do not own their human resources, so they are not motivated to invest a great deal of money in the individuals that might then leave the organization.
6. It is difficult to prove on a one-to-one cost basis the value of investing in a given training or development exercise for a particular manager.
7. Because of managerial mobility it may be a better investment to buy

already-trained managers from other organizations than to invest in training their own.

8. Human resource development costs are deferrable. An organization has to have equipment and materials to produce its products; however, training and development can be put off and the organization can still function at an acceptable level.

9. A long-term commitment of top management time, plus the money necessary to operate an adequate development program, is evidently too great for the probable returns. It seems a better strategy to have a modest program that will keep people happy than to make the effort of setting up an all-out human resources development program. Many successful organizations survive with a limited investment in human development.[11]

The opening case about Ezra, the computer programmer, clearly illustrates the limitations of development activities. The poor planning and handling of Ezra and those like him resulted in a significant expenditure of funds with little long-term return to the firm being gained.

Can you tell about at least three limitations affecting management development?

The discussion now turns from management development to another development issue—the use of Organization Development. The aim is to prepare the entire organization for change.

FORCES OF CHANGE

It has been suggested that in the last century "we have increased our speed of communication by a factor of 10, and the speed of travel by 10, our speed on data handing by 10, our ability to control diseases by 10."[12] If such major changes have come in such a relatively short period of time, human relationships obviously have been greatly affected.

The rate of social and economic change is not likely to slow in the near future. Changes in the labor force alone indicate its continuing momentum. For example, the number of people in the U. S. labor force in 1975 was about 93 million and will increase to over 100 million in the early 1980s. This labor force will be composed of a declining proportion of younger workers and an increasing number in the 25-to-44 age group. It will be composed of a growing number of females, especially working wives and mothers, and an increasing number of blacks.[13] Managers in organizations should expect changing conditions as the composition of the work force changes.

As changes of such a broad scope occur in society, personnel management is significantly affected. Organizations are in a continuous state of flux and must always be so if they are to remain in balance with a changing environment. As a result, an ongoing state of change must characterize the organization's structure, functions, work load, types of jobs, as well as employees and their qualifications, capacities, and behaviors. Developments within the organization may necessitate promotions, transfers, demotions, layoffs, or other actions affecting personnel. Think, for example, of the many reorganizations necessitated by the widespread adaptation of computers as management tools.

Is continual change necessary? Can an astute manager avoid it? Certainly not everything needs changing all the time, but forces surrounding the management of people in an organization dictate that change inevitably *does* and *will* take place. Some of the forces dictating change include:

1. Changing product life cycles
2. Material shortages or surpluses
3. International competition
4. Technological advances
5. Legislation
6. Changing values and expectations of individuals in society
7. New knowledge of human behavior and ways of organizing
8. Increasing economic independence of employees
9. Increasing government involvement in the employer-employee relationship
10. A shift by unions from a purely economic to a quasi-political position
11. The increasing complexity of organizational life.

Some of these factors will affect *every type* of organization. The change forces mentioned above can be grouped into four categories: *social and work force changes, environmental change, personnel turnover, and technological change.* Each of these will be discussed in turn.

Societal and Work Force Changes

Because an organization is comprised of people, changes affecting its people also affect the organization. A specific example of how social changes are directly affecting the work force was reported in the *Wall Street Journal.* [14] A feature story suggested that management faces increasing militancy from a traditionally docile group—white collar workers. Salaried people used to feel they were, to a degree, part of management; when they were no longer wanted they departed quietly. Recently salaried people have been resisting management's attempts to dismiss them, much like their blue-collar counterparts resist. These changes in social values and attitudes are reflected in the internal operations of many companies. Firing has become a less popular personnel tool as a result.

Age and education level changes. **Another** trend affecting personnel management is the increasing age and education of the work force. More and more occupations than ever before now include entry level educational qualifications. Those without a high school diploma are increasingly hard-pressed to find jobs. The continued importance placed on education, as well as the expansion in available educational opportunities, has resulted in a more educated labor force.

The changing age mix in the United States and its projection to 1990 is shown in Figure 11-7. The ever-increasing number of older persons will have some interesting impacts on work organization. Some of these changes are already apparent with new retirement-age laws having been enacted (see Chapter 14).

FIGURE 11-7   U.S. population: The ever-changing age mix.

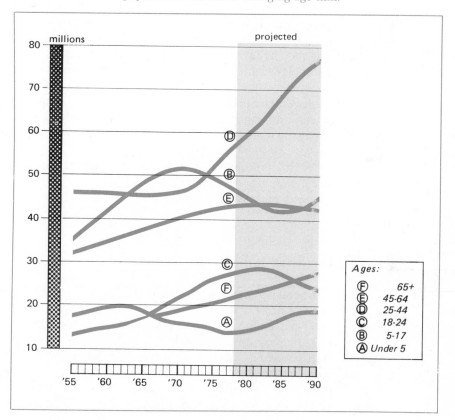

(Source: Bureau of the Census, Series II projections.)

Life-style changes and management transfers. **Other** important changes relative to the work force include changes in life-styles. Many of today's employees have a different life-style from the employees in the same age group only ten years ago and thus bring different values to the job now than employees in the 1960s.

One change taking place over the last decade has had the net result of changing development policies and practices for many organizations. There has been a growing reluctance on the part of managers to accept relocation as a part of moving up in an organization. One study found that in 617 firms surveyed, some 42 percent of the employees were saying "no" to moving. This percentage was ten times the percentage in an earlier study.[15] Another study reported a smaller percentage, but indicated 52 percent of the firms responding saw a "major" reluctance to accept transfers.[16]

Part of the reason for the reluctance to transfer is the high cost—both in direct and more hidden indirect costs—to the person being transferred. Yet many organizations, because of the wide geographic scope of their facilities and operations, rely very heavily on being able to move people where they are needed. The result of this dilemma is perhaps predictable. Many organizations have recently reviewed their transfer policies and have made changes. In one survey 42 percent of the respondents indicated that they had recently reviewed their policies regarding transfer and that the review had resulted in changes in policy.[17] Most changes were increases in the amount or type of costs the company would pay.

Movement to certain cities or areas of the country increase the reluctance of managers to move. One consultant found that a client firm had to pay a $30,000 manager a $20,000 bonus over three years to get him to relocate to New York City.[18]

As this problem and other societal changes are reflected in the work force, managers will have to change their organizations or see them changed, perhaps in undesirable ways. In addition, managers will have to adjust to environmental forces.

Environmental Changes

The social changes just described are one kind of environmental change. But the most direct environmental change for most organizations since 1960 has been the increasing involvement of government in organizational operations. Federal and state governments have agencies and statutes which can dictate wages that must be paid, certify the safety of working conditions, monitor the quality of the air surrounding many plants, provide minimum standards for hiring, and demand to see extensive records in order to scrutinize how organizations operate. This environmental change has forced managers to change personnel-related record keeping, promotion, benefits, safety, and salary practices.

Many American business organizations also are now in direct competition with foreign companies for the first time, both at home and abroad. The expansion of international trade and the desire of many American firms to move into foreign markets has lead to new personnel activities. As mentioned in Chapter 2, multinational operations require different personnel policies that cover overseas assignment, currency fluctuations, housing allowances, and family educational considerations.

Personnel Turnover

Organizations are composed of groupings of people, and people "turn over." Husbands or wives are transferred to new jobs in different cities; they find better jobs; they die; or they retire. Turnover changes old patterns of social relations and often requires alterations in the way people do their jobs. Because there will always be employee turnover, organizational change from this source is inevitable. An efficient organization will plan for, anticipate, and "manage" turnover through manpower planning and other managerial activities.

While some turnover is inevitable and even desirable, too much is an indication of organization problems. How much is too much? The answer is that "it depends." Some determining factors include the type of industry, historical trends, other employment opportunities in the community or geographical area, and the unemployment rate for the region.

In one organization, turnover has averaged 150 percent the last two years. That means that on the average, each job had to be filled one and one half times each year. This excessive turnover costs a great deal in training expenses alone, and keeps the company in a constant state of flux and turmoil. The turnover is basically a result of low wages, unpleasant work, and a low unemployment rate in the community, so discontented employees easily obtain other jobs. Turnover is discussed further in Chapter 17.

Technological Change

As noted earlier (Chapter 2), technology includes more than machinery and hardware. It is also the knowledge about organizing, the structure used to get work done, and the kind of work done on the product or service before it is marketed. In other words, technology is the sum total of the knowledge and processes used to transform raw material into finished products or services in an organization.

Changes in work schedules. Working arrangements are a part of technology as defined here. One area of working arrangements that has been in transition is the traditional eight-hour, five-day week work schedule. Organizations have been experimenting with a great many different possibilities for changing work schedules; the four-day, 40-hour week; the four-day 32-hour week; the three-day work week; and flexible scheduling. Changes of this nature require some major adjustments for organizations.

A popular change in work scheduling is *flexi-time*, or flexible scheduling. *Flexi-time usually refers to starting and quitting time variations but assumes that a constant number of hours (usually eight) are worked each day.* Employees can choose the hours to be worked in any particular day. These hours must include a *core time* when all employees must be present. Flexi-time allows management to relax some of the traditional "time clock" control of personnel. The published results of several research studies indicate that a flexible working hour schedule appears to generate favorable results.[19]

Flexi-time was developed in Germany in the 1960s and transmitted to the United States largely through European-based companies with American branches. The system, which has grown in the United States, has been applied in heavy industry, department stores, banks, insurance companies, and a wide variety of other businesses. Although the flexi-time system has mainly been confined to white-collar workers (clerical jobs) within these organizations, it has also been successfully applied to manual production work.

The use of flexi-time by U.S. firms is on the upswing. A survey reports 13 percent of all private employers with 50 or more workers now allow employees to vary start and stop times, roughly double the number in 1974.[20]

Basically, flexi-time requires each person to work the same number of hours. However, the traditional eight-hour work shift is lengthened by addition of one or more hours at the beginning and end of the normal work day. This total span of possible work hours is labeled *bandwidth time.*

Bandwidth and core times can be adjusted to fit the particular needs of an individual employer or operation. Control Data Corporation in Minneapolis, employer of 30,000 people in the United States and overseas, has three different schedules. The assembly line workers use a staggered hours system broken down into three-hour shifts. The employees start and stop work at these staggered hours, according to their preferences whenever possible. The workers with jobs dependent on specific machinery have group flexibility in which the majority's preferences prevail. The people working in research and development have individual flexibility. They may start as early as 4 A.M. if they wish, but they must report by at least 10 A.M.[21]

EDP and computerization. Another common technological change is the introduction of electronic data processing (EDP) into an organization. Many organizations have had to computerize their operations to remain competitive. Bringing the computer into an organization the first time may be a great trauma for the people who will be affected by the technological change. Many companies have handled changes of this nature very well with a minimum amount of disruption, but others have had miserable experiences with such changes. The difference is in the way the innovation was planned and implemented.

What are four broad forces causing change in organizations?

Successful changes, especially those concerned with personnel administration in an organization, do not simply happen—they are carefully planned. Planning for change requires an understanding of why people resist change.

RESISTANCE TO CHANGE

Employees resist change in many ways; wildcat strikes, quarrelling between employees and supervisors, requests for transfers, absenteeism, high turnover rates, and reduction in output are ways employees can resist change.

The Effects of Personality on Resistance to Change

Most people have a need to maintain stability or equilibrium with their environments. When a person's stablility is threatened by changes beyond his or her control, several personality forces can cause resistance. These personalitiy forces are summarized by one author as follows:[22]

1. *Homeostasis.* The human body has a built-in regulatory system for keeping fairly constant such things as temperature and blood sugar. This characteristic has been identified regarding the psychological behavior of man as well. Psychological changes may be only temporary as the organism attempts to return to its previous homeostatic state.
2. *Habit.* Habit is a preference for the familiar. Once a habit is established, its operation often becomes satisfying to the individual and it becomes very resistant to change. The familiar is preferred.
3. *Primacy.* The way in which an individual first successfully copes with the situation sets a pattern which is unusually persistent and these patterns are especially difficult to change.
4. *Selective Perception and Attention.* Once an attitude is set up, a

person responds to other situations within the framework of that established mental framework. People tend to screen out those things that do not agree with their perception of the world, or their views of things. They do not hear, do not remember, or somehow, otherwise ignore the things they find disagreeable or offensive.

5. *Dependence.*   Children as they are growing up tend to incorporate the values, attitudes and beliefs of those who care for them. Therefore, the typical adult still agrees far more than he disagrees with his parents, former teachers, or supervisors and peers on very basic items such as religion, politics, child rearing, and how a job should be done.

6. *Insecurity and Regression.*   Another personality obstacle to participation in change is the tendency to seek security in the past. When life grows difficult and frustrating, individuals tend to think with nostalgia about the happy days of the past. Even though an individual may be dissatisfied with the current situation, the prospect of change arouses even more anxiety, so people may somehow seek a road back to the old and as they now see it, a more peaceful way of life.

Resistance to Change in Work Organizations

In a work organization such basic employee concerns as *fear, inconvenience,* and *threat to interpersonal relationships* can be related to resistance to change. Fear has several sources, one of which is *economic.* For example, the employees of a clock manufacturer feared they would lose their jobs if the company changed to manufacturing electronic clocks instead of mechanical clocks.

Another fear is that a change in some way will detract from an employee's *status* and the status symbols in the organization. To illustrate, if a change meant a new job but a smaller office, a manager might resist because he or she viewed the smaller office as a loss of status or importance.

Resistance may be caused by a fear of *uncertainty.* Employees may be unwilling to learn something new because they are uncertain they will be able to do the required operations. A cashier at a supermarket resisted the change to an electronic cash register because he feared he would not be able to operate the new register rapidly and accurately.

Another cause of resistance to change is *inconvenience.* All people develop habits which provide security in a day-to-day existence. When they are thrown into a new situation, the old habits and old ways of operating may no longer apply. New patterns of behavior may have to be developed.

A final cause for resistance to change is a perceived threat to *interpersonal relationships.* When a change means becoming part of a new work group or being separated from close friends in the existing work group, a person is likely to balk. For this reason a person may hesitate at being transferred to a new job, even though it would mean a promotion and a raise. The disruption of old friendships and the effort involved in establishing new ones may cause resistance.

What are some reasons why people resist changes?

Positive Aspects of Resistance to Change

Resistance to change is not *necessarily* bad. Obviously, too much resistance to change can be disruptive for the organization and can even lead to extreme acts such as sabotage or efforts to disrupt production. However, managers can make a mistake by assuming that because people resist change, they must always be *forcing* change upon people. This view is not necessarily the case.

Too much resistance to change is an indication that something is wrong in the way the change is being introduced, just as fever indicates infection in the human body. In one manufacturing company, a new machine was installed that was expected to double output. The crew resisted the new procedures accompanying installation of the machine. Analysis showed that the crew was not cooperating because older, high status members of the crew were unhappy because they were not given the opportunity to choose their new work stations. If management had monitored for resistance, this problem would have been detected much sooner. A simple action of letting the workers choose their work stations based on seniority might have solved this problem.

A complete lack of resistance to change may indicate that employees are so afraid to oppose change or speak out that they are unwilling to express their concerns. Complete lack of resistance to change may indicate apathy and a very unfavorable organizational climate.

Managing Resistance to Change

All changes need not be violently resisted. Key components of effective change include the following management actions: planned change, consideration of human and social factors, as well as other factors, and participation by employees affected by the change *if* appropriate. Judicious application of these ideas will help managers reduce resistance to change. Poorly planned and implemented changes will be resisted, as in the case presented in Figure 11-8. In this instance, had the principals and the parents had an opportunity to participate in the decision-making process, the problems could have been significantly reduced.

FIGURE 11-8 "A Case of Poorly Managed Change."

The superintendent of schools in a medium-sized, rural school system was concerned about the "inbreeding" of elementary school principals. It was apparent that some changes were needed in the organization, because certain principals who had been in a community for many years were showing favoritism toward particular groups in the community, and toward particular teachers in the schools.

The superintendent determined that a change in administrative assignments would be in everyone's best interest. However, rather than considering how a change of this nature would be received and making some attempt to minimize negative reactions, the superintendent simply made new assignments for all 13 principals for the following year, and sent each principal a letter indicating his new assignment.

On a Friday afternoon, all 13 principals received their letters indicating that all had been reassigned to a different school. The uproar was very loud, and very immediate. By Monday morning, the superintendent had irate parents standing in line outside his office to complain about the fact that the principals they had grown accustomed to were leaving for another school. Many of the principals had prepared resignations for submission to the superintendent. By the end of the week, the superintendent had decided that discretion was the better part of valor and had withdrawn the reassignments.

Strategies for reducing resistance to change.   If good planning and consideration of the human and social factors involved have occurred and resistance still appears likely, what can a manager do to handle such resistance to change? Several strategies are available.

One possibility is to make change tentative, that is, on a *trial* basis at first. This approach is especially appropriate if the employees have had an opportunity to participate in the decision-making process. If the employees have not participated in the decision, resistance may be greater. Careful *two-way communication* can help reduce resistance. Many times resistance is based on a lack of understanding, and if managers will really listen to employees' suggestions, problems can be reduced.

Another possibility is to provide an *economic guarantee* to employees. If an employee refuses to move to a new job, a guaranteed reimbursement for all relevant costs could be offered. It is quite common in union contracts for management to guarantee that no union member will suffer economic loss as a result of technological change. Although guarantees are extremely useful in removing such opposition, they can also be expensive. However, when the cause of resistance to change is economic in nature, a manager should consider some type of economic incentive as a way to gain employee cooperation.

Can you discuss how to manage resistance to changes?

ORGANIZATION DEVELOPMENT

Even in the absence of rapid organizational change, a program to improve effectiveness or change attitudes and values may be necessary. A collection of ideas and techniques has emerged called Organizational Development (OD) which can help organizations deal with problems surrounding these changes. OD attempts to help organizations better understand current and potential problems and provides alternative methods of solving them.

> ORGANIZATION DEVELOPMENT is a value-based process of self-assessment and planned change, involving specific strategies and technology, aimed at improving the overall effectiveness of an organizational system.[23]

Can you define OD?

Systems View

A key to successful Organization Development is to view the organization as a *system*. (See Chapter 2 on organizations as systems.) This perspective implies that a recognition of the interrelated nature of organizational components and problems is necessary. For example, there is very little benefit in attempting to reduce widespread employee dissatisfaction without looking at the reward system, the kind of work, working conditions, equity in the organization, and other appropriate components in a particular situation.

Value-Based

The commonly accepted view of OD refers to efforts which have an explicitly "humanistic" bias. The values underlying most attempted OD changes are:

1. Providing opportunities for people to function as human beings rather than as resources in the productive process;

2. Providing opportunities for each employee to develop full potential;

3. Seeking to increase the effectiveness of the organization in terms of all of its goals;

4. Attempting to create an environment in which it is possible to find exciting and challenging work;

5. Providing opportunities for employees to influence the organization, the environment, and the way they relate to work;

6. Treating each employee as a person with complex needs, all of which are important at work and in life.[24]

Approaches to Organization Development

Targets for OD efforts can be:

1. people
2. technologies
3. processes and structures[25]

Entry or "intervention" into the organization may improve effectiveness either in technology, structure, or with individuals and how they relate with each other. In more traditional attempts at OD, only change in the structure or the technology of the organization is considered. In Figure 11-9 notice that an organization includes *people, technology, process,* and *structure,* all of which mesh to provide human fulfillment and to get work done.

FIGURE 11-9   Approaches to Organization Development.

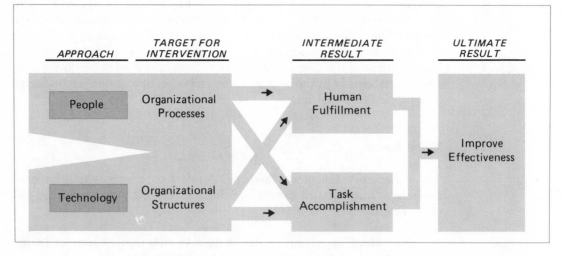

(Source: Adapted from F. Friedlander and L. D. Brown, "Organizational Development," *Annual Review of Psychology,* 1974.)

Improvements in the organization's effectiveness can be made by changing people, technology, structure, and/or the processes. For example, in the Bennett Supply Company, the productivity of the work force has been low, costs have been rising, and the absence and turnover rates are rising. Mr. Bennett is trying to decide how to reverse these trends and help the organization work better. He might appropriately begin with *action research,* an attempt to gather information on problems and make appropriate changes. He can either do this research himself or hire a consultant to help him. After changes are carefully planned, the effects on the variables under consideration can be monitored.

From this research Mr. Bennett might try to make changes in the organizational *processes* of his firm. Actions to build more "team spirit" and to develop a climate where employees can express their feelings more openly and honestly might be taken.

Or, Mr. Bennett might want to change *technology* by bringing in a new means of performing jobs in the company. He might also change *structure* variables by adding another level of management to the hierarchy. All of these "targets" for OD intervention or change are legitimate. The ones appropriate for Bennett Supply depend on that firm's particular situation and management's assessment of it.

People Approaches

OD techniques can include several types of intervention. The *survey feedback method* is a process in which data are systematically collected (usually by analysis of questionnaires from members of the organization), summarized, and the results are fed back to employees. Attitude surveys in general are discussed in Chapter 17.

Team building (group development) means developing a good working relationship among group members. Techniques such as T-group or laboratory training are useful in team building.

Intergroup development attempts to solve problems of contact between groups in an organization. For example, intergroup development might focus on minimizing or resolving conflicts between departments. These approaches (survey feedback, team building, and intergroup development) can have a number of positive effects on the attitudes of those involved.

Technological and Structural Approaches

Organization Development may focus on changes in the technology, the structure of the organization, or both. In this case, the OD approaches are deeply rooted in engineering, sociology, psychology, and economics.

One *technological approach* would be exploring the possibilities of job redesign (see Chapter 6) by increasing job scope, job depth, or both. *Structural changes* include removing levels of the management hierarchy and giving lower units in the organization more opportunity for self-direction. Creating new authority and responsibility patterns are other structural change possibilities.

What are two general approaches to OD?

Assessment of OD

As a field of study, OD has made both academicians and practitioners aware of the need for planned change. However, much more research is needed for OD to become the systematic body of knowledge OD practitioners would like it to be.

Successful change efforts.   Studies have provided valuable information on what differentiates successful and unsuccessful change. As an example of the benefits of OD and planned change efforts, one author suggests that successful change efforts have some very distinct patterns. Based on a review of several studies of organizational change, the conditions surrounding *successful* change attempts were found to be as follows:

1. The organization, and especially top management, is under considerable external and internal pressure for improvement long before an explicit organization change is contemplated. Performance and/or morale are low. Top management seems to be groping for a solution to its problems.

2. A new person, known for the ability to introduce improvements, enters the organization, either as the official head of the organization or the consultant who deals directly with the head of the organization.

3. An initial act of the new person is to encourage a re-examination of past practices and current problems within the organization.

4. The head of the organization and his immediate subordinates assume a direct and highly involved role in conducting this re-examination.

5. The new person, with top management support, engages several levels of the organization in collaborative, fact-finding, problem-solving discussions to identify and diagnose current organization problems.

6. The new person provides others with new ideas and methods for developing solutions to problems, again at many levels of the organization.

7. The solutions and decisions are developed, tested, and found creditable for solving problems on a small scale before the attempt is made to widen the scope of change to larger problems in the entire organization.

8. The change effort spreads with each success experience, and as management support grows it is gradually absorbed permanently into the organization's way of life.[26]

Unsuccessful change efforts. Unsuccessful organizational change attempts were strikingly *less consistent* than the more successful attempts. Each of the successful changes followed a similar and highly consistent route of one step building upon another. The less successful changes were much less orderly. Three interesting patterns of inconsistency are as follows:

1. The less successful changes began from a variety of starting points. This is in contrast to the successful changes which begin from a common point, i.e., strong pressure both externally and internally.

2. Another pattern of inconsistency is found in the sequence of change steps. In successful change patterns some degree of the logical consistency between steps is observed, as each seems to make the next possible. In these less successful changes, sequences contain wide and seemingly illogical gaps.

3. Another pattern of inconsistency is evident in the major approaches used to introduce change. In the successful cases, it seems fairly clear that shared approaches are used. For example, authoritative figures seek the participation of subordinates in joint decision making. In the less successful attempts, the approach is much closer to either unilateral or delegated authority rather than shared authority.[27]

In summary, OD should be seen as a very useful strategy for changing organizations, provided that change is systematic and many organizational units and members are involved. Continued research on OD may reveal new and more precise means for effectively changing organizations.

REVIEW AND PREVIEW

Organizations are constantly forced to change as a result of various pressures. Modifications in the organization are necessary because of (1) social change which alters the nature of the organization's work force, (2) environmental changes, (3) personnel turnover, and (4) technological change.

The development of managers is a critical part of being able to adapt to change as it occurs. Management development can be viewed as a subsystem within the context of the total organization. Common problems in management development can be avoided through planning, analysis, and evaluation of development efforts. The choice of a management development program should consider the managerial skills required to meet specific organizational needs.

Managers *must* be concerned with change because it ultimately requires people to work differently than before. For this and other reasons, people may react strongly and negatively to change. Resistance to change can be reduced through good planning efforts and through Organization Development where appropriate.

Organization Development is a body of knowledge, values, and humanistic goals which is currently very popular. It approaches the question of effectiveness in organizations from a systematic and applied perspective. A review of Organization Development efforts reveals that successful and unsuccessful change efforts have different patterns. Successful change patterns are more consistent and follow a systematic course.

This chapter has focused on preparing organizations for the future through management development and Organization Development. Another important series of personnel activities is appraising and paying the managers and employees who work in the organization. These issues are covered in the next section, Chapters 12, 13, and 14.

Review Questions

1. Discuss the following statement: "Management development that is not viewed within an organizational context is likely to fail."
2. What three problems do you believe are the most critical in management development efforts?
3. You are the head of a governmental agency. What two factors would affect your choice of a management development program?
4. Why is it important for managers to be aware of forces that cause organizations to change?
5. Why does resistance to change occur and how would you attempt to manage it?
6. Suppose you are a management consultant called in to assist in an Organization Development effort. What approaches would you use? What actions do you see as leading to success or to failure of your efforts?

OPENING CASE FOLLOW-UP

A real problem exists in this actual situation, but not quite the one defined by Ezra's manager. The problem is threefold in that the company is: (1) allowing the "developed" people to get away from the firm (as a result of 2 and 3 below), (2) having a rather unplanned approach to management development, and (3) failing to provide jobs into which the "developed" employees can move.

More attention should be given to the adequate utilization of those developing human resources. Better planning would have deferred the costs involved with the ten-month setback due to Ezra's departure, and also the personnel orientation and redevelopment costs needed to replace Ezra.

A specific plan of action should involve a coordination of management and the personnel administration department to ascertain the true value of potentially "promotable" people. Once this plan is developed, the personnel inventory can be completed and a corresponding program of utilization can be developed and implemented.

Case: Eastern Savings and Loan

Eastern Savings and Loan is an extremely successful operation that is only three-years old. From an initial start with eight employees the company now employs 23. Because this is a small organization, the one vice-president is in charge of all daily operations, including personnel management activities.

The bookkeeping operation started as an hour-a-day job. With the growth of ES&L, it expanded to a three-hour-a-day job, and is now a full-time job and then some. Eastern Savings and Loan first purchased a used Comptamatic posting machine which was outdated but adequate for beginning operations and was relatively inexpensive. After one year of using that machine the present equipment was purchased for $40,000. The estimated life of the new machine, which is faster than the old one, was ten years, but the growth of ES&L has been much more rapid than expected and this new machine is now outdated.

Mrs. Lee Wilson ran the bookkeeping operations from the beginning of the organizations existence until ten months ago. At that time the job became so demanding that she could not take the pressure and resigned. If everything goes smoothly, the job can be completed in eight full hours a day, five days a week. However, the organization has been continually troubled with machine breakdowns that throw the operation behind.

ES&L was able to hire another woman, Mrs. Cadwell, who had many years experience in a bookkeeping operation very similar to the one at ES&L. By working long hours she has managed to catch up so that bookkeeping operations can be handled on a day-to-day basis. However, business has continued to expand and more and more pressure is beginning to mount on Mrs. Cadwell. It is becoming increasingly more difficult for her to keep up with the work and she has mentioned this to the vice-president. He promised to discuss it with the board of directors.

During the board of directors' meeting the problem was presented, and one director suggested leasing an additional machine. The cost would be $75,000 per year, plus the salary of another operator. Another director suggested changing to a completely different system, but it was pointed out that the present machine had six years of usefulness still left. Another director suggested that an additional bookkeeper be hired who would be willing to run the operation at night. Mrs. Caldwell has warned that if management does not do something soon, she will quit. Since ES&L does not want to lose her, the directors feel that a solution must be found before the next meeting.

QUESTIONS

1. What change forces accentuate the problems with which ES&L must cope?
2. What would be the advantage of using planned change efforts in ES&L?
3. What actions would you recommend? Why?

Notes

1. The model and the discussion of it is adapted from Thomas J. Von Der-Embse, "*Choosing a Management Development Program: A Decision Made,*" *Personnel Journal, 52* (October 1973), pp. 907–912.

2. *Ibid.,* p. 912.

3. R. F. Burnaska, "The Effects of Behavior Modeling Training Upon Manager's Behavior and Employee's Perceptions," *Personnel Psychology, 29* (1976), p. 329.

4. "Imitating Models: A New Management Tool," *Business Week,* May 8, 1978, pp. 119–120.

5. J. Steven Heiner, Dorothy McGlauchlin, Constance Legeros, and Jean Freeman, "Developing the Woman Manager," *Personnel Journal, 54* (May 1975). Reprinted with permission of *Personnel Journal,* copyright May 1975.

6. *Ibid.*

7. E. B. Bolton and L. W. Humphreys, "A Training Model for Women—An Androgynous Model," *Personnel Journal, 56* (May 1977), p. 234.

8. J. F. Veiga, "Female Career Myopia," *Human Resources Management* (Winter 1976), p. 25.

9. Robert F. Pearse, *Manager to Manager: What Managers Think of Management Development* (New York: Amacom Division, American Management Association, 1974).

10. *Management Training and Development Programs,* PPF 116 (Washington, D.C.: The Bureau of National Affairs), March, 1977, p. 1.

11. Pearse, *Manager to Manager,* p. 20.

12. W. G. Bennis, *Management of Change and Conflict* (Baltimore: Penguin Books, 1972), p. 7.

13. "Jobs, Salary, Credit, Legal Status, All Focus of Woman's Year," *Commerce Today,* March 3, 1975, p. 9.

14. Ralph E. Winter, "Rough Going: More Office Workers Battle Being Fired by Suing Their Bosses," *Wall Street Journal.* Wednesday, June 18, 1975, p. 1.

15. J. H. Foegen, "If it Means Moving, Forget It," *Personnel Journal* 56 (August 1977), p. 414.

16. E. J. Bardi and J. L. Simonetti, "The Game of Management Chess—Policies and Perils of Management Transfers," *Personnel Journal* 56 (April 1977), p. 197.

17. *Ibid.*

18. Foegen, "If it Means Moving, Forget It," p. 414.

19. E. F. Huse, *Organization Development and Change* (St. Paul: West Publishing Co., 1975), pp. 296–297.

20. "Use of Flexitime," *Wall Street Journal.* April 1, 1978, p. 1.

21. "What Time Shall I Go to Work Today?" *Business Horizons,* October 1974, pp. 19–26.

22. Goodwin Watson, "Resistance to Change," in W. G. Bennis, K. D. Benne, and R. Chin, *The Planning of Change* (New York: Holt, Rhinehart and Winston, 1969), pp. 488–498.

23. This definition is taken from Newton Margulies and Anthony P. Raia, *Conceptual Foundations of Organizational Development,* (New York: McGraw–Hill Book Co., 1978), p. 24.

24. Newton Margulies and A. P. Raia, *Organization Development: Values, Process and Technology* (New York: McGraw–Hill Book Co., 1972), p. 3.

25. Frank Friedlander and L. D. Brown, "Organizational Development," *Annual Review of Psychology*, 1974, p. 314.

26. Larry E. Griener, "Patterns of Organizational Change," *Harvard Business Review*, 45:3 (May–June 1967), pp. 119–130.

27. *Ibid.*, p. 54.

Appraising and Compensating Human Resources

section

5

Once an employee has been trained to perform a job, a manager must review the employee's performance. This review is a vital part of the ongoing development of an employee. For a person to develop, that individual must receive feedback on what he or she is doing well and what areas need improvement.

The process of examining employee performance is called *performance appraisal.* Appraisals are also useful in solving some personnel problems, but the practice creates still other problems. Chapter 12 covers behavioral reactions to appraisals, common mistakes made in appraising performance, and some components of a successful appraisal process.

One major reason for appraising an employee's performance is to reward those who do more work with more *compensation.* To provide themselves with the necessities of life, most people "sell" their services to organizations for money, or pay. Pay usually means more to people than just legal tender. It can be a reward or a status symbol. But, it is still compensation for effort. People want to be compensated fairly and are concerned about equity—fair treatment in pay.

Equitable pay can be determined in a number of ways. Effective organizations use well-designed personnel systems, such as job evaluation, to see that employees are paid fairly. Systems to evaluate the worth of jobs are discussed in Chapter 13, which also includes a discussion of the legal constraints on compensation practices.

People are not only paid in money. Incentives and extra benefits are also forms of compensation. Different kinds of incentives can be designed to achieve a variety of results. Some incentive systems and guides to designing incentive systems are discussed in Chapter 14.

Now that benefits average about 35 percent of the payroll dollar, both employees and managers are concerned that benefit programs be well designed and that benefits be distributed equitably. Chapter 14 also provides details on this important area of personnel management.

chapter 12

Appraisal of
Human Resources

When you have read this chapter, you should be able to:

1. Identify the three major uses of appraisals.

2. Explain the impact of legal concerns on appraisals.

3. Discuss the behavioral aspects of appraisal from the perspective of appraisers and appraisees.

4. Identify the four basic approaches to appraisal and discuss the advantages and disadvantages of each approach.

5. Explain at least six superior rating methods.

6. Discuss the use of Management by Objectives as an appraisal approach and some of the pitfalls asssociated with it.

7. Identify three suggestions useful for improving a post-appraisal interview.

8. Explain the key considerations in developing an effective appraisal system.

Unequal-Equal Supervisors

Hubert Johnson is a department head. He has been with the company for 30 years and knows his way around quite well. He has two employees, Harriett Green and Bill White. Harriett has been with the company for 15 years and Bill has been with the company for 6 years. Harriett has always been cooperative, loyal, dependable, but not an especially good supervisor. Recently Hubert has noticed that Harriett has begun to "slip" in the performance of some of her duties. Bill, on the other hand, is a very ambitious, energetic, and dependable supervisor who grasps problems quickly and easily. Hubert has to complete performance appraisals on both individuals annually.

Ten months ago he did his appraising with a great deal of displeasure because he hated to face the unpleasantness of a negative performance appraisal review. As a result, he rated both of the employees about the same. When a discussion about the ratings was conducted, both supervisors appeared to be satisfied with the rating they had recieved.

Six months ago business began to fall off and a reduction in force was put into effect. This week, after a number of other people were laid off or demoted, it became necessary to move either Harriett Green or Bill White from the position of a supervisor to that of a worker until sales pick up. Hubert wants to keep Bill on the supervisory job, but on the basis of the appraisals there is no difference between the two. In the past when two employees have had the same ratings, the person with the most seniority receives priority. Hubert must decide today what to do.

After an employee has been selected for a job, has been trained to do it, and has worked on it for a period of time, the performance of that employee must be reviewed. The personnel unit and the appraising manager should obtain a meaningful and useful appraisal of employee performance to benefit the manager, the employee, and the organization.

The determination of how well employees do their jobs has been labeled variously as: employee rating, merit rating, employee evaluation, performance review, performance evaluation, and results appraisal, among others. This book will use the term *performance appraisal.*

PERFORMANCE APPRAISAL consists of activities related to the determination of how well employees do their jobs.

NATURE AND USES OF APPRAISAL

Appraisal focuses on assessing the usefulness of the human resources of an organization. Specifically, it attempts to measure how well employees are performing their duties and meeting their job responsibilities.

Informal vs. Systematic Appraisal

The assessment of performance may occur in two general ways, *informally* or *systematically*. The informal appraisal is conducted whenever the supervisor or personnel manager deems it necessary. All organizations use informal means to some extent, whether or not a formalized, systematic process is established. The day-to-day working relationship of a manager and an employee provides ample opportunity for the employee's performance to be judged. This judgment is communicated through conversation on the job, over coffee, or by on-the-spot examination of a particular piece of work.

A systematic appraisal system is built when the contact between manager and employee is formalized and a system is established to report supervisory impressions and observations of employee performance. When a formalized or systematic appraisal exists, the interface between the personnel unit and the appraising manager becomes important. A personnel unit can be of great assistance to a manager in seeing that appraisal is done effectively.

Appraisal interface.   The appraisal process is one that can be quite beneficial to the organization and individuals involved if done properly. It can also be the source of a great deal of discontent if not done equitably and well. In situations in which an employer must deal with a very strong union, performance appraisals may be conducted only on salaried, nonunion employees. The emphasis on seniority over merit is the major cause of this union resistance to appraisals.

FIGURE 12-1   Appraisal interface.

Personnel Unit	Managers
Designs and maintains formal system	Actually rate performance of employees
Establishes formal report system	Make formal reports
Makes sure reports are in on time	Review appraisals with employees
Trains raters	

Figure 12-1 shows that the personnel unit typically designs a more formalized appraisal system. The manager handles the actual appraising of the employee, using the systemized procedures developed by the personnel unit. As the formal system is being developed, the manager usually provides input on how the final system will work. Only rarely does a personnel specialist actually rate a manager's employees.

Timing of appraisals.   An important characteristic of a sound appraisal system is appraising employee performance on a regular basis. Typically formal appraisals are conducted every six months or annually. One study of 216 firms found that appraisals were most often conducted once a year (52 percent). The semiannual performance appraisals were used by 24 percent of the firms.[1]

This regular time interval feature of formal appraisals distinguishes them from informal appraisals. Both employees and managers are aware that performance will be reviewed on a regular basis and necessary adjustments planned. With informal appraisal procedures, performance may not be rated often enough to be beneficial, or perhaps not be rated at all. However, a formal appraisal should be conducted whenever a manager or supervisor feels it is necessary or will be useful.

Uses of Appraisal

The information provided by performance appraisal is useful in three major areas: *compensation, placement,* and *training and development.* Figure 12-2 illustrates this aspect pictorially.

Compensation.   The first and most common use of appraisals is to make adjustment in an individual's compensation package. Managers throughout the organization need performance appraisals so that individuals performing at or above expected levels can be identified and rewarded. This approach to compensation is at the heart of the traditional concept of paying on the basis of *merit* rather than seniority. *Merit* means an employee receives what is deserved on the basis of his or her past performance.

FIGURE 12-2   Uses of Performance Appraisal

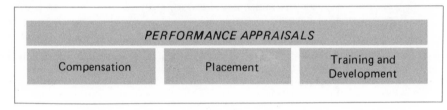

PERFORMANCE APPRAISALS		
Compensation	Placement	Training and Development

Placement.   Appraisal information also is used as input into placement decisions. When merit is used as a basis for reward and identification of potential, an individual receiving a positive appraisal rating may deserve a favorable job change or promotion. By the same token, an individual who is appraised unfavorably may be subject to discharge, demotion, or another such job movement.

Training and development.   Performance appraisal information also has a training use. The essence of this issue is captured in the statement: "Clear, current information about the strengths and weaknesses of organization members is needed if the organization is to develop appropriate and timely training programs."[2] If a manager never really considers the weaknesses or potentials of subordinates, it will be difficult to determine needed remedial training or training needed to expand the abilities of employees with high potential for advancement. Performance appraisal can be a vehicle to inform employees about their progress and to tell them what skills they need to develop to become eligible for a compensation adjustment, a promotion, or both.

There are many different performance appraisal systems designed to meet the above three uses. It is not unrealistic to say that as many performance appraisal systems and techniques exist as there are organizations with performance appraisal programs. Each organization and its managers modify various basic techniques and methods to fit particular needs and situations.

What are the three major uses of appraisals?

Discussions of appraisal techniques often emphasize orderly gathering and recording of appraisal information. While this "record-keeping" aspect is useful and important, two underlying sets of factors must be kept in mind.

Legal limitations must be considered when designing and using a performance appraisal system. The other factors are behavioral in nature and often determine some of the basic approaches and methods of appraisal. These two critical dimensions are discussed next.

LEGAL LIMITATIONS ON APPRAISAL

A growing number of court decisions have focused on performance appraisals, particularly as they relate to Equal Employment Opportunity concerns. As mentioned in Chapter 4, guidelines issued by the Equal Employment Opportunity Commission (EEOC) and other federal enforcement agencies clearly state that performance appraisals must be job-related and nondiscriminatory.

Court Cases and Appraisals

It may seem somewhat odd to emphasize that performance appraisals must be job-related because appraisals are supposed to measure how well employees are doing their jobs. Yet, in numerous cases courts have ruled that performance appraisals in use by organizations were discriminatory and were not job-related. Three important cases are summarized below.

Brito v. Zia Company (1973).[3]   In this case, Zia Company used appraisal scores to determine which workers would be laid off: those with low performance appraisals were those laid off. However, the court found that a disproportionate number of workers in protected classes were laid off. The court stated that appraisals were "tests" and subject to validation against the job duties the workers performed. Also, the court stated that appraisals were "not administered and scored under controlled and standardized conditions."[4]

Albemarle Paper v. Moody (1975).[5]   In this case, as mentioned in Chapter 4, the U.S. Supreme Court again held that performance appraisals are "tests" that are subject to EEOC guidelines. There were two important issues in this case related to performance appraisal: *subjective supervisory ratings* and the *absence of job analysis.*[6]

The problem of subjective supervisory ratings in appraisal is captured by the following quote from the court decision:

> There is no way of knowing precisely what criteria of job performance the supervisors were considering, whether each of the supervisors was considering the same criteria—or whether, indeed, any of the supervisors actually applied a focused and stable body of criteria of any kind. (p. 33)

The second part of this decision indicated that the absence of a job analysis to identify the job-specific behaviors to be appraised was a major deficiency. From earlier chapters, recall that to validate a test of any type, the test scores are compared to the person's ability to perform the duties of the job identified in a job description. Also, the job description is derived from a job analysis, the systematic investigation of the tasks, duties, and responsibilities of a job.

Basically, the court found that without clearly analyzing job duties, it was difficult to have a performance appraisal system that truly rated employees against job-performance behaviors. Using vague or general categories or rankings does not adequately tie appraisals to job duties. For example, grocery checkers should be rated on their performance of job duties, not on an overall general comparison against each other.

U.S. v. City of Chicago (1976).[7]   In this case, the courts found that the performance appraisal systems used by the Chicago Police Department discriminated against Blacks and Chicanos. Also, the officer and sergeant exams were found to be discriminatory. The court ruled that "supervisory ratings are not a fair measurement of an employee's suitability for promotion."[8] The city also was prohibited from using tests or the appraisal system and was forced to hire nonminorities according to a court-established quota system until nondiscriminatory instruments could be developed.

Legal Implications for Appraisals

The foregoing cases clearly indicate that performance appraisals must be specifically job-related and as free from subjectivity as possible. In addition to the impact of appraisals on women and minorities, the Age Discrimination Act of 1978 also forces employers to develop job-related, nonsubjective appraisals. If Inez Landon, a 63-year-old employee is to be terminated, her employer will have to show that she is no longer a satisfactory worker using a job-related appraisal system. Otherwise, Inez can charge the employer with age discrimination and might win her reinstatement and back pay. Likewise, the employer could use a sound performance appraisal system to justify retaining a 67-year-old worker to other employees.

   The impact of these legal concerns is to require performance appraisals to be tied as closely as possible to the job duties identified in a thorough job analysis. Also, the appraisal system should be designed to substitute objective performance measures instead of supervisory subjective judgments. A grocery checker should be appraised on how well the duties of a checker are performed (number of customers checked per day, amount of money shortages and overages, and so forth) instead of vague personality traits such as cooperativeness, initiative, enthusiasm, and loyalty.

What is the impact of legal concerns on appraisals?

BEHAVIORAL ASPECTS OF APPRAISAL

When appraisal is used for decisions on pay increases, promotions, discharges, and training, manager's and employees' behaviors definitely will be affected by the appraisal process. The reaction of students to grades and tests (which are both forms of performance appraisal) illustrates the emotional and behavioral implications and importance of appraisal. Students are typically very concerned with the equity of the grading process and the criteria on which they will be evaluated. Like students, employees are concerned about the fairness, consistency, and usefulness of appraisals. Some ideas crucial to an understanding of appraisal that affect both employees and managers are examined next.

Reactions of Appraising Managers and Supervisors

Managers and supervisors who must complete appraisals on their employees often resist the appraisal process. It has been stated that this typical reaction of resistance and misgiving is aroused because managers are "put in the position of playing God."[9] That is, the manager is forced to make judgmental decisions which may affect employees' careers and must communicate those judgments to the employees.

One of the major parts of a manager's role is to assist, encourage, coach, and counsel subordinates to improve their performances. However, being a judge on one hand and a coach and counselor on the other causes the manager internal conflict and confusion. It has been noted that "this conflict of roles required by most traditional appraisal systems causes the most difficulty in the appraisal process."[10]

Another reaction by some appraisers is the feeling that the time and effort involved in appraising could be used better in more direct and productive activities. Further, the fact that appraisals may be used to affect an employee's future career sometimes causes raters to alter or bias their ratings. This alteration is even more likely to occur when managers know that they will have to communicate and defend their ratings to the employees, their bosses, or personnel specialists. From the manager's viewpoint, providing negative feedback to an employee in an appraisal interview can be easily avoided by changing an employee's rating to minimize negative points. However, such actions diminish the value of the appraisal information.

Reactions such as these to what can be an unpleasant interpersonal situation are attempts, either conscious or unconscious, by the rater to avoid such unpleasantness. Eventually this avoidance helps no one. A manager owes employees a well thought-out appraisal.

Other behavioral concerns regarding appraisal are the effect of the manager's leadership style on the way appraisals are received, the lack of training most managers have in performing appraisals, and the difficulty involved in understanding all the problems associated with complex and specialized jobs some employees hold. The complications discussed above should generate an awareness of how behaviors of appraising managers are a serious concern in the appraisal process.

Reactions of the Appraised Employees

The employees who are appraised may exhibit somewhat predictable behavior when involved in the appraisal process. One of the most prominent reactions employees may demonstrate is resistance to an appraisal system, especially a newly developed or introduced system. If a new appraisal system is being implemented, employees' resistance should be anticipated and viewed as normal. By using good communication and explaining the purposes and uses of the appraisal system, normal resistance can be more easily handled.[11] Allowing a representative group of employees and managers to assist in developing an appraisal system can add to the credibility and usefulness of the appraisal information and reduce employee resistance.

Once an appraisal system is established and operational, a common reaction by employees and managers is to view appraising as a zero-sum game (there must be a winner and a loser). Employees may well see the appraisal process as a threat and feel the only way to get a high rating is for someone else to receive a low rating. This win-lose perception emerges when employees' performances are ranked or compared with one another.

Appraisals can be both zero-sum and non-zero-sum (both parties win and no one loses) in nature.[12] Emphasis on the developmental and self-improvement aspects of appraisal appears to be the most effective means to negate some of the zero-sum reactions of those involved in the appraisal process.

Another common employee reaction can be closely related to a prior example, the way students view tests. Simply because a professor prepares a test which is believed to be representative and fair, it does not necessarily follow that the students will feel the test is representative and fair. They simply see it differently. Likewise, employees being appraised will operate from somewhat different perceptual bases than the manager doing the actual appraising.

Perceptual differences are a basic fact of human psychology—different people may perceive the same event in different ways. A manager may view one set of characteristics or actions as important and representing good performance, while the appraised employees may perceive that a different set of factors is important. As discussed later in this chapter, specifically identifying the desired performance behaviors is one effective means to deal with the problem. Also, the same words have different meanings to different individuals. For example, the meanings of such words as "superior," "good," "excellent," and "satisfactory," vary among raters and among ratees.

The effects of personality traits and differences in thinking patterns compounds the perceptual confusion and distortion which occurs when employees are appraised. Traits such as "dependability," "willingness," and "initiative" are difficult to measure, define, and communicate.

These reactions of appraised employees highlight some of the behaviors resulting from appraisal. Such reactions become important considerations as appraisal systems are developed, implemented, and operated. In addition to such common reactions of appraising managers and appraised employees, other specific behavioral considerations or problems may arise. Several of the most prominent are briefly examined next.

Varying Standards Problem

When appraising employees, a manager should try to avoid using different standards and expectations for different employees performing similar jobs. For example, a student who missed 10 points on a test and received a lower grade than one who missed 20 points might become irate about the unfairness of the grading. The same reaction occurs when employees believe their boss uses different standards in appraising each individual's performance.

Even if an employee has actually been appraised on the same basis as other employees, the employee's perception is key. If Bill Spots, a student, felt a professor had graded his exam more rigorously than another student's exam, he might ask the professor for an explanation. The student's opinion or behavior might not be drastically changed by the professor's responding only that he had graded fairly. So it is with performance appraisals in a work situation. If performance appraisal information is to be valuable, employees must believe that appraising managers use the same standards and weights for every employee.

Recency Problem

The recency problem occurs in appraisal when a person's performance is rated solely on, or significantly affected by, the most recent period of time or work, instead of performance over the entire appraisal period. Just as giving a student a course grade based upon only the final examination may be incorrect, so too would giving a drill press operator a high rating because the employee made the quota only in the last two weeks of the rating period.

The recency problem is an understandably common error because of the difficulty in remembering performance two- or three-months old. Also, employees become more concerned about their performance and behavior as formal appraisal time approaches. Some employees may attempt to take advantage of the recency problem by "apple polishing" their boss shortly before an appraisal is to be completed.

One suggestion to reduce the recency problem is to have more frequent appraisals. Thus, the period of recall is compressed.[13] Another solution for a manager is to keep accurate written records and notes about an employee's performance throughout the appraisal period.

Rater Bias

Another pitfall arising in appraisal occurs when a rater's values, beliefs, or prejudices distort the ratings given. If John Harris, manager of a machine section in a tool plant, has strong dislikes for persons of certain races, this bias is likely to result in distorted appraisal information for some people. Age, religion, sex, appearance, or other arbitrary classifications may be reflected in appraisals if the appraisal process is not properly designed.

Rater bias is very difficult to overcome, especially if a manager is not aware or will not admit such bias is affecting his or her appraisals. Different methods of appraisal to be discussed later in this chapter attempt to reduce some of this bias by structuring the appraisal instrument and requiring documentation and explanations of the ratings given.

Rater Patterns

Students are well aware that some professors tend to grade more easily than other professors. Likewise, a manager may develop a similar "rating pattern." For example, Betty Wilson, office manager, tends to rate all of her employees as average or above. Even the poor performers receive an average rating from Betty. However, Jane Carr, the billing supervisor, believes that if employees are poor performers, they should be rated below average. An employee reporting to Jane who is rated average may well be a better performer than one rated average by Betty.

Another aspect of rater patterns is for appraisers to rate all employees within a narrow range (for example giving class grades which are all As and Bs), regardless of actual differences in performance by the employees. This type of error is the *central tendency error.*

Rater pattern errors are often the result of the reluctance of a superior to give a low appraisal. A study has indicated that appraisers generally find evaluating others difficult, especially if negative evaluations must be given.[14] In the same way, a professor experiences more uneasiness and reservation when having to give a student a course grade of F rather than B.

Making an appraiser aware that he or she has fallen into a pattern is one way to deal with the problem. Also, including precise and explicit definitions of categories on the rating form and allowing for considerable rating spread on each item are other means of handling rater patterns.[15]

Halo Effect

The halo effect occurs when a manager rates an employee high or low on all items because of one characteristic. For example, if a dependable worker has few absences, his supervisor might give the worker a high rating in all other areas of work, including quantity and quality of output, because of the dependability, without really thinking about other characteristics separately. Giving a female management trainee a high rating because she is attractive would also be a halo effect.

An appraisal that shows the same rating on all characteristics may be evidence of the halo effect.[16] Clearly specifying the categories to be rated, rating all employees on one characteristic at a time, and training raters are means to deal with the halo effect.

Can you discuss the impact of behavioral factors on appraisals?

FOUR BASIC APPROACHES TO APPRAISAL

Basic approaches to performance appraisal focus on who will do the actual appraising and on the managerial philosophy of an organization. This decision is based on who can best evaluate an individual's performance. The four basic approaches are as follows:

- subordinates rating their superior
- group methods
- superiors rating their subordinates
- a guided self-appraisal by the employee through the use of Management by Objectives.

The results of a survey of 216 firms showed that the immediate superior has the sole responsibility for appraisal in 78 percent of the organizations. Approximately 63 percent of the firms have a practice of having the appraisal reviewed and approved by the appraising superior's boss.[17] As is clearly revealed in these results, a superior rating subordinates is the most common method.

Subordinate Rating Approach

The concept of having superiors evaluated by subordinates is actually being used in a number of organizations today. A prime example of this type of rating is taking place in colleges and universities where students evaluate a professor's performance in the classroom. Although industry has used some subordinate rating, the main thrust has been developmental. Results are used to help superiors improve themselves or to help assess a manager's leadership potential.[18]

There are some advantages to having subordinates rate superiors. First, in situations where the superior-subordinate relationship is critical, subordinates' ratings can be quite useful in identifying competent superiors. Combat soldiers rating their leader is an example. Also, this type of rating program can help make the superior more responsive to subordinates. This advantage can quickly become a disadvantage, however, if it leads to the superior's not managing his workers, but trying only to be a "nice guy." Nice people without other qualifications may not be good managers in some situations.

Another disadvantage is the negative reaction many superiors have to being evaluated by subordinates. The fear of reprisal may be too great for employees to give realistic ratings. The principles of "proper" superior/ subordinate relations may be violated by having subordinates rate superiors. Employees may resist rating their bosses because they do not perceive it as a "proper" part of their job. And, subordinates may not be aware of the important variables in a superior's job. If this is the case, the subordinates might be rating the superior only on the way the superior treats them, and not on critical job requirements.

The problems and disadvantages associated with subordinates rating superiors seem to limit the usefulness of this appraisal approach. This approach might be somewhat useful in certain special situations such as in a university or research and development department. However, the traditional nature of most organizations seems to restrict the applicability of subordinate rating except for self-improvement purposes.

The subordinate rating of a superior is usually a group rating approach; for example, nurses may rate the head nurse and the results will be summarized before presentation to the head nurse. However, because of the special problems and characteristics of the subordinate approach, it has been treated separately from the group methods to be discussed in the following section.

Group Rating Approaches

A second basic approach to appraising consists of having a group of individuals appraise an individual's performance. The group approach has two variations. In one variation, called *multiple ratings*, persons separately rate an individual, then the separate ratings are combined. Another variation, called *committee appraisal*, involves rating of an individual by a group in a formal meeting. Group ratings can be further classified by who does the rating: *superiors* or *peers*.

Group rating by superiors. Group rating by superiors can either be by committee appraisal or multiple rating form. There are some basic advantages and disadvantages in using a group of superiors to appraise an employee's performance.

Because more people have had a chance to know and watch the individual being rated, more useful information on that person may be available. If more information is available, an organization can pinpoint better employees for promotions or future job assignments.

However, as with any personnel technique, there are some disadvantages. Having *more* information per se, does not necessarily mean *better* information. "Actual knowledge of performance is as important in such a procedure as in independent ratings, however. Without objective data to make appraisals, a committee may simply be pooling their collective ignorance."[19]

Other problems arise with committee group appraisal. It can be quite time-consuming. The choice of the committee chairman can be the crucial factor determining the efficient operation of the appraising committee, and indeed, the ultimate outcome. If the employee being rated thinks the committee members are hostile, that person will not benefit from the appraisal. Further, the committee members must realize the purpose of the appraisal session is to help an individual and that the process is genuinely valuable. If not, much is lost before the committee ever meets.[20]

The *multiple rating system* for superior's ratings is very simple. It merely requires that several superiors separately fill out rating forms on the same subordinate. The results are then tabulated to come up with an appraisal of the ratee.

Group rating of subordinates by superiors is especially appealing where the preservation of organizational status is important. A young loan officer in a bank who is responsible for loan judgments has her performance reviewed by a group of superiors comprising the bank's loan committee. This method preserves the role of judge for the superiors involved in the rating process. Unlike subordinates rating superiors, it maintains traditional authority relationships.

Group rating by peers.   The use of peer groups as raters is a special type of group performance appraisal system. The peer group technique is seldom used in committee form. If a group of salespersons met as a committee to talk about each other's ratings, future work relationships might be impaired. Also, the quality of the ratings may be diminished and the possibility of personality conflicts and alliances is increased. The peer rating approach is best used by summarizing individual ratings.

It should be noted that most of the research on peer ratings was done on military personnel at the "management or pre-management" level (officers or officer candidates). One survey of peer ratings found that: "Only two studies have been reported where investigations were made in actual industrial situations."[21]

There are several likely reasons for the scarcity of peer ratings in industry. One is that industry personnel are unfamiliar with the method. Also, members of peer groups in industry may not be as closely knit as peer groups in military training settings. Another reason is that peer ratings may be most useful at managerial levels for identifying leadership potential.

A final important reason for the absence of peer ratings in industry is the use of performance appraisal results in most nonmilitary settings. Performance appraisal results in industry are usually used as input to determine promotion or financial reward. The peer ratings "are used only for identification and counseling in military training situations, never for promotion or financial reward."[22]

In summary, the peer rating, like the group rating by superiors, appears to have some limitations. Where there is an absence of closely knit groups and of experience with this system, such ratings methods may not be appropriate. Managers considering adoption of a group appraisal system should examine and analyze their own situation before attempting either of these approaches to performance appraisal.

Superior Rating of Subordinates

The third basic approach to appraising suggests that the superior or manager is the most qualified person to evaluate a subordinate's performance realistically, objectively, and fairly. The "unity of command" notion—that every subordinate should have only one superior—remains unchanged. The methods of rating discussed below are frequently used by superiors, although they can sometimes be used in connection with previously discussed approaches.

Category rating methods. The simplest and most easily used methods are those that require a manager to indicate how an employee rates on several categories or factors. The *graphic rating scale,* the *checklist,* and *forced choice* methods are common category methods.

The *graphic rating scale* is the most commonly used method. An individual is evaluated upon various pertinent aspects of work performance and behavior. Figure 12-3 shows a typical graphic rating scale form used by managers rating office personnel. The rater checks the appropriate box for each of the factors listed. More detail can be added to the graphic scale by including phrases that describe each level of performance or each trait or factor. Also, a continuum or line with numerical values can replace the boxes, with the continuum ranging from 0–5. Another modification of the graphic rating scale is to provide space for comments following each factor rated.

There are some obvious drawbacks to the graphic rating scale. Often separate traits or factors are grouped together and the rater is given only one box to check. The rating form shown in Figure 12-3 has this flaw. Another drawback is that the descriptive words used may have different meanings to different raters. Factors or categories such as initiative and

FIGURE 12-3 Sample graphic rating form, performance review (nonexempt salaried employees).

SECTION I		Identification Data		
Last Name—First Name—Middle Initial		Employee No.	Department:	Job Title

Date of Last Review:	Covers Period: From		To	

Report Based On Work Reviewed: Reason for Review

Daily	Ninety Day Probation Period
Several Times a Week	Annual Review
Weekly	Special Review

SECTION II   Supervisor's Evaluation Of Employee

A. Cooperation   Consider: Ability and willingness to work in harmony for and with others. Does he get along with the other men? Is he pleasant to work with?

☐ Unknown

Unsatisfactory	Fair	Satisfactory	Satisfactory Plus	Excellent	Outstanding
☐	☐	☐	☐	☐	☐

B. Job Knowledge   Consider: Technical know-how, experience. Does he know what to do? Does he know the required steps to get a job done?

☐ Unknown

Unsatisfactory	Fair	Satisfactory	Satisfactory Plus	Excellent	Outstanding
☐	☐	☐	☐	☐	☐

C. Job Accomplishment   Consider: A careful worker. A thorough worker. Works quickly. Checks his work. System of work displays good jugement. Does he finish assigned work satisfactorily?

☐ Unknown

Unsatisfactory	Fair	Satisfactory	Satisfactory Plus	Excellent	Outstanding
☐	☐	☐	☐	☐	☐

D. Initiative   Consider: Ability to accomplish job with available resources. Ability to work without frequent supervision. Does he go out of his way to do a better job?

☐ Unknown

Unsatisfactory	Fair	Satisfactory	Satisfactory Plus	Excellent	Outstanding
☐	☐	☐	☐	☐	☐

E. Supervision   Consider: Ability to plan and organize work in advance. Assumes responsibility. Uses delegated authority properly. Develops teamwork.

☐ Not Applicable
☐ Unknown

Unsatisfactory	Fair	Satisfactory	Satisfactory Plus	Excellent	Outstanding
☐	☐	☐	☐	☐	☐

F. Overall Rating   Consider: Each of the above rating factors.

☐ Unknown

Unsatisfactory	Fair	Satisfactory	Satisfactory Plus	Excellent	Outstanding
☐	☐	☐	☐	☐	☐

SECTION III   Comments of Supervisor

_____

Signature of Supervisor   Date

Section IV   Comments of Reviewing Official

☐ I agree ☐ do not agree with above evaluation and have indicated my acceptance by initialling the appropriate box, and/or by presenting the following comments:

_____

Signature of Reviewing Official   Date

Used with permission.

cooperation are subject to many interpretations, especially when used in conjunction with words such as *outstanding, average,* or *poor.*

The *checklist* is a simple rating method in which the manager is given a list of statements or words and asked to check statements representing the characteristics and performance of each employee. The checklist can be modified so that varying weights can be assigned to the statements or words. The weighted checklist can then be quantified. Usually the weights are not known by the rating supervisor, but by someone else, such as a member of the personnel unit.

The difficulties with the checklist are: (1) as with the graphic rating scale, the words or statements may have different meanings and connotations to different raters; (2) the rater cannot readily discern the rating results if a weighted checklist is used; and (3) the rater does not assign the weights to each factor. These three difficulties limit the use of the information by a rater when discussing the rating with the employee. Thus, effective developmental counseling may be difficult.

The *forced choice* method is a more complex version of the checklist. The rater is required to check two of four statements: one that the employee is "most like" and one that the employee is "least like." The items are usually a mixture of positive and negative statements. The intent is to eliminate or greatly reduce the rater's personal bias.

The difficulty of constructing and validating the statements is the major limitation of the forced choice method, especially for a relatively small organization. This method is also more difficult to explain in an appraisal interview than some other methods.

Comparative methods. Another group of methods requires that managers compare the performances of all their employees. Thus, a key punch operator's performance would be appraised with and against other key punch operators by the computing supervisor.

The *ranking* method is relatively simple. The rater simply lists all of one's subordinates from highest to lowest on each factor and/or in one total listing. With ten employees, they are ranked 1 through 10—best to poorest.

The primary drawback to the ranking method is that differences between individuals are not adequately revealed. For example, there may be little difference in performance between individuals ranked second and third, but a big difference in performance between those ranked third and fourth. This can be overcome to some extent by assigning points to show the size of the gaps existing between employees.

Ranking also means that someone must be *last.* It is possible that the last ranked individual in one group would be a better employee than a higher-ranked employee in a different group under a different supervisor. This same reasoning could apply to the highest-rated individual in a group as well. Further, the basis for ranking could include rater bias or varying standards.

The rater using the *paired comparison* method formally compares each employee with every other employee in the rating group on a one-to-one basis. This can be a detailed and more complex ranking method. The number of comparisons can be calculated using the formula $N(N - 1)/2$, where N is the number of people rated. For example, a manager with 15 subordinates would have to make 105 different comparisons on each rating factor. Use of the paired comparison method provides more information about individual employees than the straight ranking method. Obviously, the large number of comparisons that must be made is the major drawback of this method.

The *forced distribution* method compares subordinates and overcomes the drawback of many comparisons involved in the paired comparison method. Using the forced distribution method, a head nurse ranges subordinate nursing personnel along a scale, placing a certain percentage of employees at various performance levels. This method assumes the widely known "bell-shaped curve," or normal distribution of performances exists in a given group.

A drawback to forced distribution is that a supervisor may resist placing any individual in the lowest (or in the highest) group. Difficulties can arise when the rater must explain to the ratee why he or she was placed in one grouping and others were placed in higher groupings. Further, with small groups there may be no reason to assume that a normal distribution of performance really exists.

Written methods.   Another group of methods requires a manager or a personnel specialist to provide written appraisal information. Documentation and description form the essence of the *critical incident*, the *essay*, and the *field review* methods.

The *critical incident* method is somewhat different in character from the previous methods because it is more a recording of employee actions than an actual rating. The manager using this system keeps a written record of the highly favorable and highly unfavorable actions illustrating an employee's performance. When something happens (a critical incident involving the employee), the manager writes it down. A list of critical incidents is kept during the entire rating period for each employee. Because the critical incident method does not necessarily have to be a rating system, it can be used in conjunction with other methods as documentation of the reasons why an employee was rated a certain way.

There are several drawbacks to using the critical incident method. First, the determination of what is a critical incident is not always uniformly understood and applied by all supervisors. Next, the requirement that a manager daily or weekly make notations about each employee's performance is a time-consuming task. Further, the critical incident method can result in employees becoming overly concerned about what the superior writes about them. Employees may begin to fear the manager's "black book." Finally, the critical incident method may result in overly close supervision because managers must be present to note "critical incidents."

The *essay* or *free-form* appraisal method requires the manager to write a short essay describing each employee's performance during the rating period. The rater is usually given a few general headings under which to categorize comments. The intent of this method is to avoid restricting the rater as other methods may do. The report in the superior's own words can convey the information which is felt necessary.

Several drawbacks of the essay method exist. First, some supervisors communicate in writing better than others. The quality of the ratings depends to a certain extent upon the writing ability of the rater. Also, the method is very time-consuming and difficult to quantify or express numerically for comparative purposes.[23]

A final method is the *field review*. This method is a modification of a superior rating a subordinate and involves the personnel unit becoming an active partner in the rating process. In a field review a member of the personnel unit interviews the manager about each employee's performance. The personnel representative then compiles the notes of each interview into a rating for each employee. The rating is then reviewed by the supervisor for needed changes. This method assumes that the representative of the personnel unit knows enough about the job setting to guide supervisors into giving more accurate and thorough appraisals.

The major limitation of the field review method is that the personnel representative has a large amount of control over the rating. While this control may be desirable from one viewpoint, supervisors may see this method as an infringement upon their managerial authority, and some managers may significantly "interpret" the information given the personnel specialist. In addition, the field review method can be very time-consuming, particularly if a supervisor has a large number of employees to be rated.

Behaviorally Anchored Rating Scales. A relatively new method is the Behaviorally Anchored Rating Scale (BARS). A BARS system is designed to overcome the problems of category methods by identifying specific examples of performance levels. These performance levels are anchored against specific job behavior an employee would typically exhibit. Figure 12-4 shows a BARS for claims interviewers and claims deputies in a state employment agency.

The heart of a BARS appraisal system is a series of behavior descriptions that describe a range of performance behaviors. Notice in Figure 12-4 that what constitutes various levels of performance is clearly defined. Clearly spelling out performance criteria and measures significantly helps to overcome problems of subjectivity and variation in meanings common in systems using vague traits such as "initiative" or "cooperation." For example, it is clearer to say that "Attendance is satisfactory when there are no more than three absences in a six-month

FIGURE 12-4   Behaviorally anchored rating scale on one performance dimension

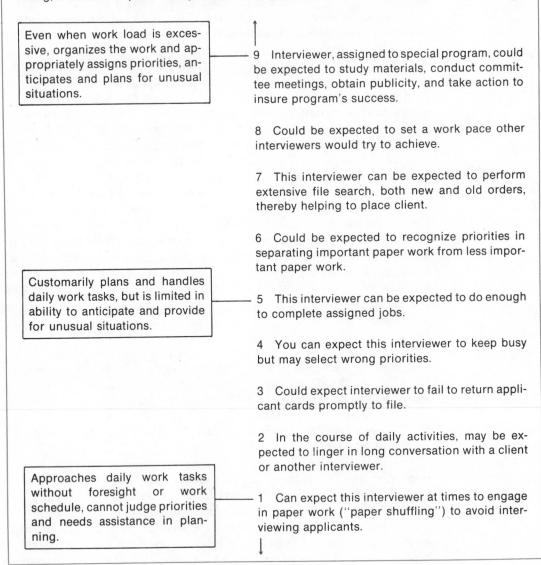

EFFECTIVE USES OF RESOURCES—plans effective use of own time and equipment.

Interviewers and Claims Deputies must plan their work far enough ahead, and in sufficient detail that important aspects are not overlooked. Some plan their work effectively, and seem to think ahead about what needs to be done. They can coordinate a great variety of tasks, such as interviews, evaluations, referrals, solicitations, and eligibility determinations. Others seem to need help in getting organized and in structuring their work efficiently. When making this rating, evaluate the person only on the basis of their planning effective work organization.

> Even when work load is excessive, organizes the work and appropriately assigns priorities, anticipates and plans for unusual situations.

9   Interviewer, assigned to special program, could be expected to study materials, conduct committee meetings, obtain publicity, and take action to insure program's success.

8   Could be expected to set a work pace other interviewers would try to achieve.

7   This interviewer can be expected to perform extensive file search, both new and old orders, thereby helping to place client.

6   Could be expected to recognize priorities in separating important paper work from less important paper work.

> Customarily plans and handles daily work tasks, but is limited in ability to anticipate and provide for unusual situations.

5   This interviewer can be expected to do enough to complete assigned jobs.

4   You can expect this interviewer to keep busy but may select wrong priorities.

3   Could expect interviewer to fail to return applicant cards promptly to file.

2   In the course of daily activities, may be expected to linger in long conversation with a client or another interviewer.

> Approaches daily work tasks without foresight or work schedule, cannot judge priorities and needs assistance in planning.

1   Can expect this interviewer at times to engage in paper work ("paper shuffling") to avoid interviewing applicants.

Used with permission.

period," than to give attendance as a category and provide boxes labeled from poor to excellent for a rater to check.

The major thrust of BARS is to tie appraisals directly to job behaviors that are consistently defined. This thrust is designed to respond to the important legal issues of job-relatedness and less subjective supervisory ratings.

While BARS appear to be a promising alternative to other methods, several problems exist with their development and usage. Performance-based appraisals require more time and effort to develop and maintain. It is likely, too, that performance-based appraisal systems may require several appraisal forms to accommodate different types of jobs in an organization. In a hospital, nurses, dieticians, and admission clerks all have different jobs. This variety should be considered in the appraisal process. Possibly having one format for clerical employees, another for sales personnel, and a third for managerial personnel would be sufficient for a department store.

BARS represent an emerging area of research and application. However, there are enough problems and unanswered questions remaining to indicate that BARS may not represent the ultimate objective, job-related appraisal system.[24]

What are six methods of appraisal that can be used by supervisors to rate subordinates?

Management by Objectives Approach

A system of guided self-appraisal called *Management by Objectives* (MBO) is a fourth basic approach to appraisal. MBO is most often used to appraise managers' performance. Disenchantment with the previously discussed approaches has increased MBO's popularity. Other names for MBO include *appraisal by results, targeting-coaching, work planning and review program, performance objectives*, and *mutual goal setting*.

MBO specifies the results and performance goals an individual hopes to attain within an appropriate length of time. The objectives each manager sets are derived from and consistent with the overall goals and objectives of the organization. Workable MBO should not be a disguised means for a superior to dictate the objectives individual managers or employees set for themselves.

Key ideas of MBO. Three key ideas underlie an MBO appraisal system. First, if an employee is really involved in planning and setting the objectives, a higher level of commitment and performance may result. Instead of having the standards and ratings set by some other person, in MBO the employee plays the key role in setting the standards and determining the

FIGURE 12-5   Sample objectives for MBO

"Submit completed regional sales report no later than the third of every month."
"Obtain orders from at least five new customers per month."
"To maintain payroll costs at 10% of sales volume."
"Have scrap loss less than 5%."
"Fill all organizational vacancies within 30 days after openings occur."

---

measurement scheme. Employee participation in determining the goals is believed to lead to greater acceptance of the goals.

Second, if what an employee is to accomplish is clearly and precisely defined, the employee will do a better job of achieving the desired results. Ambiguity and confusion may arise when superiors determine the objectives for an individual and may result in less effective performance. By having the employee set objectives, he or she gains an accurate understanding of what is expected.

A third key part of MBO is that performance objectives should be measurable, precise, and define results. Figure 12-5 contains some sample objectives. Vague generalities such as "initiative" or "cooperation" objectives common in many superior-based appraisals should be avoided. MBO objectives are specific actions to be taken or work to be accomplished.

MBO process. Implementing the guided self-appraisal system using MBO is a four-stage process. These phases are common, regardless of the title of a guided self-appraisal system. The four stages are shown in Figure 12-6 and discussed next.

FIGURE 12-6   MBO process.

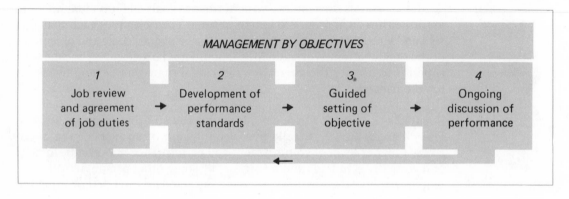

MANAGEMENT BY OBJECTIVES			
1	*2*	*3*	*4*
Job review and agreement of job duties	Development of performance standards	Guided setting of objective	Ongoing discussion of performance

1. *Job Review and Agreement.* The employee and the superior review the job description and key activities comprising the employee's job. The focus of this phase is for the employee and the superior to agree mutually on the exact components and functions of the employee's job. Included in this phase is the determination of the most important activities the employee performs.

2. *Development of Performance Standards.* Specific standards of performance must be mutually developed. This phase specifies a satisfactory level of performance. The standard is specific and definite and is established for each of the main activities agreed upon in the first step. For example, a salesperson's quota to sell five cars per month may be an appropriate performance standard. Selling that number of cars can be measured and constitutes a satisfactory level of performance. Standards should be clearly established for each managerial or employee position and should be revised as economic conditions or other variables change.

3. *Guided Objective Setting.* Objectives are established by the employee in conjunction with, and guided by, the superior. The important factor in this phase is that the employee plays the major role in setting the targets, instead of having them set by the superior as with other methods. "An objective has been defined as a desired state or accomplishment, a specified and desired result to be accomplished within a given period of time."[25] Continuing the example of the automobile salesperson, an objective might be set to challenge the employee to improve performance; the salesperson might set a new objective of selling six cars per month. Notice that the objective set may be different from the performance standard. Objectives should be set so that attainment is realistically possible.

4. *On-going Performance Discussions.* The employee and the superior use the objectives as bases for continuing discussions about the employee's performance. While a formal review session may be scheduled, the employee and the manager do not necessarily wait until the appointed time for performance discussions. Objectives are mutually modified and progress is discussed during the period.

Work planning and review (WPR). One of the earliest and most complete implementations of the guided self-appraisal—Work Planning and Review (WPR)—was developed at the General Electric Company. Because of dissatisfaction with the traditional performance appraisal, the WPR process was designed so that

(1) There are more frequent discussions of performance;

(2) there are no summary judgments or ratings made;

(3) salary action discussions are held separately;

(4) the emphasis is on mutual goal planning and problem solving.[26]

Figure 12-7 contains the descriptive steps of the WPR process and shows how an employee is guided through self-appraisal and goal setting.

FIGURE 12-7   Steps involved in WPR.

1. Review the objectives, business plans, and thrust of the company and/or part of the company in which you work. Your manager will discuss this with you and indicate areas where it is anticipated you can make a contribution. Carefully note these recommendations.

2. Review your job description or position guide. (If it is out of date or full of generalities you may wish to prepare one which will provide a solid base for discussion with your manager). Check those things you are responsible for against the business plan and note work you must do. Keep an eye open for those responsibilities you have which *should* be covered in the business plan, but are not.

3. Briefly think about your personal development during the past few months. Have you acquired knowledge, skill, or awareness of technical developments which could be applied in your work? Identify some new target you might strive for.

4. Now that you have the BIG PICTURE, sit back and dream a little. What would you really like to do? What would you need to do to dramatically increase the impact your work is presently having? What bothers you that really ought to be changed?

5. Now get back to earth and think about what is really possible. Add up your current and continuing work load, backlog of work not yet started, future commitments, and time you must reserve to meet unscheduled demands. Documenting this will then tell you how much time you have left to spend on improvements, development, and new things for which you want to use Work Planning. If, as is often the case, you find you have no time left for new things, then your job is driving you, instead of the other way around. In this case, one of your first Work Planning goals should be to create some time for *new* improvement efforts.

6. Write down two or three goals—based on the thinking you have just done—which you would like to accomplish in the next several months. To help make sure these are clearly stated, determine how you will measure accomplishment. In other words, how will you know if, how well, and when the goals have been reached?

7. Make sure these goals are both worth doing and do-able. To be sure they are worthwhile, note how they will contribute to meeting business objectives and plans. To be sure they can be done, sketch out a schedule of tasks, events, and resources necessary for their accomplishment.

You have now answered three questions: *Why is this result important? What will I produce? How will I get it done?*

(Source: Stanley C. Duffendack, *Effective Management Through Work Planning: Employee Handbook*, 2nd ed. (Schenectady, N.Y.: The Magua Co., 1971). Used with permission.)

Critique of MBO.   The basic appeal of MBO has resulted in several benefits being attributed to it. First, by removing the one-sided nature of the appraisal process and involving the employee more, increased performance, motivation, and commitment are said to result. Thus, MBO may bring about greater coordination and cooperation between superior and subordinate. Resistance to the appraisal process is replaced by an emphasis on mutual discussions about performance and goal accomplishment. MBO may open up organizations and increase the flexibility and viability they must have as society changes rapidly. Also, better planning and decision making occurs because the process includes setting realistic, attainable, and specific standards and goals. Naturally, other benefits are ascribed to MBO, but the above should indicate the nature of the advantages MBO holds for some organizations.

No management tool is perfect, and MBO has been criticized. One of the most important cautions is that MBO is not appropriate for all employees or all organizations. Jobs with little or no flexibility, such as assembly-line work, are not compatible with MBO. An assembly-line worker usually has so little job flexibility that the performance standards and objectives are already determined. The MBO process seems to be most useful with managerial personnel and employees who have a fairly wide range of flexibility and self-control in their jobs.

Another criticism of MBO is that the process of setting objectives assumes that an individual's objectives are reasonably compatible with the overall objectives of the organization. However, some managers and workers have non-job-related goals not included as a part of the MBO process.[27] A salesperson's desire to spend time with the family, a stockbroker's desire to pursue fishing, and a nurse's goal of working only with certain types of patients would not be an appropriate part of the objective setting process.

Additionally, MBO may be seen as a disguised means for managerial manipulation since it requires a climate which supports openness and a mutual orientation. When imposed upon a rigid and autocratic management system, MBO may fail. Extreme emphasis on penalties for not meeting objectives defeats the developmental and participative nature of MBO.

What is MBO and what are some criticisms of it?

In summary, MBO has some real merit and value where conditions are appropriate. However, care should be exercised so that the individuals, their jobs, and the organization are compatible with the aims and intents of the MBO process.

Can you now identify and explain the four basic approaches to appraisal?

POST-APPRAISAL INTERVIEW

Once an appraisal has been completed, it is important that the employee receive feedback. Regardless of the type of appraisal method used or who did the appraising, the results should be discussed with employees so that they have a clear understanding of how they stand in the eyes of the immediate superior and the organization. Emphasis should be placed in the post-appraisal interview on counseling and development and not solely on telling the employee, "Here is how you rate and why." Focusing on development provides a positive opportunity for manager-subordinate interaction on something important to both—the employee's performance and its improvement.

However, the appraisal interview presents both an opportunity and a difficult situation. It is an emotional experience for the manager and the employee. The manager must communicate both praise and constructive criticism. Negative information is more difficult for many managers to convey. A major concern is how to emphasize the positive aspects of the employee's performance while still discussing ways to make needed improvements. The manager also cares about how the employee will respond to the appraisal ratings and the effect the ratings and the appraisal interview will have on future performance. If the interview is handled poorly, the manager should realize that resentment and conflict may result and will likely be reflected in future work.

Employees commonly approach an appraisal interview with some concern. They are likely to perceive that performance discussions are very personal and important to their continued job success. At the same time they want to know how the manager feels they have been doing. Criticisms of performance may be taken as direct personal indictments of the individual and not just a discussion about performance. Thus, Ralph Jefferson, a bank teller, may see constructive criticisms as a commentary on his inadequacies as a person, and not a commentary on weaknesses in his performance as a bank teller.

It is fairly common for organizations to *require* that managers discuss appraisals with employees. One survey of 150 organizations found that approximately 97 percent of the surveyed firms required an appraisal interview.[28] Research and experience have revealed several tips for effective appraisal interviews. Some of the most common are listed below.

Prepare for the Interview

Managers should prepare for the appraisal interview by reviewing documents and records relating to the employee's performance. Being able to be specific and adequately justify the ratings may overcome the employee's feelings about the subjectivity and lack of factual basis for the appraisal. The manager should mentally or actually rehearse the phrasing of the difficult discussion areas. In addition to preparing for the appraisal interview, the manager should give the employee some notice an appraisal interview is planned. It seems unfair to allow the manager time to prepare without also giving the employee time to review his or her own performance.

One possibility is to give the employee a blank appraisal form for self-rating. Then, comparisons can be made, focusing on the areas of positive rating, the areas where differences occur, and the areas where improvement is needed. One reason for the spread of MBO is its focus on providing documentation of which both parties are aware.

Involve the Employee

The appraisal interview should be a mutual discussion about the performance of the employee. Research and literature review confirm the importance of subordinate participation in the appraisal interview.[29] The appraisal should not be a lecture by the manager in which the employee only answers "yes" or "no."

Focus on Performance Development

Emphasis in the appraisal interview should be placed on the development of the employee. The manager should highlight positive aspects, as well as review those areas in which improvement is needed. The appraisal interview should not be solely a criticism session. The employee should be encouraged to continue acceptable performance, as well as to overcome deficiencies. The manager should also discuss with the employee actions management can take to help the employee to perform better. For example, if a custodian is not doing the job well because needed cleaning supplies are frequently not available, the housekeeping manager should attempt to clear up the purchasing and delivery problems over which the custodian has no control.

It is generally accepted that appraisal feedback and placement or salary discussions should not be mixed. Definite discussions about raises or promotions should be excluded as much as possible from the appraisal interview. Of course, the appraisal information plays a part in making salary and placement decisions, but these decisions should be made at a separate time and not be scheduled as a part of the appraisal interview.

Mutually Determine Future Specific Employee Targets

For the interview to be developmental, the employee and the manager together should decide upon specific steps and actions the employee should take to achieve better performance. This developmental focus should indicate how the employee can get needed skills and knowledge.

For example, a secretary may be encouraged to take a refresher course in shorthand. Or, a manager may decide, together with the immediate supervisor, that the company should pay for additional education at a local university or a company-sponsored technical seminar.

Performance goals can be set and agreed upon so that the employee knows what actions lead to improved appraisal ratings. Mutually setting goals does not necessarily mean the superior has followed the entire MBO process but that specifically agreed upon targets may serve as motivational and developmental means.

Incorporating the above four ideas into the appraisal interview increases the probability that it will be effective. However, the appraisal interview will be effective only if coupled with an effective overall appraisal system. Some guidelines for effective appraisal systems follow.

How do you improve the post-appraisal interview?

ESTABLISHING AN EFFECTIVE APPRAISAL PROGRAM

The dimensions of appraisal have been examined in some detail. However, combining the various components—who is to appraise, the criteria and method to be used, and the usage of the results—into an effective appraisal program demands that managers and the personnel unit work together and in a coordinated manner. Some general guidelines for establishing and maintaining an effective appraisal system are offered below.

Support of Top Management

Regardless of the type of approach used, support and participation of upper management is vital. Unless top management also uses an appraisal system and supports the system used at lower levels, those below may resent top management's implication that: "Appraisal and performance discussions are not for us, but only for those beneath us."

Often top management plays a key role in determining the overall organization climate in which others work. Unless the appraisal system is compatible with the tone set by upper management, appraisal will be less effective. For example, if Harold Franklin, President of Franklin Manufacturing, is an autocratic and paternalistic type of executive, the appraisal system should not require much openness and mutual discussion since Mr. Franklin's style is likely to be in conflict with that type of environment. While it might be better if Mr. Franklin had a different management style, the appraisal system must be compatible with the existing organizational procedures, policies, and realities. If top management does not believe in and openly support the existing appraisal system, a consistent program should be initiated.

Involvement of Managers and Employees in Appraisal Design

In addition to top management support, those who will make the appraisals and those who will be evaluated can be involved in setting up or revising the appraisal system. While a personnel specialist may be able to design a good system, the insights of those who actually use the appraisal system are valuable. Managers and employees may see flaws or have interpretations affecting the usefulness of the appraisal information. Managers can be consulted on the method used, the criteria, and the procedures for maintaining appraisal information for personnel decision-making purposes.

Use of Performance-Based Criteria and Measures

One of the most important changes needed in many existing appraisal programs is to have performance-based criteria. The more unclear or widespread an employee's responsibilities, the more difficult it is to make a performance appraisal system meet the legal expectations discussed earlier in this chapter. The BARS approach represents an attempt to improve the job-relatedness of appraisals.

Choice of Appropriate Rater and Method

The choice of who should do the appraising (superior, a group, or subordinates) should be based on who can best provide accurate information and is in the best position to appraise performance. Rather than deciding that ratings should always be done by the supervisor, selecting the rater should be contingent upon the type of organization, the jobs performed, and other related factors. It may be appropriate to have appraisal inputs from several sources. For example, students commonly have input on their professors' appraisals, but department heads and deans have inputs as well.

The choice of a method should be one that is suitable and realistic and should consider the organization, as well as the individuals and their jobs. Time considerations, the education levels of raters and ratees, and the advantages and disadvantages of the various methods should also be considered.

Training of Appraisers

Because appraisal is important and sometimes difficult, training of appraisers is valuable. Providing managers and supervisors with some insights and ideas on rating, documenting appraisals, and making appraisal interviews increases the value and acceptance of an appraisal program.

As Figure 12-8 illustrates, the results of a survey of 216 organizations revealed that many supervisors have had little appraisal training. Training appraisers gives them confidence in their abilities to make appraisals and handle post-appraisal interviews.[30]

Communication of Appraisal Program and Its Intent to Employees

Strong effort should be made to provide employees with information on the appraisal program, and how the results will be used. If the employees are represented by a union, it is important to consult local union leaders before introducing or changing an appraisal system. Springing an appraisal system on employees is likely to cause resistance. Because employees may be uneasy and concerned during the appraisal process, providing information early allows the managers and supervisors to sell the appraisal system. Employees should be told how the appraisals will be used. The appraiser should emphasize development, noting that a key

FIGURE 12-8   Appraiser training

Type of Training	Small Organizations	Large Organizations	All
	Percent	Percent	Percent
None	54.1	55.6	54.8
Initial	24.1	16.6	20.3
Refresher	21.8	27.8	24.9
Total	100.0	100.0	100.0

(Source: Alan H. Locher and Kenneth S. Teel, "Performance Appraisal—A Survey of Current Practices," *Personnel Journal*, 56 (May 1977), pp. 245–247+. Reprinted with permission *Personnel Journal*, copyright May 1977.)

intent of the program is to give the employees feedback on how they have done and on how they can continue improving.

Revision of Appraisal Program

An appraisal system should be viewed as a dynamic program which changes and reflects the current organization and the jobs in it. Joe Kampfer, a purchasing agent may be buying a broader range of raw materials than he was last year. This change should be reflected in updated performance-based criteria. Too often appraisal programs lose their usefulness because they are never updated after they are established. A comment by a personnel director reflects this problem, "We have made no changes in our appraisal system because it was a good program when we set it up four years ago." An effective appraisal program must be monitored and adapted to changes in the organization.

What ideas should guide managers in having effective appraisal systems?

REVIEW AND PREVIEW

Appraising employee performance is vital in any organization. It not only allows managers to improve the level of performance in the organization, but it provides a basis for employees to improve themselves and their chances for career advancement.

Appraisal can take many forms; some are better suited to certain situations than others. The approaches can be classified into four categories based upon who is doing the appraising: subordinates, groups, superiors, or the employee. Within each of these areas, several techniques are available. These include category-rating methods such as graphic rating scales and checklists; comparative methods such as ranking, paired comparison, and forced choice; written methods such as critical incidents, essay, and field review; Behaviorally Anchored Rating Scales (BARS); and guided self-appraisal (MBO).

Simply appraising an employee's performance and then not communicating it is a serious mistake. Appraisal interviews are commonly used to discuss performance with the employee. Just having an appraisal system is no guarantee that it will be effective.

One of the important uses made of appraisal information is in determining an employee's compensation. However, there are several other considerations that affect the compensation an employee receives. Also, there are several different types of compensation. The next two chapters focus on compensating human resources.

REVIEW QUESTIONS

1. What are three major uses that can be made of appraisals?
2. Discuss the following statement: "Most performance appraisal systems in use today would not pass legal scrutiny."
3. Suppose you are a supervisor. What behavioral problems would you be concerned about in appraising your employees?
4. What are the four basic approaches to appraisal? Which approach would you prefer as an employee? As a manager? Why?
5. Identify six superior rating methods.
6. What is MBO? Identify some problems with MBO.
7. Construct a plan for a post-appraisal interview with an employee who has performed poorly.
8. Your boss asks you to develop an appraisal system. How would you proceed.

OPENING CASE FOLLOW-UP

Hubert is facing a very common problem. Having to distinguish between dependable, loyal service over a long period of time, and a higher quality of service from another individual over a shorter period of time is difficult. He has further complicated the unpleasant task by failing to face up to the differences in performance between the two earlier and communicating his feelings to them.

Demoting the more senior employee might be perceived by the rest of the people in the department, as well as by the individual involved, as a company slap at long-service, loyal employees. On the other hand, to demote an individual who was clearly a superior performer emphasizes longevity at the expense of performance. In addition, Hubert needs Bill on the job.

This case demonstrates the extreme need for doing performance appraisal properly. Performance appraisal can be used as the basis for making this decision, but it must be done right if it is to be both defensible and accepted by the parties involved. A poor job of performance appraisal has compounded this already difficult situation.

Case: Congratulations, and Welcome Back?

Janet Johnson joined the Customer Information section of a large manufacturing company as a secretary in December 1978. Janet's transfer to Customer Information came after a previous transfer from the Market Analysis section to the Sales Department in an attempt to improve her performance.

On November 1, 1979, Janet was given a performance appraisal. The appraisal followed counseling sessions on July 3, 1979, July 30, 1979, and September 15, 1979, as well as numerous sessions between January 1979, and July 1979. The November appraisal indicated that Janet appeared to be making improvements in her job performance; however, her performance again deteriorated, as noted by her performance appraisal in January 1980.

Her supervisor felt that Janet's poor performance was related to her personal affairs, which led to a number of activities felt to be incompatible with the efficient and effective operation of the office. The supervisor noted such activities as the following: spends an inordinate amount of time making personal telephone calls; relates her personal problems to other employees in the office; appears preoccupied with her personal problems; and frequently reports to work in a very tired state.

The supervisor felt that Janet possessed positive attributes. She had the education and skills that matched well with her secretarial duties. She worked quickly when the task was clearly stenographic. The supervisor also observed that Janet's poor performance may have been a result of her pregnancy.

It was clear to the supervisor that Janet's problems at work were related to her personal affairs, and she did not have the ability to adapt rapidly to "uncertain environments" in which resourcefulness and initiative are required. On March 4, 1980, Janet left the company on a maternity leave of absence. The supervisor has just received word that Janet gave birth to a 7 pound, 6 ounce baby boy, and wants to return to work in six weeks.

QUESTIONS

1. What problems existed in this case?
2. Were additional courses of action open to the supervisor in order for Janet to improve her performance?
3. In what ways does the fact that the employee is female and pregnant affect the appraisal and the supervisor's choice of action?
4. As the supervisor, what would you do?

Notes

1. Alan H. Locher and Kenneth S. Teel, "Performance Appraisal—A Survey of Current Practices," *Personnel Journal*, 56 (May 1977), pp. 245–247+.

2. Edgar F. Huse, "Performance Appraisal—A New Look," *Personnel Administration*, March–April 1967, pp. 3–5ff.

3. *Brito* v. *Zia Company*, 478 F2d. 1200 (1973).

4. Robert I. Lazer, "The Discrimination Danger in Performance Appraisal," *The Conference Board Record* (March 1976), p. 62.

5. *Albermarle Paper Co.* v. *Moody*, 74–389 (1975).

6. Lazer, "Performance Appraisal," p. 61.

7. *U.S.* v. *City of Chicago.*

8. Keith J. Edwards, "Performance Appraisal and the Law: Legal Requirements and Practical Guidelines," paper presented at the American Psychological Association, Division 14 meeting; Washington, D.C.: September 1976, p. 6.

9. Douglas McGregor, "An Uneasy Look at Performance Appraisal," *Harvard Business Review*, May-June 1957, pp. 89–94.

10. Robert J. Hayden, "Performance Appraisal: A Better Way," *Personnel Journal*, 52 (July 1973), p. 609.

11. M. H. Phillips, "Merit Rating for Skilled and Semi-skilled Workers," *Personnel Management*, 44 (1962), pp. 120–128.

12. Paul H. Thompson, and Gene W. Dalton, "Performance Appraisal: Managers Beware," *Harvard Business Review* (January–February 1970), p. 152.

13. John B. Miner, "Management Appraisal: A Capsule Review and Current References," *Business Horizons* (May 1968), pp. 83–96.

14. Thomas H. Stone, "An Examination of Six Prevalent Assumptions Concerning Performance Appraisal," *Public Personnel Management*, 2 (November–December 1973), pp. 408–414.

15. Ronald J. Burke and Linda J. Kemball, "Performance Appraisal: Some Issues in the Process," *The Canadian Personnel* (November 1971), pp. 25–34.

16. L. L. Cummings and Donald P. Schwab, *Performance in Organizations: Determinants and Appraisal* (Glenview, Ill.: Scott, Foresman and Company, 1973), p. 79.

17. Locher and Teal, "Performance Appraisal," p. 247.

18. Cummings and Schwab, *Performance in Organizations*, p. 107.

19. Wendell French, *The Personnel Management Process*, 4th ed. (Boston: Houghton Mifflin Co., 1978), p. 311.

20. Virgil K. Rowland, "The Mechanics of Group Appraisal," *Personnel*, May–June, 1958, pp. 36–43.

21. Eugene C. Mayfield, "Management Selection: Buddy Nominations Revisited," *Personnel Psychology* 23 (1970), pp. 377–391.

22. Walter Poehler Hutchins, "Peer Ratings as a Predictor of Success in Pilot Training" (unpublished Master's thesis, University of Colorado, 1962), pp. 17–18.

23. Marion W. Richardson, "The Free-Written Rating," in Thomas L. Whisler and Shirley F. Harper, eds., *Performance Appraisal: Research and Practice* (New York: Holt, Rinehart and Winston, 1962), pp. 220–221.

24. For a review of BARS literature, see Donald Schwab, Herbert Heneman III,

and T. A. DeCotiis, "Behaviorally Anchored Rating Scales: A Review of the Literature," *Personnel Psychology*, 28 (1975), pp. 549–562.

A critique of BARS is contained in Robert S. Atkin and Edward J. Conlon, "Behaviorally Anchored Rating Scales: Some Theoretical Issues," *The Academy of Management Review*, 3 (January, 1978), pp. 119–128.

25. Anthony P. Raia, *Managing by Objectives* (Glenview, Ill: Scott, Foresman and Co., 1974), p. 56.

26. Herbert H. Meyer, Emanuel Kay, and John R. P. French, Jr., "Split Roles in Performance Appraisal," *Harvard Business Review*, January–February 1965, p. 127.

27. Harry Levinson, "Management by Whose Objectives?", *Harvard Business Review*, July–August 1970, pp. 125–134.

28. *Employee Performance: Evaluation and Control*, PPF #108, February 1975, p. 6 (Washington, D.C.: The Bureau of National Affairs).

29. Ronald J. Burke and Douglas S. Wilcox, "Characteristics of Effective Employee Performance Review and Development Interviews," *Personnel Psychology*, 22 (1969), pp. 291–309.

30. Burke and Kemball, "Performance Appraisal," p. 29.

chapter 13

Compensating Jobs and Work

When you have read this chapter, you should be able to:

1. Identify the three meanings of compensation for employees.

2. Discuss the importance of equity in compensation.

3. List the key provisions of four basic laws dealing with compensation.

4. Contrast and compare the three bases of compensation.

5. Define job evaluation and its purpose.

6. Explain briefly four methods of job evaluation.

7. Identify the stages involved in developing a pay system.

The Campus Store

The Campus Store is located across the street from a large midwestern university. It is one of 15 stores in a chain of stores located in major university towns across the country. There are two managers of the store at State University—a manager and an assistant manager. Also, there are 18 full-time female employees, and four part-time college boys who work as stock clerks. All employees, with the exception of the two managers, are paid hourly.

The home office of the Campus Store is located 800 miles away. This office handles most of the bookkeeping and payroll paperwork for all the stores in the company. Employee time cards are sent to the home office and all payroll checks are prepared there. Because the company is nationwide, the stores are all subject to the federal wage and hour laws.

The home office has a company policy that the payroll figures for each store must not exceed 10 percent of the gross sales of that store. Because the Campus Store is only two-years old, its payroll has been running about 11 percent. The home office usually allows each new store a two-year grace period before it demands the 10 percent figure be met. The Campus Store must meet the 10 percent figure during the current year.

It is now February 1. The federal wage law required the company to raise the minimum wage 10 cents per hour on January 1. When the new wage law took effect, the wages of all employees who made above the minimum originally were raised to achieve the same relative level. The increased wage level resulted in the monthly payroll figure for the Capus Store to jump to 12.3 percent of gross sales. This jump caused great consternation within the management structure of both the store and the home office, which urged the store managers to either refrain from hiring additional employees until the sales could rise enough to get the store down to the 10 percent level or to cut the number of employees.

In addition, the home office has a company policy of paying the minimum wage for six months, and then giving a raise if warranted. But, this raise is not automatic. Also, it is company policy that no hourly employee may receive more than one raise every six months. Because of the policy of paying minimum wage for the first six months, the store has an extremely high turnover rate within the first year of an employee's service to the store.

You are the store manager who must deal with the problems caused by the company's compensation policies and the minimum-wage increase. Frankly, you feel that if you cut the number of employees necessary to get down to the 10 percent ratio between payroll to sales, you will not be able to serve the customers who patronize the store, and the drop in service will result in more shoplifting and lower sales.

TYPES OF COMPENSATION

People work to gain rewards for their efforts. This exchange of labor for financial reward is the heart of the compensation process.

Formal compensation can be offered using three types of rewards, as Figure 13–1 illustrates.

FIGURE 13–1   Formal compensation components.

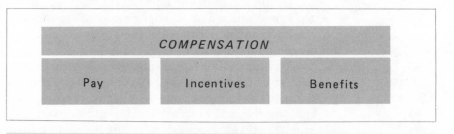

PAY is the basic compensation employees receive, usually a wage or salary.

INCENTIVES are rewards designed to encourage and reimburse employees for effort beyond normal performance expectations.

BENEFITS are rewards available to employees or a group of employees as a part of organizational membership.

Compensation forms such as bonuses, commissions, and profit-sharing plans are designed to give employees an incentive to produce results. Health insurance, vacation pay, or retirement pensions are examples of benefits. This chapter deals with issues in the overall compensation process and the basic pay personnel receive. Because incentives and benefits are special types of compensation, they are discussed in a separate chapter, Chapter 14.

Compensation Interface

Compensation costs are significant expenditures in most firms. As the opening case illustrates, compensation policies and practices also may be one of the biggest headaches for managers and personnel specialists.

Figure 13–2 illustrates a typical compensation interface. Personnel specialists usually guide the overall development and administration of an organization's compensation system by conducting job evaluations and wage surveys. Also, because of the technical complexity involved, personnel specialists are typically the ones to develop incentive and benefit systems. On the other hand, managers try to match employees' efforts with rewards, using the job evaluation and wage survey information as guidelines when recommending pay rates and pay increases. Much managerial activity goes into monitoring employee attendance and productivity. Because time and/or productivity are the bases for compensation, this monitoring is a vital part of any manager's job.

Successful compensation depends on the meaning of the rewards to the employees of an organization. As mentioned in Chapter 3, an employee's motivation is closely related to compensation, whether that reward is pay, benefits, or internal satisfaction. The behavioral dimensions of compensation cannot be separated from the process, nor can they be ignored by managers. When people work they expect to receive fair value (that is, *equity*) for their labors. This perception of fair value, briefly described in Chapter 3, has a significant impact on the satisfaction and performance of employees.

BEHAVIORAL ASPECTS OF COMPENSATION

The basic compensation or pay employees receive is often the prime reason for working. With the pay received, the necessities and luxuries of life in a modern society are bought. However, pay usually has several other meanings to employees.

FIGURE 13–2   Compensation interface.

Personnel Unit	Managers
Develops and administers compensation system	Attempt to match performance and rewards
Conducts job evaluation and wage survey	Recommend pay rates and pay increases
Develops incentive and benefit systems	Monitor attendance and productivity for pay and incentive compensation

Meaning of Compensation to Employees

There are three basic areas in which compensation and base pay have meaning: *economic, psychosocial,* and *growth and motivation.* Each is discussed next.

Economic.   The *economic* meaning of basic pay is the most obvious because pay serves as a way of obtaining the necessities and luxuries people need and want. Relatively few people have an independent source of income through inheritance, accumulation, or illegal action (such as bank robbery). Some disadvantaged individuals who are unable to work, or a few individuals who choose not to work, receive money from government agencies. For most people, employment in organizations is the way to obtain economic resources which can be exchanged for such items as food, house payments, a car, clothes, furniture, vacations, and countless other goods and services.

Psychosocial.   A second meaning of compensation is *psychosocial* in nature. Pay and other types of compensation provide means for "keeping score" and psychological satisfaction of achievement. If Ed Schwinn receives a raise, he may see his change in compensation as recognition for his efforts and he may derive a sense of achievement from his work. This internal satisfaction may mean more to him than what he can buy with the additional money. Conversely, the absence of adequate compensation may cause Ed to become discouraged or dissatisfied. One author suggests that research on pay indicates that the satisfaction of psychological and social needs such as status, achievement, esteem, and recognition are affected by the pay a person receives.[1]

Status is the relative social ranking of a person to others. That compensation acts as a status symbol is well-known. As confirmed by research, people compare their base pay to determine how they "rank" in the social structure. As a measure of status, compensation gives highly rewarded individuals high social standing and importance. This relative "ranking" can significantly affect individuals' satisfaction, and possibly even their performance.[2]

Ranking can occur within work groups. A division manager might compare her pay to that of other employees in the division and with other division managers. She may be satisfied with her pay when comparing it to other division managers. Or, she may feel that based on pay, there are higher status and lower status division managers.

Growth and motivation.   Compensation is also a means to *growth and motivation.* From the viewpoint of the organization, people are compensated for performance. It is to be hoped that compensation can be used as one measure of how well employees have grown in their performance and capabilities. It can also serve as a means for motivating higher performance. Increased compensation can serve as a goal for which people will strive if they see that greater effort brings the increased pay, and if they want the increased pay.[3] However, the amount of money that serves to motivate one employee to produce more may not motivate another employee.

What are the three meanings of compensation?

The various meanings that compensation can have for employees and managers alike are quite complex and have been subject to continuing research. The multifaceted nature of financial rewards is summarized well by the following statement from a research study:

> Money does appear to have a good deal of symbolic value, and it does mean different things to groups of people having differing biographies or backgrounds or training or experience.[4]

Equity Issue

The notion of "A fair day's work for a fair day's pay" is voiced often by employers, employees, and unions. The equity issue deals with fairness, or the lack of it. The individual's view of fair value is critical to the relationship between performance and job satisfaction.

EQUITY is defined as the perceived fairness of what the person does (inputs) compared with what the person receives (outputs).

Inputs are what a person brings to the organization and include educational level, age, experience, productivity, and other skills or efforts. The items received by a person, or the *outputs,* are the rewards obtained in exchange for the inputs. Outputs include pay, benefits, recognition, achievement, prestige, and any other rewards received. Note that the output can be either actual and tangible (that is, the economic meaning) or intangible (that is, internal to the person).

Equity and inequity. Equity is an exchange and comparison process.[5] Patricia George, a laboratory technician in a hospital, is an example. She exchanges her talents and efforts for the tangible and intangible rewards the hospital gives her. She then compares her inputs—what she did—to her outputs—what she received—to determine the equity of her compensation.

The comparison process also includes the individual's comparison of his or her inputs to the inputs of other individuals. Thus, Patricia George will also compare her talents, skills, and efforts to those of other laboratory technicians or other hospital employees. Her perception—correct or incorrect—significantly affects her valuation of her inputs and outputs. *Inequity* occurs when there is an imbalance between the inputs and the outputs as a result of the comparison process.

If inputs exceed outputs.   One review of equity theory research suggests that if an employee is underpaid (more inputs than outputs), the employee will tend to reduce his or her inputs.[6] If the lab technician mentioned above feels that she has received fewer rewards than her inputs, she will attempt to resolve the inequity. Her reactions can include some or all of the following: increased dissatisfaction, attempts to get compensation raised, quitting the job for a more equitable one, changing her perceptual comparison, or reducing her productivity. All of these actions are attempts to reduce the inequity.

If outputs exceed inputs.   One obvious way a person may attempt to resolve this type of inequity is by putting forth more effort. If the lab technician feels that she has received more rewards than she deserves, she might work harder in order to justify her "overpayment." Or, she might process the same number of laboratory samples, but do so more accurately and produce higher quality results. Other actions she could take could include a recomparison, whereby she might decide she evaluated her efforts inaccurately, and she really was *not* overpaid.

Regardless of the action she takes, she will make some attempt to relieve the inequity tension. Research evidence of the type of action she is most likely to take is mixed. The type of payment methods also makes a difference.[7]

Pay Secrecy

Because comparison is such a critical part of the equity issue, some academicians and practicing managers have pointed out the need to provide pay information to employees. Pay information typically kept secret includes how much others make, what raises others have received, and the pay policies of the organization. A survey of 184 organizations indicated that in only 18 percent of the companies did a manager officially know about the salaries of other managers.[8]

One reason for secret or closed pay systems is the fear that open pay systems will create discontent, petty complaining, and tension. If an accountant knows for sure that he is paid less than another accountant, he may become dissatisfied and feel he is receiving "inequitable" treatment. Also, an open pay system forces managers to explain and justify pay differences. If there are not good reasons for the differences, personnel problems can increase.

An open pay system provides the basis for discussion and accurate comparison. Research on pay secrecy has revealed that in some situations, open policies on pay are related to high motivation and performance. In other settings open policies on pay have caused low satisfaction, low motivation, and conflict between managers and their employees. The implication is that an open pay system can be used if: (1) performance can be measured, (2) individuals work fairly independently, and (3) there is a means to tie an individual's inputs and effort to the outputs and rewards.[9]

To illustrate, pay openness between certain types of sales representatives might be appropriate. Sales representatives do have objective performance measures (amount of sales, number of customers contacted, etc.), they work independently, and their pay can be tied fairly closely to sales effort. Often, sales representatives are shown each month what the level of sales (and therefore commissions) of everyone in the sales group has been.

Managers should be aware of the pay secrecy issue and avoid keeping pay secret when it would be advantageous to use an open system. By providing pay information, employees do have the information needed to make more accurate equity comparisons. An open pay system requires that managers be able to explain satisfactorily any pay differences that exist.

Can you explain the importance of equity in compensating employees?

Behavioral Summary

The importance of the above behavioral dimensions of compensation should be evident. A manager who does not consider the meaning of compensation to employees, the perceived fairness (equity) of the compensation, and the pay secrecy issue cannot develop a sound compensation system. As important as the behavioral aspects of compensation are, managers must also be aware of external constraints on compensation imposed by federal and state governments.

LEGAL CONSTRAINTS ON COMPENSATION

Several legal constraints or laws deal with personnel compensation in the United States. These laws affect employee compensation and personnel management directly because they deal with the rewards employees receive and the financial costs to employers. Laws affecting minimum-wage standards and hours of work are two important areas of governmental influence on compensation.

Fair Labor Standards Act of 1938

The major law on compensation is the Fair Labor Standards Act of 1938 (FLSA) and its amendments. This act has three major objectives: (1) establish a minimum-wage floor, (2) encourage limits on the number of weekly hours employees work through overtime provisions, (3) discourage oppressive child labor. The first two objectives are most relevant to current personnel management practices.

Minimum wage.   The FLSA set a minimum wage to be paid a broad spectrum of employees. Numerous groups were exempted from coverage under the 1938 Act. In 1966 the FLSA was amended to update the act and to include more employees and industries. Currently, most organizations and employees are covered, with the exception of executive, professional, and administrative personnel. Also, local, state, and federal government employees are not covered by the FLSA. The basic minimum wage effective January 1, 1979, is $2.90 per hour and it increases to $3.10 per hour in 1980 and $3.35 per hour in 1981.

Overtime.   The FLSA also contains overtime pay requirements. Under the 1938 version and still in effect are provisions setting overtime pay at one and a half times the regular pay rate for all hours in excess of 40 per week. Figure 13–3 shows the wage calculations for an employee who is covered by the act that worked 44 hours in a week.

The work week is defined as a consecutive period of 168 hours (24 hours × 7 days) and does not have to be a calendar week. Hospitals are allowed to use a 14-day period instead of the seven-day workweek as long as overtime is paid for hours more than 80 in a 14-day period. Overtime provisions do not apply to farm workers, who also have a lower minimum

FIGURE 13–3   Wage calculations under Fair Labor Standards Act.

Employee	Regular Pay Rate	Hours Worked/week
Judy Jones	$4.00/hr.	44 hrs.

Computations		
Regular:	$4.00/hr. × 40 hrs.	= $160.00
	($4.00/hr. × 1½) = $6.00/hr. × 4 hrs.	= 24.00
	Total gross pay	= $184.00

wage schedule. No daily number of hours requiring overtime is set, except for special provisions relating to hospitals and other specially designated organizations. Thus, if a manufacturing firm has a four day/ten hour schedule, no overtime pay is required by the act.

Equal Pay Act of 1963

As a part of amendments to the FLSA in 1963, 1968, and 1972, the Equal Pay Act is an attempt to prohibit wage discrimination on the basis of sex. As discussed in Chapter 5, the major intent is to provide fair and equitable pay for women. As the Wage and Hour Division of the U.S. Labor Department states, "Men and women performing equal work in the same establishment under similar conditions must receive the same pay if their jobs require *equal skill, equal effort,* and *equal responsibility.*"[10] Jobs must be "substantially" the same, but not necessarily identical. Pay differentials on the basis of merit or seniority are not prohibited if they are not based on sex discrimination.

The lower pay that women have traditionally received can no longer be justified on the basis of future promotability. Paying a male more because the employer believes the male has a greater possibility of staying with the organization is not allowed. In the past some felt women should be paid less because they would quit to marry, they might become pregnant, or have to move because their spouses were transferred, but such concerns, even if true, cannot be used to justify pay differences.

The costs of settling claims under this act can have a significant financial impact on an employer. For example, Corning Glass Works had to make a $1 million retroactive payment to women employees and American Telephone and Telegraph had to make a $30 million settlement payment, primarily to women employees, for violation of the Equal Pay Act and related discrimination.[11] Building on this act, most states have passed laws that prohibit sex-based pay differences.

Walsh-Healey Act of 1936

Many of the provisions of the Walsh-Healey Act of 1936 were incorporated into the FLSA passed two years later. However, the Walsh-Healey Act requires companies with *federal supply contracts* exceeding $10,000 to pay a minimum wage. This act applies only to those working directly on the contract or who substantially affect its performance. For example, if a company has a contract to supply shoes to the Army, those employees directly involved in making and supplying the shoes have to be paid a minimum wage. Executive, administrative, and maintenance employees are not covered by the act.

A difference between the Walsh-Healey Act and the FLSA is that the

FIGURE 13–4   Wage calculations under Walsh-Healey Act.

Employee	Regular Pay Rate	Hours Worked
Tom Taylor	$5.00/hr.	10/day Monday–Thursday = 40/week

Computations

Regular:	8 hrs/day × 4 days = 32 × $5.00/hr	= $160.00
Overtime:	2 hrs/day × 4 days = 8 × 7.50/hr.	= 60.00
	($5.00 × 1½)	
	Total gross pay	$220.00

former requires overtime payment for hours over 8 per day or 40 per week, but the latter requires overtime pay only for those over 40 per week and includes no clause about number of daily hours. As Figure 13–4 shows, an employee working on a federal contract with a four-day/ten-hour schedule would have to be paid overtime for two hours per day under the Walsh-Healey Act, even though the weekly hours would be kept to 40 hours.

Davis-Bacon Act of 1931

The Davis-Bacon Act of 1931 affects compensation paid by firms engaged in federal construction projects valued in excess of $2,000. It deals only with *federal construction projects* and does not contain specific minimum wage provisions. However, it does require that the *prevailing wage rate* be paid on all federal construction projects. The prevailing wage actually may be, and frequently is, the average union rate for the local area where the construction is being done. Thus, if the average rate for carpenters in a city is $7 per hour, the carpenters building a new post office in the city must be paid at least $7 per hour.

What are four laws that affect compensation?

State Laws

Modified versions of these compensation-related federal laws have been enacted by many states and municipal governmental bodies. These laws tend to cover workers included in intrastate commerce not covered by federal laws. A survey revealed that 39 states and the District of Columbia had minimum-wage laws and minimum-wage rate provisions in effect.[12]

Most states formerly had laws which limited the number of hours women could work. However, these laws have generally been held to be discriminatory in a variety of court cases. Consequently, most states have dropped such laws.

COMPENSATION BASES

Several forms of compensation are available for managers and employees to use in developing an overall remuneration program for the organization. Minimization of cost and matching effort and reward to achieve equity are important in choosing a method of compensation.

The basic means of payment are usually chosen by the managers when an organization is formed or a job is created. Of course, the presence of a union is also likely to influence the types of compensation methods used. Each payment method has some advantages and disadvantages.

Managers should choose the method which best fits a particular type of situation. Tailoring compensation may well mean that there could be different kinds for people in different positions in the organization. Because a method of payment can directly affect the equity perceptions of employees, managers should carefully choose a method consistent with both the tasks performed and the individuals performing them. Picking an incorrect or inappropriate method can affect the productivity and turnover rate of personnel. There are three bases for compensation: *time, productivity,* and a *combination of time and productivity.*

Time

Employees may be paid for the amount of time they are on the job. There are three pay classes in many organizations, identified according to the way pay is distributed and the nature of jobs. The classifications are

- *salaried exempt,*
- *salaried nonexempt,*
- *hourly.*

The most common means of payment based on time is *hourly* and employees paid hourly are said to receive *wages.* To compute this type of pay, the number of hours an individual works is multiplied by the wage rate to determine gross pay.

WAGES are pay directly calculated on the amount of time worked.

Salary is another means of paying people for time worked.

> SALARY is compensation that is consistent from period to period and is not directly related to the amount of hours worked by the individual.

Under the provisions of the FLSA each salaried position must be identified as *salaried exempt* or *salaried nonexempt*. Employees in positions classified as salaried nonexempt are covered by the overtime provisions of the FLSA, and therefore must be paid overtime. Typical salaried nonexempt positions would include secretarial, clerical, or manufacturing positions. Figure 13–5 illustrates calculation of overtime for a nonexempt employee paid a salary.

Individuals holding *salaried exempt* positions are exempt from the coverage of the FLSA overtime provisions and are not required by law to receive overtime payment. Salaried-exempt positions include professional, managerial, and outside sales employees.

Being on salary typically has carried higher status and importance for employees than being on wages. A fairly recent development is for those manufacturing and clerical personnel typically paid on an hourly basis to be paid a salary. Eaton Corporation has used an "all-salaried" approach in some of its plants with success. A common reason for this switch is to create a sense of loyalty and organizational commitment among employees who may not have that orientation. Putting blue-collar workers on salary is a drastic change from historical patterns of pay.

One reason for paying on the basis of time is the ease of record keeping. A payroll clerk can compute pay from time clock cards. Another reason for time-based payment is that it may be difficult in some positions to pay employees for what they produce rather than how long they work. Some clerical jobs may be of this nature.

FIGURE 13–5   Computing salaried nonexempt overtime pay.

Helen Gibson, a keypunch operator, received $140/week.
   $140 ÷ 40 hrs per week = $3.50/hour
Assume she works 44 hours; she is due 4 hours of overtime.
Overtime rate (1½ × $3.50) = $5.25
   Total pay = 40 hours × $3.50 = $140
                    4 hours × $5.25 =   21
Helen's gross pay for the week $161

Productivity

Another method of paying individuals is to pay according to the amount an employee produces. This means of compensation, called *piece-rate*, is one of the oldest means of tying productivity and effort together. An employee who works in an electronics plant packaging radios is paid on the basis of productivity. If the employee is paid 30 cents for each radio packaged, and is expected to package 80 radios a day, the employee receives $24.

The piece-rate system can be easily explained to workers. Total pay can be calculated readily and effort is tied directly to productivity. If some individuals want to work faster than others, they can choose their own speed. Employees who want to earn more can produce more units or work at a faster pace.

A productivity-based pay system should be developed with caution so that quality is also encouraged. For example, paying the radio packager only on the basis of quantity might lead to some radios being carelessly packed, sacrificing quality. Another possible drawback to a piece-rate system is that the piece-rate, or productivity compensation rate, must be determined for each specific job. These rates are determined through motion and time studies, described in Chapter 6. If minimum-wage requirements change or an individual's compensation must change, the productivity rate must also be changed. The piece-rate can also be applied to other types of jobs. For example, paying a door-to-door salesperson $1.50 for each magazine subscription sold is another form of piece-rate or productivity pay.

Other methods of piece-rate pay have been developed at various times. "Modified" piece-rate plans sometimes offer workers the opportunity to receive higher pay for units produced above a quota. For example, since the radio packager's standard is to package 80 radios per day, the employee might be paid 10 cents extra for each radio packaged above the standard.

Combination Methods

Employees can also be paid by combining time methods with a productivity method. The salary plus commission available to sales representatives is most familiar. Assume that a sales representative for a consumer products company manufacturing shaving cream is paid $1,000 a month plus 1 percent of the dollar value of all merchandise he sells. Combining salary with a productivity reward is designed to motivate the sales representative to sell more but recognizes that not everything done can be measured. Executive-level managers typically receive a salary plus some type of bonus plan for sales, production, or profitability. These combination systems will be examined in more detail in Chapter 14 on incentives.

What are three bases used in compensating employees?

Compensation and Task Structure

The type of task done should be matched with the type of compensation appropriate for it. Individuals paid on an hourly basis, such as production workers or clerical workers, typically have more routine and shorter job cycles. If the task is such that individual productivity can be determined, a piece-rate or some incentive type of system can be utilized. It has been suggested that "piece-rate plans can be used whenever the work is within the control of the worker and is repetitive, measurable, and the plan is acceptable to the worker."[13]

A combination plan might be useful in a situation where income can fluctuate but it is also desirable to tie productivity to effort. For example, a sales representative's income can fluctuate significantly over the course of a year. By paying a base salary each month, the sales representative is assured a continuity of income each month; but adding a commission or productivity reward encourages extra sales effort.

Overall, the important point to be made in compensation and task structure is that the task and work done by individual employees should be examined and the compensation methods used should fit the types of tasks and the work done. The method of paying individuals should be fair and should reflect the different levels of effort and skills necessary to perform jobs. A useful system for identifying differences in jobs for compensation purposes is job evaluation.

JOB EVALUATION

> JOB EVALUATION is the systematic determination of the relative worth of jobs within an organization.

The key thrust of job evaluation is to provide an equitable basis for the comparison of jobs. Systematic evaluation of jobs is an attempt to reduce favoritism and leads to a formal, coordinated pay system.

Job Evaluation Process

Job evaluation flows from the job analysis process and uses job descriptions as its base. Figure 13–6 depicts the job evaluation process.

FIGURE 13–6 Job evaluation process.

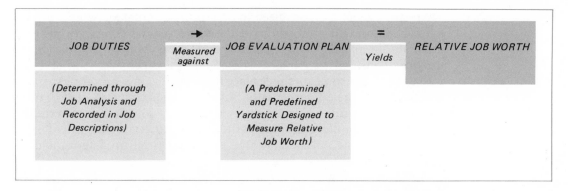

(Source: Reprinted by permission of the publisher from *Compensation* by Robert E. Sibson. ©
1974 by AMACOM, a divison of American Management Associations.)

The beginning point for evaluation is the job description. As mentioned in Chapter 6, a job description describes the job "in abstract," not
the individual performing the job. The job description of every job in an
organization is examined using a predetermined means by comparing:

1. The relative importance,
2. The relative skills needed to perform the job, and
3. The difficulty of one job versus other jobs.

Though job evaluation uses a systematic approach, managers should be
aware that job evaluation can never be totally objective. Subjective judgments cannot be avoided and must be explained to employees if the
resulting compensation system is to be useful.

Job evaluation systems should be clearly communicated so that employee misunderstandings and complaints about perceived inequity will
be reduced. Managers and personnel specialists should make sure the job
evaluation system is not overemphasized and the real meaning of what is
being done is not underemphasized. Managers should also be aware that
some individuals will always feel themselves to be treated unfairly, but
that job evaluation is an attempt to overcome as much of this perception
as possible. One study reported that union reaction to job evaluation was
found to be negative because union leaders viewed job evaluation with
distrust and as a way to limit collective bargaining over wages.[14] Managers of unionized employees must also deal with this concern, regardless
of the job evaluation method used.

Can you define job evaluation and tell its purpose?

JOB EVALUATION METHODS

There are several methods used to determine internal job worth through job evaluation. All methods have the same general objective, but each method differs in its complexity and measurement means. Some methods consider the job as a whole and others consider it as divisible into units. Also, some methods place numerical values on various aspects of jobs and others do not. Finally, some methods compare a job to other jobs directly, while other methods compare a job to a predetermined standard.[15] Regardless of the method used however, the intent is to develop a useable, measurable, and realistic system to determine compensation in an organization.

A survey of employers revealed that some methods are more popular than others. In Figure 13–7 notice that the point system is the most widely used method and ranking methods the least used. The Hay plan listed in Figure 13–7 is a type of factor comparison system.

FIGURE 13–7   Job evaluation procedures.

Evaluation Method Used	Exempt Only or all Employees (N = 84)	Nonexempt or Office only (N = 63)	Plant Only (N = 25)	All Plans (N = 172)
Pointsystem	46	56	68	53
Factor comparison	31	35	36	33
Job classification	24	22	32	24
Market pricing	15	11	0	12
Hay Associates plan	23	2	0	12
Simple ranking	17	13	4	9
Forced-choice ranking	5	8	0	5

(Source: "Personnel Policies Forum," *Job Evaluation Policies and Procedures*, PPF Survey # 113 [Washington, D.C.: Bureau of National Affairs, June 1976], p. 4.)

Although discussed as a job evaluation method, market pricing does not truly consider the relative internal worth of a job. Instead, it simply assumes that the pay set by other employers is an accurate reflection of a job's worth. One difficulty with this approach is the assumption that jobs are the same in another organization. Also, direct market pricing does not adequately consider the impact of economic conditions, employer size, and other variables. To illustrate, in one midwestern U.S. city, one of the major employers is a highly unionized company. The clerical pay is based on the pay scale in the unionized part of the company. A beginning secretary is paid $900 per month; consequently, the firm constantly has a waiting list of extremely experienced and qualified persons available. A small insurance agency manager who is hiring a secretary would have extreme difficulty justifying such an expenditure. That manager might hire someone with less experience for considerably less money. This example illustrates that using market pricing exclusively has some definite pitfalls and why more complex methods have developed.

Ranking Method

The ranking method is one of the simplest methods used. Managers and personnel specialists using the ranking method place jobs in order ranging from highest to lowest in value. The entire job is considered rather than the individual components.

Variations on straight ranking can be used. *Alternation ranking* and *paired comparison* ranking are two common variations. In alternation ranking all jobs are listed and the evaluator works from top to bottom as well as bottom to top. The evaluator identifies the highest-rated job, the lowest-rated job, and then the second-highest, the second-lowest, and so on until all jobs are listed. The job in the middle is the last one identified. The paired comparison method compares all jobs to every other job in the organization, one at a time. After summation a total list of jobs can be ranked.[16]

Advantages and disadvantages. Ranking methods are extremely subjective and managers may have difficulty explaining why one job is ranked higher than another to employees, especially since these rankings will ultimately affect the pay individuals on those jobs receive. Also, when there are a large number of jobs, the ranking method can be very awkward and unwieldy. Consider a personnel specialist in an automobile parts manufacturing concern who must rank 250 different jobs. This method would be almost impossible to use in a way that could be justified to most employees. Therefore, the job ranking method is limited in use and is more appropriate to a small organization having relatively few jobs.

Classification or Grading Method

The job classification method of job evaluation is found in the U.S. Civil Service System for its civilian employees. The GS grades are developed through a job classification or grading method.

A number of classes or grades for jobs are defined. Then the various jobs in the organization are put into the classes according to common factors found in jobs, such as degree of responsibility, abilities or skills, knowledge, duties, volume of work, and experience needed. The classes are then ranked into an overall system.

There are five basic steps to classifying jobs.[17] In the first step necessary information is taken from job descriptions and job specifications. The next step is to separate jobs into types (like sales jobs, manufacturing jobs, clerical jobs, etc.). The third step is to identify the job factors to be used to grade or classify the jobs. Several factors are often used. Fourth, descriptions of job classes are made by writing statements that indicate: "Jobs falling in this classification have the following characteristics." Finally, individual jobs are placed in the appropriate classification. Often the fourth and fifth stages are combined because it is difficult to write a grade description without also considering the job descriptions that are to be placed in that grade.

Advantages and disadvantages.   One of the major reasons that the job classification method is widely used in government and other organizations is that it is a system employees and managers can understand. Also, the classification method has some flexibility. As evidence of this flexibility to handle a wide variety of jobs, consider the U.S. Civil Service System and the large variety and number of jobs classified according to GS grades.

The major difficulty with the classification method is the subjective judgment needed to develop the grade descriptions and to accurately place jobs in them. With a large variety of jobs and generally written grade descriptions, some jobs may appear to fall into two or three different grades. Thus, some subjective judgments must be made. Another problem with the job grading or classification is that it relies heavily on job titles and duties and assumes they are similar from one organization to another. For example, a social welfare supervisor in a state governmental agency in one county might have different job responsibilities than a social welfare supervisor in a smaller county or a different governmental agency. If both are evaluated using a classification system, there may be some inappropriate grading of responsibilities involved. For these reasons some federal, state, and local governmental agencies are shifting to the use of a point system.

Point Method

The point method, the most widely used job evaluation method, breaks jobs down into various identifiable components and places weights or points on these components. The point method is more sophisticated than the ranking and classification methods because of the way each job is broken down. Because the different job components carry different weights, each is assigned a numerical value. The values of the various components are then added for each job and compared to other jobs.

Figure 13–8 shows a point chart for evaluating jobs. The individual using the chart on Figure 13–8 will take the job description and then attempt to determine how much of each element is necessary to perform the job satisfactorily. To minimize bias, this determination should be made by a group of people familiar with the job.

The manager using the chart in Figure 13–8 would take a job description and decide which degree for each element is appropriate for the job. Once all jobs have had point totals determined, they are grouped together into pay grades.

Advantages and disadvantages. The major reason the point method has grown in popularity is because it is a relatively simple system to use. It considers the components of jobs rather than just the total job, and it is a much more comprehensive system than either the ranking or classification method. Once points have been determined and a job evaluation point manual has been developed, the method can easily be used by nonspecialists. A definite advantage is that the system can be understood by managers and employees.

Another reason for the widespread usage of the point method is that it does not consider current pay for a job. It evaluates the components of a job and total points are determined before the current wage structure is considered. In this way some realistic assessment of relative worth can be determined instead of just relying on *past patterns* of worth.

One major drawback to the point method is the time needed to develop a point system. For this reason point manuals and systems developed by management consultants or other organizations are used by many employers. Another disadvantage is that even though the point system does attempt to be objective, managers must still make subjective judgments to determine what degree and how many points should be allotted for each element. Human error through misinterpretation or misjudgment is definitely a possibility. Even though the point system is not perfect, in several respects it is probably better than the two previous systems because it does consider and attempt to quantify job elements.

Factor Comparison

The factor comparison method, which is very quantitative, involves determining the *key jobs* in an organization. A key job is one generally seen by employees and managers as being a standard type of job, correctly priced, and representative of major factors in most jobs in the organization. A key job can be identified in some situations as one performed by many individuals or having special significance to the organization. For example, one key job in a retail store might be a clothing salesclerk.

To develop the factor comparison method, five factors are used to evaluate all jobs: mental requirements, skill requirements, physical re-

FIGURE 13–8   Point method charts.

| Skill | Clerical Group | | | | |
	1st Degree	2nd Degree	3rd Degree	4th Degree	5th Degree
1. Education	14	28	42	56	
2. Experience	22	44	66	88	110
3. Initiative & ingenuity	14	28	42	56	
4. Contacts with others	14	28	42	56	
Responsibility					
5. Supervision received	10	20	35	50	
6. Latitude & depth	20	40	70	100	
7. Work of others	5	10	15	20	
8. Trust imposed	10	20	35	50	70
9. Performance	7	14	21	28	35
Other					
10. Work environment	10	25	45		
11. Mental or visual demand	10	20	35		
12. Physical effort	28				

The specific degrees and points for Education, Trust Imposed, and Work Environment are as follows:

Education   Education is the basic *prerequisite* knowledge that is essential to satisfactorily perform the job. This knowledge may have been acquired through formal schooling such as grammar school, high school, college, night school, correspondence courses, company education programs, or through equivalent experience in allied fields. Analyze the minimum *requirements of the job and not the formal education of individuals performing it.*

1st Degree   Requires knowledge usually equivalent to a two-year high school education. Requires ability to read, write, and follow simple written or oral instructions, use simple arithmetic processes involving counting, adding, subtracting, dividing and multiplying whole numbers. May require basic typing ability.

2nd Degree   Requires knowledge equivalent to a four-year high school education in order to perform work requiring advanced arithmetic processes involving adding, subtracting, dividing, and multiplying of decimals and fractions; maintain or prepare routine correspondence, records, and reports. May require knowledge of advanced typing and/or basic knowledge of shorthand, bookkeeping, drafting, etc.

3rd Degree Requires knowledge equivalent to four-year high school education plus some specialized knowledge in a particular field such as advanced stenographic, secretarial or business training, elementary accounting or a general knowledge of blueprint reading or engineering practices.

4th Degree Requires knowledge equivalent to two years of college education in order to understand and perform work requiring general engineering or accounting theory. Must be able to originate and compile statistics and interpretive reports, and prepare correspondence of a difficult or technical nature.

Responsibility for Trust Imposed This factor appraises the extent to which the job requires responsibility for safeguarding confidential information and the effect of such disclosure on the Company's relations with employees, customers or competitors.

1st Degree Negligible. Little or no confidential data involved.

2nd Degree Some access to confidential information but where responsibility is limited or where the full import is not apparent.

3rd Degree Occasional access to confidential information where the full import is apparent and where disclosure may have an adverse effect on the Company's external or internal affairs.

4th Degree Regularly works with and has access to confidential data which if disclosed could seriously affect the Company's internal or external affairs or undermine its competitive position.

5th Degree Full and complete access to reports, policies, records and plans of Company-wide programs, including financial cost and engineering data. Requires the utmost discretion and integrity to safeguard the Company's interests.

Work Environment This factor appraises the physical surroundings and the degree to which noise is present at the work location. Consider the extent of distraction and commotion caused by the sounds.

1st Degree Normal office conditions. Noise limited to the usual sounds of typewriters and other equipment.

2nd Degree More than average noise due to the intermittent operation by several employees of adding machines, calculators, typewriters, or duplicating machines.

3rd Degree Considerable noise generated by constant machine operation such as is present in the Data Processing section.

(Source: *Wage and Salary Administration: A Guide to Current Policies and Practices* [Chicago: The Dartnell Corp., 1969], pp. 135–141. Used with permission. Revision published every three years.)

quirements, responsibility, and working conditions.[18] All jobs are then compared factor by factor against the key jobs. The factor comparison method is actually a combination of the ranking and point methods.

Between 10 and 20 key jobs are initially identified both for comparison and for the types of jobs in the organization. Then the individual doing the evaluation compares these positions in terms of the above factors and ranks them according to the importance of the factors in each job. Monetary values are then assigned to each one of the factors and compared with the existing monetary scales for the key jobs. Finally, evaluations of all other jobs in the organization are made by comparing them to the key jobs.[19]

Hay Plan.   A special type of factor comparison method used by a consulting firm, Hay and Associates, has received widespread application. As Figure 13–7 noted, approximately 12 percent of the firms surveyed were using the Hay Plan. However, it is interesting to note that most usage of the Hay Plan is with exempt only or with all employees. The Hay Plan uses three factors: *know-how, problem-solving,* and *accountability* and numerically measures the degree to which each of these three elements is required in each job.[20]

Advantages and disadvantages.   One of the major advantages of the factor comparison method is that it is tied very specifically to one organization. Each organization must develop its own key jobs and its own factors. For this reason buying a packaged system which may not be appropriate for an organization should be avoided. The factor comparison method does establish quantitative weights as the point method does, but it also builds in a definite comparison. It requires the evaluator to make a specific comparative identification of the weights assigned. Finally, factor comparison not only tells which jobs are worth more, but it also indicates *how much* more, so the factor values can be more easily converted to the monetary wages.

The major disadvantage of the factor comparison method is its difficulty and complexity. It is not an easy system to explain to employees and it is time-consuming to establish and develop. A factor comparison system may not be appropriate for an organization with many similar jobs. As an example, some organizations have had difficulty using the Hay Plan with nonexempt employees, primarily because many clerical jobs vary very little on accountability.

Extensive space is not being devoted in this text to factor comparison because it is an extremely complex system. Managers attempting to use the method should consult a specialist or one of the more detailed compensation books or manuals.[21]

Can you identify and briefly discuss four job evaluation methods?

DEVELOPING AND ADMINISTERING
A PAY SYSTEM

Once internal equity is determined through job evaluation, the basis for developing a total pay system is available. The development of a pay system requires consideration of an organization's pay policies and how they are to be administered. As a part of the administration process, managers should compare the pay their organizations are offering to what other employers in the community and region are paying employees for similar types of jobs through a wage survey. Once wage survey information is collected, wage curves and labor grades can be developed and jobs can be priced.

Figure 13–9 shows the relationship of job evaluation and wage surveys to a total pay system. Each of the steps in this figure will be discussed next.

Wage Survey

The purpose of a wage survey is to insure external equity in a pay system.

A WAGE SURVEY is a means of gathering data on the existing compensation rates for employees performing similar jobs in other organizations.

FIGURE 13–9   Pay system components.

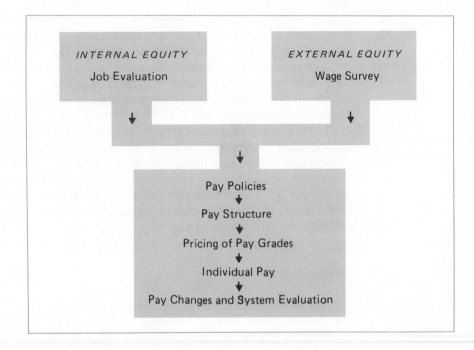

An employer may choose to use wage surveys conducted by other organizations or may decide to conduct its own survey.

Using prepared wage surveys.   Several sources for pay information are available including government surveys, trade associations, unions, and consulting services. As an example, in numerous communities employers participate in a wage survey sponsored by the Chamber of Commerce. This information is also needed by new employers interested in locating in a community. National surveys on many jobs and industries are available through the U.S. Department of Labor, Bureau of Labor Statistics, or through national trade associations. If the wage information the organization needs is not already available, the organization can undertake its own wage survey.

Developing a wage survey.   If an organization conducts its own survey, employers with comparable positions should be selected. Employers considered to be "representative of the community" should also be surveyed. If the organization conducting the survey is not unionized, the wage survey should examine unionized as well as nonunion companies. Developing wages competitive with union wages may deter employees from joining a union.

Another decision the manager must make is what positions are to be surveyed. Not all jobs in all organizations can be surveyed and not all jobs in all organizations will be the same. An accounting clerk in a city government might perform a different job than an accounting clerk in a credit billing firm. Therefore, managers should select jobs that can be easily compared and that have common job elements.

The next phase of the wage survey is for the managers to decide what compensation information on various jobs is needed. Information such as starting pay, base pay, overtime rate, vacation-holiday pay and policies, and bonus plans can all be included in a wage survey. Care should be taken that too much information is not requested. Asking for too much information may discourage survey returns because of the time respondents must take to answer.[22]

The results of the wage survey may have to be made available to those participating in the survey in order to gain their cooperation. Some surveys specify confidentiality, but in others, organizations are identified along with what they pay for various jobs. Often different job levels are included and the wages are presented both in total and by cities to reflect cost differences. Sometimes included is a list of job descriptions to generally indicate the nature of the various job titles.

Pay Policies

Organizations must develop policies or general guidelines to govern the pay system. Uniform policies are needed for coordination, consistency, and fairness in compensating employees. One of the policy decisions that must be made is *the comparative level of pay* the organization tries to maintain. Specifically, if Arrow Stores has a policy such as "paying the going-rate" or "paying above area averages for similar jobs," the policy reflects the organization's philosophy as an employer. Arrow Stores, or any other employer, should try to follow the pay level policy, and not let it become a meaningless phrase in a company handbook.

Another policy decision involves specific company or organizational policies about the relationship between pay expenditures and productivity, sales, number of customers, and so on. The opening case illustrated a policy of maintaining wage and salary expenditures at 10 percent of gross sales volume. A policy such as this and the reasons for it should be explained to employees.

Pay increase policies.   Another policy decision is how pay increases are to be distributed. Seniority or time with the company, time on a particular job, merit (performance), or some combination of time and merit should be identified. Similarly, many employers have policies that indicate the minimum time persons must be employed before they are eligible for a pay increase. If across-the-board or cost-of-living increases are to be given, this policy needs to be specified. Also, how often these or other automatic increases are given (for instance, once a year) should be identified.

One common pay raise practice is the use of a so-called "cost of living adjustment." The theory underlying this approach is that giving employees a standard percentage figure enables them to maintain the same real wages in a period of economic inflation. Unfortunately some employers give across-the-board raises and call them "merit raises." If all employees get a 7 percent pay increase as a minimum raise, the frequent reaction is to view this raise as a cost-of-living adjustment that has very little tie to "merit" and good performance. For this reason employers giving a basic percentage increase to all employees should avoid the term "merit" for it. The merit or performance part should be identified as that amount above the standard raise.

These areas represent a sample of the types of pay policy decisions that must be made. A critical factor in administering a pay system is the pay that an employee could receive elsewhere, as revealed in a wage survey. It is natural for employees to compare their pay to what they *believe* others in similar jobs in other organizations receive.

Pay Structure

Once wage survey data have been gathered, and pay policies determined, the organization's pay structure can be developed by combining that information with job evaluation data. One means for tying wage survey information to grade prices is through a *wage curve,* which is statistically determined by charting job evaluation points to current pay or wage survey rates for all jobs. If current pay of employees is used, the employer is assuming that current pay generally is realistic and fair. Usage of wage survey data puts more emphasis on external market conditions. In this way the distribution of pay can be shown and a trend line using the least squares regression method can be drawn to plot a wage trend line, which shows the relationship between job value or points and wage survey rates. An example is shown in Figure 13–10. Using all of the information above, labor grades are developed.

> LABOR GRADES are used to group individual jobs having approximately the same job worth together.

By using labor grades, an organization can develop a coordinated pay system. The intent is to avoid having to determine a separate pay rate for each position in the organization. A firm using a point method of job evaluation would group jobs having about the same number of points into one labor grade. As discussed previously, the factor comparison method uses monetary values. An organization using that method can easily establish and price the labor grades. A vital part of the classification method is developing grades, and the ranking method can be converted to labor grades by grouping several ranks together. Basic to setting up labor grades is deciding how many grades are to be established. Seven to 16 grades generally are used, with 11 grades being the average number used.[23]

Pricing of Jobs

Having established the labor grades, managers and/or personnel specialists must price them; that is, establish the monetary pay rate for each grade. A decision must be made if each job in a labor grade is to receive the same pay rate or if there is to be a range of pay. Figure 13–11 shows the labor grades determined through a typical point system and the pay for clerical employees that accompanies each grade. The same information is also presented graphically in Figure 13–10.

Individual Pay

Once rate ranges for pay grades are determined, the specific pay for individuals can be determined. Setting up a *pay range* for each labor grade provides flexibility by allowing individuals to progress in grade instead of having to be moved to a new grade each time they receive a raise. Also, a pay range allows some flexibility to reward more highly the better per-

FIGURE 13–10 Pay structure depicted graphically.

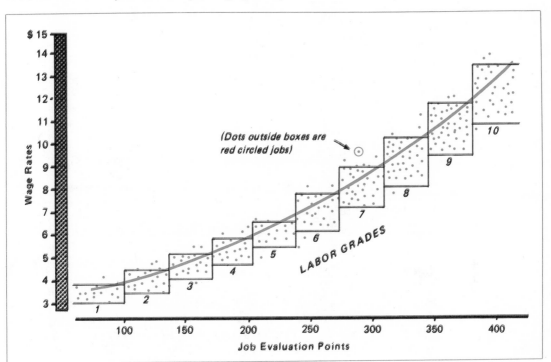

forming employees, while maintaining the integrity of the pay system. Labor grades can also have an overlap between grades, as those in Figure 13–11 do.

As previously mentioned, job evaluation determines the relative *worth* of jobs. The evaluated worth of a job may be different from the pay an individual receives for that job. If skilled people are in short supply, for example, welders, the worth of a job may be evaluated at $6 an hour, but the going rate for welders in the community may be $8 an hour. In order to fill the position, the firm must pay $8 an hour.

"Red circle" rate. A job whose pay rate is out of grade or range is identified as a *red circle rate.* A red-circled job is noted on the graph in Figure 13–10. For example, assume Paul Train's current pay is $4.80 per hour, but the labor grade price is between $5.02 and $5.20. Paul's job would be red circled and attempts would be made over a period of time to bring Paul's rate into grade.

A pay rate more than the determined pay rate is also red-circled. An attempt should be made to bring these rates into grade also. Occasionally managers may have to deviate from the priced grades to hire scarce skills or to consider competitive market shortages of particular job skills.

FIGURE 13-11   Example of priced labor grades.

Grade	Point Range	Hourly Pay Range*
1	100 and under	$3.10–3.87
2	101–135	3.57–4.46
3	136–170	4.11–5.13
4	171–205	4.73–5.91
5	206–240	5.44–6.80
6	241–275	6.26–7.82
7	276–310	7.20–9.00
8	311–345	8.28–10.35
9	346–380	9.52–11.90
10	over 380	10.95–13.69

* Note: 15 percent between grade minimums, with a 25 percent grade spread.

Changing Pay

An organization changing from an informal and uncoordinated pay system to a formalized pay structure should try to make the transition as smoothly as possible. The behavioral reactions of employees must definitely be considered. Clear communication to employees, an explanation of the new pay system, and the need for change are all important actions to be taken. Whether or not the system is new, changes in the pay system should be phased in gradually. Attempts to institute radical and immediate changes in pay are likely to cause strong employee reactions.

Care must be taken to monitor a pay system once it has been implemented. A pay system that does not change after it has been established is likely to become obsolete. Technological, social, product, or competitive conditions can all cause the need for a pay system to change. Internal changes including organizational shifts, expansion, and new products or services might necessitate changes in a pay system. The effort involved in establishing a coordinated pay system is likely to be partially wasted if it is not continually monitored and updated.

Can you describe the process of developing a pay system?

REVIEW AND PREVIEW

The compensation provided by an organization is a major means for attracting and holding employees. Because financial compensation is a major organizational cost, managers need an awareness of the meaning compensation has to employees. Whether the compensation has economic, psychosocial, and/or growth meanings to employees, managers should be concerned with the individual's perceived fairness or equity of the compensation. Key to compensating human resources is the providing of adequate rewards in exchange for employees' inputs.

To insure internal equity, job evaluation is necessary. Job evaluation is concerned with determining the relative worth of jobs, and it can be done through ranking, classification, point, or factor comparison methods.

Once the job evaluation process has been completed, an organizational pay system must be developed and administered. Wage survey data must be collected, pay policies identified, and the pay structure calculated and composed. To have an effective pay system, changes will have to be expected and made on a continuing basis.

This chapter has dealt with compensation as a major area of personnel management and has focused on the basic pay employees and managers receive. The next chapter examines two other types of compensation—incentives and benefits.

Review Questions

1. What did compensation mean to you in your most recent job?
2. "Equity is the most important aspect of all compensation activities." Discuss.
3. In what ways are the following laws different: (a) Fair Labor Standards Act, (b) Walsh-Healey Act, (c) Davis-Bacon Act?
4. People can be paid in three basic ways. What are they and what are the advantages of each?
5. What is job evaluation? Considering all methods, why do you believe the point method is the most widely used job evaluation method?
6. You have been named compensation manager for a hospital. How would you establish a pay system?

OPENING CASE FOLLOW-UP

The need for balancing compensation expenditures with other business demands in a relatively new organization is important. However, the problems in this case are made more severe because of the local managers' lack of control. They have no control over the wages employees can be initially offered. Thus, their ability to deal with the turnover problem is limited. With high turnover, it is difficult to keep trained employees who might be more efficient. Also, the restrictions on raises may have negative effects on the motivation of employees by providing mainly an economic meaning to compensation.

Having all checks made up in the home office prevents the local managers from knowing their payroll expenditures until after they have been made, when their payroll/sales ratio is already out of line. The federal minimum-wage increase should be taken into consideration by the home office as a factor over which managers have no control either. The wage structure in the area might be different from the wage structure in the home office area or in other areas of the country.

There are no easy answers to this case. One would hope that the logical arguments against current compensation policies would cause the home office to change them. Without significant changes, the store will continue to experience problems.

Case: Scientific Turmoil

Joan is the director of scientific computing at a large utility company. The people she supervises are all college graduates with backgrounds in science, engineering, or math. These people do systems work and computer programming that is more problem-oriented than other programmers in the company. In fact, there is much rivalry between the Business and Scientific Programming departments. Partially because of this attitude, the people in the Scientific Department are quite close knit.

Joan hired Fred into the group from the Engineering Department. Fred, who had worked for the company for seven years, learned the programming easily and was doing quite well. One year later Bob was hired into the group by Joan. Bob and Fred both assimilated into the group quickly.

About a month later, Joan's problems began. Information was quite freely shared by members of the group, especially job-related information such as salary. When Fred learned that Bob was making more money than he was, he was quite upset. Bob was doing the same kind of work with less experience at this new job. He also had less total working time with the company—only four years.

When Fred voiced his concern to his boss, he was told that the company had specific guidelines for raises and wide salary ranges for each job level. Bob was just on the high side of his old job's salary range and received a hefty raise when he was promoted to this new job. Fred was not pleased with the setup because he had received a raise just before Bob came and knew that it would be a year before he would get another one. In Fred's mind, he was now qualified, more experienced, had better knowledge of the company, and, if nothing else, more seniority than Bob. Fred's attitude and discontent was apparent in his work, and although Joan could not really prove it, Fred caused serious delays in projects. Also, new errors seemed to be cropping up in the computer programs that come out of Joan's section.

QUESTIONS

1. What role does equity play in this case?
2. Should companies demand that individuals not reveal their salaries? Why or why not?
3. Comment on the salary system and weaknesses you see in it.
4. As the director, how would you handle Fred?

Notes

1. Edward E. Lawler III, *Pay and Organizational Effectiveness* (New York: McGraw-Hill Book, 1971).

2. Edward E. Lawler III, "Managers' Perception of Their Subordinates' Pay and of Their Supervisors' Pay," *Personnel Psychology*, 23 (1970), pp. 591–604.

3. Jay R. Schuster and Barbara Clark, "Individual Differences Related to Feelings Toward Pay," *Personnel Psychology*, 23 (1970), pp. 591–604.

4. Paul F. Wernimont and Susan Fitzpatrick, "The Meaning of Money," *Journal of Applied Psychology*, 56 (1972), pp. 218–226.

5. For a concise explanation of equity theory, see Michael R. Carrell and John E. Dittrich, "Equity Theory: The Recent Literature, Methodological Considerations, and New Directions," *The Academy of Management Review*, 3 (April 1978) pp. 202–210.

6. *Ibid.*

7. Paul S. Goodman and Abraham Friedman, "An Examination of Adams' Theory of Inequity," *Administrative Science Quarterly*, 16 (1971), pp. 271–288.

8. Mary G. Miner, "Pay Policies: Secret or Open? And Why?" *Personnel Journal*, 53 (1974), pp. 110–115.

9. Paul Thompson and John Pronsky, "Secrecy or Disclosure in Management Compensation?" *Business Horizons*, June 1975, pp. 67–74.

10. Wage and Hour Division, U.S. Dept. of Labor, *Equal Pay*, U.S. Dept. of Labor, WH Publication 1320 (Washington, D.C.: U.S. Governmental Printing Office, 1973), p. 4.

11. *Fair Employment Digest* (Berea, Ohio: American Society for Personnel Administration, 1974).

12. U.S. Dept. of Labor, *State Minimum Wage Laws: A Chartbook on Basic Provisions*, U.S. Dept. of Labor, Employment Standards Administration, Labor Law Series #4A (Washington, D.C.: U.S. Governmental Printing Office, 1974).

13. Herbert G. Zollitsch, "Productivity, Time Study, and Incentive-Pay Plans," in Dale Yoder and Herbert G. Heneman, Jr., eds., *ASPA Handbook of Personnel and Industrial Relations*, vol. 2, *Motivation and Commitment* (Washington, D.C.: The Bureau of National Affairs, 1975), pp. 6–62.

14. Harold D. Jones, "Issues in Job Evaluation: The Union View," *Personnel Journal*, 51 (1972), pp. 675–679.

15. Robert E. Sibson, *Compensation* (New York: AMACOM Division, American Management Association, 1974), chapter 4.

16. For more details see Allan N. Nash and Stephen J. Carroll, *The Management of Compensation* (Monterey, Calif.: Brooks/Cole Publishing, 1975), pp. 123–128.

17. David W. Belcher, *Compensation Administration* (Englewood Cliffs, N.J.: Prentice-Hall, 1974), pp. 151–153.

18. Eugene J. Benge, "Using Factor Methods to Measure Jobs," in Milton L. Rock, ed., *Handbook of Wage and Salary Administration* (New York: McGraw-Hill, 1972), pp. 2–42 through 2–55.

19. Herbert G. Zollitsch and Adolph Langsner, *Wage and Salary Administration*, 2d ed. (Cincinnati: Southwestern Publishing, 1970), pp. 179–183.

20. For more information on the Hay Plan see W. F. Younger, "The Hay-MSL System," in Angela Bowey, ed., *Handbook of Salary and Wage Systems.* (Epping, Essex, Great Britain: Gower Press, 1975), pp. 173–180.

21. For example, see Zollitsch and Langsner, *Wage and Salary Administration,* or Belcher, *Compensation Administration.*

22. A good description of how to prepare a wage survey is contained in Bruce R. Ellig, "Salary Surveys: Design to Application," *The Personnel Administrator* (October 1977), pp. 41–48.

23. Charles W. Brennan, *Wage Administration,* rev. ed. (Homewood, Ill.: Richard D. Irwin, 1963), p. 190.

chapter 14

Incentives and Benefits

When you have read this chapter, you should be able to:

1. Define incentive and benefit and differentiate between them.

2. Discuss two behavioral problems with individual incentives and indicate two types of individual incentives.

3. Discuss the purpose of group and organizational incentives, and identify at least two types of group or organizational incentive systems.

4. List the five key ideas in an effective incentive system.

5. Identify and briefly explain at least four of the major types of benefits.

6. Explain the cafeteria-style benefit system.

7. Discuss two general pension-related issues.

8. Write a concise description of the Employee Retirement Income Security Act of 1974.

9. Explain the impact of changes in laws dealing with retirement.

10. Discuss the issues of early retirement and pre-retirement counseling.

Cash Is Good, Card Is Bad

Arlow's, a retail store located in a major midwestern city, is part of a regional chain of fine department stores. Because of its reputation, Arlow's has been able to attract highly competent professional sales help. All salesclerks are salaried, nonexempt employees who are well-paid, but who do not receive commissions.

Recently sales have flattened out because of slower economic conditions. Thinking that an extra incentive would help Arlow's through the economic dip, the store manager decided to institute a 2 percent commission on *cash sales only*. Because of the 3½ percent service charge made by the bank charge card plan on all charge sales, Arlow's manager felt that this incentive plan would appeal to the salesclerks and be advantageous to the firm.

The manager was right—too right in fact. Some of the salesclerks have become so enthusiastic about getting their 2 percent that they are being very pushy and insulting to customers who refuse to pay cash and try to use a bank charge card. Consequently, the manager has received several complaints in the last few days from irate customers who loudly promise to "never shop here again."

Incentives and benefits are two types of compensation which go beyond the basic pay an individual receives. Both are forms of rewarding employees in exchange for their efforts. However, incentives and benefits each have a different emphasis from the basic pay an individual receives.

> An INCENTIVE is *additional* compensation related to performance.

It provides additional compensation for those employees who perform well and attempts to tie additional compensation as directly as possible to employee productivity.

> A BENEFIT is additional compensation given to employees as a condition of organizational membership.

The major difference between a benefit and an incentive is that individuals receive benefits as long as they are employees of the organization. An incentive, however, is tied directly to performance and is only given for above-average performance. An individual who does not perform well will not receive as much in incentive compensation but will receive approximately the same benefit compensation as another employee who has been with the firm the same length of time and has the same general job responsibilities. To more fully explore the various aspects of incentives and benefits, each is examined in a separate part of the chapter.

Can you distinguish between an incentive and a benefit?

As pointed out in the previous chapter, the personnel unit and other managers play varying roles in compensation. Figure 14–1 shows a typical compensation interface and identifies sample roles of each party concerning incentives and benefits.

Notice the primary role of the personnel unit in the incentive and benefit areas. The role of the manager is more general supervision than direct involvement. The technical nature of many incentives and benefits gives the personnel unit a larger role to play.

INCENTIVES

For centuries compensation has been related to performance. The main purpose of incentives is to tie employees' rewards closely to their achievements, which is done by providing more compensation for better performance. It is generally assumed that better performance will follow from greater effort.

As pointed out in earlier chapters, whether or not an individual worker

FIGURE 14–1   Incentives and benefit portion of compensation interface.

Personnel Unit	Managers
Develops incentive systems	Assist in developing incentive systems
	Monitor attendance and productivity for incentive compensation
Develops benefit systems	Encourage and coach employees to obtain incentives
Answers employee's technical questions on benefits	Answer simple questions on benefits
Assists employees in claiming benefits	Maintain liason with personnel specialists on benefits
Coordinates special preretirement programs	Maintain good communications with employees near retirement

will strive for increased output or productivity, and thus receive additional rewards, depends upon several factors. One prime factor is whether or not the employee wants the additional rewards that follow from the increased performance. Using money as an incentive to motivate people to work harder will be successful only if they *want* more money. For example, some people may prefer some extra time-off rather than more money.

The three basic types of incentive systems: *individual, group,* and *organizational*, will be examined next. Often organizations use a combination of systems.

INDIVIDUAL INCENTIVES

Many different types of individual incentive systems are available, but they all attempt to relate individual effort to individual reward. For a salesclerk who works on a salary plus commission, the commission portion represents individual incentive compensation.

Individual incentive may have to be tailored to individual desires; thus, if a worker wants additional time-off instead of additional take-home pay, the incentive system may have to provide that option to be effective. An individual incentive system may also be used as a means of measuring individual capabilities and initiative. Those who have special abilities and exert more effort can be identified for promotions or transfers to other more demanding and rewarding jobs.

Problems with Individual Incentives

A major concern with an individual incentive system is *keeping the system current.* A bonus payment to a salesclerk on the basis of the dollar value of sales may require changes to compensate for inflation, changes in the product line, or the types of merchandise sold.

Another concern is that *employee competition* for incentives may produce undesirable results. Paying salesclerks in a retail store a commission may result in some clerks "fighting" over customers. Some salesclerks may be reluctant to work in departments that sell lesser valued items if their commissions are figured on the basis of total sales. For example, clerks in a department store may overconcentrate on selling major appliances without giving adequate attention to the small household appliances.

Any incentive system requires a climate of *trust and cooperation* between the employers and workers. If the workers believe that the incentive system is just a management scheme designed to make them work harder and that they ultimately will receive less pay, the individual incentive system *will not* be effective.

Individual incentive systems may be *resisted by unions.* Many unions are built on security, seniority, and group solidarity instead of the total productivity of an individual. Also, incentive systems may favor only the highly motivated, competent workers and actually depress the average workers' earnings.

Employees must see that their increased efforts do result in increased pay and that they receive equity for their additional efforts. One author warns that incentives can be misdirected.[1] An employee in a mattress factory who receives incentive compensation based on the number of units produced may turn out a large number of mattresses, but of lower quality. Another example of a misdirected incentive system is rewarding a department store manager only for keeping costs down. As a result, the manager may not make some really necessary expenditures.

Legal changes such as the Tax Reform Act of 1976 have far-reaching effects on incentive plans. The act affected the way in which deferred income is taxed. The new tax structure imposes stiffer taxes on deferred income incentive programs and has caused many companies to reevaluate their incentive programs.[2] Types of individual incentives include piece-rate and bonus plans.

Can you identify two behavioral problems associated with individual incentives?

Piece-Rate

The most basic individual incentive system is the piece-rate system. Under the *straight piecework system,* wages are determined by multiplying the number of units produced (garments sewn, customers contacted, etc.) by the piece-rate for one unit, as expressed by

$$\underset{\text{(Number of units)}}{N} \times \underset{\text{unit rate}}{R} = \underset{\text{wages}}{W}$$

Regardless of the number of pieces produced, the incentive compensation for each piece does not change. The wage payment for each employee is easy to figure, and labor cost may be accurately predicted since the cost is the same for each unit.

Another type of piece-rate system, the *differential piece-rate system,* pays employees at one piece-rate if they produce less than a standard output, and at a higher piece-rate if they produce more than the standard. This play, developed by Frederick W. Taylor in the late 1800s, was designed to stimulate employees to achieve or exceed established standards of production. A manager can determine the quota or standard through time and motion studies or by deciding what *standard* performance for a particular job should be. A worker whose standard is 50 units and is paid 10 cents for each unit, might receive 15 cents for each unit produced over the standard.[3]

Despite its incentive value, piecework usage is declining. One reason is that for many types of jobs standards are difficult and costly to determine, and in some instances the cost of determining and maintaining the standard may be greater than the benefits derived from piecework. Jobs where individuals have little control over output or where high standards of quality are necessary may also be unsuited to piecework. However, in certain industries such as the garment industry, it is still widely used.

Bonus

Another type of individual incentive is the bonus. Although bonuses can be developed for groups and for entire organizations, the individual bonus is somewhat unique in that it rewards only high performing individuals. Providing the salesperson who sells the most new cars a trip to Las Vegas would be an example of a bonus. Sales contests, productivity contests, and other incentive schemes can be conducted so that individual employees receive a bonus or something extra in the way of compensation.

The bonus form of individual incentive compensation is often used at the executive or upper management levels of an organization. Because of the broad nature of executive responsibilities, many executives have their individual bonuses based on corporate or divisional performance.

Many bonuses are similar to profit-sharing plans except that the bonus incentives usually are limited to upper-level managers instead of being shared with many employees. A survey of organizations found that 46 percent of the companies surveyed paid bonuses to middle-level executives, and 59 percent paid bonuses to top executives. This same survey revealed that executive bonuses were tied to both profits and individual performance, with profits having more weight than individual performance.[4] One research study found that the level of executive compensation was not significantly related to corporate performance.[5] Because executive performance is difficult to determine, bonus compensation for executives must reflect some kind of performance measure if it is to be meaningful.

An annual individual bonus can be determined by using a percentage of an individual's base salary. Though technically this type of bonus is individual, it comes very close to being a group or organizationwide system since it is based on group or organizationwide performance. To pay a division manager a bonus based on the profits of the division, the total performance of the division and its employees must be considered. A logical extension of this thinking is to offer group or organizationwide incentive systems.

What are two types of individual incentive systems?

GROUP AND ORGANIZATIONAL
INCENTIVE SYSTEMS

A group or organizational incentive provides rewards to *all* employees in a unit. This type is designed to overcome some of the limitations of the individual incentive system and to promote cooperation and coordinated effort within the group or organization.

One result of a group incentive system may be to overcome the resistance of co-workers to an individual who produces more. A group incentive system, however, may not lead to higher productivity because individual effort is not as directly tied to the rewards. One critical factor in the group incentive system is the size of the group. If it becomes too large, employees may feel their individual effort will have little or no effect on the total performance of the group and the group incentive.

Small-group incentive plans are a direct result of a growing number of complex and interdependent jobs. Small-group plans may encourage teamwork in groups of as many as 40 employees; however, there is nothing to encourage cooperation between groups. Groups, like individuals, may restrict output, resist revision of standards, and seek gain at the expense of other groups. In a group incentive plan, group size, group stability, and type of work are critical factors.[6]

Compensating individual employee groups with incentives may cause them to overemphasize certain efforts to the detriment of overall organizational good. For example, the conflict between the marketing and production branches of many organizations occurs because marketing's incentive compensation is based upon what is sold, while production's incentive compensation is based upon keeping unit production costs as low as possible. Marketing representatives may want to tailor products to customers needs to increase their sales, but production managers want long productions runs to lower costs. The overall company good may take second place. To deal with problems such as those, organizational incentive systems have been developed.

An *organizationwide* incentive system compensates all employees in the organization based upon how well the organization *as a whole* does during the year. Consider a simple example: If profits were up 10 percent over the previous year, all employees might receive an incentive payment of 10 percent of their regular monthly pay. The example cited earlier about conflict between marketing and production might be overcome by using an organizational incentive that emphasizes organizational profit and productivity.

The basic concept underlying organizationwide incentive plans is that overall efficiency depends on organization or plantwide cooperation. The purpose of these plans is to produce teamwork. Organizationwide incentive plans are most successful in small organizations with stable product lines, competent supervision, cooperative union management relations, strong top management and effective employee management communication.[7] These plans include profit-sharing and Scanlon-type plans.

What is the purpose of group and organizationwide
incentives?

Profit-sharing

As implied by its name, profit-sharing distributes a portion of profits of
the organization to the employees. One author estimates that there are
more than 25,000 profit-sharing plans in the United States, and they are
growing at a rapid rate.[8] Typically, the percentage of the profits to be set
aside for distribution to employees is agreed upon by the end of the year
before profits are distributed.

The major objectives of profit-sharing plans are to make employees
more profit conscience, to encourage cooperation and teamwork, and to
involve employees in the organization's success. In some profit-sharing
plans, employees receive their portion of the profits at the end of the year;
in others, the profits are deferred and placed into a fund which is available
to employees upon retirement or upon leaving an organization.

Employee stock option plan.   A common type of profit-sharing plan is
the Employee Stock Option Plan (ESOP). As ESOP is designed to give
employees some ownership of the company they work for, thereby increasing their commitment, loyalty, and effort. In a typical ESOP, the
employing organization provides a large block of stock for distribution to
employees based on the length of service, salaries, and organizational
performance during the fiscal year.

Basically, the ESOP allows employees to purchase stock in their employing organization at a set price that is generally significantly lower
than the market value of the stock in a future time period.[9] In order to
exercise the stock option the employee must ultimately accumulate the
money to purchase the stock at the set price. If the stock is purchased and
then does not perform as expected, the employee may become disenchanted with the option as comepnsation. Lack of funds to purchase
stock also may limit the employee's perceived value of an ESOP.

Scanlon plan.   A unique type of organizationwide incentive plan is the
Scanlon plan. Since its development in 1927, Scanlon plans have been
implemented in many companies; however, they have never been installed in a large company such as General Motors.

The basic concept underlying the Scanlon plan is that efficiency depends on teamwork and plantwide cooperation. The plan has two main
features: a direct incentive to employees to improve efficiency, and a
system of departmental committees and a plant screening committee to
evaluate all cost-saving suggestions. Calculation, by any of several for-
mulas, of the standard and normal costs of production results in a formula
upon which the Scanlon plan incentives are based. The incentive bonus is
usually a ratio of past payroll to sales value of production (plus or minus

inventory adjustment) compared to actual payroll. Any saving between actual and expected payroll is placed in a bonus fund. A predetermined percentage of this fund is split between employees and the company.

The departmental committees receive and review cost-saving suggestions. Suggestions beyond the level of authority of departmental committees are passed to the plant committee for review. Savings that result from submitted suggestions are passed on to members of the organization. The Scanlon plan is not a true profit-sharing plan because employees receive incentive compensation for reducing labor costs, regardless of whether or not the organization ultimately makes a profit.[10]

Where the Scanlon plan has been implemented, some firms have experienced an increase in productivity and a decrease in labor costs. Also, employee attitudes have become more favorable, and there has been greater cooperation between management and the workers.

The success of the Scanlon plan can be significantly affected by union opposition and the attitudes of the managers toward employees and employee participation. In a survey of employees who work under the Scanlon plan, positive employee attitudes were found: employees do appear to have greater knowledge about the company and higher cooperative relationships.[11]

Can you identify at least two types of group or organizational incentives?

GUIDELINES FOR AN EFFECTIVE INCENTIVE PROGRAM

As indicated in the above discussion, incentive systems can be complex and may take many forms. Managers should consider the following general guidelines when establishing and maintaining incentive systems:

1. *Incentive systems should be tied as much as possible to performance.* If an incentive is actually to spur increased performance and effort, employees must see a direct relationship between their efforts and their rewards. Further, both workers and managers must see the incentive rewards as equitable and desirable. If a group incentive system is to be used, it should be compatible with employees' desires and should reflect employees' efforts as a group of individuals.

2. *Incentive plans should provide for individual differences.* Recognition of the complex-man concept (Chapter 3) requires that a variety of incentive systems may have to be developed to appeal to various organizational groups and individuals. Not everybody will want the same type of incentive rewards. For example, one writer suggests that incentive systems for salespersons be self-tailored, and "each

plan must be designed for a specific purpose and with the characteristics of the specific salesmen in mind."[12]

3. *Incentive systems should be designed to reflect the type of work that is done and the type of structure in the organization.* One research study found that the type of incentive compensation should vary with the organization structure and the amount of freedom that divisional managers have. Where great freedom exists, the incentive system for division general managers should be based entirely on objective performance measures. When a division has little freedom, payoffs may be more varied, and subjective as well as objective measures may be used.[13]

4. *The incentive system chosen should be consistent with the climate and constraints of an organization.* A manager should recognize the basic incompatibility in attempting to devise a Scanlon plan for an organization in which there is strict adherence to traditional procedures and rules. The incentive plan should also be consistent with organizational resources and be developed in close consultation with the financial officers to determine how much incentive compensation an organization can afford.

5. *An incentive system should be consistently monitored to determine if it is being fairly administered and is accurately reflecting current technological and organizational conditions.* Offering an incentive for clothing salesclerks to sell outdated merchandise would be more appropriate than offering one for selling only current fashion items that are already good sellers.

Incentive systems should continually be reviewed to determine whether they are operating as designed. Follow-up through an attitude survey or other means will determine if the incentive system is actually encouraging employees to perform better. If it is not, then managers should seriously consider changing the system. Any incentive system should be based on performance; otherwise, it becomes a benefit.

What are five key aspects of an effective incentive system?

BENEFITS

Unlike incentive systems, *benefits* are available to all members of the organization, regardless of differences in individual performance. As was emphasized earlier, benefits are available to employees as long as they are members of the organization. For example, if an employee is performing poorly but is still employed, he or she is entitled to the medical insurance and other benefits. Only when the employee resigns or is "dehired" does the individual lose benefits.

Benefit Costs

A benefit is frequently a nontaxable form of compensation provided by an employer. Although benefits are not considered part of an individual's compensation for tax purposes, they do represent a significant expenditure from the organization's point of view.

Every two years the U.S. Chamber of Commerce surveys a large number of industries to determine the extent of benefit payment. In the most recent survey, as of the writing of this book, an employer in American industry averaged paying 35.4 percent of total payroll in benefits. The significance of this average figure is that an average employee making $12,000 per year receives $4,248 in benefits per year. The amount of benefits provided varied significantly. An employee in the hospital industry averaged 24 percent benefits to total pay, while an employee in the chemical manufacturing industry received 42.2 percent benefits to total pay.[14]

There are many different types of benefits provided employees. For ease of discussion, they are grouped into several types:

- required security
- voluntary security
- time-off related
- insurance and financial
- social
- recreational and miscellaneous other benefits
- retirement-related benefits

Each of these is examined, with required security benefits being discussed first.

Required Security Benefits

Some benefits are required by various federal and state laws. *Workmen's compensation* and *unemployment compensation* are the most important of the required security benefits. Retirement funding through Social Security and pensions are discussed later in this chapter.

Workmen's compensation.   The Federal Employee's Compensation Act of 1908 provided injury insurance to government workers. From that act and workmen's compensation laws enacted by California, New Jersey, Washington, and Wisconsin in 1911, workmen's compensation laws have spread to all the remaining states. The aim of workmen's compensation is to provide cash benefits to any person injured on the job. Workmen's compensation costs are born entirely by the employer on the theory that industrial accidents should be considered one of the costs of production.

Workmen's compensation laws may be either compulsory or elective. Figure 14–2 indicates those states having *compulsory or elective law.* Every employer subject to compulsory law must comply with its provisions for compensation of work injuries. Under an elective law, employers have the option of accepting or rejecting the act. If employers reject the act, they lose the customary common law defenses of assumed risk of employment, negligence of a fellow servant, and contributing negligence. Under elective law, if an employer has rejected the act, an employee injured on the job may be unable to get compensation unless he sues for damages.

Workmen's compensation provides two types of payments to injured workers or to a killed worker's next of kin. Payment can be either *direct cash* or it can be *reimbursement for medical expenses, pain, and suffering.*

Employers pay premiums for workmen's compensation through participation in a private insurance fund or in a state-operated workmen's compensation plan. Employer compensation rates are often related to job risk and safety records. The amount of compensation paid to employees depends upon the nature and severity of injury and varies from state to state. Because of the wide variation in state benefits, organized labor and others have pushed for the federal government to provide more control and more standardized benefits. As yet, these attempts have not been successful.

Workmen's compensation plans originally provided only for physical injury. They have been expanded in many areas to cover emotional impairments that may have resulted from a physical injury. Also, emotional illnesses caused by job-induced strain, stress, anxiety, or pressure may be covered.

Unemployment compensation. The second form of legally required benefits is unemployment compensation, which was established as part of the Social Security Act of 1935. Each state operates its own unemployment compensation system, and the provisions differ significantly from state to state.

Employers finance this benefit by paying a percentage tax on their total payrolls to state and federal unemployment compensation funds. If an employee is out of work and is actively looking for employment, he or she may receive up to 26 or 30 weeks of pay, at the rate of 50 to 80 percent of normal pay.

Voluntary Security Benefits

In addition to security benefits required by law, employers can offer security benefits voluntarily or through provisions in a management/union contract. Two common voluntary security benefits are supplemental unemployment benefits (SUB) and severance pay.

Figure 14–2 Workmen's compensation: compulsory or elective?

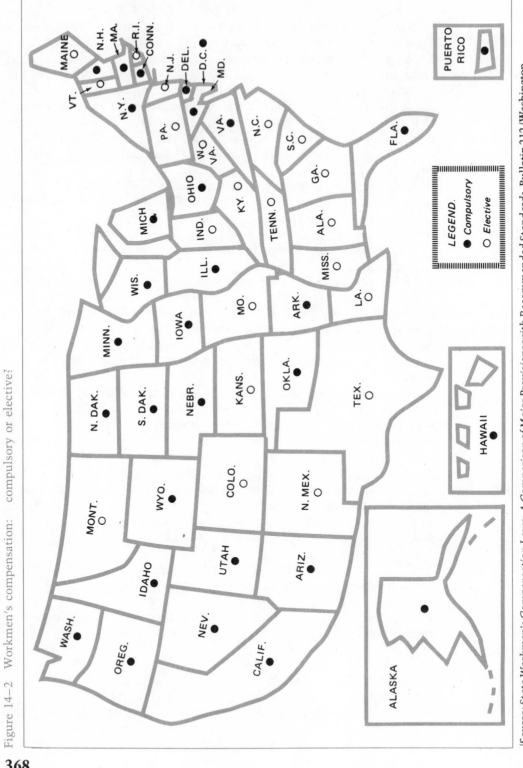

(Source: *State Workmen's Compensation Laws: A Comparison of Major Provisions with Recommended Standards*, Bulletin 212 (Washington, D.C.: U.S. Department of Labor, 1971 rev.), p. 3.)

Supplemental unemployment benefits (SUB).   Supplemental Unemployment Benefits (SUB) are closely related to unemployment compensation but are not required by law. First obtained by the United Auto Workers in 1955, SUB is a benefit provision negotiated by a union with an employer as a part of the collective bargaining process. The provision requires company contributions to a fund, which supplements the unemployment compensation available to employees from federal and/or state sources or both. However, employers do not have unlimited financial responsibilities to SUBs; during the 1974–1975 recession, the SUB fund for several automobile manufacturers was exhausted because of the large number of workers laid off.

SUB programs attempt to guarantee employees who are laid off or temporarily unemployed an amount close to their normal take-home pay for a limited amount of time. For example, one SUB plan provides laid-off employees 90 percent of their take-home pay for 26 weeks. The SUB payment is added to normal unemployment compensation up to the 90 percent figure. Figure 14–3 shows a sample calculation for a SUB plan.

FIGURE 14–3   Sample supplemental unemployment benefit calculation.

Normal pay $5/hr and 40/hr week	=	$200/wk
90% of normal pay	=	$180/wk
State unemployment compensation	=	$ 82/wk
SUB pay		$ 98/wk

Severence pay.   Severence pay is a security benefit offered by some employers. Employees who lose their jobs permanently may receive a lump sum payment if they are terminated by the employer. For example, if a plant closes because it is outmoded and no longer economically profitable to operate, the employees who lose their jobs receive a lump-sum payment based on their years of service because their employment with that company is permanently severed. Severance pay provisions often appear in union/management agreements and usually provide larger payment for employees with longer service.

Time-Off Related Benefits

Several benefits provide pay for time-off. *Holiday pay* is very common for such established holidays such as Labor Day, Memorial Day, Christmas, New Year's, and July 4. Federal legislation designating many holidays to fall on Mondays creates many three-day weekends. Other holidays are offered to some employees by selected state laws or union contracts.

FIGURE 14–4   Sample graduated vacation plan.

Length of Service	Paid Vacation Time
At least 9 months to 2 years	1 week (5 days off)
2 years to 7 years	2 weeks (10 days off)
7 years to 15 years	3 weeks (15 days off)
More than 15 years	4 weeks (20 days off)

Vacations with pay are a very common benefit. Employees often have graduated vacation time based on length of service. Figure 14–4 is an example of a graduated paid-vacation scheme.

Sick pay is another common type of pay for time not worked. Many employers allow their employees to miss a limited number of days because of sickness or illness without losing pay. Some sick-pay plans contain provisions whereby employees receive pay for sick days not taken.

Time-off with pay is also given many employees serving on jury duty, serving with the military reserves, assisting with elections, or voting. All of these time-off benefits add to employer costs.

Insurance and Financial Benefits

Another major group of benefits provided by employers are financial in nature. A variety of different types of insurance and financial services are contained in benefit packages.

Insurance.   The three most common types of insurance are health, life, and sickness and disability. Figure 14–5 shows the results of a survey of 152 employers. Notice that most employers, regardless of size or industry, offer group life and hospital/surgical insurance.

Group insurance benefits offered by some employers include automobile insurance, dental insurance, legal insurance, prescription drug insurance, and eye-care insurance. The major advantage to employees is that many employers may pay some or all of the cost of these plans. Also, cheaper insurance rates are available through a group program.

Health Maintenance Organization.   A unique form of health care may be made available through a Health Maintenance Organization (HMO), an organized form of health care providing services for a fixed period and group on a prepaid basis. Unlike other health care benefits, the HMO emphasizes prevention as well as correction.[15]

An HMO is composed of a group of doctors and other professionals

FIGURE 14–5   Insurance benefits survey.

Benefit/Employee Group Covered	Types of Benefits Provided (% of Responding Companies)					
	Size		Industry			All
	Large	Small	Mfg.	Nonmfg.	Nonbus.	Companies
Group Life Insurance						
Production/Maintenance	99	99	100	100	94	99
Office/Clerical	99	99	100	100	94	99
Management	99	99	100	100	94	99
Hospital/Surgical Insurance						
Production/Maintenance	99	97	99	97	97	98
Office/Clerical	99	97	99	97	97	98
Management	99	97	99	97	97	98
Major Medical Plan						
Production/Maintenance	84	70	75	78	79	77
Office/Clerical	93	90	90	97	88	91
Management	95	91	91	97	91	93
Hospitalization and Major Medical are combined in Comprehensive coverage						
Production/Maintenance	53	37	44	51	41	45
Office/Clerical	56	43	48	59	44	50
Management	59	45	50	59	47	51
Sickness & Accident Disability						
a. Short-term						
Production/Maintenance	55	61	84	30	26	58
Office/Clerical	47	49	63	35	26	48
Management	43	42	58	27	24	42
b. Long-term						
Production/Maintenance	25	22	14	35	35	24
Office/Clerical	36	38	26	57	41	37
Management	43	47	35	68	44	45

(Source: Personnel Policies Forum, *Employee Health and Welfare Benefits*, PPF Survey #107 (Washington, D.C.: Bureau of National Affairs, October 1974), p. 2. Used with permission).

who provide basic and additional health care. Some employers offer this benefit because HMOs encourage broader health care services at a reasonable cost for employees. This form of health care should be examined by managers in the future as an alternative to traditional health insurance systems.

Financial. Financial benefits can include a wide variety of items. A *credit union* provides savings and lending services for employees. *Purchase discounts* allow employees to buy goods or services from their employer at a reduced rate. For example, a furniture manufacturer may allow employees to buy furniture at wholesale cost plus 10 percent. Or, a state bank may offer the use of a safety deposit box and free checking to its employees.

Employee *thrift, saving,* or *stock investment plans* may be made available. Some employers match a portion of the employee's contribution. These plans are especially attractive to executive and managerial personnel. To illustrate, in a stock purchase plan, the corporation may provide funds equal to the amount invested by the employee to purchase that stock. In this way, employees can benefit from the future growth of the corporation. Another aim is that employees will develop a greater loyalty and interest in the company and its success.

Financial planning and counseling is a valuable benefit to executives. They may need information on investments, tax sheltering, and comprehensive financial counseling because of their higher compensation.

Numerous other financial-related benefits can be cited. The use of a company car, company expense accounts, and help in buying or selling a house when transferred are other common financial-related benefits. Those listed above show the variety of financial benefits that can be offered.

Social, Recreational, and Other Services

Another group of benefits and services provided are social and recreational in nature, such as bowling leagues, picnics, parties, sponsored athletic teams, organizationally-owned and provided recreational lodges, and sponsored activities and interest groups. Dances, banquets, cocktail hours, and other social events provide an opportunity for personnel to become better acquainted and strengthen interpersonal relationships. The employer should retain control of all events associated with the organization because of possible legal responsibility.

Strong emphasis on numerous social and recreation programs is designed to encourage employee happiness and team spirit. Employees may appreciate this type of benefit, but managers should not expect increased job productivity or job satisfaction to result.

Counseling services are an important part of many organizational benefit programs. Although supervisors are expected to counsel subordinates, most organizations recognize that there will be employees whose problems require qualified counselors. Many organizations refer such individuals to church organizations, family counseling, or marriage counselors and mental health clinics. Some organizations, like the Utah Copper Division of Kennecott Copper Corporation, have 24-hour counseling services. The program, called INSIGHT, allows employees or members of their families to arrange for counseling service simply by dialing a Salt Lake City area telephone day or night.[16] Smaller organizations may benefit from working with community institutions.

Other benefits far too numerous to mention here are made available by various employers. Food services, child-care services, paid professional memberships, lunch period entertainment, and organizationally provided uniforms are just a few. Applicable benefits must be developed into a coordinated and effective benefits program. A recent approach to benefit coordination is the cafeteria approach to benefits.

Can you identify and discuss at least four major types of benefits?

Cafeteria-style Benefit System

The cafeteria-style approach to benefits is likely to be one of the next major steps in the evolution of employee benefits. It recognizes that individual situations differ because of age, family status and life-style. This approach utilizes the data-handling capabilities of computers and allows each employee to have an individual combination of benefits within some overall limit. The organization makes a variety of "dishes," or benefits, available. Each employee or group of employees can "select" desired benefits. Sometimes known as *variable benefits*, employees can even be offered the option of taking the cost of the benefits as part of their pay.

Advantages. The cafeteria-style approach has several advantages. One is that this scheme takes into consideration the complex-man idea. Because employees in an organization have different desires and needs, they can tailor benefit packages to fit their individual life situations. One research study found significant differences among workers' preferences for various benefit and compensation options. Younger workers preferred a family dental insurance plan, while older people preferred a pension increase.[17] Another advantage to the variable-benefit approach is heightened employee awareness of the cost and the value of their benefits. By having to determine the benefits they will receive, employees know what they receive and what the trade-off options are.[18]

Drawbacks. The cafeteria-style approach to benefits is not without some drawbacks. One problem is the complexity of keeping track of what each individual chooses, especially if there are a large number of employees. Another problem is that employees may not always pick the benefit package that would be in their best long-term interest. A young male construction worker might not choose disability benefits; however, if he is injured, his family may suffer financial hardships. Part of this problem can be overcome by requiring employees to select a core set of benefits (that is, life, health, and disability insurance) and offering options on other benefits.[19] A third problem is that as more benefits are made available, employees may not be able to understand the options because a benefit structure and its provisions can often become quite complicated. This complexity is especially true for executive benefits and options.[20] The cafeteria-style approach appears to offer an interesting way to tailor benefits to individual employees or employee groups.

Can you explain the cafeteria-style benefit system?

RETIREMENT-RELATED BENEFITS

A widespread benefit offered by most employers attempts to provide income security for employees when they retire. Few people have independent reserves to use when they retire. Thus, financial resources must be set aside throughout their work careers. Some retirement-related benefits are required *by law*.

Governmentally Provided Retirement Benefits

The Social Security Act of 1935 with its later amendments, established a system providing old-age, survivors, disability, and retirement benefits. Administered by the U.S. government through the Social Security Administration, this program provides benefits to previously employed individuals. Both employees and employers share in the cost of Social Security by paying a tax on the employees' wages or salaries. Individuals may retire at age 62 with reduced benefits, or full benefits at age 65 or after.

Because the Social Security System affects a large number of individuals and is governmentally operated, it is a very politically sensitive program and increases in Social Security benefits are often voted by legislators. Within the last few years, Social Security payments have been tied to the cost of living (through the Consumer Price Index). This action, plus the increasing number of persons covered by the Social Security System, has resulted in concern about the availability of future funds from which to pay benefits. Also, the changing makeup of the population and the increased longevity of many persons has placed severe strains on the system.

In order to receive benefits under Social Security an individual must have engaged in some form of employment covered by the act. This act includes most private enterprises, most types of self-employment including farming, active military service, and employment in some nonprofit organizations and government agencies. Some groups of employees, including railroad workers and United States Civil Service employees who are covered by their own systems, generally are exempted from the act.[21]

Pensions

A second group of retirement benefits are provided through private pension plans established and funded by employers and employees. Private and government-administered pension plans cover more than 51 million people.[22] The number of persons covered by private pension plans is expected to grow as the work force expands.

Pension planning is a complex and specialized field which often confuses both managers and employees. Note that pensions are considered rewards for long service and are not incentives to work more efficiently or effectively. They are deferred wages and are perceived as a right earned by employees, not as a gift given by the employer. It is interesting to observe that many persons covered by private pension plans have not drawn and may never draw benefits from pension plans because of job mobility. Many employees do not stay with one employer long enough to receive the pension benefits of this service.[23] A brief presentation of some of the basic terms and types of pension requirements follow.

Pension funding.   Funds for paying pension benefits can be accumulated in two basic ways: funded and unfunded. An *unfunded plan* pays pension benefits out of current income to the organization. Therefore, an unfunded plan relies on present income or sales dollars to generate the money necessary to pay pensions. Obviously, the unfunded plan depends very much on economic conditions of the organization. Employees and former employees may be left without adequate pension benefits if current revenues are insufficient to pay these benefits.

The *funded method* provides pension benefits over a long period from funds accumulated ahead of time. By amassing funds and interest prior to actual need, employers can insure employees that this pension will actually be available. For this reason, the funded plan is preferred and is more widely used.

Pension contribution.   Pension plans can be either contributory or noncontributory. In a *contributory plan*, the money for pension benefits is contributed by both employees and employers. In a *noncontributory plan*, the employer provides all of the funds. Obviously, the noncontributory plan is preferred by employees and labor unions.

Pension rights. Certain rights are attached to employee pension plans, including vesting and portability. *Vesting* is the right of employees to receive benefits from their pension plans. Typically, vesting allows employees to be assured of receiving a certain pension, providing that they have worked a minimum number of years. If an employee resigns or is terminated before he or she vests (that is before an individual has been employed for the required time), no pension rights accrue to the person except to receive the funds he or she has contributed. If employees stay the allotted time, they retain their pension rights.

Portability is another feature of employee pensions that allows employees to move their pension benefit rights from one employer to another. For example, a plan that is portable within the paper industry will allow workers to move from one paper company to another without losing pension benefits. A commonly used portable pension system in colleges and universities is the Teacher Insurance Annuity Association (TIAA) System. Under this system, any faculty or staff member who accumulates pension benefits at one university can transfer those benefits to another university within the TIAA system.

If individuals are not in a portable system, they must take a *lump-sum settlement* of the money they contributed to the plan plus accumulated interest on their contributions. The employee does not always receive the employer's contribution, however.

Pension insurance. If funds from a pension plan are accumulated in a trust fund or through a bank, it is often a "trusteed" or uninsured plan. *Uninsured* means that the benefits at retirement are determined by calculations that consider the age of the employee, years worked, and other factors. An *insured plan* is one administered through insurance companies or similar institutions which buy retirement annuity policies. The pension rate is more or less guaranteed.

Because pensions are so complex, employees often do not bother to learn about the provisions in their pensions and the advantages of various plans. Widespread criticism of pension plans led to the federal government passing a law in 1974 to regulate private pension plans. The underlying purpose of this law is to assure that employees who put money into pension plans, or depend upon a pension for retirement funds, will actually receive that money when they retire.

Can you discuss two general pension related issues?

Employee Retirement Income Security Act of 1974

The Employee Retirement Income Security Act of 1974 (ERISA) is a technically worded and complex act that established a federal agency to administer its provisions. It covers six major areas, which are summarized in Figure 14–6.

FIGURE 14–6   Employee Retirement Income Security Act of 1974: basic areas of coverage.

1. Fiduciary Standards

   A fiduciary is an entity controlling or holding property for someone else's benefit. The law established restrictions on fiduciaries and says that they must act as "a prudent man would."

2. Reporting and Disclosure

   Employers and fiduciaries are required to maintain extensive records and to disclose to employees and the regulating federal agency the status of pension plans.

3. Participation

   Generally the act states that an employee with one year's service and who is at least 25 years of age must be covered if a pension plan is offered by an employer.

4. Vesting

   Three types of vesting provisions are provided. Once the type is chosen by the employer and an employee vests, the employee is guaranteed the right to the appropriate pension benefits. Detailed provisions governing vesting provisions are also established.

5. Funding

   Minimum funding requirements are established for unfunded plans, and mandatory guides are set whereby employers must "catch-up" their unfunded pension liabilities.

6. Plan Termination Insurance

   The Pension Benefit Guaranty Corporation is set up to protect employees who might lose their benefits by their pension plan going out of existence. All plans covered by the law are required to purchase the insurance. If a plan fails, the Guaranty Corporation will pay vested benefits up to $750/month to the employees whose pension plan is terminated.

(Source: Adapted from information in Kenneth R. Huggins, "The New Pension Security Law," *Omaha Business Review*, 2 (Spring 1975), pp. 1–3. *Used with permission.*)

The complexity of the law and the subject it deals with has resulted in much confusion for employers, banks, insurance companies, and other fiduciaries. ERISA has had the effect of increasing paperwork and generally increasing the costs of pension plan administration. However, most companies complying with ERISA requirements indicate that there have been no drastic changes in existing plans.

Although a few companies terminated their pension plans, the majority tailored existing plans to meet the ERISA requirements. Of particular concern was the vesting of benefits, funding, and eligibility for enrollment. Nearly four-fifths of all pension plans are financed entirely by the employer, and more than two-thirds are administered solely by the employer. In more than one-half of the plans, employees are eligible for enrollment after completing one year of employment.[24]

ERISA provides employees increased security through regulation of pension plans. Employees who contribute to a pension plan can have more confidence that they will receive their benefits upon retirement. Vesting requirements have changed as a result of ERISA, with approximately 86 percent of the plans providing for full vesting of employee pension rights in ten years or less, compared with 38 percent in 1973. The most common eligibility requirements for a full pension benefit are either age 65 or ten years of service. Also, 86 percent of the pension plans have early retirement provisions, 64 percent provide disability requirements, and 94 percent provide survivor benefits.[25]

Impact of ERISA.　By combining the benefits from government pensions, private pensions, and Social Security, many individuals are able to look forward to a reasonably secure retirement. Companies that terminated their pension plans because of ERISA requirements did so because compliance would have been too costly.

The most significant difficulty in complying with ERISA seems to be the voluminous paperwork involved in record keeping and reporting requirements. There are also problems with disclosure requirements, defining breaks in service, and with eligibility requirements and vesting.

Changes recommended in ERISA.　Over half of the companies complying with ERISA recommended changes in reporting requirements, and 42 percent suggested changes in disclosure requirements. Other suggested changes involved fiduciary responsibilities, eligibility provisions, and minimum standards for vesting and/or funding. Most suggested that any changes made now would only add more confusion to what is a chaotic situation. All emphasized that many of the regulations should be simplified and made more logical.[26]

Can you write a concise description of ERISA and what it requires?

Retirement and the Age Discrimination Act (1978 Revisions)

A 1978 amendment to the 1967 Age Discrimination Act stated that, beginning January 1, 1979, employees in private businesses having at least 20 persons on the payroll can no longer be forced to retire prior to age 70. Federal workers cannot be forced to retire at any age. Pension law, however, requires full vesting of pension rights no later than age 65 if the employee has at least ten years service. Employees may continue to retire at age 65 with full benefits if they desire. Business can, however, retire high-level executives with retirement incomes of $27,000 or more at age 65, as long as he or she is in a "high-level policy-making position," and had been in that job for two years.

This act does not suggest that people over 65 cannot be terminated if they are no longer doing their jobs. Older workers who are poor performers can be terminated like anyone else. However, studies have reasonably well confirmed that a person's ability to do a job does not necessarily decrease with increased age. Performance depends on the person and on the job involved.[27] Unless the jobs require heavy, physical labor, workers from 65 to 75 generally perform as well as younger workers. Older workers tend to be more accurate, can compensate for age difficulties with experience, have increased responsibility, and tend to turnover and be absent less than younger workers. However, they have less ability to work at high speed, less capacity to memorize, and a slower rate of learning.[28]

Impact of changes.   The full impact of the change in mandatory retirement age will have to be assessed some years in the future. Some companies are convinced the new law will have little effect because the trend is toward early retirement. Chrysler Corporation which has an early retirement policy (age 55) feels that auto workers want to retire as quickly as possible. Sears Roebuck, on the other hand, surveyed workers who would have retired at 65 and found 45 percent want to stay on the job.[29]

Peter Drucker feels that requiring a senior executive to retire at age 65 while others stay simply will not work.[30] He feels that able people at age 55 and over may choose *not* to accept upper-level executive jobs if it means retirement at 65. He suggests that a sensible policy might be to provide for a senior person to leave the executive suite at age 65 but to continue on as an individual professional "counselor" or "consultant." This practice is already standard at some companies such as Westinghouse.

Discrimination in Pension Plans

Pension plans which require that women contribute more because they live longer as a group have been found to be illegal by the Supreme Court because they violate the Civil Rights Act of 1964. Some think this ruling will force pension plan administrators to rely on "unisex" mortality tables instead of the separate tables for men and women that have traditionally been used.

Can you explain some changes in laws affecting retirement?

Early Retirement

Provisions for early retirement are currently included in 86 percent of all pension plans and reflects a recent trend toward allowing emplyees to retire early and receive most or all of their benefits. The most common age requirement for early retirement is 55 with varying amounts of required service time.[31]

There are numerous reasons for early retirement. Early retirement provides opportunities for people to get away from a long-term job. Individuals who have spent 25 or 30 years working for the same employer may wish to use their talents in another area. From the employers' viewpoint, replacing older and higher-paid workers with younger and lower-paid workers can be a way to cut costs in an economic slump.[32] This tactic can turn out to be a disadvantage because a firm may lose a large number of skilled and loyal employees in a very short period of time.

A vital part of retirement is an awareness of the special needs and anxieties of managers and workers as they approach retirement. These problems may be dealt with through a pre-retirement counseling program.

Pre-retirement Counseling

Pre-retirement counseling is aimed at easing employee's anxieties and preparing them for retirement, and the benefits associated with it. The biological changes of aging may cause an individual concern, but suddenly not having a job as a basis from which to order one's life can cause even more anxiety. Pre-retirement counseling recognizes that retirement involves a mental adjustment for which employees need to be prepared. One authority defines the purpose of pre-retirement counseling as follows: "It prepares the employee to make the best possible decisions pertaining to his assets and objectives before his retirement."[33]

The thrust of pre-retirement counseling is twofold. One aim is to have people begin their financial planning before they retire. Employees need to be aware of the amount of resources they will have, where these resources come from, their health and insurance benefits, and related assistance available through governmental and private sources. A second aim is to make older employees aware of the psychological changes caused by retirement. Employees should be encouraged to think about how they are going to use their time, the types of activities in which they will be involved, and employment and housing opportunities for older persons. The results of a survey on pre-retirement counseling are presented in Figure 14–7.

Pre-retirement counseling should not begin *immediately* before retirement, but should be a systematic process of gradual preparation. A good approach is to begin pre-retirement counseling several years before employees actually retire and to increase counseling opportunities as retirement approaches. Extensive counseling depends upon whether or not

FIGURE 14–7   Retirement counseling survey results.

	Number	Percentage
Companies sent questionnaire	160	100.0
Companies responding	112	70.0
From respondees:		
Those that counsel	95	84.8
Those that counsel informally	85	75.9
Those that counsel for all employees	89	79.5
How many:		
Retain an outside organization to counsel	1	.9
Are considering engaging a consultant	12	10.7
Provide Counseling in the following areas		
Pension Options	86	76.8
Profit Sharing Distributions	37	33.0
Group Insurance Conversion	90	80.1
Medicare	83	74.1
Medicare Supplements	74	66.1
Social Security	83	74.1
Veterans Benefits	19	17.0
Budgeting	9	8.0
Survivorship Planning	34	30.4
Personal Insurance	19	17.0
Personal Assets	8	7.1
Retirement Communities	5	4.5
Retirement Publications	21	18.6
Retirement Organizations	13	11.6

(Source: Don Pellicano, "Overview of Corporate Pre-Retirement Counseling," *Personnel Journal*, 56 (May 1977), pp. 235–237 +. Reprinted with permission *Personnel Journal*, Copyright May 1977.)

the organization is large enough to afford this type of program. If an organization cannot afford it, managers can encourage the pre-retiree to check state and federal agencies which might offer pre-retirement assistance and information. Also, associations such as the American Association of Retired Persons are available and helpful.

Can you discuss early retirement and preretirement counseling?

REVIEW AND PREVIEW

Incentives and benefits are two types of additional compensation, each with a different purpose. Incentives attempt to tie increased performance to increased rewards. Benefits are available as part of organizational membership and are not directly related to performance.

Incentive systems that emphasize individual, group, or organizational performance rewards can be developed. Regardless of the system used, the incentives should be designed to actually reward extra effort.

A wide range of benefits can be offered by employers. Some are required by law; others, including voluntary security benefits, insurance and financial benefits, and social and recreational benefits, can be voluntarily offered to employees.

A final set of benefits are retirement-related. Through the federal Social Security System and private pensions, employees are provided financial benefits necessary during retirement. The increased regulation of private pension plans is designed to insure that employees receive the retirement benefits they expect. The pension area is necessarily complex and the overview contained in this chapter is designed to highlight some general information about pensions. Management should be aware of the concerns of a person who considers retiring early or who is approaching retirement by providing pre-retirement counseling.

An important part of personnel management is the maintenance of a healthy and safe work environment. This maintenance concern includes both the emotional and physical health and safety of employees. These concerns are covered next in Chapter 15.

Review Questions

1. Distinguish between an incentive and a benefit.
2. Identify two types of incentives and indicate some behavioral problems that can occur with each.
3. Why are group and organizational incentives used? What are several types?
4. Describe how you would establish an effective incentive system.
5. Which four types of benefits and services would you most prefer? Relate this answer to the "cafeteria approach" to benefits.
6. Describe two types of retirement-related benefits and indicate the impact the Employee Retirement Income Security Act might have on them.
7. What do you feel are the major issues in early retirement and in pre-retirement counseling?

OPENING CASE FOLLOW UP:

The incentive scheme described in the case has resulted in problems. By placing emphasis on how the sale is paid for, instead of on the sale itself, the manager has generated counterproductive results. The incentive is not directly tied to the results that the manager wants—increased sales. Also, clerks in departments stocking lower-cost items are at an obvious advantage because customers are more likely to pay cash. A clerk who sells luggage is at a disadvantage when compared to a clerk selling lingerie.

The manager should drastically rethink this incentive plan. One possibility is to reduce the commission to 1½ percent, but have it apply to all sales. Or, the manager might want to implement some type of group incentive system that would be based on departmental sales increase or profitability figures.

Case: Early Retirement?

Small Oil, Inc., has a reputation for not being especially sympathetic to its longer service employees. In fact, in the last three years five employees with only two years to go to retirement have been fired. While the company would certainly never agree, employees are convinced the actions have been taken to avoid paying pensions (over and above that part that is already vested).

QUESTIONS

1. What is the nature of the relationship most people feel between long service with an organization and retirement? Could this be the basis for the idea that you cannot fire anyone approaching retirement age?
2. How is a reputation like this in the benefits area likely to affect Small Oil, Inc.?

Notes

1. Edwin C. Duerr, "The Effect of Misdirected Incentives on Employee Behavior," *Personnel Journal*, 53 (December 1974), pp. 890–93.

2. Ernest C. Miller, ed., *The Compensation Review*, 9 (first quarter 1977), p. 2.

3. There are many possible variations of straight and differential piece-rate systems. Combinations are possible, too.

4. "The Status of Today's Executive," ASPA-BNA Survey No. 28, *Bulletin to Management*, July 17, 1975 (Washington, D.C.: Bureau of National Affairs, 1975).

5. K. R. Srinivasa Murthy and Malcolm S. Salter, "Should CEO Pay be Limited to Results?" *Harvard Business Review* (May-June 1975), pp. 66–73.

6. T. H. Patten, Jr., *Pay: Employee Compensation and Incentive Plans*, (London: Free Press, 1977), pp. 416–418.

7. D. W. Belcher, *Compensation Administration* (Englewood Cliffs: Prentice-Hall 1974), p. 301.

8. Herbert G. Zollitsch, "Productivity Time Study, and Incentive-Pay Plans," in *ASPA Handbook of Personnel*, vol. 2, *Motivation and Commitment* (Washington, D.C.: Bureau of National Affairs 1975), pp. 6–67.

9. "Every Employee an Owner? Old Idea Gets a New Boost," *U.S.News and World Report*, June 9, 1975, pp. 68–69.

10. Herbert G. Zollitsch, "Productivity, Time Study, and Incentive Pay Plans," p. 6–69.

11. Robert K. Goodman, J. H. Wakely, and R. H. Ruh, "What Employees Think of the Scanlon Plan," *Personnel* (September 1972), pp. 22–29.

12. David M. Gardner and Kendrith Rowland, "A Self-Tailored Approach to Incentives," *Personnel Journal*, 49 (November 1970), pp. 911–917.

13. Robert A. Pitts, "Incentive Compensation and Organization Design," *Personnel Journal*, 53 (May 1974), pp. 338–344.

14. U.S. Chamber of Commerce, *Employee Benefits 1975* (Wahsington, D.C.: U.S. Chamber of Commerce, 1976).

15. Paul Snider, "Health Maintenance Organizations—A Can of Worms?" *Personnel* (November-December 1974), pp. 36–44.

16. *Labor Policy and Practice—Personnel Management* (Washington, D.C.: Bureau of National Affairs 1974), pp. 101–106.

17. J. Brad Chapman and Robert Ottemann, "Employee Preferences for Various Compensation and Fringe Benefit Options," *The Personnel Administrator* (November-December 1975), pp. 31–36.

18. William B. Werther, "A New Direction in Rethinking Fringe Benefits," *MSU Business Topics* (Winter 1974), pp. 35–40.

19. David J. Thomsen, "Introducing Cafeteria Compensation in Your Company," *Personnel Journal,* 56 (March 1977), pp. 124–131.

20. Robert V. Goode, "Complications at the Cafeteria Checkout Line," *Personnel* (November-December 1974), pp. 45–49.

21. *Labor Course* (Englewood Cliffs, N.J.: Prentice-Hall 1978).

22. *Life Insurance Fact Book*, 1974, p. 36.

23. Patten, *Pay*, p. 533.

24. *Pension Plans and the Impact of ERISA*, PPF Survey No. 119 (October 1977) (Washington, D.C. Bureau of National Affairs), p. 1.

25. *Ibid*.

26. *Ibid*.

27. R. J. Paul, "Mandatory Retirement—Some Research Findings," Paper presented 1978 Midwest Business Administration Association, Chicago.

28. *Ibid*.

29. "Firms Split on Later Retirement," *Denver Post*, March 24, 1978, p. 60.

30. Peter Drucker, "Executives and Mandatory Retirement," *Wall Street Journal*, April 6, 1978.

31. *Pension Plans and the Impact of ERISA*, p. 10.

32. Ralph E. Winter, "The Gentle Boot: To Tighten Operations, Firms Force Men in 50's and 60's to Retire Early," *Wall Street Journal*, March 15, 1972, p. 1.

33. Don Pellicano, "Retirement Counseling," *Personnel Journal,* 42 (July 1973), p. 615.

section
6

Organizational Maintenance

Healthy and safe employees are likely to be more productive than those who are affected by unhealthy or unsafe occurrences. Every year organizations lose money because of illnesses, accidents, and injuries on the job. A part of personnel management is to provide employees with working environments that are safe and to insure that employees with health problems receive help.

Traditionally, safety received only minor attention in many organizations. The Occupational Safety and Health Act of 1970 has changed this outlook and added a new dimension to personnel management responsibilities. The regulations contained in the act are complex and sometimes compliance is difficult. Managers must also maintain an atmosphere of safety consciousness in the organization through continuous communication. Suggestions on dealing with the problems of health and safety and some details of the Occupational Safety and Health Act are included in Chapter 15.

Coordination of personnel efforts requires policies and rules. However, if not well designed and enforced, policies and rules can be sources of irritation and may rightly be targets of criticism. Chapter 16 deals with organizational coordination as it is affected by personnel policies and rules and formal personnel communication.

Vital to personnel coordination efforts are adequate personnel records. These records are necessary for day-to-day monitoring of personnel activities. In addition, personnel records serve as a major source of personnel research data. Personnel research activities provide the organization with a more analytical perspective for decision making than just managerial intuition. Personnel records and research are discussed in Chapter 17.

chapter 15

Personnel Health and Safety

When you have read this chapter, you should be able to:

1. Define health and safety and explain their importance in an organization.

2. Discuss several factors affecting health and safety in organizations.

3. Explain the impact of four health problems in organizations.

4. Discuss the basic provisions of the Occupational Safety and Health Act of 1970.

5. Identify and briefly explain the basic components of a systems approach to safety.

Near Proximity?

Peter Schultz is personnel director for Mid-Coastal Freight and Trucking, Inc. Recently Peter had a "visit" from Herman Medina, an OSHA compliance officer. On a tour of the warehouse Herman found no violations.

However, when Herman got to the loading dock he stopped to talk to two of the men loading a truck. Since the men had just finished loading some fairly heavy boxes, Herman asked them if they had ever gotten hurt loading boxes that size. Clyde Cutler, one of the loaders, said, "Sometimes we drop one and maybe we cut our hands or arms some. But some mercurochrome and a gauze bandage from the first-aid box usually stops the bleeding and it heals pretty quick."

Herman asked Peter if he was trained in first-aid and Peter said, "No." Herman then asked if anyone at the warehouse had been certified by the Red Cross in first-aid. Peter said no, primarily because a hospital is located about 15 to 20 blocks away. Herman said that was not sufficient because somebody injured would be at least ten minutes from treatment. Herman then described OSHA standard 42,1910 (72c) on first-aid: "At least one employee must be Red Cross certified if an infirmary, clinic, or hospital is not in near proximity to the workplace." Peter groaned when Herman handed him a violation statement.

Organizations are obligated to provide employees with a safe and healthful environment. Requiring employees to work with unsafe equipment or in areas where hazards are not controlled is a highly questionable practice. Employees can perform their jobs better in safe environments with proper tools.

This chapter looks at ways organizations can maintain safe working environments for employees. Both managers and personnel specialists are involved in health and safety in an organization.

DISTINCTION BETWEEN HEALTH AND SAFETY

The terms "health" and "safety" are very closely related. Although they are often used in the same context, a distinction should be made.

HEALTH refers to a general state of physical, mental, and emotional well-being.

Health is a broader and somewhat more nebulous term than safety. A healthy person is one who is free of illness or injury. Mental or emotional health refers to the absence of mental or emotional problems which impair normal human functions. Unhealthy employees cannot perform as effectively as healthy ones. However, exactly what is healthy or normal behavior is open to interpretation. Health maintenance or management refers to maintaining the overall well-being of an individual.

Typically, safety concerns physical well-being instead of mental or emotional well-being. The main purpose of effective safety programs in organizations is to *prevent* work-related injuries and accidents.

SAFETY refers to protection of the physical health of people.

The two objectives of health and safety policies are the protection of personnel and the safe interaction of people and the working environment. Because many employers' efforts to meet these objectives were inadequate, a federal law entitled the Occupational Safety and Health Act of 1970 was passed. This act has had a tremendous impact and any person interested in personnel management should develop a working knowledge of the act's provisions and implications.

Can you define health and safety?

Health and Safety Interface

As Figure 15–1 indicates, the primary safety responsibility in an organization usually falls on supervisors and managers. A personnel unit specialist or safety specialist can help investigate accidents, produce safety program materials, and conduct formal safety training. However, the manager is critical in maintaining healthful and safe working conditions and a sound work force.

The supervisor or manager is on the "front line" for maintaining a healthy work environment. Bill Cargill, a supervisor in a ball-bearing plant, has several health and safety related responsibilities. Examples of some of his responsibilities are: reminding an employee to wear safety glasses; checking on the cleanliness of the work area; observing his employees' behaviors to see if any of them have alcohol, drug, or emotional problems which affect their work behavior; and recommending equipment changes (such as screens, railings, or guards) to specialists in the organization.

Harriett Maykin, a personnel safety specialist in the same plant, has other safety responsibilities: maintaining government required health

FIGURE 15–1 Health and safety interface.

Personnel Unit	Managers
Coordinates health and safety programs	Monitor health and safety of employees daily
Develops safety reporting system	Coach employees to be safety conscious
Provides accident investigation expertise	Investigate accidents
Provides technical expertise on accident research and prevention	Observe health and safety behavior of employees daily

and safety records; coordinating a safety training class for new employees; assisting Bill in investigating an accident in which an employee injured his hand; and developing plantwide safety communication and information materials. The interface between a supervisor such as Bill and a personnel specialist such as Harriett is important for a coordinated maintenance effort.

NATURE OF HEALTH AND SAFETY

Every year employers lose an astounding amount of money and resources because of accidents. A Bureau of Labor Statistics Survey for a recent one-year period provides some rather startling statistics.[1]

1. On the average, about one of every 11 workers in private industry experienced a job-related injury or illness.
2. About 4.8 million work-related injuries and illnesses occurred.
3. Work-related fatalities declined from 5,900 in the previous year to 5,300.
4. Of the nearly 5 million recordable work-related injuries that occurred during the year in private industries, 97 percent were injuries, 3 percent illnesses.
5. Lost work days totaled 29.8 million days, equivalent to 53.1 lost work days/100 workers.

With problems of this magnitude, health and safety must be a prime concern in the management of human resources. Knowledge about factors affecting employee health and safety are important.

Worker Attitudes and Accidents

Because health and safety deal with individual well-being, employees' attitudes about safety should be considered in planning safety programs. Employees' attitudes toward their working conditions, accidents, and jobs should be analyzed when an organization's health and safety activities are examined. Many more problems are caused by careless employees than by machines or employer negligence. The safety director for a supermarket chain estimated that "80% of wholesale and retail-related accidents are due to unsafe acts by employees versus 20% due to unsafe physical conditions."[2]

At one time, it was thought that workers who were dissatisfied with their jobs would have a higher accident rate. However, this assumption has been questioned in recent years. One study of accident proneness found that younger and less-experienced employees were involved in more injuries and accidents. This same study suggested that there were some personality and emotional differences between people who had no accidents and those who had repeated accidents.[3] Another study concluded there was little significant relationship between the number of accidents and the psychological factors of the people involved.[4] Together, these studies suggest that while employees' personalities and attitudes may have an effect on accidents, a cause-and-effect relationship is very difficult to establish.

Worker Boredom and Monotony

Employees doing the same job repeatedly each day can become bored. Two results are that they either begin to pay less attention to the task or develop bad habits which can cause accidents and injuries. Some accidents can be prevented by designing machines and equipment areas so that workers who may daydream periodically or who perform rather mechanical jobs cannot injure themselves or others.

Another way to deal with worker boredom is to relieve the monotony by redesigning the job. Elements of job design such as job scope and job depth were discussed in Chapter 6.

Working Conditions and Health and Safety

As noted above, one of the best ways to prevent accidents is to construct the working environment so that it is very difficult for employees to injure themselves. Providing safety equipment and guards on machinery and installing emergency switches are equipment changes which are often made to prevent accidents. To prevent Mary Bents, a punch-press operator, from mashing her finger, a guard is attached to a machine so her hand cannot accidentally slip into the machine. Actions such as providing safety rails; keeping aisles clear; and providing adequate ventilation, lighting, heating, and air conditioning all can help make the work environment safer.

A specialized field which has developed to engineer the work environment is *ergonomics*. Ergonomics comes from the word *"ergon,"* meaning *"work"* and *"omics,"* meaning *"management of."* Ergonomics is an approach which examines the interaction between the worker, the job, and the working environment.[5] An ergonomist studies the physiological, psychological, and engineering design aspects of a job. Other aspects such as fatigue factors, lighting, tools, equipment layouts, and placement of controls are also considered by an ergonomist.

What are factors that may affect health and safety?

HEALTH

Employee health problems are inevitable in all organizations. These problems can range from illnesses such as a cold or flu to serious injuries on the job or elsewhere. Some employees have emotional problems; others have drinking or drug problems. All these affect organizational opeartions.

Health Problems

There are four major health problem areas which may have direct relevance to personnel management: *physical illness, emotional illness, alcoholism,* and *drug abuse.*

Physical illness.   Physical illnesses and problems may reduce an employee's ability to perform a job. As was pointed out in Chapter 14, organizations help employees with physical illnesses and problems by providing hospitalization and health insurance. However, most health programs focus on helping employees to *get well* rather than *preventing* them from getting sick or minimizing problems. The Health Maintenance Organization, mentioned in Chapter 14, is an exception which deals specifically with illness prevention.

Some organizations have staff medical professionals such as doctors or nurses to treat minor illnesses and job-related injuries. If a claims clerk at a large insurance company came to work feeling rather weak because he had a cold, the company doctor could prescribe some medication to help the clerk feel better. Many larger companies provide on-site medical assistance because the Occupational Safety and Health Act of 1970 (to be discussed later) requires certain first-aid treatment and health services to be available in a "close proximity" to work stations.

Employers may sponsor general physical examinations yearly or on a regular basis. Organizations providing this service are investing in the physical health of employees who may not see a doctor regularly because of work schedules, personal reluctance, or lack of money. One company provides check-ups for employees so that they have the opportunity for good physical health and hygiene examinations. With the vigilance of the health team, potential problems can be treated early. The firm's management believes that the company can benefit financially and organizationally if healthier employees are on the job.

One survey showed that 53 percent of 447 companies surveyed had company-sponsored health examinations for their executives.[6] For many executives the physical demands are often great because of extensive travel and work pressures. Attempting to pinpoint potential health problems and deal with them early allows an employer to have the continued service of a valuable individual. Sometimes physical health and hygiene problems are caused by emotional or mental health factors.

Emotional illness.　　Emotional or mental illnesses and hygiene problems can be caused by many complex and interacting factors. Causes of these problems can be related to an individual's personality, job, personal conduct, or contact with others. For example, extreme anxiety and emotional disturbance might be related to the death of a loved one, divorce, or physical changes due to age.

When an emotional problem becomes so severe that it disrupts an employee's ability to function normally, the employee should be directed to appropriate professionals for help. Because emotional problems are very difficult to diagnose, supervisors and managers should not become deeply involved in them. Assume that a quality control inspector is emotionally upset because of his marital difficulties. His supervisor does not want to get personally involved in trying to solve the employee's problems. Even though genuinely concerned about the employee, the supervisor should know that the employee's problems are beyond the scope of direct company assistance. Most supervisors and managers are concerned about employees' problems, but realize that appropriate professionals are better qualified to help them.

One method that organizations are using to deal with employee emotional problems is an *employee assistance program.* In such a program, an employer establishes a liason relationship with a social service counseling agency. Employees who have problems may then contact the agency, either voluntarily or by employer referral, for assistance with a broad range of problems. Much or all of the counseling costs are paid for by the employer up to a preestablished limit.

Alcoholism. Alcoholism is a costly health problem. It has been estimated that the problem drinker on the payroll costs American industry approximately $10 billion a year in lost production, mishandling of resources, sick pay, absenteeism, and other costs. Approximately 6 to 10 percent of the American work force suffers from various degrees of alcoholism.[7]

Because of the problems and costs involved, organizations are sponsoring programs to deal with alcoholic managers and workers. Usually these programs are enthusiastically supported by unions. Some health insurance coverage includes alcoholism as a disease so that employees are helped to pay for treatment of their drinking problems. By dealing with alcoholism, employers are able to retain otherwise good workers who are disabled by drinking problems.

The director of the alcoholism program for the New York City Police Department indicated that an employee program resulted in increased productivity and significant savings in training costs. The program director indicated that the program helped 618 police officers save their jobs, and 75 percent of those officers returned to full duty.[8] Insurance companies have been very active in providing comprehensive programs dealing with alcoholism. The Kemper, Equitable, Traveler's, and Prudential Insurance companies have employee programs which consider alcoholism as a disease that can be treated.

One process for dealing with problem drinkers is shown in Figure 15–2. Managers and supervisors should encourage employees with drinking problems to seek specialized treatment. This treatment can be made available through a company program, a cooperative program between an employer and a union, a private agency, state or local health and social service agencies, or voluntary organizations such as Alcoholics Anonymous.

Assisting employees who have drinking problems is a part of good personnel management. Although some alcoholic employees may resist treatment at first, alcohol rehabilitation programs generally have had a success rate of 50 to 75 percent.[9] Instead of immediately firing an employee with a drinking problem, many employers are recognizing their responsibilities in dealing with alcoholism.

Drug abuse. The impact of drug abuse is evident throughout society— and in organizations. These problems cover the full range, from the use of minor drugs, such as marijuana, to the overuse of legal drugs, such as barbituates and tranquilizers, and illegal hard drugs, such as heroin. In a survey of 222 companies, 117 reported they found some type of drug abuse among their employees.[10] Employers have recently begun to respond to their employees' drug-related problems. It has been estimated that approximately 100 U.S. corporations have an active drug-abuse control program.[11]

Managers attempting to deal with the problem of employee drug abuse should be aware of drug-induced changes in an employee's behavior.

FIGURE 15–2 Policy on problem drinking.

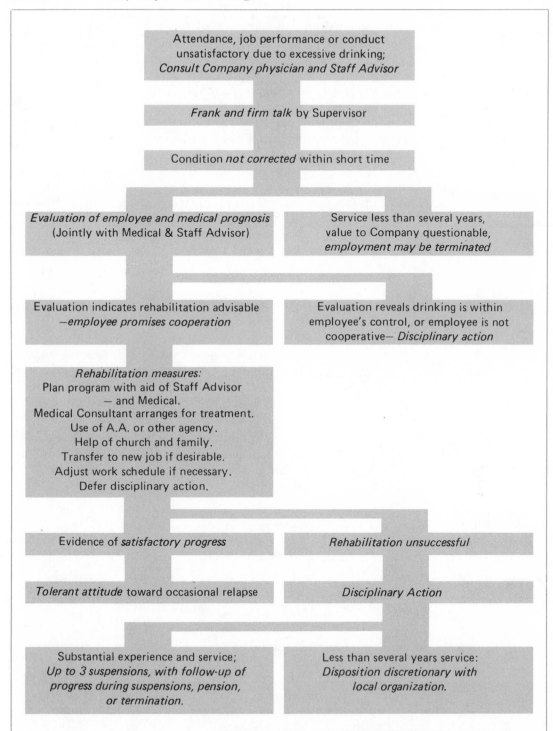

Attendance, job performance or conduct
unsatisfactory due to excessive drinking;
Consult Company physician and Staff Advisor

Frank and firm talk by Supervisor

Condition *not corrected* within short time

Evaluation of employee and medical prognosis
(Jointly with Medical & Staff Advisor)

Service less than several years,
value to Company questionable,
employment may be terminated

Evaluation indicates rehabilitation advisable
—*employee promises cooperation*

Evaluation reveals drinking is within
employee's control, or employee is not
cooperative— *Disciplinary action*

Rehabilitation measures:
Plan program with aid of Staff Advisor
— and Medical.
Medical Consultant arranges for treatment.
Use of A.A. or other agency.
Help of church and family.
Transfer to new job if desirable.
Adjust work schedule if necessary.
Defer disciplinary action.

Evidence of *satisfactory progress*

Rehabilitation unsuccessful

Tolerant attitude toward occasional relapse

Disciplinary Action

Substantial experience and service;
*Up to 3 suspensions, with follow-up of
progress during suspensions, pension,
or termination.*

Less than several years service:
*Disposition discretionary with
local organization.*

(Source: August Ralston, "Employee Alcoholism: Response of the Largest Industrials," *The Personnel Administrator,* August 1977, p. 52. Reprinted with permission.)

Possible tip-offs to drug abuse are excessive absenteeism, increased tardiness, decreasing job performance, and unexplained personality and behavior changes. However, a supervisor or manager can do little other than inform the company physician or counseling specialist about the problem and direct the employee to appropriate professionals.

Policies on drug abuse and how to deal with it are needed in many organizations. Improving selection procedures to screen out persons who abuse drugs is a possible solution. Some firms utilize urinalysis tests as a part of their selection process. This screening is very imprecise and may discriminate against persons who once had a drug problem but have overcome it. Another difficulty is defining exactly what constitutes a drug problem. Obviously, smoking marijuana occasionally is a different matter than being hooked on heroin. To deal with drug problems, organizations need to: (1) develop an awareness of drug problems, and (2) develop organizational policies and responses to cope with drug abuse.

Personnel Management and Health Maintenance

The various health problems discussed above are legitimate and real concerns in many organizations. At one extreme, responses can include ignoring or firing problem employees. At the other extreme, managers and organizations can provide special programs and services for employees with health problems. A survey of methods used in dealing with a variety of employee problems is capsuled in Figure 15–3.

Providing work conditions conducive to good employee health is a necessary part of personnel management. Safety is a subset of maintaining the health of the human resources in an organization.

Can you identify and discuss four health problems facing organizations?

SAFETY

A safe work environment should be a prime concern for all managers and employees. The statistics mentioned earlier reflect the costs in lost productivity and human suffering. Safety was one of the most neglected areas of personnel management for years. The Williams-Steiger Occupational Safety and Health Act of 1970 was passed to require employers to be more health and safety conscious.

FIGURE 15–3 Methods for dealing with problem employees.

	Alcoholism	Marijuana Abuse	Prescription drug abuse	Hard drug addiction	Emotional illness	Personal crises
Consultation with supervisor	55%	40%	32%	26%	43%	55%
Discipline short of discharge	35(49)	15(17)	12	8(11)	9(16)	12
Discharge	29(15)	28(27)	15	25(33)	9 (7)	9
In-house counseling	45(67)	20(21)	22	15(18)	43(43)	55
Referral to outside agency	60(65)	38(21)	31	35(20)	55(67)	58
Other (Please describe)	14	8	6	8	9	8
No Response	12	37	48	48	28	18

Note: Figures are percentages of companies using specified method for each problem. Figures in parentheses are results of 1970 survey

(Source: "Counseling Policies and Programs for Employed With Problems," ASPA-BNA Survey #34, *Bulletin to Management*, March 23, 1978, p. (Washington, D.C.: The Bureau of National Affairs). BNA Policy & Practice Series The Bureau of National Affairs, Inc.)

Occupational Safety and Health Act of 1970

The Occupational Safety and Health Act, which became effective in 1971, is a part of the nation's labor law. The purpose of the act is "to assure so far as possible every working man or woman in the Nation safe and healthful working conditions and to preserve our human resources."[12] Every employer engaged in commerce who has one or more employees is covered by the act. Farmers having fewer than ten employees are exempt from the act. Also covered under other health and safety acts are some employers in specific industries such as coal mining. Federal, state, and local government employees are covered by separate provisions of the act.

Basic provisions. The act established the Occupational Safety and Health Administration, known as OSHA. To implement the act, numerous specific standards were established concerning equipment and working environment regulations. OSHA often uses national standards developed by engineering and quality control groups but they are not *voluntary* standards that the employer pledges to meet. Employers are *required* to meet the provisions and standards under OSHA. The act also established the National Institute of Occupational Safety and Health (NIOSH)

FIGURE 15–4 Sample OSHA construction standards.

Potable water. Where single service cups (to be used but once) are supplied, both a sanitary container for the unused cups and a receptacle for disposing of the used cups shall be provided.

If the variations in noise level involve maxima at intervals of 1 second or less, it is to be considered continuous.

Helmets for the head protection of employees exposed to high voltage electrical shock and burns shall meet the specifications contained in American National Standards Institute, Z89.2–1971.

Guardrails, made of lumber not less than 2 × 4 inches (or other material providing equivalent protection), approximately 42 inches high, with a midrail of 1 × 6 inch lumber (or other material providing equivalent protection), and toeboard shall be installed at all open sides and ends on all scaffolds more than 10 feet above the ground or floor. Toeboards shall be a minimum of 4 inches in height. Wire mesh shall be installed in accordance with paragraph (a)(6) of this section.

Mason's adjustable multiple-point suspension scaffolds. (1) The scaffold shall be capable of sustaining a working load of 50 pounds per square foot and shall not be loaded in excess of that figure.

(Source: Occupational Safety and Health Administration, U.S. Department of Labor, "Construction Safety and Health Regulations," *Federal Register*, vol. 39, no. 122 (Washington, D.C.: U.S. Government Printing Office, June 24, 1974), pp. 22809, 22910, 22836, 22837.)

as a supporting body to do research and develop standards. Figure 15–4 gives some examples of some rather specific OSHA standards.

It is easy to see that these standards contain precise conditions for compliance. Employers are responsible for knowing about and informing their employees of safety and health standards established by OSHA. In addition, they are required to enforce the use of personal protective equipment and to provide safety communication to employees so they are aware of safety considerations. Employees who report safety violations to OSHA cannot be punished or discharged.

Record-keeping requirements. OSHA has established a standard national system for recording occupational injuries, accidents, and fatalities. Employers are required to maintain an annual detailed record of the various types of accidents for inspection by OSHA representatives and for submission to the agency.

Figure 15–5 shows the basic form that is required by OSHA for reporting accidents that do occur. There are several types of injuries or illnesses defined by the act:

1. *Injury or illness-related deaths.*
2. *Lost-time or disabling injuries:* disabling or job-related injuries

FIGURE 15–5   OSHA form.

OSHA No. 101
Case or File No. _____

Form approved
OMB No. 44R 1453

Supplementary Record of Occupational Injuries and Illnesses

EMPLOYER

1. Name _____

2. Mail address _____
   (No. and street)   (City or town)   (State)

3. Location, if different from mail address _____

INJURED OR ILL EMPLOYEE

4. Name _____ Social Security No. _____
   (First name)   (Middle name)   (Last name)

5. Home address _____
   (No. and street)   (City or town)   (State)

6. Age _____   7. Sex: Male_____ Female_____ (Check one)

8. Occupation _____
   (Enter regular job title, *not* the specific activity he was performing at time of injury.)

9. Department _____
   (Enter name of department or division in which the injured person is regularly employed, even
   though he may have been temporarily working in another department at the time of injury.)

THE ACCIDENT OR EXPOSURE TO OCCUPATIONAL ILLNESS

10. Place of accident or exposure _____
    (No. and street)   (City or town)   (State)
    If accident or exposure occurred on employer's premises, give address of plant or establishment in which
    it occurred. Do not indicate department or division within the plant or establishment. If accident oc-
    curred outside employer's premises at an identifiable address, give that address. If it occurred on a pub-
    lic highway or at any other place which cannot be identified by number and street, please provide place
    references locating the place of injury as accurately as possible.

11. Was place of accident or exposure on employer's premises? _____ (Yes or No)

12. What was the employee doing when injured? _____
    (Be specific. If he was using tools or equipment or handling material,
    _____
    name them and tell what he was doing with them.)
    _____

13. How did the accident occur? _____
    (Describe fully the events which resulted in the injury or occupational illness. Tell what
    _____
    happened and how it happened. Name any objects or substances involved and tell how they were involved. Give
    _____
    full details on all factors which led or contributed to the accident. Use separate sheet for additional space.)

OCCUPATIONAL INJURY OR OCCUPATIONAL ILLNESS

14. Describe the injury or illness in detail and indicate the part of body affected. _____
    (e.g.: amputation of right index finger
    _____
    at second joint; fracture of ribs; lead poisoning; dermatitis of left hand, etc.)

15. Name the object or substance which directly injured the employee. (For example, the machine or thing
    he struck against or which struck him; the vapor or poison he inhaled or swallowed; the chemical or ra-
    diation which irritated his skin; or in cases of strains, hernias, etc., the thing he was lifting, pulling, etc.)
    _____
    _____

16. Date of injury or initial diagnosis of occupational illness _____
    (Date)

17. Did employee die? _____ (Yes or No)

OTHER

18. Name and address of physician _____

19. If hospitalized, name and address of hospital _____
    _____

    Date of report _____ Prepared by _____
    Official position _____

which cause an employee to miss his or her regularly scheduled work on the day following the accident.

3. *Medical care injuries:* injuries requiring treatment by a physician but that do not cause an employee to miss a regularly scheduled work turn.

4. *Minor injuries:* injuries which require first-aid treatment and do not cause an employee to miss the next regularly scheduled work turn.

The record-keeping requirements under OSHA are summarized in Figure 15–6. Notice that only minor injuries do not have to be recorded for OSHA.

Criticism of OSHA's record-keeping requirements resulted in significant changes in 1977. Many small employers having less than ten employees were exempted from having to complete the summary records. Only those small firms meeting the following conditions must complete OSHA Form 200, the basic reporting document: (1) those firms

FIGURE 15–6   Guide to recordability of cases under the Occupational Safety and Health Act.

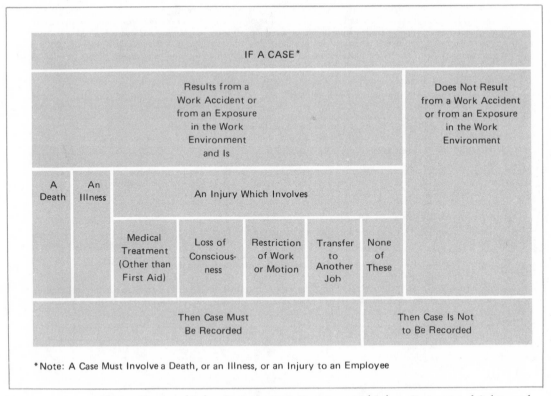

(Source: Bureau of Labor Statistics, U.S. Department of Labor, *Occupational Safety and Health Statistics: Concepts and Methods* (Washington, D.C.: U.S. Government Printing Office, 1975), p. 2.)

having frequent hospitalization injuries or illnesses, (2) those firms having work-related deaths; (3) those firms included in OSHA's annual labor statistics survey.

Managers may go to extreme lengths to avoid lost-time or medical care injuries. For example, if several managers are trained in first-aid, some injuries can be treated on the work site. In one situation an employee's back injuries were treated with heat packs to avoid counting the accident as a medical care injury.

Until OSHA tightened regulations, many employers would move injured employees to other jobs to avoid counting an injury as a lost-time injury. Assume a seamstress in a clothing factory injured her hand on the job so that she could not operate her sewing machine. Her employer had her carry thread to other operators and perform other "make work" jobs so that she did not miss work. Current regulations attempt to control this type of subterfuge by requiring employees to perform the same type of job.

There are several major reasons why employers try to make injuries appear less severe for reporting purposes. An abnormal number of lost-time or medical care injuries are warning flags to OSHA representatives and may lead to intensive investigations. Also, an employer's workmen's compensation and liability insurance coverage costs may be affected by increased injuries and accidents.

Accident frequency and severity rates also must be calculated. OSHA regulations require organizations to calculate injury frequency rates per 100 full-time employees on an annual basis. The *accident frequency rate* is figured as follows:[13]

$$\frac{N}{MH} \times 200,000$$

where N = number of occupational injuries and illnesses
MH = total hours worked by all employees during reference year
200,000 = base for 100 full-time equivalent workers (working 40 hours per week, 50 weeks per year).

Accident severity rates are computed by figuring the number of lost-time cases, the number of lost workdays, and the number of deaths. These figures are then related to total man hours/100 full-time employees, and compared to industrywide rates and other employers rates.

Inspection requirements. The 1970 act provides for on-the-spot inspection by OSHA agents, known as *compliance officers or inspectors*. In the original act an employer *could not refuse* entry to an OSHA inspector. Furthermore, the original act prohibited a compliance officer from giving prior notification of an inspection. This provision was included to allow inspection of normal operations, instead of allowing an employer to "tidy up." This so-called no-knock provision was challenged in numerous court suits. Finally, in 1978, the U.S. Supreme Court made a definite ruling on this issue.

Marshall v. Barlow's Inc.[14]   In this case, an Idaho plumbing and air conditioning firm, Barlow's, refused entry to an OSHA inspector. The employer argued that the no-knock provision violated the Fourth Amendment of the U.S. Constitution, which deals with "unreasonable search and seizure." The government, through Ray Marshall, the Secretary of Labor, argued that the no-knock provision was necessary for enforcement of the 1970 act and that the Fourth Amendment did not apply to a business situation with employees and customers having access to the firm.

The Supreme Court rejected the government's arguments and held that safety inspectors must produce a search warrant if an employer refuses to allow an inspector voluntarily. However, the Court ruled that an inspector does not have to prove probable cause to obtain a search warrant. A warrant can be obtained if a search is part of a general enforcement plan.

Although this decision was initially viewed as a victory for employers, later analysis of the decision revealed that the Supreme Court took a "middle-of-the-road" position. Inspectors no longer must be admitted through the no-knock provision. However, warrants are relatively easy to obtain because of the "general enforcement plan" aspects of the decision. An employer can refuse admittance, but the process of obtaining a warrant for OSHA is not extremely restrictive.

Conduct of inspection.   When the compliance officer arrives, the manager should request to see the inspector's credentials. After entering, the OSHA officer typically requests a meeting with the top representative or manager in the organization. The officer also may request that a union representative, an employee, and a company representative be present as the inspection is conducted. The OSHA inspector checks an organization's records to see if they are being maintained and how many accidents have occurred. Following this review of the safety records, the inspector conducts an on-the-spot inspection and may use a wide variety of equipment to test compliance with the standards.

Figure 15–7 provides a list of some of the equipment that may be used by an OSHA compliance officer. Following the inspection, the compliance officer can issue citations for violations of standards and provisions of the act.

Violations.   The type of citations issued depends on the severity and extent of the violation and the employer's knowledge of possible violations. There are basically five types:

FIGURE 15–7   What the OSHA inspector carries.

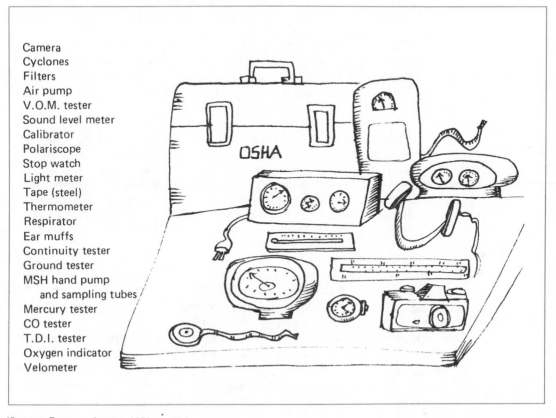

Camera
Cyclones
Filters
Air pump
V.O.M. tester
Sound level meter
Calibrator
Polariscope
Stop watch
Light meter
Tape (steel)
Thermometer
Respirator
Ear muffs
Continuity tester
Ground tester
MSH hand pump
    and sampling tubes
Mercury tester
CO tester
T.D.I. tester
Oxygen indicator
Velometer

(Source: Factory, August 1972, p. 28.)

1. *Imminent Danger.* An imminent danger violation is issued if there is reasonable certainty the condition will cause death or serious physical harm if it is not corrected immediately. Imminent danger violations are handled on the highest priority basis. They are reviewed by a regional OSHA director, and the condition must be corrected immediately. If the violation is serious enough and the employer does not cooperate, a representative of OSHA may go to a federal judge and obtain an injunction to close down the company until the violation is corrected. The absence of any guard railings to prevent an employee from falling three stories into heavy machinery could be classified an imminent danger violation.

2. *Serious.* A serious violation is issued if there is great probability the condition could cause death or serious physical harm and the employer should know of the condition. Examples would be the absence of a protective screen on a lathe, allowing an employee to easily mangle a hand, or the lack of a safety cover on an electric saw.

3. *Other-than-serious.* This type of violation is one that could have an impact on employees' health or safety but probably would not cause death or serious harm. Having loose ropes in a work area on which people could trip and hurt themselves might be classified as a nonserious violation.

4. *De minimis.* A *De minimis* violation is one that does not have direct and immediate relationship to the employees' safety or health. A citation is not issued but a notice of the violation is given to the employer. For example, lack of doors on toilet stalls would be a *De minimis* violation.

5. *Willful and Repeated.* This type of violation is somewhat different from the others. Willful and repeated violations deal with employers who have been previously cited for violations. If an employer knew about a safety violation and/or had been warned for a violation and did not correct the problem, a second citation is issued. The penalty for a willful and repeated violation can go as high as $10,000. If death results from a willful violation, a jail term of six months can be imposed.

In place of a rather rigid fine system, OSHA inspectors now use a regulated penalty calculation process. This process, which is somewhat complex, considers the probability of occurrences and the severity of possible injury. Then a penalty is calculated.

One significant change OSHA made in 1977 is that no fines are levied if there are ten or less violations which are "other than serious." Thus, a machine shop owner who had eight of the lesser violations would be given a citation, but no penalty would be imposed if the violations were corrected by the next inspection.

Safety consultation.   OSHA, in conjunction with state governments, has established a safety consultation service. An employer can contact the state agency and have a state safety consultant conduct an advisory inspection. This state official cannot issue citations or penalties and generally is prohibited from providing OSHA with any information obtained during the consultation visit. Such a visit provides an employer an opportunity to receive a report useful in preventing future difficulties when OSHA does conduct an inspection.

Effects of OSHA

OSHA has had a significant impact on the operation of American organizations. It has been able to accomplish, at least partially, some of its goals for reducing accident and injury rates. In response to the query, "Has the act been effective?", the answer has to be discussed on several fronts. Although the effect on injury rates is still somewhat unclear, it appears that OSHA has been able to reduce the number of accidents and injuries in some cases. A study of the meat-packing industry in one state found that the application of OSHA standards in the meat and meat products industry was significant in reducing the frequency of employee injuries.[15]

OSHA has definitely increased the safety consciousness of employers. Because an organization must always be prepared for an OSHA inspection, managers are forced to serve as constant safety monitors. This safety awareness is evident in managers' attempts to improve the safety consciousness and orientation of their employees.

Criticisms of OSHA

Most employers agree with the act's intent to provide healthy and safe working conditions for all employees. However, criticism of OSHA has emerged for several reasons.

One reason is that *some standards are vague* and it is difficult to know whether or not one is complying. In the opening case a standard required that a plant having a certain number of workers have qualified medical personnel "in close proximity" to the work area. This standard has been the subject of several OSHA violations and cases; but what is "close proximity?" Is it in the work area? In the plant? Is it a hospital ten minutes away?

Secondly, the *rules are often very complicated and technical.* Often small-business owners and managers who do not have a safety specialist find the standards very difficult to read and understand. The presence of many very minor standards also hurt OSHA's credibility. To counter such criticism, in 1978, OSHA proposed the revocation of about 1,100 minor or confusing standards.

A third major criticism is that the OSHA inspector *cannot serve as a safety counselor.* However, with the establishment of the consultation program, this criticism loses some strength.

A fourth concern is that the *cost of correcting violations* may be prohibitive for many employers. Requiring a small employer to make major structural changes in a building may not be financially possible. The employer may have to close down the operation. The cost of compliance may not be realistic given the cost of the violation. For example, requiring a small employer with ten employees to reconstruct its restroom facilities with partitions, split toilet seats, and so on, may not be realistic because of the employer's limited financial resources.

A fifth problem with OSHA is different in perspective. With so many employers to inspect, many employers have only a relatively *small probability of being inspected.* Labor unions and others have criticized OSHA and Congress for not providing enough inspectors. One interesting study revealed that with the probability of being inspected and receiving a fine so low, many employers pay little attention to OSHA enforcement efforts.[16]

In summary, it can be said that OSHA has had a significant impact on organizations. However, not all of the results have been of a positive nature. Some fine tuning of the law and enforcement efforts is likely. As changes are made, continuing compliance with OSHA should be a major focus of any organization's efforts. To do this, safety programs should be approached systematically and comprehensively.

Can you discuss the nature and provisions of OSHA?

A SYSTEMS APPROACH TO SAFETY

Effective safety management considers the type of safety problems, accidents, employees, and technology in the organizational setting. Furthermore, the systems approach to safety recognizes the importance of the human element in safety. Simply attempting to engineer machines, without dealing with the behavioral reactions of employees and without trying to encourage safe behavior, would be "compartmentalizing" the safety effort. There are several basic components in a systematic approach to safety.

Organizational Commitment

Any comprehensive and systematic approach to safety begins with an organization's commitment to a comprehensive safety effort. This effort should be coordinated from the top to involve all members of the organization and be reflected in their actions and work. One safety expert states, "The interest and involvement of top-management in safety measures is the most important factor in the reduction of accidents."[17] If the president of a small electrical manufacturing firm does not wear a hard hat in the manufacturing shop, he can hardly expect to enforce a requirement that all employees wear hard hats in the shop. Unfortunately, sincere support of top management for a safety program often is missing from many safety programs.

Coordinated Safety Efforts

Once a commitment is made to organizational safety, planning efforts must be coordinated with duties assigned to supervisors, managers, safety specialists, and personnel specialists. Naturally, the types of duties would vary according to the size of the firm and the industry. For this reason, it is inappropriate to suggest a single proper mixture of responsibilities.

Certainly, the primary thrust of any systematic approach to safety revolves around the continued diligence of workers, supervisors, and managerial personnel. Employees who are not reminded of safety violations, who are not encouraged to be safety conscious, or who violate company safety rules and policies are not likely to be safe employees. The safety emphasis must be consistently made and enforced. Properly coordinated efforts between the personnel unit and managers will aid in developing safety-conscious and safety-motivated employees.

Employee Safety Motivation

Encouraging employees to continually keep safety standards in mind while performing their jobs is difficult. Often, employees think safety measures are bothersome and unnecessary until an accident or injury occurs. For example, requiring employees to wear safety glasses in a laboratory may be necessary most of the time. However, the glasses are awkward and employees resist using them even when they know they should have protection. Some employees may have worked for years without them and think this new requirement is a nuisance.

One way to encourage employee safety is to involve all employees at various times in safety training and committees. One study of worker participation in safety programs found that employees could be involved in safety by allowing a cross section of workers to serve on safety inspection teams.[18] Another means to encourage safety is to hold frequent safety meetings with employees.

Accident Investigation

When accidents or injuries do occur, a detailed investigation of the cause must be made and ways to prevent similar accidents from occuring in the future are studied. It has been noted that accident investigation consists of three major parts: (1) the scene, (2) the interview, (3) the report.[19]

In investigating *the scene* of an accident, an attempt is made to determine the physical and environmental conditions that contributed to the accident. Poor lighting, poor ventilation, and wet floors are all possible considerations at the scene. Investigation at the scene of the accident should be done as soon as possible after the accident so that conditions have not significantly changed. One way to obtain an accurate view of an accident scene is to photograph or videotape the scene.

The second phase of the investigation is *the interview*. The injured employee, his or her supervisor, and witnesses to the accident should be interviewed. The interviewer attempts to determine what happened and how the accident was caused. These interviews may also generate some suggestions as to how to prevent similar accidents from occurring in the future.

The third phase of any good accident investigation is the *accident report*. Completion of an accident investigation report provides the data necessary to fill out the forms and records required by OSHA. One of the more humorous accident reports encountered is included as Figure 15–8.

As a part of an investigation, recommendations should be made on how the accident could have been prevented and necessary changes to prevent further accidents. Identifying why an accident occurred is useful, but identifying steps to prevent it from occurring again is the important part of systematic safety.

Accident Research

Closely related to accident investigation is accident research to determine ways to prevent accidents. Employing safety engineers, ergonomists, or having outside experts evaluate the safety of working conditions is useful. If a large number of the same type of accidents seem to be occurring in an organizational unit, a safety education training program may be necessary to emphasize the importance of working safely. Assume that a publishing company reports a greater-than-average number of back injuries caused by employees lifting heavy boxes. Safety training on the proper way to lift heavy objects could be initiated.

Safety Publicity

In addition to safety training, continuous communication programs to develop safety consciousness is necessary. Posting safety policies and rules is part of this effort. Contests, incentives, and posters are additional ways employers can heighten safety awareness. Changing safety posters, continually updating company bulletin boards, and attractively posting company safety information in high traffic areas are recommended actions. Merely sending safety memos is a very inadequate approach to the problem.

One common way to communicate safety ideas is through safety films and videotapes. Clark Equipment Company uses a film to develop safety consciousness and awareness in its forklift truck operators.[20] Viewing possible unsafe situations and the accidents that can result is good exposure to the need for safety.

Evaluation of Safety Efforts

Organizations need to monitor their safety efforts. Just as a firm's accounting records are audited, periodic audits of a firm's safety efforts

FIGURE 15–8   Accident report.

Getting It Coming and Going

One hour after beginning a new job which involved moving a pile of bricks from the top of a two-story house to the ground, a construction worker in Peterborough, Ontario, suffered an accident which hospitalized him. He was instructed by his employer to fill out an accident report. It read:

"Thinking I could save time, I rigged a beam with a pulley at the top of the house, and a rope leading to the ground. I tied an empty barrel on one end of the rope, pulled it to the top of the house, and then fastened the other end of the rope to a tree. Going up to the top of the house, I filled the barrel with bricks.

"Then I went down and unfastened the rope to let the barrel down. Unfortunately, the barrel of bricks was now heavier than I, and before I knew what was happening, the barrel jerked me up in the air.

"I hung on to the rope, and halfway up I met the barrel coming down, receiving a severe blow on the left shoulder.

"I then continued on up to the top, banging my head on the beam and jamming my fingers in the pulley.

"When the barrel hit the ground, the bottom burst, spilling the bricks. As I was now heavier than the barrel, I started down at high speed.

"Halfway down, I met the empty barrel coming up, receiving several cuts and contusions from the sharp edges of the bricks.

At this point, I must have become confused, because I let go of the rope. The barrel came down, striking me on the head, and I woke up in the hospital.

"I respectfully request sick leave."

(Source: Toronto Star (R. J. Griffiths), from *National Lampoon.*)

should also be made. Accident and injury statistics should be compared to previous accident patterns to determine if any significant changes have occurred. This analysis should be designed to measure progress in safety management. A manager at a hospital might measure its safety efforts by comparing the hospital's accident rates to hospital-industry figures and to the rates at other hospitals of the same size in the area.

Another part of safety evaulation is updating safety materials and safety training aids. Also, the accident investigation procedures and accident reporting methods should be evaluated continually to see that these are actually generating ideas useful in reducing accidents. Safety policies and regulations should be reviewed to be sure they comply with both existing and new standards set up by OSHA, state, and professional agencies.

What are the major components of a safety system?

A systematic safety program requires continual effort to maintain safe working environments. Managers and specialists should continually examine the organization's progress in developing a safe and healthful environment for its people.

REVIEW AND PREVIEW

This chapter has examined the importance of personnel health and safety. Maintaining the general well-being of employees requires that an organization look closely at its working conditions and its workers' attitudes toward those conditions. General health and its more applied component safety are both important.

Health problems may be a result of off-the-job illnesses and problems. A manager becomes involved with employee health problems when they hamper the organization's operations. Physical illnesses, emotional illnesses, alcoholism, and drug abuse are four types of employee health problems. Responses by managers to these problems should be to direct employees to appropriate professional help, either inside or outside the organization.

Safety is a direct and applied process that has become more important since the passage of the Occupational Safety and Health Act of 1970. Through the enforcement of this act, the federal government has made personnel health and safety a mandatory concern for managers. OSHA appears to have been a factor in heightening safety awareness and in reducing work-related injuries and accidents, even though some valid criticisms of the act have brought about some modifications.

Meeting the safety requirements of OSHA can be accomplished by a systematic and comprehensive safety effort. An organization must be committed to safety and develop a coordinated safety effort to motivate its employees to be more safety conscious. Through investigation of accidents and evaluation of the organization's safety efforts, managers focus on preventing future accidents and injuries.

Actions aimed at maintaining the health and safety of personnel are one part of organizational maintenance. Another part is the development and maintenance of personnel policies and rules to achieve organizational consistency and coordination. Personnel coordination is facilitated by communicating matters dealing with personnel-related activities. Personnel coordination is examined in Chapter 16.

Review Questions

1. Differentiate between health and safety as personnel activities. Then identify some factors that affect health and safety.
2. Discuss the following statement by a supervisor: "I feel it's my duty to get involved with my employees and their personal problems to show that I truly care about them."
3. Why should a firm be concerned about alcohol and drug usage by employees?
4. Describe the Occupational Safety and Health Act and some of its key provisions.
5. Discuss the following comment: "OSHA should be abolished because it serves to just harrass small businesses."
6. Why is a systems approach to safety important?

OPENING CASE FOLLOW-UP

This case is a narrative description of an actual OSHA case and illustrates the demands that OSHA can place on managers and personnel specialists. In the actual situation the company received a violation and was assessed a $50 fine. However, the employer appealed the violation and it was overturned in a two-to-one decision by the OSHA Review Commission. The majority ruled that the term "near proximity" was too vague. The minority commissioner said the company should be penalized because "near proximity" appears in other standards that have been updated. Also, the minority commissioner emphasized the need for using fairly broad terms that could cover a wide variety of work places and situations.

The impact of OSHA is clearly demonstrated in this case. The advantage of having a trained first-aid individual or very accessible emergency care is an important part of protecting workers. However, the vagueness of the standard led to the employer and the inspector misinterpreting the compliance requirement.

Case: Hairy Harry

Harry H. Harrison's supervisor considered Harry his best subordinate. Harry seemed to enjoy his work as a machine operator, a job he has held at the Miller Manufacturing Company for just over two years now. He has by far the best productivity record of all 22 machine operators. It was only after the accident that Harry's supervisor and others questioned whether Harry's superior speed of performance was hazardous to Harry's health.

The accident occurred when Harry's hair inadvertently became entangled in his machine while he was operating it. Harry suffered a severe and painful scalping of the left side of his head as a result. Harry downplayed the accident and seemed embarrassed by it. It was only after Harry had begun to see the medical bills that Harry decided to notify OSHA. Harry charged specifically that the company should have provided a mechanical guard to prevent hair from being able to enter the machine.

In response to Harry's complaint, an inspection of the company was made by OSHA. The company answered Harry's charges by claiming that it had provided protective caps for workers and countercharged that Harry was the one who was negligent since he would not wear a cap. Harry explained that he did not want to wear the ugly and unpopular cap and that he was somehow under the impression that only women were required to wear the caps. The company showed the OSHA inspector a copy of the company safety rules, one item of which stated that machine operators with hair longer than six inches are required to wear the caps. The safety rules had been read and signed by Harry at the beginning of his employment. Further, the company representative indicated that the company's interpretation of an OSHA regulation was that caps had to be provided but did not require that they be worn. The OSHA inspector and the company safety specialist are now in conference.

QUESTIONS

1. Without having read the specific standard, do you think the firm should receive a citation? If yes, which type?

2. How sound is the company's defense?

3. As a safety specialist, what would you do to get Harry and the other employees to wear the caps that are provided for their own protection?

Notes

1. Bureau of Labor Statistics, U.S. Department of Labor, "BLS Reports Results of Survey of Occupational Injuries and Illnesses for 1975," USDL 74–687, December 8, 1977.

2. "The OSHA Tangle," *Chain Store Age Executive* (April 1975), p. 15.

3. John B. Miner and Mary G. Miner, *Personnel and Industrial Relations*, 3rd ed. (New York: Macmillan, 1977), pp. 433–438.

4. George V. Nichols, "An Exploratory Study of Some of the Psychological Factors Related to Safety," *ASSE Journal* (November 1972), pp. 12–18.

5. "Ergonomics: What's It All About?" *Occupational Hazards* (September 1967), pp. 37–39.

6. "Company-Sponsored Executive Health Examinations—Why?" *Personnel Journal* 52 (November 1973), pp. 994–995.

7. August Ralston, "Employee Alcoholism: Response of the Largest Industrials," *The Personnel Administrator* (August 1977), pp. 50–56.

8. Kevin W. Kane, "The Corporate Responsibility in the Area of Alcoholism," *Personnel Journal*, 54 (July 1975), pp. 380–384.

9. Stanley E. Kaden, "Compassion or Cover-Up, The Alcoholic Employee," *Personnel Journal*, 56 (July 1977), pp. 356–358.

10. Barry Kramer, "National Survey of Drug Abuse in Industry Finds Incidence To Be Fairly Widespread," *Wall Street Journal*, March 12, 1971, p. 6.

11. Doris Baldwin, "The Trouble with Drugs," *Job Safety and Health* (February 1975), p. 4.

12. Occupational Safety and Health Administration, U.S. Department of Labor, *All About OSHA*, OSHA #2056 (Washington, D.C.: U.S. Government Printing Office) p. 3.

13. Bureau of Labor Statistics, U.S. Department of Labor, *Occupational Injuries and Illnesses by Industry*, July 1–December 31, 1971, Bulletin #1798 (Washington, D.C.: U.S. Government Printing Office, 1973), p. 30.

14. *Marshall v. Barlow's Inc.*, 76–1143 (1978).

15. Lawrence P. Ettkin and J. Brad Chapman, "Is OSHA Effective in Reducing Industrial Injuries," *Labor Law Journal*, 28 (April 1975), pp. 236–242.

16. John M. Gleason and Darold T. Barnum, "Effectiveness of OSHA Sanctions in Influencing Employee Behavior: Single and Multi-Period Decision Models," *Accident Analysis and Prevention*, 10 (1978), pp. 35–49.

17. Robert E. McClay, "Professionalizing the Safety Function," *Personnel Journal*, 56 (February 1977), p. 73.

18. Roderick A. Forsgren, "Developing Employee Psychological Advantage through Safety Management," *Environmental Control and Safety Management* (December 1970), pp. 26–30.

19. W. G. Bufkin, "Accident Investigation," *National Safety News* (September 1971), pp. 49–51.

20. "Safety Cinema Strikes Emotional Response," *National Safety News* (January 1975), p. 68.

| chapter 16 | # Personnel Policies and Coordination |

When you have read this chapter, you should be able to:

1. Define the purpose of personnel policies.
2. List and briefly explain at least four forms of formal personnel communications.
3. Describe the three stages in the life cycle of a rule.
4. Explain the nature of progressive discipline.
5. Identify and describe at least four guidelines for developing effective personnel policies and rules.

I Want a Leave

An employee, Linda, wanted to take a day's leave on the Friday after Thanksgiving; this leave would allow her a four-day weekend to visit relatives. Though Linda asked for the day off three weeks in advance, her supervisor, Bob, refused to grant her the leave. The main reason he refused her request was a heavy workload.

Linda complained that this action was unfair and discriminatory because another employee in the section was granted annual leave on that Friday. Furthermore, Linda felt that since she had the annual leave on the books, she was entitled to use it.

Bob replied that the employee who was scheduled to be off that Friday had asked for the leave time at the beginning of the year. Also, while Linda was a clerk/typist, the other employee was an accounting technician and the jobs were dissimilar. Bob stated that company policy gives him the authority to grant leave; and due to the heavy workload, he needed all of his remaining employees.

Linda first complained to Bob's supervisor and requested annual leave, but the supervisor "washed his hands" of the situation by saying the decision belonged entirely to Bob. Next Linda talked with someone in the employee relations section. She again received little sympathy; the employee relations specialist also recited the supervisor's right to request a worker's presence whenever the work load requires it.

Linda then requested an interview with the local union representative, who after listening to Linda's problem, agreed to speak to Bob and his supervisor. The discussion became quite heated and the union representative sides with Linda.

In the following weeks, Bob, his supervisor, and several employees of the section were repeatedly called into conference about Linda's situation. The basic issue of debate was whether or not Bob had the authority and the need to require Linda's attendance on the Friday in question.

Achieving personnel objectives in the organization requires a *coordination* of the efforts and actions of the departments and individuals involved. This coordination does not simply happen. It requires "coordinating mechanisms" and an appropriate communication climate if the activities of a number of different entities are all to be guided in roughly the same direction. If everyone went his or her own way, there would be a great deal of confusion.

The policies and coordination interface is shown in Figure 16–1. Because overall organization policies require input from the personnel unit, and personnel policies require input from other managers as well,

FIGURE 16–1   Personnel policies and coordination interface.

Designs formal mechanisms for coordinating personnel policies	Help in developing personnel policies and rules
Provides advice in development of companywide personnel policies and rules	Review policies and rules with employees
Provides information on proper disciplinary procedures	Enforce employees' observation of rules through discipline
May help explain personnel rules and policies to managers	Serve as first source of explanation of rules and policies for employees

this interface is especially important. Policies and coordination must be developed and managed well if consistency, continuity, and fairness is to exist for the human resources in an organization.

The personnel unit helps to achieve organizational objectives, as well as its own objectives. For example, if the organization has a policy of nondiscrimination in its hiring practice, and an objective of having as many minority individuals in the work force as their proportion in the general population, the personnel unit must design its selection, training, and other programs to help accomplish these objectives. Both *within* the personnel unit and in activities *between* that unit and others in the organization, coordination will be necessary to achieve the objective.

Also, the personnel unit is generally considered the first source of inputs for organizationwide personnel policies. It should be seen as a necessary source of inputs on disciplinary policies and procedures.

Because managers are the main users and enforcers of rules and policies, they should receive some training and explanation in how to use policies and rules effectively. Unless the personnel unit and managers work together in a coordinated manner, there exists the possibility of conflict detrimental to the total organization. In the opening case, the personnel unit and Bob, the supervisor, took a unified and coordinated position on Linda's request. While it is not necessary for the personnel unit to always support other managers, it is critical that any conflict between the two entities be resolved so that employees receive a fair and coordinated response. This coordination of organizational effort requires the development of personnel policies.

POLICIES AND PERSONNEL

Personnel policies may come from many different sources. Policies may be (in effect) imposed from outside the organization. For example, competition for skilled labor may lead to a policy to pay above the area wage for certain classifications of employees.

Long-run objectives of the organization may help dictate personnel policy too. For example, an objective of doubling the organization's size and output in ten years may dictate personnel policies regarding management development and recruiting practices. But, whatever the source of personnel policies, they serve to guide the actions of organizational members.

> POLICIES are general guidelines that regulate organizational actions.

The role policies play in guiding organizational decision requires that they be reviewed regularly. Obsolete policies can cause poor decisions and poor coordination. Also, failure to review, add to, or delete policies as situations change may lead to problems in the future.

To illustrate, some employers in the past followed policies that an employee having alcohol or drug problems should be fired. However, because of social changes and the practices of other employers, many organizations have changed their personnel policies regarding "troubled employees"—those with alcohol, drug, or emotional problems. Figure 16–2 shows a policy statement and supporting procedures for dealing with troubled employees.

What is the nature and purpose of personnel policies?

A variety of personnel coordination activities are built upon personnel policies. The next section examines several important ones.

PERSONNEL COORDINATING MECHANISMS

Organizational activities are coordinated through the interaction of employees, supervisors, and managers. A primary coordination tool is *communication.* Channels from manager to employee, or executive to subordinates, or among managers, or rank-and-file employees must be open. Without effective communication about the efforts of everyone in the organization, progress is difficult. Our purpose in dealing with communication in this chapter is not to replace the kind of material usually covered in organizational behavior or interpersonal communication courses. Rather, the emphasis will be on some formal communication means that are usually thought of as being specifically personnel management in nature. That is, *house organs, employee handbooks, em-*

FIGURE 16–2 Employee assistance program for the troubled employee (Large Northern Manufacturer).

POLICY

The company recognizes that a wide range of human problems which are not directly associated with job functions can affect an employee's work performance. These problems include physical illness, mental or emotional upset, alcoholism, drug abuse, and other concerns. The company has several medical programs which address themselves to these problems with the intent of identifying them at the earliest possible moment and recommending appropriate treatment on an individual and confidential basis.

PROCEDURES
1. The initiation of any action with respect to an employee is contingent upon unsatisfactory job performance resulting from apparent medical or behavioral abnormalities. Judgments regarding unsatisfactory work performance remain the prerogative of cognizant supervision, which has the responsibility of seeking medical assistance through the Medical Department.
2. In the event an employee refuses to undergo diagnosis and treatment, the Employee Relations Division shall be notified.

(Source: ASPA-BNA Survey #34, "Counseling Policies and Programs for Employees with Problems," March 23, 1978p p. 9. BNA Policy & Practice Series, The Bureau of National Affairs, Inc. Used with permission.)

ployee communications committees, suggestion systems, and an *ombudsman* are all formal personnel communication activities.

Rules are also coordination mechanisms. They are more specific behavioral guidelines than policies. For example, one welding company has a policy that states management intends to provide the highest-quality welding service in the area. One of the rules that helps operationalize that policy is that a welder with fewer than five years of welder experience will not be hired. This rule constrains personnel selection decisions. An organization usually has rules for many different phases of operations.

Finally, the need for rules leads to the need to enforce those rules. *Discipline* is a necessary part of every manager's job. Often personnel specialists become involved in either interpreting disciplinary procedures or, in some instances, doing some of the disciplining. Therefore, the last coordinating mechanism considered will be "progressive" discipline.

Coordination through Formal Communication

Formal communication is a necessary component if coordination is to occur. To be effective, this communication must allow the flow of information both up and down in the organization. Personnel information can be formally communicated in several different ways. *Employee handbooks, suggestion systems, employee communication committees,* an *organizational ombudsman,* and numerous *house organs,* such as newspapers and magazines, are some that can be used.

Employee handbook. Providing personnel information through a handbook gives employees a reference source for company policies and rules. The main purpose of an employee handbook is to help employees to function effectively in an organization. Figure 16–3 indicates some items contained in a typical handbook.

Blue Cross of Southern California studied their internal communications and discovered some interesting facts about employee knowledge of the company. Most employees were not familiar with corporate policies and were confused about the organizational structure. To overcome this information deficiency, an employee handbook was published.[1]

FIGURE 16–3   Contents of typical employee handbooks.

Company A
   Who we are—What we do
   History of our company
   Hours of work
   Salary review
   Promotions
   Holidays and vacations
   Illness and accidents; hospital and medical bills; group insurance
   Termination of employment
   Use of the telephone
   Our pension plan

Company B
   Company history
   Pictures of plants and products
   You and your job
   Employee benefits and services
   Company policies and rules
   An insert of the union contract

   A letter explaining the handbook
   Company history
   Organization charts
   Your earnings and your hours
   Your working conditions
   Your security and your future

(Source: Richard M. Machal and Edgar M. Buttenheim, "Employee Handbooks," in Joseph J. Famularo, ed., *Handbook of Modern Personnel Administration* (New York: McGraw-Hill, 1972), p. 74–2. Used with permission.)

One problem with employee handbooks is that the specialists preparing them may not write on the reading level of those who will read them. A study comparing identical company handbooks from 1950 and 1964 showed only a small increase in their readability.[2] One solution is to test the readability of the handbook on a sample of employees before it is published.

Another important factor which should be considered in preparing an employee handbook is its use. Simply giving an employee a handbook and saying, "Here's all the information you need to know," is not sufficient. Some organizations distribute handbooks as part of their orientation process (see Chapter 9). One company periodically gives all employees a written test on the company handbook. Questions consistently missed become the focus of personnel communication efforts. These tests are also used to update the handbook.

Suggestion system. A suggestion system is a formal way to push communication upward through the organization. The opportunity for employees to suggest changes or ways to improve operations may develop loyalty and commitment to the organization. Often an employee in the work unit knows more about how waste can be eliminated or how hazards can be controlled than managers, who are not as close to the job.

A suggestion system should be publicized, and good suggestions should be used. The suggestions should be collected often and evaluated by a suggestion committee, usually composed of managers and nonmanagerial personnel. Suggestions selected by this committee are then passed on to upper management.

Employees submitting useful suggestions should receive a reward. Some rewards are a flat fee such as a savings bond, or a percentage of the savings resulting from the suggestion. For example, a computer programmer whom the authors know works in a hospital. Noticing that the hospital was throwing away all the old computer printouts of patient rosters, she suggested that these printouts be sold to a paper recycling firm. Her suggestion was accepted and she now gets 5 percent of the $1,500 the hospital receives annually for the paper. In one survey of about 1,400 companies with approximately 7½ million employees, over 3½ million suggestions were received and over $42 million in suggestion awards were paid.[3]

The oldest continuously operating suggestion system in the United States is at Eastman Kodak Corporation. It began in 1898 with a $2 award to a man who pointed out the advantages of washing windows in a production department. Since then, over 1.8 million suggestions have been made, 600,000 accepted, and Kodak employees receive over 1.5 million a year for their ideas.[4]

A good suggestion system provides prompt feedback to all employees submitting suggestions. If employees are not told why their suggestions are accepted or rejected, much of the underlying momentum will be lost.

Further, the system should encourage a few meaningful suggestions instead of a large number of trivial ones. A true measure of the success of a suggestion system is the utility of the suggestions received.

Employee communications committees. Some firms have established formal communication committees composed primarily of nonmanagerial employees. The General Electric Company has made effective use of what is called "an employee sounding board" at its large Maryland appliance complex. According to a GE spokesman, current personnel practices and work activities are the most frequent subjects covered by this group.[5]

An approach somewhat similar is in use at Norton Company, an industrial manufacturing firm in Massachusetts. In this firm, 21 in-plant "employee counselors" have been appointed who assist first-line supervisors by providing information to other workers on company personnel policies and practices. These communication counselors also provide some employee assistance counseling on personal job-related problems. The personnel director for Norton Company comments: "The In-Plant Counselor Program is eroding many barriers to effective communications that have existed and helped build a solid relationship between Norton Company and its employees."[6]

Both of these programs further illustrate the advantage of involving nonmanagerial employees in formal personnel communications. Other formats are in use in other firms, and all are designed to enhance personnel coordination.

Organizational ombudsman. The ombudsman, a concept originating in Sweden, is a person outside the normal chain of command who serves as a "public defender" or problem solver for management and the employees. Providing an ombudsman in the organization gives employees a place to turn with complaints, problems, frustrations, and feelings of inequity or injustice.

Xerox Corporation uses an ombudsman to resolve complaints from employees which cannot be settled through the employee's supervisor or the personnel department. The ombudsman reviews the employee's information and complaint. After the problems are discussed with other individuals, such as the employee's supervisor or a representative of the personnel department, the ombudsman recommends a solution to the problem.[7] Making this separate individual available gives the opportunity for employees to talk freely about complaints and frustrations. Some of these complaints may not otherwise surface until they become serious problems.

The concept has been slow to gain acceptance in the United States, although General Electric and Boeing Vertol Company have also tried ombudsmen. A major problem has been finding an appropriate niche in the organizational structure for such a person. Some managers and supervisors may resent the ombudsman's privilege of hearing their employees' problems.

An ombudsman must have exceptional human-relations skills and training in behavioral sciences or counseling in order to improve communication and create a more open atmosphere. One writer strongly states that the ombudsman concept should not be a short-term program or gimmick, for "the role of the ombudsman is to serve as embodiment of the corporate conscience."[8] Establishing an ombudsman position may indicate the organization is aware of the long-range effect of good personnel relations on organizational effectiveness.

The most frequent problems faced by an ombudsman are over salary, performance, appraisals, intercompany job movements, layoffs, and benefits. General Electric's ombudsman estimated that in only about 10 percent of the cases could nothing be done to resolve the problem.[9]

Ombudsmen can provide a good source of information that can be used to revise policies and procedures. It is one way management can check if current policies are working properly. The complaints may indicate, for example, that a job posting system is required or that the performance appraisal system is not working, and changes then can be made.

House organs. Organizations also communicate with employees through internal publications called *house organs.* These include newspapers, company magazines, or organizational newsletters. These publications frequently contain feature stories, on employees and their families, including news of promotions, retirements, and awards and news about the organization and its operations. Some very elaborate hours organs in larger companies require a full-time public relations staff. In smaller organizations a secretary in the personnel department may prepare a mimeographed newsletter.

The publication should be an honest attempt to communicate information employees need to know. It should not be solely a public relations tool to build the image of the company. Bad news, as well as good news, should be reported objectively in a readable style. Cartoons, drawings, and photographs improve the graphic appearance of publications and draw employee interest.

An airline house organ has a question-and-answer section where employees anonymously submit tough questions to management. Management's answers are printed with the questions in every issue. Because every effort is made to give completely honest answers to these questions, this section has been very useful. This idea fizzled in another large company because the questions were answered with "the company line" and employees soon lost interest in the less-than-candid replies.

Attention should be paid to whether the house organ is doing what management would like it to do. Two cases illustrate this quite clearly.[10] In one large pharmaceutical company, one entire division considers itself neglected by corporate management. This feeling is partially generated because the company's monthly newspaper fails to give this division the coverage it gives other divisions. In another company with six plants, the company paper had a lot of personal news about employees from all the plants. The objective was to provide the feeling of one "big happy family," even though the plants were far apart. A study showed that the workers did not care about people in other plants and simply were not interested in the newspaper. The solution was six separate newspapers, which increased the costs and time involved.

It has been suggested that the publisher of a house organ and the manager in charge must know:

1. What the publication is trying to achieve.
2. Exactly who is the audience being reached.
3. How the publication can involve the audience in its purposes.
4. Whether the cost of the whole process is worth the benefit.[11]

Other formal communications methods related to house organs are bulletin boards, posters, movies, and slides. Organizational communication is much broader than the above forms of formal personnel communication, although the formal techniques covered here can play a part in improving the coordination of personnel activities in the organization.

What are four forms of formal personnel communication?

Rules

Rules serve several purposes in organizations. They coordinate activities, maintain stability, and serve as handy decision guides so that routine decisions do not have to be made again and again. However, rules can pose problems as well. They can block new ways of doing work, can become excuses rather than reasons, and may add to the red tape in organizations.

> RULES are specific guidelines that regulate and restrict the behavior of individuals.

Rules like policies need occasional audits and changes. It may be useful to think about rules in terms of a "life cycle." Figure 16–4 shows the life cycle of a rule.

In Stage I the rule-making process begins because of a need to limit behavior or coordinate activities. In Stage II the rule is accepted and obeyed because it is seen as fulfilling an organizational need. In Stage III the rule is rejected because situations have changed or it is no longer helpful in getting the job done. People start to deviate from the behaviors prescribed in the rule. This deviation may be accompanied by a reduction in the enforcement of the rule. Before a rule reaches this point in its life cycle, it should be changed to fit the current situation—hence rule 1_A in Figure 16–4.

What is the life cycle of a rule?

Enforcement problems can result if policies and rules are completely unacceptable to employees. If a rule is not enforced, it will not be useful. For example, simply having a plant rule which prohibits smoking is insufficient. One factory has had a no-smoking rule for years, but the rule has not been enforced because the superintendent is a three-pack-a-day man. Other workers who feel they are in a safe area sneak a smoke when

FIGURE 16–4   The life cycle of a rule.

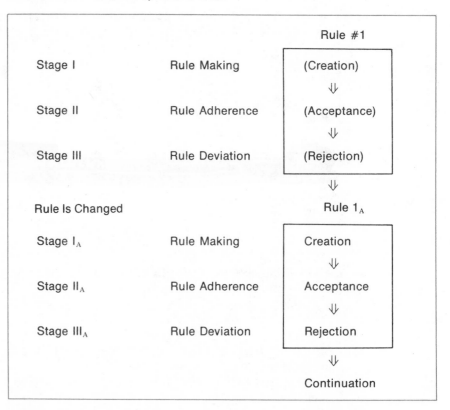

(Source: Adapted from J. H. Jackson and S. W. Adams, "The Life Cycle of a Rule," *Academy of Management Review* 4 (1979)).

they can because they see the rule violated in the office. To be effective, rules must be enforced or changed.

DISCIPLINE

Discipline is a form of training that enforces the organization's rules. It can be approached in two basic ways: *preventive* and *punitive.* Although these approaches may sound like conflicting terms, they are related.

The purpose of *preventive discipline* is to heighten employees' awareness of company policies and rules in their work experiences. Knowledge of disciplinary actions may prevent violations. The emphasis on preventive discipline is similar to the emphasis on preventing accidents. A fair warning by a supervisor in a work unit who must abide by the same rule as employees has much the same effect as a warning to prevent accidents by someone in a potentially dangerous situation. One author suggests that the best discipline is self-discipline.[12] Developing an awareness of acceptable behavior to prevent discipline problems is better than the punitive approach.

The *punitive* approach is used when violations or discipline problems occur. The hope is that through punishment, employees will not repeat the undesired behaviors. Most organizations use both these approaches to emphasize that rules must be followed.

Figure 16–5 shows the results of a survey of 185 firms on employee conduct and discipline. Notice that different offenses carry a more severe punishment for second and third offenses. For instance, smoking in unauthorized areas is not punished as severely as theft.

Equity, or fairness, must be considered in designing discipline systems to enforce rules. Few problems arise if employees understand the reasons and fairness behind policies and rules.

Organizational discipline is issued in different degrees of severity: *oral reprimand, written reprimand, formal written warning, suspension,* and *discharge.* The "progressive" nature of good discipline gives employees a chance to correct their ways. In this sense, discipline is training because for each failure to learn, the penalty is more severe.

Progressive Discipline

Progressive discipline is best viewed as the training or shaping of behavior in order to modify unacceptable behavior. This shaping may include punishment or it may not. Discipline is certainly not limited to punishment, as was noted earlier.

The concept of progressive discipline suggests that the attempts to modify behavior get more severe as the employee continues to exhibit

FIGURE 16–5 Patterns of disciplinary action for various offenses.*

Type of Offense	First Offense			Second Offense			Third Offense			Fourth Offense		
	W	S	D	W	S	D	W	S	D	W	S	D
Attendance problems												
Unexcused absence	84	21	3	60	28	3	13	47	26	2	11	52
Chronic absenteeism	88	3	2	55	32	4	8	44	38	1	4	50
Unexcused/excessive lateness	92	1	0	68	24	1	20	53	21	4	12	55
Leaving without permission	78	10	7	33	37	20	6	30	34	0	3	30
On-the-job behavior problems												
Intoxication at work	28	33	36	8	22	32	2	5	22	1	0	7
Insubordination	36	28	34	9	22	35	1	8	22	0	1	7
Horseplay	77	13	4	29	42	16	6	24	42	2	2	25
Smoking in unauthorized places	65	10	5	28	32	15	4	23	28	16	3	18
Fighting	16	25	54	4	9	30	1	1	11	0	0	2
Gambling	39	21	27	11	19	30	4	8	17	1	1	10
Failure to use safety devices	81	2	2	46	31	6	12	30	32	4	8	27
Failure to report injuries	6	10	46	1	2	12	0	1	3	0	0	1
Carelessness	89	3	0	55	31	4	12	44	30	2	5	50
Sleeping on the job	40	34	24	8	23	42	1	5	26	0	1	9
Abusive or threatening language to supervision	34	33	30	8	24	37	1	6	23	0	0	7
Possession of narcotics	10	11	70	3	3	13	1	1	3	1	0	1
Possession of firearms or other weapons	9	10	63	2	4	12	0	1	4	0	0	1
Dishonesty and related problems												
Theft	2	6	90	1	0	9	0	0	1	0	0	0
Falsifying employment application	6	0	88	1	1	2	0	0	1	0	0	0
Willful damage to company property	17	17	64	4	11	21	0	2	13	0	0	4
Punching another employee's time card	19	21	40	4	10	38	2	4	8	0	0	5
Falsifying work records	15	18	58	3	4	28	1	2	5	0	0	2
Subversive activity	12	5	41	2	6	8	0	1	6	0	0	2
Other problems												
Unauthorized soliciting	78	6	8	28	38	13	4	22	40	1	3	23
Slowdown of production	50	11	22	16	25	19	4	9	27	0	2	13
Unauthorized strike activity	6	10	46	1	2	12	0	1	3	0	0	1
Wage garnishment	52	0	0	35	13	3	15	18	13	9	6	18
Outside criminal activities	9	10	49	2	5	8	1	1	5	1	0	1
Working for competing company	23	0	28	1	8	14	0	0	9	0	0	0

W = Warning; S = suspension; D = discharge.

• Percentages are of all companies responding to checklist (N = 160). Figures do not add to 100 because of nonresponses in instances where company takes no disciplinary action for a particular offense, has had no experience with the disciplinary problem involved, and/or has no specific rule concerning a particular offense. In some instances, no formal action is taken for the first (and sometimes second) offense with the result there is a no response in these categories. In cases where employees are discharged for the first (or second) offense, there is no response in the third and fourth offense categories.

(Source: Personnel Policies Forum, *Employee Conduct and Discipline,* PPF Survey #102 (Washington, D.C.: Bureau of National Affairs, Inc., August 1973), p. 6. Used with permission.)

improper behavior. Figure 16–6 shows steps in a typical progressive discipline system. As suggested above, any discipline is best viewed as training. An employee should be given an opportunity to correct deficiencies before being dismissed. This opportunity includes, at a minimum, steps 1, 2, and 4 in Figure 16–6. These steps insure that both the nature and seriousness of the problem have been communicated to the employee.

Defensible Dismissal

Special note should be made of the last step in the progressive discipline procedures—discharge or dismissal. While dismissing an employee is never a pleasant prospect, it sometimes must be done. However, defensible personnel practice demands that termination be properly done as the terminal point of a progressive discipline procedure.

In this sense, unionized organizations have an advantage over nonunionized organizations. A unionized organization almost always has a series of disciplinary steps as a part of its labor contract. These steps are agreed upon as fair by both union and management as a result of collective bargaining. Elements of the progressive discipline model described here are the basis of most union contract agreements on discipline and are widely accepted by management professionals as an appropriate route to dismissal.

Nonunion organizations may design a dismissal procedure in keeping with the models developed by unionized firms. They may use a procedure that is generally accepted as equitable, or they may act in some other fashion. Unfortunately, many poorly managed organizations, public and private, fail to consider the issue of an equitable dismissal system until a dismissal has been made and they are *forced* to consider it. Many firms do not have a formal discipline procedure at all.

A progressive discipline procedure is not designed to make it difficult to dismiss an employee who is not doing the job. Rather, it is designed to

FIGURE 16–6 Progressive discipline.

A progressive discipline system includes:

1. Verbal cautions (with notes in employee's file)
2. Written reprimand (copies for both parties)
*3. Short suspension
4. Demotion and/or withholding pay raise
*5. Longer suspension
6. Discharge

* *May be omitted in certain instances or certain procedures.*

force the manager to document the efforts made to work with the employee's problem. When there is no third party to represent the employee such as a union, this process also helps insure that the employee is not the victim of arbitrary action on the part of a given manager.

Can you explain the nature and importance of progressive discipline?

GUIDELINES TO EFFECTIVE PERSONNEL POLICIES AND RULES

The following guidelines suggest that well-designed personnel policies and rules should be *consistent, reasonable, necessary, applicable, understandable,* and *distributed and communicated.*

Consistent

Rules should be consistent with the organization's policies, and policies should be consistent with the organization's goal. Managers should try to avoid having conflicting policies. The principal intent of policies is to provide written guidelines and specify actions. If some policies and rules are enforced and others are not, then all tend to lose their effectiveness.

Reasonable

Ideally, employees should be able to see policies as being fair and realistic. Policies and rules which are so inflexible that individuals are penalized unfairly should be reevaluated. Apex Corporation has a policy that anyone to be promoted to vice-president must have a college degree. This policy might be seen as unfair and unreasonable for someone who began working for the company 20 years ago and knows how to handle the job. Adding a provision such as "Only in exceptional cases can experience substitute for formal education," might be perceived as more reasonable and fair.

A rule forbidding workers to use the company telephone for personal calls might be unreasonable because emergency phone calls are occasionally necessary. Limiting the amount of time the telphone can be used for personal business and the number of calls can make the rule reasonable. Figure 16–7 contains a list of humorous policies most people would agree are unreasonable.

FIGURE 16–7   Policy change memorandum.

Memorandum

To: All Personnel

Subject: New Sick Leave Policy

It has been brought to my attention that the attendance record of this department is a disgrace to our gracious benefactor, who, at your own request, has given you your job. Due to lack of consideration for your jobs with so fine a department, as shown by such absenteeism, it has become necessary for us to revise some of our policies. The following changes are in effect immediately.

1. SICKNESS:
    No excuse . . . We will no longer accept your doctor's statement as proof, as we believe that if you are able to go to the doctor, you are able to come to work.

2. DEATH:
    (Other than your own) . . . This is no excuse. There is nothing you can do for them, and we are sure that someone else with a lesser position can attend to the arrangements. However, if the funeral can be held in the late afternoon, we will be glad to let you off one hour early; provided that your share of the work is ahead enough to keep the job going in your absence.

3. LEAVE OF ABSENCE:
    (For an operation) . . . We are no longer allowing this practice. We wish to discourage any thoughts that you may need an operation, as we believe that as long as you are an employee here that you will need all of whatever you have and you should not, under any circumstances, consider having anything removed. We hired you as you are and to have anything removed would certainly make you less than we bargained for.

4. DEATH:
    (Your own) . . . This will be accepted as an excuse, but we would like two weeks notice as we feel it is your duty to train someone else for your job.

ALSO, entirely too much time is being spent in the restroom. In the future, we will follow the practice of going in alphabetical order. For instance, those whose names being with "A" will go from 8:00–8:15, "B" will go from 8:15 to 8:30, and so on. If you are unable to go at your time, it will be necessary to wait until the next day when your turn comes again.

Policies and rules should not be so inflexible that necessary exceptions are excluded. A company policy requiring all sales representatives to limit air travel to coach class may need exceptions. For example, an employee may need to fly to another city to confer with a client when no seats are available in coach class. Requiring the employee to pay the difference in fare would be unreasonable and unfair.

Some of the most ticklish company policies and rules involve employee dress. Dress codes are frequently attacked, and organizations that have them should be able to justify them to the satisfaction of both employees and outside sources that might question them. A great amount of time should not be required to check enforcement of such rules.

Necessary

Personnel policies and rules should be of value to employees; to this end, managers should confirm the intent and necessity of proposed rules and eliminate obsolete ones. If a railroad changes from coal-powered to diesel-powered engines, work rules for the engines should be changed to apply to diesel-powered engines. Policies and rules should be reviewed whenever there is a major organizational change. Unfortunately this review is not always done, and many outdated rules are still on the books in many organizations.

Applicable

Because personnel policies are general guidelines to action, they are applicable to a large group of employees in the organization. If this is not so, then the applicable areas must be identified. For instance, if a sick leave policy is only applicable to nonexempt employees, it should be specified in the company handbook. Policies and rules that apply only to one unit or type of job should be developed as part of specific guidelines for that unit or job.

Understandable

Personnel policies and rules should be written so that employees can clearly understand them. One way to determine if policies and rules are understandable is to ask a cross-section of employees with various positions, education levels, and job responsibilities to explain the intent and meaning of a rule. If the answers are extremely varied, the rule should be rewritten.

To illustrate, at Environmental Products, a policy was drafted stating: "Employees will remain in the company's employ as long as their work merits it." Another policy said: "If a layoff is necessary, *merit* rating is the basis for deciding who remains." Conversations with a number of different employees showed a variety of interpretations of what would be done if a layoff occurred. Some thought that merit would be considered only when a decision had to be made between two people with equal seniority. The office workers thought the rule applied only to workers in the plant. Supervisors had another interpretation. The personnel manager decided that clarification was needed.

Distributed and Communicated

Personnel policies must be distributed and communicated to employees to be effective. Employee handbooks can be creatively designed to explain detailed policies and rules so that people can refer to a handbook at times when someone is not available to answer a question. Supervisors and managers can maintain discipline by reminding their employees about policies and rules.

REVIEW AND PREVIEW

Personnel policies and coordination are vital parts of maintenance in an organization. Coordinating efforts are partially accomplished through formal personnel communciations.

As a part of the broad organizational communications system, managers and personnel specialists can make use of several types of formal personnel communications. Employee handbooks, suggestion systems, employee communication committees, an organizational ombudsman, and house organs are all means available to formally communicate with the personnel in an organization.

Coordination efforts are also accomplished by the development and enforcement of personnel policies and rules. Progressive discipline and equity underlie successful enforcement efforts. To be effective, personnel policies and rules must be developed following some general guidelines. Policies and rules should be consistent, reasonable, necessary, applicable, understandable, and distributed and communicated.

Effective personnel coordination requires the maintenance of personnel records. Without a sound personnel records system, coordination will be significantly reduced. From these records and other sources, personnel research can be done to identify problems and changes needed in an organization. Chapter 16 focuses on personnel records and research.

Review Questions

1. What is the intent of personnel coordination activities?
2. You are a department manager in a discount store. Describe two situations: one in which you would use preventive discipline and one in which you would use punitive discipline.

3. If you had to establish a formal means of communicating personnel policies in a community college, what means would you use? Why?

4. Discuss the following statement: "Rules are always the basis for increased red tape in an organization."

5. Why might a progressive discipline procedure be seen as a logical extension of a policy of giving employees fair and equitable treatment while employed?

6. You have been assigned the task of writing a personnel policy manual. What general guidelines for writing policies would you use?

OPENING CASE FOLLOW-UP

The actual outcome of the problem was that Linda *was required* to work on that Friday. She *did attend* work that day.

This case illustrates the value of personnel policies and the importance of coordination. Giving Linda the day off on such relatively short notice could easily have triggered a multitude of requests for annual leave for that Friday.

The leave policy was flexible enough to allow Bob, the supervisor, some latitude in making leave decisions. However, a problem with the leave policy was that it did not indicate how far in advance requests had to be made. Addition of such a clause would aid supervisors by providing them adequate notice of a request and give them more time to adjust work schedules. The differences in job duties is important only in that the two individuals had differing work loads.

Case: "It's Time to Travel"

Eastern Valley State College is a regional state college with approximately 6,000 students. The Department of Business has seven faculty members. The policy manual for faculty contains the following statement: "Faculty members are expected to maintain their professional competence and the college affirms a policy of supporting faculty in this regard."

One of the main ways faculty maintain currentness in their professional fields is by attending professional meetings. When hired, Professor Hargraves was told that the college pays for a faculty member to attend one professional meeting each academic year. Because of his teaching responsibilities, Professor Hargraves waited until April 2 to apply to attend the Southern Business Meeting. He was told by his department chairman that the department was low on travel funds because another faculty member had attended two other meetings to present research papers. Therefore, the department chairman denied Professor Hargraves' request. Professor Hargraves was naturally upset, especially since there had been no written notice provided the faculty about the travel funding situation. Professor Hargraves returned to his office very disgruntled and started preparing his credentials sheet to use in applying for a job at another college.

Questions

1. Evaluate the policy statement about professional competence and the formal communication system relating to it.
2. Discuss the apparent inequity present in applying the policy and how the policy could be rewritten and better implemented.

Notes

1. Paula Cowan, "Establishing a Communication Chain: The Development and Distribution of an Employee Handbook," *Personnel Journal*, 54 (June 1975), pp. 342–349.

2. Keith Davis, "Readability Changes in Employee Handbooks of Identical Companies During a Fifteen-Year Period," *Personnel Psychology*, 21 (Winter 1968), pp. 413–420.

3. John E. Hein, "Employee Suggestion Systems Pay," *Personnel Journal*, 52 (March 1973), pp. 218–221.

4. A. W. Bergerson, "Employee Suggestion Plan Still Going Strong at Kodak," *Supervisory Management* (May 1977), pp. 32–33.

5. Douglas G. Curley, "Employee Sounding Boards: Answering the Participants Need," *The Personnel Administrator* (May 1978), pp. 69–73+.

6. P. B. Marshall, "Employee Counselors: Opening New Lines of Communication," *The Personnel Administrator* (November 1976), pp. 44–48.

7. "How the Xerox Ombudsman Helps Xerox," *Business Week*, May 12, 1973, pp. 188–190.

8. Isidore Silver, "The Corporate Ombudsman," *Harvard Business Review* (May-June 1967), p. 87.

9. "Where Ombudsman Work Out," *Business Week*, May 3, 1976, p. 114.

10. Jim Mann, "Is Your House Organ a Vital Organ?" *Personnel Journal*, 56 (September 1977), pp. 461–462.

11. *Ibid.*

12. S. J. Schwartz, "Discipline as Self-Discipline," *Supervisory Management* (June 1972), pp. 26–30.

chapter 17

Personnel Records and Research

When you have read this chapter, you should be able to:

1. Explain how personnel records fit with personnel research.

2. Diagram a personnel information system.

3. List cautions to be observed in assuring the privacy of personnel records.

4. Identify two basic modes for researching personnel problems and two methods in each mode.

5. Describe why absenteeism and turnover are important concerns in organizations.

6. Define and briefly discuss the concepts of a personnel audit and human resource accounting.

The New Personnel Director

Jerry Spence graduated a year and a half ago from a general business program at State University. He took a job that spring with Applied Systems Corporation, an organization of about 300 employees that designs and manufactures peripheral computer hardware. Jerry started as a general management trainee and impressed his fellow workers with his drive, interest, and ability to learn. As part of the management training program Jerry was rotated from department to department. He spent six months in sales, three months in productions, and three months in accounting prior to his latest move to the personnel department.

There he has acted as assistant personnel director to Ted Quantry. Ted was an older fellow who was 64 and approaching retirement. Ted was not particularly energetic or innovative and saw personnel as a record keeping and employment function. Last week, at home, Ted had a massive heart attack and died. Yesterday after the funeral, Ted's boss called Jerry and informed him that he had been picked as Ted's replacement.

Having only been with the company a year and a half, Jerry was a little overwhelmed with the responsibility involved, but his boss's encouragement made him feel he could handle the job. Jerry wishes now that he had taken a personnel management course or two in college, but the courses were not required and he had wanted to finish as soon as possible. Jerry has some vague ideas about areas that need some examination in the organization, but he is not sure how some of these areas tie together. For example, he knows that the turnover rate is about 30 percent, which he feels is above average for this type of operation. Also, he and his boss recognize that absenteeism is something of a problem during certain periods of the year. In addition, certain things in the organization that should be done have been put off, such as revising or, in most cases, preparing job descriptions. As he stares at the big picture on the wall across from his desk in his new office, Jerry wonders where to begin.

Only by studying personnel activities can managers determine program effectiveness, the quality and extent of employee performance, and the need for new practices and systems. Research on personnel management activities provides an understanding of what works, what does not work, and what needs to be done.

PERSONNEL RESEARCH analyzes both the problems and successes managers have had by comparing past and present practices with criteria or standards.

Such research is ongoing and requires that good records be kept. In addition, the government has imposed record-keeping requirements on most business organizations. It has been suggested "The extent to which an organization can tolerate such impartial scrutiny and learn from it, may itself be a measure of the degree of professionalism of management in that organization."[1]

Figure 17–1 shows the records and research interface. The personnel unit and operating managers share the responsibility for good personnel records and research. The personnel unit usually guides the design and collection of data, while managers provide assistance and necessary information. This chapter considers basics of personnel record keeping and formal research and their importance to an organization's current personnel management operations.

PERSONNEL RECORDS

One of the only functions of early personnel departments was that of record-keeper. It should be apparent by this point in the book that the

FIGURE 17–1 Personnel records and research interface.

Personnel Unit	Managers
Designs personnel information systems	Have access to personnel information system as needed
Keeps required records	
Provides expertise to design and evaluate data gathering	Provide information on people in the work units
Provides overview of organization climate	Assist in gathering data on organizational climate
Evaluates turnover and absenteeism throughout the organization	Control absenteeism and turnover in own work unit
Conducts personnel audit	Cooperate in personnel audit

contemporary personnel department has many more activities today, but the need for keeping personnel records has taken on much greater importance with increased government demands and such new sophisticated personnel techniques as manpower forecasting.

Personnel-related records and data provide an excellent source of information for auditing or assessing the effectiveness of a personnel department or any unit. They also provide the basis for doing research into possible causes of problems the organization may be experiencing. Figure 17–2 shows some of the kinds of personnel records and data that may be available in many organizations.

Personnel records also serve as important documentation in certain cases. For example, a new employee stated that he had a driver's license on the employment application blank and was hired to drive a delivery truck. Examination later revealed the new employee did *not* have a driver's license and he was fired for falsifying the application. Without the record of the falsified application, proving he had lied would have been difficult because he claimed he had never said he had a driver's license.

How do personnel records and personnel research fit together?

Records and the Government

Federal, state, and local laws *require* numerous records be kept on employees. The requirements are so varied as to exactly what should be kept

FIGURE 17–2   Some kinds of personnel records and data sources.

Accident Records	Termination Records
Employment Requisition Records	Job Specification
Personnel Inventories	Job Descriptions
Applicant Records	Salary Increase Records
Interview Records	Training Records
Turnover Records	Personal History Records
Transfer Records	Affirmative Action Records
Payroll Records	Medical Records
Work Schedule Records	Insurance Records
Test Score Records	Other Benefit Records
Performance Records	Committee Meeting Records
Grievance Records	Retired Employee Records
Arbitration Awards	Personal Interest Records
Occupational Health Records	Attitude/Morale Data
Job Bidding Records	Open Jobs Records
Exit Interview Records	Labor Market Data
Employee Expense Records	

and for how long that each specific case must be dealt with separately. A good source to consult is the *Federal Register*, March 10, 1975, 40 (No. 47) beginning with page 11262. In this source all federal government reporting requirements are listed and the length of time records must be retained is noted.

Generally, records relating to wages, basic employment, work schedules, job evaluations, merit and seniority systems, sex, occupation, deductions, and Affirmative Action programs must be kept by all employers who are subject to provisions of the Fair Labor Standards Act. The most commonly required retention time for such records is three years. However, this limit varies and should be carefully checked.

In addition, other records may be required on issues relating to EEO, OSHA, or the Age Discrimination Act. Such new record-keeping requirements have not been accepted easily by managers who must adapt to the additional paperwork. In addition to the time and expense of keeping records, many managers feel that records can be a source of major trouble by allowing the past actions of management to be questioned. There probably *is* a point beyond which it costs more to keep records than can be gained by doing so. However, the major problem presented by personnel record-keeping is more commonly the inability to retrieve needed information without major difficulties.

For example, better personnel decisions can be made if good information is available on the nature, causes, and severity of accidents, the reasons for absenteeism, the availability of experience, the distribution of performance appraisals, and so forth. But for many organizations such information is not *readily* available. A solution to the problems associated with record-keeping and getting useful information easily from the records that are kept is a well-designed personnel information system.

Personnel Information Systems

A PERSONNEL INFORMATION SYSTEM is an integrated man/ machine system that is designed to provide information to be used in making personnel decisions.

It usually utilizes a computer and its attendant hardware and software and a data base. Figure 17–3 shows a very simple model of a personnel information system.

Most of the records/data sources listed in Figure 17–2 lend themselves to quantification; that is, they can be stated in numerical terms. These numbers then can be combined or manipulated by the personnel manager or a computer programmer to provide the type of information necessary for planning, controlling, making decisions, or preparing reports.

FIGURE 17–3   A simple model of a personnel information system.

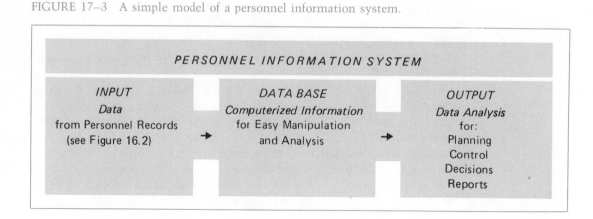

The computer has vastly simplified the task of analyzing vast amounts of data and can be an invaluable aid in every aspect of personnel management from payroll processing to record retention. But, it must be understood that the computer is only a machine, a tool. If it is given bad information, it returns in kind. Extracting useful information from raw data requires knowledgeable approaches and a good bit of common sense. In short, the computer is a tremendous aid to the personnel manager but can never replace the manager.

One study of government and business organizations found that computers operating for personnel purposes were not used to their full potential. According to this study, some of the common uses that personnel had for computers were: (1) payroll records and reports, (2) pay statistics and reports, and (3) personnel statistics and reports.[2]

Personnel information systems are used extensively in employee benefit programs. As these programs become more complex, computerization is necessary to maintain accurate records of the various benefits and options employees select. Another major use of computers is in manpower planning and forecasting. Computers make it easier to build manpower models and project work force demands and availability for the next five years. Computerization is not limited to use by large corporations. Smaller computer systems and desk-top computer units can be invaluable to small organizations which must store and quickly retrieve amounts of information.

Figure 17–4 shows some practical guidelines for developing and using a personnel information system. All of the guides underscore the importance of having a system that is flexible, responsive, and user oriented. Ideally, the personnel department should be able to use the information system with very little help from computer programmers after it has been set up.

FIGURE 17–4   Practical guides to development and use of a personnel information system.

1. Information has little value unless it can be used to make comparisons, ratios, or draw trends from which causality can be inferred.

2. Effective personnel information systems must emphasize the user of the information not the computer. The most elegant hardware and software available will not be of any use unless the end result is better decisions by the people using the information.

3. Both the users of the information and top management should be involved in the design of the system so it will meet their needs.

4. The system should have clear cut objectives and measures of effectiveness established from the start.

5. Changes to the system when needed should be made easily and quickly.

6. Access should be easy for authorized persons. It should not require a computer programmer to get information from the system.

7. Employees should know what information on them is on the system and should have at least an annual opportunity to see their files.**

** Source: Adapted from E. E. Burack and R. Smith *Personnel Management* (St. Paul: West Publishing, 1977), p. 439. Used with permission.

Diagram a personnel information system.

Privacy and Personnel Records

As a result of governmental concern regarding the protection of individuals' rights to privacy, the Privacy Act of 1974 (Public Law 92–579) was passed. This law applies to federal agencies and companies supplying services to the federal government, but numerous state laws have been passed, and it appears that additional federal legislation in this area may be forthcoming. In addition to privacy provisions affecting selection (see Chapter 8), there are also provisions affecting personnel records systems.

All the specific details on how exactly the privacy laws will affect personnel records and personnel information systems have not yet been determined. But one example of an organization attempting to deal with the spirit of the laws is IBM's establishment of four principles of privacy. These principles can serve as a guide in this area until more specific details are agreed upon:

1. Individuals should have access to information about themselves in record-keeping systems.

2. There should be a way for an individual to correct or amend an inaccurate record.
3. An individual should be able to prevent information from being improperly disclosed or used for other than authorized purposes.
4. There should be reasonable precautions to be sure that data are reliable and not misused.[3]

Seeing that these principles are adhered to may require some rethinking and reorganizing of many existing record-keeping systems in personnel units, but doing so is likely to minimize problems later. For example, one proposal is that no negative information on an employee could be retained and used if it is more than two-years old.

The records that are kept on personnel in organizations provide an excellent source for doing research inside the organization. Personnel research, as was suggested earlier, provides management with the information it uses to make adjustments or to continue with the status quo if adjustments are not needed.

What cautions should be observed in assuring privacy of personnel records?

PERSONNEL RESEARCH

The current state of an organization and its employees can be researched in two basic ways. One way, *primary research*, is research conducted mainly within the organization. Information is systematically collected from employee records or surveys, and this information is used in managerial decision making. Another way, *secondary research*, is research conducted using sources outside the organization to provide insights on improving operations. For instance, a manager may read about other organizations and their sick-pay policies to determine an acceptable policy on paid sick leave.

RESEARCH IN THE ORGANIZATION

To the extent that each organization's problems are unique, each must conduct primary research as a basis for managerial decisions. Employee participation in research projects may help a manager obtain accurate input from employees. For example, employees of the State Education Agency completed an attitude survey on job satisfaction in their unit. This survey pointed out problem areas which would not have been discovered otherwise, such as dissatisfaction with supervision and promotion policies. There are numerous primary ways to research the status of personnel management in an organization. Some of the most important ones follow.

Employee questionnaires. One type of primary research can be done by using an employee questionnaire, often one that examines a limited topic. This device gives employees an opportunity to voice their opinions about rather specific personnel management activities. For example, questionnaires may be sent to employees regarding the organization's performance appraisal system to collect ideas for revising it. Or, employees may be asked to evaluate specific organizational communication methods, such as the employee handbook or the company suggestion system. Figure 17-5 shows a variety of possible questionnaire items.

Questionnaires can be distributed and collected by supervisors; or surveys can be distributed with employee paychecks or mailed to their homes. Better information can be obtained if employees are not required to identify themselves on a questionnaire and if they can return completed questionnaires anonymously. For example, Linda Stice, a manager in a large insurance company, was considered to be a very tough supervisor; her section consistently had more grievances than the others. When the personnel department designed a survey to pinpoint problems in the company, Linda was instructed to distribute and collect the questionnaires. The employees felt sure Linda would look at their answers before returning the forms to the personnel department; consequently, they did not answer the questions honestly.

Attitude surveys. Attitude surveys focus on feelings and motives to pinpoint the employees' underlying opinions about their working environment. One source suggests three basic purposes for conducting attitude surveys: (1) for use as a base for comparing other surveys; (2) as a measurement of the effect of change before and after the change occurs;

FIGURE 17–5 Sample employee questionnaire items.

1. How would you describe the benefits in the organization?
   Excellent ____ Good ____ Average ____ Fair ____ Poor ____
2. How do you feel about the company policy of "buying back" sick leave?
   Like it ____ Dislike it ____ Don't know ____ Why?
3. Would you use a company tuition reimbursement plan at local educational institutions?
   Yes ____ No ____ Not sure ____
4. Would you be in favor of a flexible work week schedule?
   Yes ____ Undecided ____ No ____

(3) to determine the nature and extent of employee feelings regarding specific organizational issues and the organization in general.[4]

The topics of attitude surveys may vary. Surveys serve as a soundingboard for employees' feelings about their jobs, supervisors, co-workers, organizational policies and practices, and the organization in general. Many prepared attitude surveys are available. One should be careful, however, to see published reliability and validity statistics before using a prepared test. (See Chapter 4 for a discussion of reliability and validity.) Only acceptably valid and reliable surveys really measure attitudes accurately. Often a "research" survey that is self-developed by a manager is poorly structured, asks questions in a confusing manner, or "leads" the employees to respond in a manner to give the manager the "results" he or she wants.

Organizational climate.   One recent research development is the measurement of organizational "climate." *Organizational climate is the characteristics of an organization as seen from the employees' viewpoint.*[5] It attempts to determine how employees feel about the organization or certain specific aspects of it. For instance, in one company, employees liked the work they did, but problems with the company's structure and policies hampered their job performances and satisfactions. In this particular case, employee satisfaction with their work differed from their satisfaction with the company.[6] The value of an organizational climate study is that it can be used to diagnose the current state of an organization and indicate where changes are needed. An overall view of the organization's climate can be displayed graphically, as in Figure 17–6.

It is important to remember that an organization's climate varies from one unit to another. The climate of the housekeeping unit might be different from the climate of the intensive care unit in a hospital. When researching organizational climate, the results should be identified both by subunits and as a whole to provide an overall organizational picture. Dimensions of organizational climate commonly measured include[7]:

1. *Structure*—feelings about rules, procedures, and constraints
2. *Responsibility*—feelings about individual's decision-making freedom
3. *Reward*—degree to which employees perceive fairness in pay and other rewards
4. *Risk*—sense of challenge and risk
5. *Team Spirit*—feeling of group friendliness and identification with the organization
6. *Standards*—emphasis perceived on goal attainment and achievement of performance standards

FIGURE 17–6　Sales corporation organization climate.

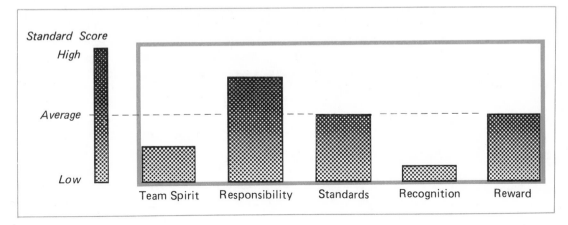

Organizational climate may be measured and the results used as a diagnostic tool for managers or consultants. A large Chicago bank used organizational climate research to measure the current level of employees' feelings in one unit of the bank and recommended changes based upon the results.[8] Climate surveys are action research devices used to intervene in an organization and provide a basis for making changes. Such research is likely to be an increasingly important part of personnel management.

Research interviews.　　The personal interview is an alternative to the opinion survey and may focus on a wide variety of problems. One type of interview widely used is the *exit interview*. Persons leaving the organization are interviewed and asked to identify problems that caused them to resign. This information can be used to correct problems so that others will not leave. Personnel specialists usually conduct exit interviews rather than supervisors, and a skillful interviewer can gain useful information. One problem with the exit interview is that resigning employees may be reluctant to divulge their real reasons for leaving because they do not want to "burn any bridges." They may also fear that candid responses will hinder their chances of receiving favorable references.

The major reason an employee usually gives for leaving a job is an offer of more pay somewhere else. While this reason is considered to be acceptable, more pay may not be the only factor involved. Former employees may be more willing to provide more information on a questionnaire mailed to their home or in a telephone conversation sometime after leaving.

Experiments. Experiments can also provide useful data. Two formats for setting up experiments are: (1) measuring conditions before and after a change is made, and (2) having some employees perform a job in a new way while others perform the same job in the old way and compare the results. Persons trained in experimental design and statistics are usually needed to conduct such studies and interpret the results.

What are two internal means for researching personnel problems?

ABSENTEEISM AND TURNOVER

Absenteeism and turnover are major concerns in most organizations. These two personnel problems are universally watched and studied by managers because they affect the organization's operations. If a manager needs 12 people to work in a unit to get the work done, and 4 of the 12 are absent most of the time, the unit's work likely will not get done. Research on the reasons for absenteeism should be done using an organization's own records.

Absenteeism

Employees can be absent from work for several reasons. Illness, death in the family, or other personal reasons are unavoidable and understandable; however, excessive absences may cause organizational coordination problems. Many employers have sick-leave policies which allow employees a certain number of paid days per year on which they may be absent. Employees who miss fewer days are reimbursed with sick pay. A formula for computing absenteeism rates suggested by the U.S. Department of Labor is as follows:

$$\frac{\text{Number of person-days lost through job absence during period}}{(\text{Average number of employees}) \times (\text{Number of work days})} \times 100$$

The rate can be computed based on the number of hours instead of days. In one study of 136 organizations the absentee rate ranged from 1.8 percent to 11.4 percent, with the average being 4 percent.[9]

Organizations have noted that there are consistently more absences on Fridays and Mondays than on other days. One reason for this is that some employees stretch the weekend to three or four days. Other causes for absenteeism can be suggested. As mentioned in Chapter 6, a relationship between absenteeism and job satisfaction has been found. Employees with higher job satisfaction will probably be absent less than those who are dissatisfied with their jobs.

Dealing with absenteeism must begin with continuous monitoring of absenteeism statistics in work units. This monitoring will help managers pinpoint employees who are frequently absent and units with excessive absenteeism. Offering rewards for good attendance, giving bonuses for missing fewer than a certain number of days, and buying unused sick leave are all methods of reducing absenteeism. If absenteeism is excessive, the problem employees can be "dehired." Organizational policies on absenteeism should be clearly stated in the employee handbook and stressed by supervisors and managers. Employee counseling and discussion may correct some of the problems that make people reluctant to come to work and may suggest positive actions to be taken.

Turnover

> TURNOVER refers to the process of employees leaving the organization and having to be replaced.

Turnover can be a very costly problem. One firm had a turnover rate of over 120 percent per year. It cost the company $1.5 million per year in lost productivity, increased training time, increased personnel selection time, lost worker efficiency, and other indirect costs. The turnover rate for an organization can be computed using the following formula from the U.S. Department of Labor (separations are people who left the organization):

$$\frac{\text{Number of employee separations during the month}}{\text{Total number of employees at midmonth}} \times 100$$

A national survey found that turnover ranged from 2 percent to 32.5 percent per year. The average turnover rate was about 3 percent per year.[10] It is important to note that turnover rates vary among industries. Organizations requiring little skill among entry-level personnel are likely to have a higher turnover rate among those employees than among managerial personnel. Therefore, it is important that turnover rates be computed by work units. One organization's companywide turnover rate was not severe. However, 80 percent of the turnover occurred within one department. This imbalance indicated that some action was needed to deal with problems in that unit.

Turnover can be dealt with in several ways. Because it is related to job satisfaction, matching an employee's expectations of rewards and satisfaction may help reduce turnover problems. A good way to eliminate turnover is to improve selection and matching of applicants to jobs. By hiring people who are more likely to stay through fine-tuning the selection process, managers can increase the possibility that fewer employees will leave. Good employee orientation also will help reduce turnover. Employees who are properly introduced into the company and are well-trained tend to be less likely to leave. If people receive some basic information about the company and the job to be performed, they can determine early whether or not they want to stay. Another reason for turnover is that individuals believe there is no opportunity for career advancement. Career planning and internal promotion can help an organization keep career personnel.

A fair and equitable pay system can help prevent turnover.[11] An employee who is underpaid relative to employees in other jobs with similar skills may leave. As mentioned in an earlier chapter, pay is one of the major reasons that people work.

Managers who maintain open communications can help resolve turnover problems. An awareness of employee problems and dissatisfactions may provide a manager with opportunities to resolve them before they become so severe that employees leave. Turnover problems can be pinpointed by researching personnel records. In this effort, computer-based personnel information systems are invaluable.

Why are absenteeism and turnover important concerns in organizations?

RESEARCH OUTSIDE THE ORGANIZATION

Managers and personnel specialists can gain useful information by consulting sources outside the organization. Some common ones are discussed next.

Other Organizations

Personnel specialists can gain new insights from managers and specialists in other organizations by participating in professional personnel groups. The most prominent professional organizations are the American Society for Personnel Administration (ASPA) and the International Personnel Management Association (IPMA). These organizations publish professional journals and newsletters, conduct annual meetings and conferences, and provide many other services, often through local chapters. ASPA is composed of public and private personnel administrators, whereas members of IPMA are primarily personnel managers from local, state, and federal government agencies.

Private management consulting firms and local colleges and universities also provide assistance in personnel research. These outside researchers may be more knowledgeable and unbiased than persons inside the organization. Consultants skilled in questionnaire design and data analysis can provide expert advice on personnel research. Appendix B contains a list of organizations and agencies having information useful to personnel specialists and other managers.

National or area surveys. Surveys by other organizations can provide some perspectives on a company's internal research. Some professional organizations like the Bureau of National Affairs and the National Industrial Conference Board, sponsor surveys on personnel practices in communities, states, regions, and in the nation. The survey results are then distributed to participating organizations. Or, an organization may conduct its own comparative outside surveys such as wage surveys.

Current literature. Professional personnel journals and publications provide useful communication between managers, personnel specialists, researchers, and other practitioners. Figure 17-7 is a list of journals which often publish personnel management information.

Importance of Personnel Research

Effective personnel management decisions are assisted by personnel research because there are no pat answers to personnel problems. Good personnel management comes through analyzing problems and applying experience and knowledge to *particular situations.* A manager who "supposes" that something may happen is not likely to be effective. In some organizations personnel research is formalized through a personnel audit.

PERSONNEL AUDIT

A PERSONNEL AUDIT is a formal research effort to evaluate the current state of personnel management in an organization.

A personnel audit is similar in purpose to the financial audit, which examines, verifies, evaluates, and investigates an organization's current financial status. Many of the research sources mentioned earlier are

FIGURE 17–7   Current literature in personnel management.

A.   Research Oriented Journals

(These journals contain articles that report on original research. Normally these journals contain rather sophisticated writing and/or quantitative verifications of authors' findings.)

Academy of Management Journal
Academy of Management Review
Administrative Science Quarterly
American Journal of Sociology
American Sociological Review
Behavioral Science
Human Organization
Human Relations
Industrial & Labor Relations Review
Industrial Relations
Journal of Applied Behavioral
   Science

Journal of Applied Psychology
Journal of Business
Journal of Business
   Communications
Journal of Communications
Journal of Industrial Relations
Journal of Management Studies
Journal of Social Psychology
Journal of Social Issues
Management Science
Organizational Behavior & Human
   Performance
Personnel Psychology
Research Management
Sloan Management Review
Social Forces
Social Science Research
Sociometry

B.   Management Oriented Journals

(These journals generally cover a wide range of subjects. Articles in these publications normally are aimed at the practitioner and are written to interpret, summarize, or discuss past, present, and future research and administrative applications. Not all of the articles in these publications are personnel-oriented.)

Across the Board
Administrative Management
Advanced Management Journal
Business Horizons
California Management Review
Canadian Personnel
Columbia Journal of World
   Business
Dun's Review
Fortune
Harvard Business Review

Human Behavior
Human Resource Management
Labor Law Journal
Management Review
Michigan Business Review
Michigan State University Business
   Topics
Monthly Labor Review
Nation's Business
Organizational Dynamics

Personnel
Personnel Administration
Personnel Journal
Personnel Management
Public Personnel Management
Psychology Today
The Personnel Administrator
Supervisory Management
Training and Development Journal

C.   For assistance in locating articles, some of the following indices and abstracts contain subject matter of interest.

Applied Science and Technology
   Index
Business Periodicals Index
Dissertation Abstracts
Employee Relations Index
Index to Legal Periodicals
Index to Social Sciences and
   Humanities

Management Abstracts
Personnel Management Abstracts
Psychological Abstracts
Reader's Guide to Periodical
   Literature
Sociological Abstracts

452

used in personnel audits. These sources can tell top executives, personnel specialists, and managers how well the organization is managing its human resources.

Using statistical reports and research data, personnel audits evaluate how well personnel activities have been performed. A formal comprehensive audit can examine many areas including employment records, selection, placement, the maintenance of personnel records, employee benefits, training, employee services, safety and health, labor relations, and public relations.[12] Another form of comprehensive evaluation of personnel management activities is human resource accounting.

HUMAN RESOURCE ACCOUNTING

> HUMAN RESOURCE ACCOUNTING is a specialized personnel audit which continually attempts to quantify the value of an organization's human resources.

Human resource accounting is similar in principle to an accounting statement. Just as financial accounting reflects the cost of capital assets such as machinery and buildings, human resource accounting, typically done either once a year or at regular intervals, attempts to place a value on an organization's human resources by formulating a human resource "balance sheet." This instrument demonstrates that human resources are an asset instead of a common expense and that they should therefore be computed as part of an organization's total worth.

Human resource accounting shows the investment the organization makes in its people and how the value of these people changes over time—the acquisition cost of employees is compared to the replacement cost. The value of employees is increased by training and experience over a period of time. For example, a chemical firm fired 200 of its employees to save $250,000 in direct costs. However, by considering human resources as assets, a researcher determined that the value of the company's human resources decreased by $1 million. Ultimately, the plant lost $1 million when the employees were fired.[13]

The importance of human resource accounting is illustrated by the effect a change in human resources has on the stock market. If a change occurs in a company's top management or key personnel, the price of that company's stock can go up or down. The board of directors of a large food company decided to remove the president, vice-president, and controller. When this news reached the stock market, the price of the company's stock soared because the market viewed this action as a major improvement in the company's operations. That illustrates the value placed on the top management team—in this case it was low.

Use of human resources accounting is limited because it is difficult to establish how much organizations increase or decrease the value of their human assets. Also, different accounting approaches can be used to measure human resources.[14]

In sum, human resource accounting is a sophisticated way to measure the effectiveness of personnel management activities and the use of people in an organization. It is presented here as an illustration of attempts to measure the effectiveness of personnel activities.

Compare the concepts of personnel audit and human resources accounting.

REVIEW AND PREVIEW

In order to judge how effectively an organization is being managed, managers and personnel specialists attempt to evaluate how well the human resources have been used. This research provides information and insights for improving personnel management.

Personnel records are an important part of this process. Personnel records contain a variety of information, but the government has mandated that certain records be kept. Personnel information systems can help greatly in managing great masses of personnel records. However, privacy of personnel records is becoming a greater concern.

Two basic research sources can be used to evaluate personnel management actions. One mode uses internal sources or organizational information, such as employee questionnaires, attitude surveys, research interviews, experiments, and personnel records. Absenteeism and turnover are two key areas for evaluation, and computer-based personnel information systems aid in analyzing data quickly and accurately.

The second mode relies on sources outside the organization for research information. Common secondary sources are other organizations, surveys, and current literature.

Personnel research is an important part of good personnel management. In some organizations, this research has been formalized through a personnel audit and human resource accounting. These methods evaluate how well an organization's human resources have been managed.

The past section has considered activities that are part of the maintenance interface. Attention now turns to the interface with formal labor organizations, which provides some special challenges to personnel management.

Review Questions

1. Discuss the following statement: "Privacy concerns will have a significant impact on personnel recordkeeping systems."

2. You are a personnel director for Consolidated Widgets. What means would you use to conduct personnel research on turnover and absenteeism problems?

3. Why would you be concerned about turnover and absenteeism problems?

4. A personnel audit and human resource accounting are somewhat different in thrust. Differentiate between them.

OPENING CASE FOLLOW-UP

Jerry is in the uncomfortable position of having been thrust into a situation with which he is not familiar. One suggestion would be for him to conduct a personnel audit to get a formal and fairly comprehensive reading on the current state of personnel activities in ASC. Then he might be able to determine the areas that really need immediate attention with which he is not very familiar. It is safe to say that Ted's benign neglect of many personnel activities has resulted in many areas that need considerable work.

Jerry is in an interesting position because if he can make the most of this opportunity, which became available considerably ahead of schedule, he will have aided his career. His lack of knowledge of personnel management may hinder him, but there are many sources to which he can turn to learn about personnel: trade publications, professional publications, professional consultants, and personnel associations, to name some. Both a personnel audit and a familiarity with personnel activities are important for Jerry at this point. Also, he has a number of personnel records available to him that have probably been kept because of government requirements. These include job evaluations, performance appraisals, age, sex, occupation, training, and other data.

Case: Too Little Turnover?

At Milton Manufacturing Company the newly installed personnel information system is turning up some interesting information. For example, the company has less than 1 percent per year turnover in its management group. And, those that have been leaving do so primarily because they have been retired. However, the level of cross-training (managers able to handle their own assignment and another at the same level) is quite low. Further, the number of qualified candidates for upper-level management jobs (which require cross training) is quite low. This information combined with less than acceptable levels of organizational performance has upper management concerned.

QUESTIONS

1. Is there such a thing as too little turnover?
2. What might be the relationship between low turnover in management and poor performance?

Notes

1. Wilmar F. Bernthal, "New Challenges Demand that 'WE' Change Roles," *The Personnel Administrator* (November–December 1968), pp. 33–38.

2. Edward A. Tomeski and Harold Lazarus, "Computerized Information Systems in Personnel—A Comparative Analysis of the State of the Art in Government and Business," *Academy of Management Journal*, 17 (March 1974), pp. 168–172.

3. Virginia E. Schein, "Privacy and Personnel: A Time for Action," *Personnel Journal* (December 1976), p. 606.

4. Rene V. Dawis and William Weitzel, "Worker Attitudes and Expectations," in Dale Yoder and Herbert G. Heneman, Jr., eds., *ASPA Handbook of Personnel and Industrial Relations, volume 2, Motivation and Commitment* (Washington, D.C.: The Bureau of National Affairs, 1975), pp. 6–40.

5. This definition closely resembles one given in Don Hellriegel and John W. Slocum, "Organizational Climate: Measures, Research and Contingencies," *Academy of Management Journal*, 17 (June 1974), pp. 255–280.

6. Support for this view is contained in Benjamin Schneider and Robert A. Snyder, "Some Relationships Between Job Satisfaction and Organizational Climate," *Journal of Applied Psychology*, 60 (March 1975), pp. 318–328.

7. The dimensions in this form are suggested in an organizational climate instrument developed by George H. Litwin and Robert A. Stringer, *Motivation and Organizational Climate* (Cambridge, Mass.: Harvard University Press, 1968).

8. Charles E. Becker, "Deciding When It's Time for a Change in Organizational Climate," *Personnel* (May–June 1975), pp. 25–31.

9. Personnel Policies Forum, *Employee Absenteeism and Turnover*, PPF #106, (Washington, D.C.: Bureau of National Affairs, May 1974), p. 3.

456

10. *Ibid.,* p. 9.

11. George C. Gorden, "Putting the Brakes on Turnover," *Personnel Journal,* 53 (February 1974), pp. 141–144.

12. For a detailed guide of areas that can be audited, see Geneva Seybold, *Personnel Audits and Reports to Top Management,* Personnel Policy Study #191 (New York: National Industrial Conference Board, 1964).

13. "A New Twist to 'People Accounting,'" *Business Week*, October 21, 1972, pp. 67–68.

14. For an overview of the various methods of measuring human resource values, see Lee White and Kenneth Van Voorhis, "Human Resource Accounting: Behavioral Whim or Management Tool?," paper presented at Southern Management Assn. meeting, New Orleans, La., November 1975; and Philip H. Mirvis and Barry A. Macy, "Human Resource Accounting: A Measurement Perspective," *Academy of Management Proceedings of 35th Annual Meeting,* New Orleans, La., August 1975.

section 7

Organization/Union Interfaces

Some organizations formally interact with their employees through unions. To understand the basis of this relationship, the history of the labor movement and labor legislation must be studied. Chapter 18 provides a useful synopsis of the evolution of unionism and labor legislation in the United States. The process of unionization in an organization is one that is often misunderstood, but an understanding of the steps in the process are an important part of a manager's knowledge.

If an organization is unionized, a labor contract is the basis for the relationship between an employer and a union. The process of reaching a contract agreement is known as collective bargaining, an important part of labor/management relations. The bargaining process and typical issues in collective bargaining are discussed in Chapter 19.

Grievance procedures and arbitration are methods union members use to solve problems with the organization. In Chapter 19, the daily administration of a labor agreement through the grievance procedure is discussed. If grievances cannot be settled, then an arbitrator may be selected to decide what must be done. An analysis of some common problems arbitrators face and the relationship between a manager's behavior and grievance rates are also discussed in Chapter 19.

459

chapter
18

Nature of
Union/Management Relations

When you have read this chapter, you should be able to:

1. Compare and contrast the philosophy of U.S. and European unions.

2. Trace the evolution of labor unions in the United States from 1800 to 1935.

3. Explain the acts which make up the National Labor Code.

4. Identify the stages in the unionization process.

5. Depict the general structure of unions.

6. Describe three current trends in unionism.

You Ungrateful *?!

George Gottlieb is the founder, owner, and president of Computer Service Bureau (CSB). Eight years ago George started CSB as a time-sharing and computer services company. A combination of George's sales ability and his hiring of several extremely good computer systems analysts resulted in CSB becoming very profitable and growing rapidly. Currently CSB has 200 employees, about half of whom hold clerical and key-punch jobs.

Most of those holding those lower-paid jobs are female, under the age of 30, and fairly mobile. Because of the short training period and a very high turnover rate (100 percent per year), CSB starts new lower-level employees at 5 percent below the wage rate for similar jobs in other local employers. However, the local labor market is fairly loose, so CSB has had no difficulty hiring entry-level employees.

Currently, George is angry. One of his supervisors just showed him a leaflet that an employee received at home. This leaflet urged the employee to sign a card indicating that the employee wants to vote on joining the International Office Workers Union (IOWU).

After a rather long tirade in which George referred to the employees as "ungrateful * ?! ," he told the supervisor he would send out a letter to all employees. In the letter he plans to say that anyone who signs a union card will be fired. Also, he plans to contact a labor attorney to help him "beat the union."

Some people contend that unions present an "outside force" with which an organization's management must deal. As the opening case illustrates, managers often resent the idea that employees need "outside" representation. Others argue that the union is an internal force because it is made up of employees of the organization. Regardless of the internal/external issue, the existence of a union presents additional personnel management challenges.

Figure 18–1 shows a typical set of responsibilities the personnel unit and operating managers have in dealing with unions. It should be noted that this interface may vary in different organizations. In some organizations, the personnel unit does not become involved at all with labor relations because the operating management handles them. In other organizations, the personnel unit is almost completely in charge of labor relations. The breakdown of responsibilities shown in 18–1 is a midpoint between these extremes.

In this chapter, some basics about American unions will be covered to acquaint the reader with some of the terms and philosophies associated with unionism. Then the evolution and history of unions, current trends, union structure, and unionism in the public sector will be discussed.

FIGURE 18–1   Union relations interface.

Personnel Unit	Managers
May be involved in dealing with organizing attempts at the company level	Provide conditions conducive to a positive relationship with employees
May help negotiate labor agreement	Administer the labor agreement on a daily basis
Provides detailed knowledge of labor legislation as may be necessary	Deal with specific problems in the relationship between management and the union members

Unions

The existence of a union usually means formal *collective bargaining* between management and union representatives over certain issues. *Grievances* are formal complaints filed by workers with management. Collective bargaining and grievance procedures are two of the important interfaces between management and labor unions once a union has gained recognition as a legal representative of employee interests. Those two areas are examined in the next chapter.

AMERICAN UNIONISM

Unions in the United States have been characterized as:

1. *Organized groups* usually representing either members in many different companies throughout an industry (such as the auto industry) or occupational grouping (such as carpenters);
2. Institutions developed beyond the working life of individuals—that is, the union is concerned with *more than just the on-the-job behavior* of its members;
3. An employer regulation device which can be viewed as a *countervailing force* to management.[1]

Philosophies of Unionism

Part of the philosophy of unionism in the United States has come from philosophies and ideas about organized labor in Western Europe, especially England. The Industrial Revolution encouraged both employers and employees to seek personal advancement through collective action because individual effort was inadequate.

Unionism in the United States has followed a somewhat different pattern than in other countries, where the union movement has been at the forefront of various political trends. For the most part this politicalization has not been the case in the United States. Perhaps the reason is that workers tend to identify with the American free enterprise system. Further, there is not the degree of class consciousness and conflict between the worker class and the management class in the United States that exists in European countries. Ownership of private property by both management and union members is a further mediating influence in the United States.

Job-centered emphasis.   Perhaps the union philosophy in the United States is best expressed by a former labor leader, Samuel Gompers, who said:

> The ground work principle of America's labor movement has been to recognize that first things must come first. The primary essential in our mission has been the protection of the wage earner, now; to improve the safety and the sanitary conditions of the workshop; to free him from the tyranies, petty or otherwise, which serve to make his existence slavery. These in the nature of things, I repeat, were and are the objectives of trade unions.[2]

The primary purpose voiced in this philosophy of unionism in the United States has been the collective pursuit of "bread-and-butter" issues: higher wages, job security, and good working conditions. A contemporary illustration is a proposal by the United Steelworkers for lifetime wage and salary security.[3]

To aid in the protection of workers' security, large unions in the United States have become politically active, although such activity traditionally has been oriented more toward workplace issues than broad social concerns. However, since the mid-1960s unions have taken positions on economic issues, on full employment, and on some social issues. Nevertheless, American unionism has focused primarily on wages, working hours, and working conditions.

European emphasis.   Unions in a number of European countries have a somewhat different emphasis. They tend to be very ideological and political because they see themselves representing the working class. One writer notes that European unions:

> embarked upon a course of advancing the entire working class by transforming the total society, in contrast to the emphasis of the American movement on the immediate specifics of wages, hours, and working conditions for its members only.[4]

In Europe, political parties and trade unions merge together, and in some countries such as Great Britain, one of the major political parties is actually called the Labour Party. In France and Italy in recent years national general labor strikes have been called to reinforce the political and social aims of these labor parties.

Another facet of foreign unions that has not been widely adopted in the United States is the notion of worker involvement in managerial decision making.

> Most European unions have not been content to limit their plant objectives to wages, hours, and working conditions. Socialist influence and tradition have led most of the labor movements to inscribe high on their platforms the doctrine of workers' control over industry, in the sense of industrial decisions on production, investment, and marketing.[5]

This involvement, called co-determination, is discussed later in this chapter, although it is mentioned here to show the extent of involvement that unions can have in managerial decision making.

One interesting speculation is that the two philosophies are being merged. As a result of widespread international trade and multinational firms, cross-fertilization is increasing. International labor organizations may be labor's response to the multinational corporation. Already automobile workers' unions in Europe and the United States are discussing cooperative efforts. However, it is not likely that a labor party as such would be formed in the United States or that the labor unions in Europe would drastically change. It would appear that some interchange and adaptations will occur, but the European and American unions will still retain some distinctly different characteristics.

What are philosophical differences between U.S. and European unionism?

Unions as a Countervailing Force

Managements and unions, through their respective representatives, spend a great deal of time and effort disagreeing with one another. This disagreement is to be expected because of the nature of their built-in adversary roles. For example, publications from the United States Chamber of Commerce, a management organization, and the AFL/CIO *American Federationist*, a labor publication, discuss the "facts" about strikes. The management group suggests that:

> Some unions exert monopolistic power by closing down an entire industry simultaneously; others bring their multi-industry union against just one employer at a time, forcing each to capitulate and fall in line by the wage-leader technique. International unions at times combine to coerce industry to adopt a uniform wage package.[6]

The union viewpoint on the other hand suggests:

The United States could not have achieved its vast productive growth and widespread well-being without collective bargaining. . . . . . . Basic to the success of the system of free collective bargaining is the right to strike—the right of workers collectively to lay down their tools. Yet, this right is continually challenged. . . . In this country, strikes are a collective bargaining weapon of absolute last resort when workers and their unions find the bargaining table leaves them no choice. Strikes are the exception, not the rule, of U.S. labor/management relations.[7]

These two extremely divergent views on strikes clearly indicate that management and union have institutionalized their disagreements. Yet, it is naive to suppose that either position or group is right *all of the time,* nor is it correct to assume that there are always serious disagreements that lead to strikes. Figure 18–2 indicates that work stoppages because of strikes or lockouts are, and have been, a relative small percentage of total work time. The U.S. figures are considerably lower than those of many other countries.

Perhaps the most beneficial view of unions is as a *countervailing force* to help keep management "honest" and make management consider the impact of its policies upon its employees. However, a rather delicate

FIGURE 18–2   Work stoppages, 1962–1977.

Year	Number of Stoppages	Workers Involved (thousands)	Days Idle (thousands)	Percent of Estimated Working Time
1962	3,614	1,230	18,600	.13
1963	3,362	941	16,100	.11
1964	3,655	1,640	22,900	.15
1965	3,963	1,550	13,300	.15
1966	4,405	1,960	25,400	.15
1967	4,595	2,870	42,100	.25
1968	5,045	2,649	49,018	.28
1969	5,700	2,481	42,869	.24
1970	5,716	3,305	66,414	.37
1971	5,138	3,280	47,589	.26
1972	5,010	1,714	27,066	.15
1973	5,353	2,251	27,948	.14
1974	6,074	2,778	47,991	.24
1975	5,031	1,746	31,237	.16
1976	5,648	2,420	37,895	.19
1977	5,600	2,300	36,000	.17

(Source: U.S., Department of Labor, Bureau of Labor Statistics, *Monthly Labor Review*, 101 (May 1978), p. 115.)

balance exists between management power and union power in an organization. It is very easy for this balance to be tipped one way or the other.

While the management/union relationship is quite acceptable as a countervailing-forces situation, it can become difficult when either side clearly gains the upper hand, determined to use its power to "conquer" the other. The effect of labor legislation passed over the years in this country has been to maintain a reasonable balance in the bargaining relationship. The legal foundation of the collective bargaining relationship in the United States will be discussed later in the chapter. First, a look at the historical emergence of the American labor union movement is needed.

Early Evolution of U.S. Unions

It has been suggested that the labor movement in the United States arose when craftsmen in similar occupations banded together voluntarily to protect their jobs.[8] Voluntary union membership is based on *job consciousness*: jobs are a scarce resource and union members must protect them. Under this line of reasoning, the union's chief concern is *job control*: a union must control the tasks making up the jobs under the union's jurisdiction, such as plumbing, electrical work, or carpentry. Job control has been one of the cornerstones of American unionism.

As early as 1794 in the United States, shoemakers organized into a union and conducted strikes and picketing. However, in the early days, unions in the United States received very little support from the courts. In 1805, when the shoemakers' union struck for higher wages, a Philadelphia court found union members guilty of engaging in a *criminal conspiracy* to raise wages.

Commonwealth v. Hunt.   In 1842 a very important legal landmark, the case of *Commonwealth* v. *Hunt*, was decided. The Massachusetts Supreme Court ruled that: "For a union to be guilty of conspiracy, either its objective or the means used to reach it must be criminal or unlawful."[9] As a result of this decision, unions were no longer seen as illegal conspiracies in the eyes of the courts and the conspiracy idea lost favor.

Post–Civil War period.   The end of the Civil War in 1865 was followed by rapid industrial expansion and a growth of giant business trusts. The 1870s were characterized by industrial unrest, low wages, long hours, and considerable unemployment. In 1877, great railroad strikes spread through the major U.S. railroad lines in protest against the practices of railroad management. Eight years earlier, a group of workers formed the *Knights of Labor*. The goals of the Knights of Labor were: (1) to establish one big union embracing all workers, and (2) to establish a cooperative economic system to replace capitalism. They emphasized "political reform" and the establishment of "work cooperatives." However, the Knights, after their peak in 1885, soon faded from the labor scene.

In 1886, the American Federation of Labor (AFL) was formed as a federation of independent national unions. Its basic principle was to organize *skilled craft workers*, like carpenters and plumbers, to bargain for such "bread-and-butter" issues as wages and working conditions. The AFL emphasized collective bargaining as a primary means of obtaining these immediate objectives. Samuel Gompers was the AFL's chief spokesman and served as president until his death in 1924.

At first, the AFL grew very slowly. Six years after its formation, its total membership amounted to only 250,000. However, it managed to survive in the face of adversity while other parts of the labor movement withered and died.

While *craft unions* (made up of skilled craftsmen) survived and the AFL continued, the Civil War gave factories a big boost. Factory mass-production methods, using semiskilled or unskilled workers, were necessary to supply the armies. Though factories provided a potential area of expansion for unions, they were very hard to organize. Unions found they could not control entry to factory jobs because most of the jobs were filled by semiskilled workers who had no tradition of unionism. This difference ultimately led to the founding of the Congress for Industrial Organization (CIO) in 1938. So unionism outside the skilled crafts remained very uncertain, with the consequence that *industrial unions* were formed much later than *craft unions*.

Early Labor Legislation

It has been suggested that if unconstrained superior economic strength can be used to prevent labor unions from forming, the *right to organize* means very little. To be meaningful, a "right" must be respected.[10] The right to collective bargaining is of little value if workers are not free to exercise it. As evidence shows, management has used practices calculated to prevent workers from using this right, and the federal government has taken action to either hamper unions or protect them.

The passage of the Sherman Antitrust Act in 1890 forbade monopolies and efforts to illegally restrain trade. As a result of a 1908 Supreme Court Case (Danbury Hatters case—*Loewe* v. *Lawlor*), union boycott efforts were classed as attempts to restrain trade.

Several years later, in 1914, the Clayton Act was passed which limited the use of injunctions in labor disputes, but it had little effect on the labor movement in the United States. The courts interpreted the Clayton Act to mean that the *activities* of a union determined whether or not it was in violation of the law. This interpretation never really changed labor's situation. As a result, union strength declined through the 1920s.

Railway Labor Act (1926). The Railway Labor Act is significant because it represents a shift in governmental regulation of unions. As a result of a joint effort of railroad management and unions to reduce the possibilities of transportation strikes, this act gave railroad employees "the right to organize and bargain collectively through representatives of their own choosing." In 1936, airlines and their employees were added to those covered by this act. Both of these industries are still covered by this act instead of others passed later.

The act set up a rather complex series of steps to prevent work stoppages. Although a detailed explanation is beyond the scope of this book, it should be noted that many labor experts today feel that the airline and railroad industries should be covered under the same laws as all other industries. Because times have changed, they argue that the Railway Labor Act should be eliminated.[11]

Norris-LaGuardia Act (1932). In 1932 Congress passed the Norris-LaGuardia Act which guaranteed workers' right to organize and restricted the issuance of court injunction in labor disputes. The Norris-LaGuardia Act substantially freed union activity from court interference and made the infamous "yellow dog" contract illegal. Under this contract, signed by the worker as a condition of employment, the employee agreed not to join a union upon penalty of discharge. It was called a yellow dog contract because, according to union sympathizers, only a "yellow dog" would take a job under such conditions.

In 1933 the National Industrial Recovery Act (NIRA) was passed. It contained, among other things, provisions extending the policies of the Railway Labor Act for railroad employees into interstate commerce. Also, the act set up election machinery permitting employees to choose collective bargaining representatives. The NIRA was declared unconstitutional in 1935, and it was replaced by the Wagner Act.

Can you sketch U.S. labor history from 1800–1932?

The progress made by unions up to the early 1930s provided the basis for the development and passage of several acts: 1) *Wagner Act*, 2) *Taft-Hartley Act*, and 3) the *Landrum-Griffin Act*. These later acts have the most direct and continuing impact on employers and unions today and form the *National Labor Code*.

NATIONAL LABOR CODE

Each of the acts in the National Labor Code was enacted to protect some entity in the union/management relationship. Figure 18–3 shows each of

FIGURE 18–3   National Labor Code.

NATIONAL LABOR CODE		
Wagner Act	Taft-Hartley Act	Landrum-Griffin Act
Unions	*Management*	*Union Members*

the segments of the code and which party received the greatest protection. The nature of this protection will become clearer as each of the acts is discussed.

The Wagner Act

The National Labor Relations Act (or Wagner Act) of 1935 has been called the "Magna Carta" of labor and forms the first of three parts of the *National Labor Code*. The Wagner Act was, by anyone's standards, *pro-union*. It was Congress' effort to bring about industrial peace and to encourage union growth in three ways: (1) by establishing the *right to organize*, unhampered by management interference; (2) by providing definitions of *unfair labor practices* on the part of management; and (3) by setting up an agency—the *National Labor Relations Board*—to see that the rules were followed.

In setting up the National Labor Relations Board to administer the act, Congress established the principle that employees should be *protected* in their rights to form a union and to *bargain collectively* on wages and working conditions. To do this, the act made it an unfair labor practice for an *employer* to do any of the following:

1. Interfere with, restrain, or coerce employees in the exercise of their rights to organize, bargain collectively, and engage in other concerted activities for their mutual aid or protection.

2. Dominate or interfere with the formation or administration of any labor organization or contribute financial or other support to it.

3. Encourage or discourage membership in any labor organization by discrimination with regard to hiring or tenure or conditions of employment, subject to an exception for valid union security agreement.

4. Discharge or otherwise discriminate against an employee because he filed charges or gave testimony under the act.

5. Refuse to bargain collectively with the majority of representatives of his employees.[12]

The Taft-Hartley Act

When World War II ended, the pent-up demand for goods was frustrated by numerous strikes. There were about three times the number of strikes as before the war. These conditions led to the passage of the *Taft-Hartley Act* in 1947.

The Taft-Hartley Act was an attempt to balance the collective bargaining equation. It was designed to offset the pro-union Wagner Act by limiting union tactics and was considered to be *pro-management*. It provided the second part of the *National Labor Code*.

The new law was built upon the Wagner Act, but all of the Wagner Act's major provisions were amended or qualified in some respect, and an entirely new code of conduct for unions was established. The Taft-Hartley Act forbade a series of unfair labor practices by unions. It became unlawful for a *union* to:

1. Restrain or coerce employees in the exercise of their rights under the act; restrain or coerce any employer in the selection of his bargaining or grievance representative;
2. Cause or attempt to cause an employer to discriminate against an employee on account of membership or nonmembership in a labor organization, subject to an exception for a valid union shop agreement;
3. Refuse to bargain collectively in good faith with an employer if the union has been designated as bargaining agent by a majority of the employees;
4. Induce or encourage employees to stop work for the object of forcing an employer or self-employed person to join a union or enforcing an employer or other person to stop doing business with any other person (boycott provisions);
5. Induce or encourage employees to stop work for the object of forcing an employer to assign particular work to members of a union instead of members of another union (jurisdictional strike);
6. Charge an excessive or discriminatory fee as a condition to becoming a member of the union;
7. Cause or attempt to cause an employer to pay for services that are not performed or are not to be performed (feather-bedding).[13]

One specific provision in the Taft-Hartley Act deserves special explanation. This provision is Section 14B, the so-called "right-to work" provision which outlaws the closed shop and allows states to pass "right-to-work laws." A *closed shop* requires employees to join a union before they can be hired. The act *did* allow the *union shop*, which requires that an employee join the union, usually 30–60 days after being hired.

"Right-to-work" laws are state laws that prohibit both the closed shop and the union shop. They were so named because they allow a person the right to work without having to join a union. As of 1978, 20 states had enacted these laws.

The Landrum-Griffin Act

In 1959, the third segment of the *National Labor Code*, the *Landrum-Griffin Act*, was passed as a result of a congressional committee's findings on union corruption. This law was aimed at protecting *individual union members* by requiring a bill of rights, reporting procedures, election supervision, and tightening the secondary boycott provisions of the Taft-Hartley Act. Among provisions of the Landrum-Griffin Act are:

1. Every labor organization is required to have a constitution and by-laws containing certain minimum standards and safeguards.
2. Reports on the union's policies and procedures as well as an annual financial report must be filed with the Secretary of Labor and must be disclosed to the union's members.
3. Union members must have a bill of rights to protect their rights within the unions.
4. Standards are established for union trusteeship and union elections.
5. Reports on trusteeships must be made to the Secretary of Labor.
6. A fiduciary relationship is imposed upon union officers.
7. They are required to file reports with the Secretary of Labor on conflict of interest transactions.
8. The Secretary of Labor is made a watch-dog of union conduct. He is a custodian of reports from unions and their officers and he is given the power to investigate and prosecute violations of many of the provisions of the act.[14]

What are the acts in the National Labor Code?

As society's needs change, the National Labor Code will continue to evolve. The collective bargaining relationship may need to be revised again. Proposed extensions of the National Labor Code include: compulsory arbitration; extended injunction powers for the President in national emergency situations; and some kind of extension of the price-wage control system to include management/union agreements. The important point is that this legal foundation of labor/management relations *does* change with time.

THE UNIONIZATION PROCESS

All of the provisions of the above laws focus on two areas:

1. Procedures whereby employees decide whether or not to join a union, and

2. The collective bargaining process whereby ongoing union/management agreements are reached.

The first of these issues is discussed below and collective bargaining is discussed in detail in the next chapter. Figure 18-4 depicts the stages in a typical unionization effort. The first stage is handbilling.

Handbilling

This stage serves the same purpose that advertising does for a product: to create interest in "buying" the union. Brochures, leaflets, or circulars are all types of handbills. These items can be passed out to employees as they leave work, mailed to their homes, or even attached to their vehicles. Their purpose is to convince employees to sign an authorization card.

Authorization Card

This card, which is signed by an employee, indicates the employee's desire to vote on having a union. It does not necessarily mean that the employee is in favor of a union, but that he or she would like to have the opportunity to vote on having one. One reason employees who do not want a union might sign an authorization card is to get management's attention that employees are disgruntled.

A listing by the United Steelworkers of America of key factors leading to success in organizing white-collar workers reads like a checklist of "management don't's." Important areas of employee discontent that can lead to unionization include:

1. A lack of communication between employees and management;
2. Management's ignorance of workers' problems;
3. Lower salary scales than most in the same geographical area;
4. Inequities in salaries with people doing identical work receiving different rates;
5. Inequities in promotions with regard to seniority;

FIGURE 18–4 Unionization process.

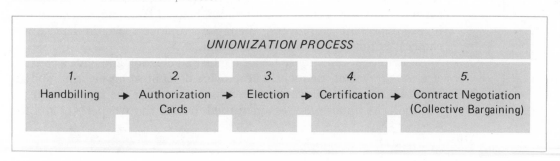

6. The absence of medical, surgical, sick leave, or pension plans for employees on a noncontributory basis;
7. Poor working conditions;
8. Overtime work without compensation;
9. Constant pressure and harassment for work completion;
10. Management's treating employees as if the employees were unintelligent.[15]

The Office and Professional Employees International Union expands upon the list in a publication that lists the following items for its organizers to consider when determining if an organization is "ripe" for a union.[16]

Location of the plant or office	Sick and accident policy
Female/male ratio	Group insurance plan
Location of parking lots	How was overtime distributed?
Number of shifts	Is seniority followed?
Starting and quitting times	What is promotional policy?
What is the wage structure?	Can employees transfer?
When are employees paid?	Leave of absence policy
Do they get a bonus?	Lay-off practices
Shift premiums	Recall procedures
Overtime practices	Disciplinary procedures
Vacation entitlement	Tactics of the company toward unions

According to federal labor law, if 30 percent of the employees in a proposed bargaining unit have signed cards, the union may petition the National Labor Relations Board (NLRB) or a similar appropriate agency for an election. Disagreements between the employer and the union as to who should and who should not be included in the bargaining unit can lead to lengthy legal battles before the NLRB and in the courts. If the NLRB determines that an appropriate number of cards have been signed, then that agency will order and supervise an election.

Representation Election

An election to determine if a union will represent the employees is supervised by the NLRB or another legal body. If two unions are attempting to represent employees, then the employees would have three choices: union A, union B, or no union.

An employer can choose to not contest an election and have a *consent election*. However, frequently employers do contest an election and attempt to provide employees information to convince them not to vote for a union. The unfair practices identified in both the Wagner Act and the

Taft-Hartley Act place restrictions on the actions of both an employer and the union.

Assuming an election is held, the union only needs to receive a *majority of those voting* in the election. For example, if a group of 200 employees is the identified unit and only 50 people vote, only 26 employees would need to vote "yes" in order for a union to be named as the representative of all 200. If either side believes that unfair labor practices have been used by the other side, the election results can be appealed to the NLRB. If the NLRB finds that unfair practices were used, it can order a new election. Assuming that no unfair practices have been used and the union obtains a majority in the election, the union then petitions the NLRB for certification.

Certification

Official certification of a union as the legal representative for employees is given by the NLRB, or the relevant body, after reviewing the results of the election. Once certified, the union attempts to negotiate a contract with the employer.

Employees who have a union and no longer wish to be represented by it can utilize the same process. An attempt to remove a union as the employees' representative is called *decertification*. Most of the same procedures and regulations apply to decertification efforts.

Contract Negotiation (Collective Bargaining)

Negotiation of a labor contract is one of the most important methods used by unions to obtain their major goals. The Taft-Hartley Act defines collective bargaining as:

> The performance of the mutual obligation of the employer and the representative of the employees to *meet* at reasonable times and *confer in good faith* with respect to wages, hours, and other terms and conditions of employment, or the negotiations of agreement, or any question arising thereunder and the execution of a written contract incorporating any agreement reached if requested by either party. But such obligation does not compel either party to agree to a proposal or require the making of any concession.[17] (italics added)

In the process of collective bargaining, strikes are also an important tool for unions. A *strike is basically a shutdown of work and production that can be used by the union to show its power and to gain concessions from management.* A strike imposes certain *costs* on management for disagreeing with union demands, and it extracts costs from the union's members as well. A general discussion of collective bargaining is contained in the next chapter.

This brief overview of the unionization process is designed to familiarize you with how unions become employee representatives. Unionism has been a very important force in the management of personnel in the United States. In the last 60 years, workers have participated in determining such personnel policies as wages, hours, and benefits. Today, most union contracts contain provisions for nine or more annual holidays, leaves of absence, sick-leave plans, insurance, pension, supplemental unemployment benefits, and more. These provisions were not common benefits before unions became "protected" by federal law and used their resources to spread their representation of employees.

How does a union become a representative of employees?

UNION STRUCTURE

Unions have become multilevel organizational structures. Members of local unions are at the bottom of the organization chart, regional or district offices in the middle, and the national or international union headquarters at the top of the hierarchy. In 1955, a merger of the American Federation of Labor and the Congress of Industrial Organizations formed the AFL-CIO (see Figure 18–5).

Local Unions

Local unions may be centered around a particular employer organization or around a particular geographical location. For example, the Communication Workers of America local for Dallas, Texas, might include all the nonexempt telephone company employees in Dallas. (As mentioned in Chapter 13, nonexempt employees are subject to the overtime provisions of federal wage and hour laws).

The policy-making process of the local union is generally democratic in form. Members vote on suggestions by either the membership or the officers. Normally, secret ballots are used. Officers in local unions are elected by the membership and are subject to removal if they do not perform satisfactorily. For this reason, local union officers tend to be very concerned with the effect of their actions on the membership. They tend to react to situations much as politicians would react because they, too, are concerned with obtaining votes.

Some unions have *business agents*, full-time union officials who are usually elected. The agent may run the local headquarters, help negotiate contracts with management, and may become involved in organization attempts. *Shop stewards* are usually elected by the local union membership and represent the lowest elected level in the local union. They

FIGURE 18–5   Structure of the AFL-CIO.

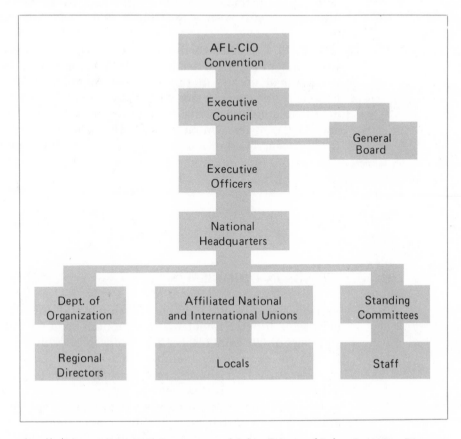

(Source: Adapted from U.S. Department of Labor, Bureau of Labor Statistics, *Directory of National Unions and Employee Associations*, Bulletin 1750 (Washington, D.C.: U.S. Government Printing Office, 1971).)

usually negotiate grievances with supervisors and generally represent the workers at the work site.

Union Hierarchy

Intermediate union organizational units coordinate the activities of a number of local units. All of the local unions in a state, or in several may be grouped together with some type of joint governing board. Such organizations may be city-wide, state-wide, or multi-state-wide.

At the top of the union hierarchy are the national or international unions. (The terms mean essentially the same.) These are very powerful levels of the organization, designed to provide services to the local unions, as well as to determine union policy on a national scale. They help maintain financial records, provide a base from which additional organization drives may take place, and control the money for strike funds.

The AFL-CIO is a rather loose confederation of national unions, each of which is semiautonomous. The AFL-CIO represents nearly two-thirds of the national unions in this country. Approximately one-third of the nationals, however, are not affiliated with the AFL-CIO. The two largest unaffiliated unions in this grouping are the United Automobile Workers and the Teamsters Union. The United Mine Workers and the International Brotherhood of Longshoremen also are not members of the AFL-CIO.

How are unions in the U.S. typically structured?

TRENDS IN UNIONISM

Reliable statistics on union membership in the United States are historically very difficult to obtain. Some unions tend to exaggerate membership reports to gain respect for themselves. Other unions have been known to report fewer members than they actually have for financial reasons, such as trying to avoid making higher payments to the labor federations to which they belong.[18]

However, the most current figures available from the Bureau of Labor Statistics showed that membership in *labor unions* and public and professional *employee associations* headquartered in the United States was 22.5 million in 1976, a decrease of 767,000, or 4 percent, over 1974 figures.[19]

Figure 18–6 traces the membership in U.S. unions from 1960 through 1976. The total number of union members has increased during those years; however, the number of union members as a percent of the total work force has actually declined somewhat from 23.6 percent in 1960 to 20.1 percent in 1976. This decline is partially due to a growing work force. But it is also of concern to union leaders because it shows they are not penetrating the work force as fast as new employees are added.

Other figures show the percentage and number of white-collar and women workers in unions and associations has been rising. In recent years unions have been quite interested in organizing workers in these categories. However, these workers have shown a great deal of resistance to joining unions. During the last few years the trend seems to be reversing itself, but overall figures can be somewhat deceiving. Specifically, almost *half* of the nation's 31 million blue-collar workers (craftsmen, operatives, etc.) are now unionized. This number includes at least 80 percent of the workers in transportation, construction, municipal

FIGURE 18–6   U.S. union membership, 1960–1976 (selected years).

Year	Total Membership* (thousands)	Total Labor Force		Employees in Nonagricultural Establishments	
		Number (thousands)	Percent Union Members	Number (thousands)	Percent Union Members
1960	17,049	72,142	23.6	54,234	31.4
1962	16,586	73,442	22.6	55,596	29.8
1964	16,841	75,830	22.0	58,331	28.9
1966	17,940	78,893	22.7	63,955	28.1
1968	18,916	82,272	23.0	67,951**	27.8**
1970	19,381	85,903	22.6	70,920**	27.3**
1972	19,435	88,991	21.8	73,711**	26.4**
1974	20,096	93,240	21.6	78,334	25.7
1976	19,432	96,917	20.1	79,443	24.5

*Membership includes total reported membership excluding Canada. Also included are members of directly affiliated local unions. Members of single-firm unions are excluded.
**Revised.

(Source: U.S. Department of Labor, "Labor Union and Employee Association Membership—1976," press release, September 4, 1978.)

utilities, and somewhat over two-thirds of the blue-collar workers in manufacturing and mining.[20] Almost all manual workers in some manufacturing industries including steel, automobiles, rubber, aerospace, meatpacking, agricultural implements, brewing, paper, needle trades, and a few others have been organized. A substantial percent of the blue-collar employees in the printing, oil, chemical, shoe, electric, electronic, and pharmaceutical industries have also been unionized.[21]

Therefore, the overall figure that something less than 25 percent of the work force is unionized can be somewhat misleading. Certain industries are quite heavily unionized, whereas others are hardly unionized at all.

Unionism in the Public Sector

In 1962, the emergence of employee organizations in the national government became an important factor for the first time and started a new era in public personnel administration. Since then, unionism has spread to state and local governments as well.

Unionism and the federal government.   President Kennedy in 1962 issued Executive Order 10988 which, for the first time in the United States' history, supported the unionization of federal employees.

In 1966, Congress passed legislation allowing postal employees to organize and have exclusive recognition. In 1969, through Executive

Order 11491, President Nixon revised Executive Order 10988 to increase the rights of employee organizations. Executive Order 11491 set up a federal labor relations council to administer and interpret the order, a grievance procedure process, a code of unfair labor practices, and exclusive recognition to unions. Although Executive Order 11491 still limits unionism, it does establish realistic methods pertaining to labor/management relations within the federal government, which are similar to methods used in the private sector.

Allowing federal employees to organize and join unions presents new problems and challenges for personnel administration in the federal government. Unions in the federal government hold the same basic philosophy as unions in the private sector. Most individuals who join a union in the federal government feel that it protects their individual freedom and rights in the organization and provides a means for increasing wages and fringe benefits.[22] However, unions in the federal government do *differ* somewhat from unions in the private sector. For example, the Civil Service Commission still has considerable control over personnel policies and regulations. Because of limits on collective bargaining, federal government unions cannot bargain over wages. Also, white-collar workers fill the majority of government positions, and therefore the majority of the union-member slots.[24]

State and local government unionism.   Union growth has been even more rapid at the state and local level than at the federal level. As Figure 18–7 reveals, union membership at the state and local levels now exceeds 1.7 million workers. Much of the total union membership growth has come in this sector.

Unionism in this sector of the economy presents some unique problems and challenges. First, many of the unionized local government employees are in exclusive and critical service areas. Police officers, fire fighters, and sanitation workers all provide essential services in most cities. Allowing these workers to go on strike endangers public health and safety. Consequently, 37 states have laws prohibiting public employee

FIGURE 18–7   Governmental union membership.

Level of Government	Number of Unionized Employees (in thousands)		
	1972	1974	1976
U.S. Federal	1,355	1,391	1,300
State and Local	1,105	1,529	1,710

(Source: U.S. Department of Labor, "Labor Union and Employee Association Membership—1976," press release, September 4, 1978.)

work stoppages.[23] The impact of work stoppages has led to numerous methods of impasse resolution including arbitration.

The impact of public employee wage increases on taxes is another concern. As the 1978 tax referendum in California and other states emphasized, the general public is increasingly skeptical of state and local government tax expenditures. Thus wage demands by public employees are often met with distrust and are becoming political issues.

Another problem is that state and local governmental unions often face widely varying laws and hiring policies from city to city and state to state. The widespread existence of civil service and so-called "merit systems" provides a vastly different environment in the public sector. The result is that "the bargaining environment of the public sector is characterized by complexity, lack of clarity, and change."[24]

White-Collar Union Movement

The American labor movement has long had the image of being a blue-collar movement. However, a large number of white-collar workers are joining unions, and the trend can be expected to accelerate in the years ahead. White-collar workers represented about 27 percent of the total unionized work force in 1976, compared to 24.3 percent in 1974.[25] In addition, unions have been winning a higher percentage of white-collar elections—about 57 percent—than in other areas.[26] Six of the ten largest AFL-CIO unions are mainly composed of white-collar workers.[27]

The reasons behind this growth are rather complex. One reason is that changes in technology have boosted the number of white-collar workers in the work force. With the total employees in white-collar jobs increasing relative to manufacturing jobs, unions have had to focus on white-collar areas in order to maintain membership.

Further, union leaders feel there is a growing realization among professionals that their employment problems are not too different from those of production workers in the areas of pay, job security, and grievances.[28] Also, professionals in areas such as nursing, teaching, and engineering are turning to unions in increasing numbers. Unionization among such employees, who have not typically been union-oriented, presents a definite challenge for managers in a wide range of organizations.

CO-DETERMINATION

An idea receiving widespread use in Europe is *co-determination*. Under this concept union or worker representatives are given positions on a company's board of directors or on a firm's management advisory board. This example is only one element in a trend toward greater worker influence and corporate management that has swept through much of Western Europe.

Different countries have different forms of co-determination. In Germany workers sit on the board of directors and exercise some veto power over certain proposals by management.[29] In Britain and Italy, where chronic labor/management strife endangers efforts to revive the national economies, major corporations are taking the initiative to urge sharing the decision-making process with workers.[30]

The idea of joint management may or may not be appropriate for labor/management relations in the United States, but it does illustrate a very interesting attempt at labor/management relations in Europe. Working cooperation between management and union can provide benefits for both, especially in the area of job design. As an example, a joint labor/management committee at a Rockwell International plant in Michigan helped design the new plant.[31]

REVIEW AND PREVIEW

The conditions surrounding labor relations in this country reflect the historical development of U.S. unions and U.S. labor legislation. The National Labor Code provides a three-pronged base for current labor/management relationships in this country. The Wagner Act was pro-union; the Taft-Hartley, pro-management; and the Landrum-Griffin, pro-individual union members.

An awareness of the process of certification is vital in order to respond to union efforts. Trends in unionism also need to be considered if organizations are to effectively manage the union interface.

Labor/management relationships can span a spectrum from constant conflict to outright collaboration. Most relationships in this country currently fall between the two extremes, but examples of both extremes can sometimes be found. The next chapter looks at collective bargaining as another part of the management relationship. It also examines one of the most important interfaces between the union and management, that of the grievance procedure.

Review Questions

1. Discuss: "Unions in the United States and Europe are and always will be distinctly different."
2. List five key events that occurred in U.S. labor history before 1935.
3. Identify the three parts of the National Labor Code and the key elements of each act.

4. One of your employees has just brought you a union leaflet urging the employee to sign a card. What events would you expect from that point?

5. What is the meaning of a "confederation" of unions? What are the levels within a union confederation?

6. Unionism in the United States is undergoing some changes. What are some of the current trends and changes?

OPENING CASE FOLLOW-UP

The reaction exhibited by George Gottlieb, founder of Computer Service Bureau (CSB), is typically seen in managers and entrepreneurs. However, George would be better served if he realized that his employees might feel they need an outside force to deal with some of their problems. In addition, George's ignorance of labor law may lead him to take illegal action by threatening employees with dismissal if they sign an authorization card.

George should take action on two fronts. First, he should contact his labor attorney before taking any action so that he knows what he legally can and cannot do. Secondly, he needs to find out what problems employees have. One reason for the lack of a union attempt earlier was the high turnover: employees did not stay with CSB long enough to become interested in a union.

It is apparent that George does not want to deal with unionized employees. However, employees may need a union or a unionization effort to affect necessary changes in wages and other job conditions.

Case: Witchcraft*

One of the most interesting cases in the history of the National Labor Relations Board involved a union election in Puerto Rico. The General Cigar Company (GCC) filed an unfair practices charge against the International Association of Machinists and Aerospace Workers (IAM). The final election results were 255 for the IAM, 222 for no union and 6 challenged votes, but the GCC asked the NLRB to void the election for several reasons:

1. An IAM supporter persuaded some other workers to smell the contents of a bottle of magic potion bought from a local "bujera" (witch or sorceress) and then told them they could not vote against the union without repercussions.
2. A publicly-acknowledged witch was paid $150 by the wife of another employee to work for the union.
3. A male midget was hired by another pro-union employee to persuade employees to vote for the IAM.
4. The weather before and after the election was clear and sunny. However, during the election a torrential rainstorm hit.

The GCC also charged the IAM with threatening and bribing employees to vote pro-union. The IAM called the charges ludicrous and said the complaints showed the need for a union to protect employees from management.

QUESTIONS

1. If you were on the NLRB, what laws would you need to consider?
2. Would you rule for GCC or the IAM? Why?

* Adapted from information in *Business Week*, October 19, 1968, p. 132.

Notes

1. E. W. Baake, "Some Basic Characteristics of Unions," in E. W. Baake, Clark Kerr, and Charles Anrod, eds. *Unions, Management and the Public*, 3d ed. (New York: Harcourt Brace Jovanovich, 1967), pp. 139–142.

2. Samuel Gompers, "The Philosophy of Trade Unionism," in E. W. Baake, Clark Kerr, and Charles Anrod, eds. *Unions, Management and the Public*, 3d ed. (New York: Harcourt Brace Jovanovich, 1967), p. 42.

3. "Developments in Industrial Relations," *Monthly Labor Review*, 101 (June 1977), pp. 62–64.

4. Everett M. Kassalow, "The Development of Western Labor Movements: Some Comparative Considerations," in Richard Lester, ed., *Labor: Readings on Major Issues* (New York: Random House, 1965), p. 74.

5. *Ibid.*, p. 84.

6. *The Anti-Trust Approach to Union Monopoly* (Washington, D.C.: U.S. Chamber of Commerce, n.d.).

7. "Why Strikes? Facts vs. Fiction," *Economic Trends and Outlook*, prepared by the AFL/CIO Department of Research, Washington, D.C. reprinted from *AFL/ CIO American Federationist* (November 1965).

8. S. Perlman, *A History of Trade Unionism in the United States* (New York: Macmillan, 1929).

9. Marten Estey, *The Unions: Structure, Development, and Management.* (New York: Harcourt Brace Jovanovich, 1967), pp. 94–95.

10. B. J. Taylor and F. Whitney, *Labor Relations Law*, 2d ed. (Englewood Cliffs, N.J.: Prentice-Hall, 1975), p. 118.

11. For more details on the act, see Eugene C. Hagburg and Marvin J. Levine, *Labor Relations: An Integrated Perspective* (St. Paul, Minn.: West Publishing, 1978), chapter 10.

12. Reprinted by permission from *Primer of Labor Relations*, 17th ed., copyright 1969 by The Bureau of National Affairs, Inc., Washington, D.C. 20037.

13. Reprinted by permission from *Primer of Labor Relations*, 17th ed., copyright 1969 by The Bureau of National Affairs, Inc., Washington, D.C. 20037.

14. Reprinted by permission from *Primer of Labor Relations*, 17th ed., copyright 1969 by The Bureau of National Affairs, Inc., Washington, D.C. 20037.

15. "White Collar Unionization," *Generation* (September-October 1970), pp. 20–21.

16. Office and Professional Employees International Union, AFL-CIO CLC, *Now Let's Get Out and Organize*, pp. 5–6.

17. 29 U.S. Code 158. Also found in 61 U.S. Statutes 160, June 23, 1947.

18. A. A. Sloane and F. Whitney, *Labor Relations*, 2d ed. (Englewood Cliffs, N.J.: Prentice-Hall, 1972), p. 6.

19. U.S. Department of Labor, "Labor Union and Employee Association Membership—1976," press release, September 4, 1978.

20. Sloane and Whitney, *Labor Relations*, p. 7.

21. *Ibid.*, p. 7.

22. L. V. Imundo, Jr., "Why Federal Employees Join Unions: A Study of AFGE Local 916," *Public Personnel Management* (January-February 1973), pp. 23–28.

23. Charles Redenius, "Public Employees: A Survey of Some Critical Problems on the Frontier of Collective Bargaining," *Labor Law Journal*, 27 (September 1976), pp. 588–599.

24. *Ibid.*, p. 591.

25. U.S. Department of Labor, "Labor Union Membership."

26. Alan Kistler, "Trends in Union Growth," *Labor Law Journal*, 28 (August 1977), pp. 539–545.

27. "Labor Letter," *Wall Street Journal*, December 13, 1977, p. 1.

28. "More Middle-Class Workers Rush to Join Unions," *U.S. News and World Report* (October 1974), p. 68.

29. Reyer A. Swaak, "Industrial Democracy: An Update," *The Personnel Administrator* (April 1978) pp. 34–41.

30. "Co-determination When Workers Help Manage," *Business Week*, July 14, 1975, p. 133.

31. William L. Batt, Jr. and Edgar Weinberg, "Labor-Management Cooperation Today," *Harvard Business Review* (January-February 1978), pp. 96–104.

<table>
<tr><td>chapter
19</td><td># Collective Bargaining
and Effective
Union-Management Relations</td></tr>
</table>

When you have read this chapter, you should be able to:

1. Define collective bargaining.

2. Identify some collective bargaining relationships and structures which can exist.

3. Describe a typical bargaining process.

4. Distinguish between a grievance and a complaint.

5. Discuss the basic steps in a grievance procedure.

6. Define and discuss arbitration as the final phase of the grievance procedure.

7. Identify at least four grievances that can be resolved through arbitration.

8. Contrast the legal and behavioral approaches to grievance resolution.

The Clean-up Grievance

The Willis Welding Company is a six-year-old welding equipment supply firm. The nonmanagerial workforce is unionized. Yesterday the union filed a grievance on behalf of Raymond Anzalone.

The union contract contains a clause that states: "Employees will be allowed reasonable time to clean up at the end of a work shift with pay." Two days ago Raymond's supervisor, Marshall Warren, found Raymond cleaning up 40 minutes before quitting time. Marshall said, "What are you doing quitting so early? If you don't get back to work, you'll be docked pay." Raymond replied, "I just finished filling the Acme order, which is a big job, and the next order is the Apex order, another big one. I didn't see any point in starting it for only a few minutes since I would probably have to start again tomorrow anyway to check where I was. Besides, our contract says we get clean up time." Marshall returned to his office and made a notation on Raymond's time card that 30 minutes should be deducted from Raymond's hours.

You are the plant manager and you are to meet with the shop steward this afternoon.

The broad issues of unionism discussed in the previous chapter become focused in an organization following a successful unionization attempt. As noted in Chapter 18, the final stage of the unionization process is the negotiation and signing of a contractual agreement between a union and an employer. This chapter discusses the process of contract negotiation through collective bargaining. Then it examines one of the most important areas of day-to-day union/management relations—grievances.

COLLECTIVE BARGAINING

Collective bargaining is somewhat different in the United States than in other countries, due to different philosophical and political origins for the collective bargaining system. Different legal frameworks for collective bargaining also exist in different countries.

COLLECTIVE BARGAINING is the process whereby representatives of management and representatives of the workers come together and negotiate over such items as wages, hours, and conditions of employment.

Types of Bargaining Relationships

Management/union relationships in collective bargaining can follow one of several different types:[1]

Conflict. This uncompromising management attitude is fast fading from the labor scene. However, it existed on a wide scale prior to World War II.

An armed truce attitude. Company representatives are motivated by the logic that they are well aware of the vital interests of the company and the unions are poles away and they always will be. This does not mean that forcing head-on conflict is in the best interests of either. Even today, many union-management relationships have made no more progress than this.

Power bargaining. Managers engaged in a power bargaining relationship can accept the union and in fact many pride themselves on their sense of "realism" which forces them to acknowledge the union's power. Management philosophy here assumes that management's task is to increase and then use their power to offset that of the other side where possible.

Accommodation. Accommodation is hardly the same thing as cooperation. Accommodation involves evolving routines and learning to adjust to one another and attempt to minimize conflict, to conciliate whenever necessary, and to tolerate one another. This in no way suggests that management goes out of its way to help organized labor.

Cooperation. This involves full acceptance of the union as an active partner in a formal plan and is a rare occurrence. In cooperation, management supports not only the right but the desirability of union participation in certain areas of decision making. The two parties jointly deal with personnel and production problems as they occur.

Collusion. This is a form of mutual interest monopoly which frankly is unconcerned with every interest except its own. These situations are relatively rare in American labor history because they have been deemed illegal.

"Good Faith"

Provisions in federal labor law suggest that employers' and employees' bargaining representatives be obligated to bargain "in good faith." *Good faith* means that the parties *agree* to bargain and that they send negotiators who are in a position to make decisions, not someone who does not have the authority to commit either group to a decision. Good faith means that the *decisions* are not changed after they are made and the *meetings* between the parties are not scheduled at ridiculous hours. It means not refusing to have a *written contract* and not using blatantly anti-union or anti-management propaganda during the bargaining process. The specifics of the collective bargaining "good faith" relationship are defined by a series of NLRB rulings and court rulings.

Collective bargaining is intended as a mutual give-and-take between representatives of two organizations to the mutual benefit of both. The power relationship contained in collective bargaining has the aspect of mutual threat. There is interdependence involved, but the threat of conflict seems necessary to maintain the relationship. Perhaps the most important aspect of collective bargaining, however, is that it is *on-going*. It is not a relationship that will be extinguished immediately after the agreement is reached.

Bargaining Structures

Bargaining structures come in many forms. The *one-employer/one-union structure* is the simplest. A more complex model is the *multi-union bargaining structure*, as in the construction industry, where one employer may face several different building trade unions representing a number of different crafts.

Another variation, *multi-employer bargaining*, developed in the coal mining and garment industries. In some cases, bargaining has been formally structured as a two-tier system, with a "master contract" supplemented by a local contract dealing with plant site issues.[2]

A bargaining structure changes over time as a result of unions attempting to stay up to date with changes in the organization's structure or technology. To maintain an effective bargaining position, union structures change and bargaining structures generally become more centralized and broader in scope.[3] These changes essentially follow the patterns in corporate organizations.

What are some possible bargaining relationships and structures?

Typical Bargaining Process

Typical bargaining includes an initial presentation of expectations (sometimes called *demands*) by both sides. Each tries to allow itself some flexibility to "trade-off" less important demands for more critical ones.

After opening positions have been taken, each side attempts to determine what the other side values highly and to reach the best bargain possible. For example, the union may be asking for dental benefits to be paid by the company as part of a package that also includes wage demands and retirement benefits. However, the union is *basically* interested in the wages and retirement benefits and would be willing to trade the dental payments for more wages. The company, however, has to determine what the union wants most and decide just exactly what it must give up.

After an initial agreement has been made, the two sides usually return to their respective constituencies to determine if what they have informally agreed on is acceptable. If it is, this agreement then usually becomes part of the formal written labor agreement, often referred to as *the contract.* Typical subjects for inclusion in a formal labor agreement, or contract, are shown in Figure 19–1.

Bargaining Deadlocks

Regardless of the structure of the bargaining process, labor and management do not always reach agreement on the issues. In such cases, a deadlock may result in *strikes by the union* or a *lockout by management.* Efforts to forestall such drastic actions on the part of either party can take the form of *conciliation/mediation* or *arbitration.*

FIGURE 19–1   Typical items in a labor "contract."

1. Purpose of agreement
2. Nondiscrimination clause
3. Management rights
4. Recognition of the union
5. Wages
6. Incentives
7. Hours of work
8. Vacations
9. Sick leave
10. Leaves of absence
11. Separation allowance
12. Seniority
13. Bulletin boards
14. Pension and insurance
15. Grievance procedure
16. Definitions
17. Terms of the contract (dates)
18. Appendices

Conciliation or mediation.　**Conciliation or mediation efforts occur when an outside individual attempts to help two deadlocked parties continue negotiations and arrive at a solution.** The mediator does not attempt to impose an external solution upon the parties but merely tries to keep them talking and may suggest compromise situations. A good example of this process was the work done by a federal mediator to keep the National Football League owners' and players' association at the bargaining table.

Arbitration.　**An arbitrator is an impartial individual whose job is to determine the relative merits of each argument and then make a decision, called an *award.*** Contract arbitration is very rare except in parts of the public sector such as police and firemen in some cities. Most arbitration is grievance arbitration. Some relatively recent court decisions have granted the arbitrator essentially the status of a legal judge, in that arbitration awards are not subject to change by the courts.

Can you generally describe a bargaining process?

Complexity of Collective Bargaining

Collective bargaining is a subject with so many ramifications that it is a separate technical area of study at many universities. This brief discussion of collective bargaining presents some of the important issues involved. The collective bargaining actually may or may not be handled by the personnel department (see Chapter 2, Figure 2–7). Exactly what the personnel unit does handle varies from employer to employer. However, the study referred to in Figure 2–7 found that many managers felt the collective-bargaining activities should be handled by operating managers rather than personnel executives.

CONTRACT "MANAGEMENT" AND GRIEVANCES

Once a collective bargaining contract is signed, then that contract is the main governing document. The typical contract details what management can and cannot do and what the responsibilities of the union are.

　The day-to-day administration of a contract most often focuses on employee and employer rights. When a unionized employee feels his or her rights under the contract have been violated, then that employee can file a grievance. The distinction between a grievance and a complaint should be made.

A GRIEVANCE is a specific, formal dissatisfaction expressed through an identified procedure.

A complaint, on the other hand, is merely an employee dissatisfaction which has *not* taken the formal grievance settlement route. Management should be concerned with both grievances and complaints because many complaints can become grievances; and, complaints are good indicators of potential problems within the workforce.

Can you differentiate between a complaint and a grievance?

Alert management knows that an unsettled dissatisfaction, whether real or imaginary, expressed or unexpressed, is a serious potential source of trouble. Hidden dissatisfactions grow and soon arouse an emotional state which may be completely out of proportion to the original complaint. A dissatisfaction can pervade the entire organization, and before long, workers' attitudes can be seriously affected. Therefore, it is important that grievances be handled properly.

Grievance Interface

Figure 19–2 shows possible division of responsibilities between the personnel unit and the managers. These responsibilities vary considerably from one organization to another, but the personnel unit usually has a more general responsibility. Managers must live with the grievance procedure as a possible constraint on some of their decisions.

In the organization where a union exists, grievances might occur over several different matters: interpretation of the contract, disputes not covered in the contract, and personal employee grievances. In non-unionized companies, complaints also tend to relate to a variety of individual concerns: wages, benefits, working conditions, and equity.

Extent of Grievance Procedures

Grievance procedures are almost always included in labor/management contracts. One study found that about 96 percent of the contracts studied contained grievance provisions.[4] However, many organizations that do not have unions do not have formal grievance procedures. Another study reported that only 22 percent of the sampled non-unionized companies had grievance procedures for hourly workers.[5]

FIGURE 19–2   Grievance interface.

Personnel Unit	Managers
Assists in designing the grievance procedure	Operate within the grievance procedure
Monitors trends in grievance rates for the organization	Attempt to resolve grievances where possible as "person closest to the problem"
May assist preparation of grievance cases for arbitration	Document grievance cases at own level for the grievance procedure
May have responsibility for settling grievances	Have responsibility for grievance prevention

Union

Ideally, a grievance procedure should not be necessary. A "super manager" should be able to maintain open channels of communication and quickly spot and rectify any troubles that might become grievances. However, "super managers" who have this communication ability are very rare.

Management commonly insists it has an "open-door policy"—if anything is bothering employees, all they have to do is to come to management and talk. However, employees are often skeptical of this approach, feeling that their complaint would probably be viewed as unnecessary "rocking of the boat." An "open-door" policy is *not* a sufficient grievance procedure.

A GRIEVANCE PROCEDURE

Grievance procedures are usually designed so that grievances can be settled as close to the problem as possible. First-line supervisors are usually closest to the problem; however, the supervisor is concerned with many other matters besides one employee's grievance and may even be the subject of an employee's grievance.

Supervisory involvement presents some very real problems in solving a grievance at this level. For example, William Dunn is 27-years-old and a lathe operator at Baker's Machine Shop. On Monday morning, his foreman, Joe Bass, approached him, told him that his production was lower than his quota, and advised him to catch up. William reported that there was a part on his lathe needing repair and requested that the mechanics examine and repair it. Joe informed William that the mechanics were too busy and that he must repair it himself to maintain his production. William refused and a heated argument ensued, with the result that Joe ordered William home for the day.

This illustration shows the ease with which an encounter between an employee and a supervisor can lead to a breakdown in the relationship. This breakdown or failure to communicate effectively can be costly to William if he loses his job, a day's wages, or his pride. It can be costly to Joe, who represents management, and to the owner of Baker's Machine Shop if production is delayed or halted. To resolve such conflicts, a formal channel of communication, called a *grievance procedure,* must exist for use between employers and employees.

Assume that Baker's Machine Shop had a contract with the International Brotherhood of Lathe Operators, of which William was a member. Further, the contract specifically stated that the company *plant mechanics* were to repair all manufacturing equipment. Then there is a clear violation of the union contract. What is William's next step? He may begin to use the appeals machinery provided for him in the contract. The actual grievance procedure is different in each organization. It depends on what the employer and the union have agreed upon and what is written into the labor contract.

Steps in a Grievance Procedure

As Figure 19–3 depicts, several basic steps exist in *most* grievance procedures. The grievance can be settled at any stage.

1. The employee discusses the grievance with the immediate supervisor.
2. The employee then discusses the grievance with the union steward and the supervisor.
3. The union *chief* steward discusses it with the supervisor's manager.
4. The union grievance committee discusses the grievance with the unit plant manager or the employer's industrial relations department.
5. The national union representative discusses it with the general company manager.
6. The final step may be reference to an impartial umpire or arbitrator for ultimate disposition of the grievance.

Employee and supervisor. In our example, William has already discussed his grievance with the foreman. This first step should eliminate the majority of gripes and complaints employees may view as legitimate grievances.

Supervisors are generally responsible for understanding the contract so that they can administer it fairly on a day-to-day basis. They must be

FIGURE 19–3 A grievance procedure.

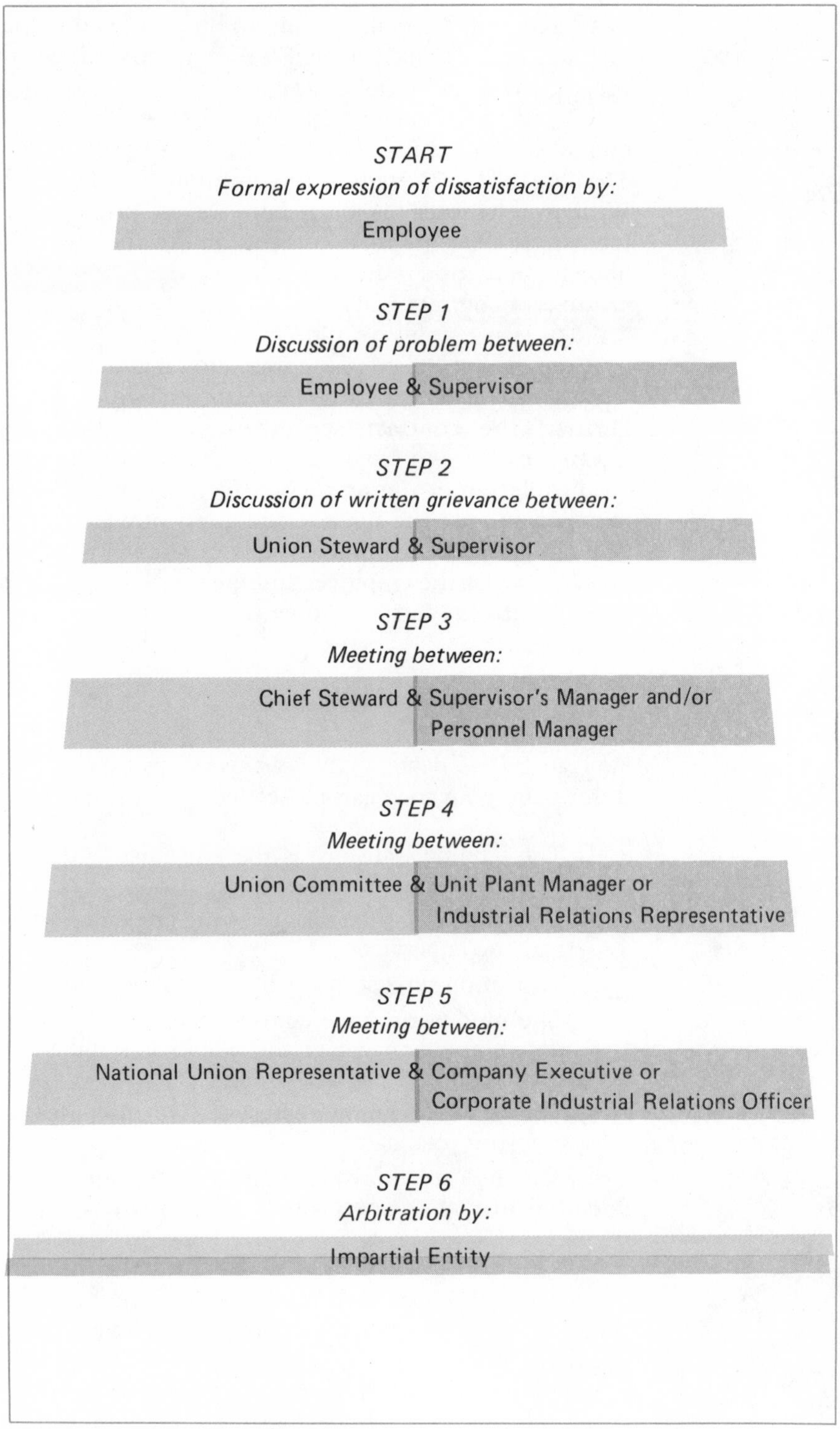

START
Formal expression of dissatisfaction by:

Employee

STEP 1
Discussion of problem between:

Employee & Supervisor

STEP 2
Discussion of written grievance between:

Union Steward & Supervisor

STEP 3
Meeting between:

Chief Steward & Supervisor's Manager and/or
Personnel Manager

STEP 4
Meeting between:

Union Committee & Unit Plant Manager or
Industrial Relations Representative

STEP 5
Meeting between:

National Union Representative & Company Executive or
Corporate Industrial Relations Officer

STEP 6
Arbitration by:

Impartial Entity

accessible to employees for grievance investigation and must gather all the pertinent facts and carefully investigate the causes, symptoms, and results.

Union steward and supervisor.   The second step involves the union steward. The main task here is to present the grievances of the union's members such as William to management. However, the responsibility rests not only with the individual steward but also, to a large degree, with the union membership as a whole. The effect of this grievance on the relationship between the union and management must be determined.

Assume the grievance remains unsettled after the second step. The steward takes it to the chief steward who contacts the supervisor's boss and/or the unit's personnel manager. In most grievance procedures, the grievance is documented, and until it is settled, much of the communication between management and the union is in writing. This written communication is important because it provides a record of each succeeding step in the procedure and constitutes a history for review at each subsequent step. The department manager (who is Joe's boss) backs Joe against the chief steward, so the grievance goes to the next step.

Union grievance committee and unit manager.   Pressure tends to build with each successive step because grievances which are *not* precedent-setting or difficult are screened out earlier in the process. The fourth stage involves the local union/management grievance committee. In our case, the grievance committee of the union convinces the plant manager that Joe violated the contract and William should be brought back to work and paid for the time he missed. The plant manager gave in partly because he thought the company had a weak case, and partly because if the grievance continued past him, it would probably go to arbitration, and he did not feel the issue was worth the cost. Although in William's case a grievance committee was used, not all grievance procedures use committees. This step may be omitted in many procedures.

National representatives and arbitrator.   If the grievance had remained unsettled, national representatives for both sides would have met to try to resolve the conflict. An arbitrator would have been selected and asked to make a decision on the matter. The manner of selecting an arbitrator varies but usually involves each party eliminating names from a list of potential arbitrator candidates until only one name remains.

What are the steps in a grievance procedure?

Importance of a Grievance Procedure

Grievance procedures are very important for effective employee/employer relations. The chance of a union successfully organizing a company's employees is much greater if a firm has no formal procedure to hear employee grievances.[6] Without a grievance procedure, management may not know about employee discontent in important areas, and therefore be vulnerable to organizing attempts.

Union organizers often conduct a careful survey before attempting to organize any company. A survey reveals more about the feelings of a company's employees than many managers are aware of through daily relationships with these people. Such information does not always *automatically* come to the attention of management. A great deal of it is dismissed at lower levels, and it never gets to levels where decisions can be made to rectify some of the problems. For these reasons, a formal grievance procedure can be a very valuable communication tool for management in providing workers a fair hearing for their problems.

Grievances and Job Security

It has been suggested that American workers are primarily concerned with the protection of their jobs.[7] Most formal grievances are disputes arising out of the meaning and intent of the collective bargaining contract. However, these disputes can be viewed easily as job security problems. Suppose that an employee named Paula Wilson filed a grievance when an employee with a lower job classification was promoted instead of her. Paula claimed that the contract stipulated *seniority* would be the first consideration in promotion. Paula really is not concerned about the meaning and intent of the contract. She knows employees in higher job classifications are less likely to be laid off during slack periods. The basis for her grievance is her own long-run security.

A system for the settlement of grievances aids the preservation of job security.[8] People's need for security is a recognized behavioral fact and formal grievance procedures can be an aid in reducing security fears.

GRIEVANCE ARBITRATION

Grievance arbitration is a means of settling disputes arising from different interpretations of a contract. This dispute resolution is not to be confused with contract arbitration, which is arbitration to determine how a contract will be written. Grievance arbitration is a deeply ingrained part of the collective bargaining system, although it was not always so. For the most part, arbitration was not a useful part of the process of settling labor disputes in earlier times.

With the passage of the Wagner Act in 1935, collective bargaining was officially sanctioned in the United States. During war years, the War Labor Board did a great deal to facilitate both collective bargaining and arbitration. With a "peace-at-any-price" philosophy in labor relations, arbitration became an important tool in maintaining stability.

In 1957, another era began in the history of arbitration as a grievance-settling device. A court decision which established the right of unions to *sue* for specific performance of arbitration awards gave arbitration new strength. Later court cases added more strength to arbitration. It was ruled that a company had to arbitrate *all* issues not specifically excluded in the contract. Courts were directed *not* to rule on the appropriateness of an arbitration award unless misinformation, fraud, or negligence were involved.

Arbitration is very flexible. It can be applicable to almost any kind of controversy except criminal questions. Voluntary arbitration may be used either in the negotiation of agreements or in interpretation of clauses in existing agreements, or both. However, labor and management, for the most part, agree that disputes over negotiations of a new contract should not be arbitrated. So arbitration plays its most important part in labor relations as a *final point* in the grievance procedure.

Arbitration and the Contract

The grievance procedure is the union member's most tangible contact with collective bargaining. The procedure set up in the contract is likely to have a visible, direct, immediate, and personal influence on the union member.

A very important part of arbitration is the wording of the contract clause which accurately expresses each party's intent relative to arbitration. It is important to spell out the types of disputes which may be taken to arbitration. Most collective bargaining contracts suggest that either party may start arbitration proceedings. Others, however, provide that only the union can initiate arbitration proceedings. Still others permit arbitration only when both parties mutually agree.

The Individual and the Union

Individual union members do not always feel their best interests are properly served by the union. Workers and unions may not agree on the interpretation of a contract clause. Some workers may doubt whether the union's bureaucratic structure will carry an individual's grievance to a satisfactory conclusion.[9] For example, Bill Jones feels strongly that the case of his suspension for drinking was not sufficiently represented by the union because the shop steward is a teetotaler. What is Bill to do?

If the individual does not feel the union has properly and vigorously pursued the grievance, he or she may have recourse to the federal court system. More cases will arise regarding the question of individual rights in the grievance procedure. These cases attempt to pinpoint individual rights inside the bargaining unit, and also to determine what those rights are if a person has been denied due process through the grievance procedure.[10]

> During the past 15 years, the questions of arbitration enforcement and individual rights have become clearer through Supreme Court decisions. Normally, the parties in the contract grant the arbitrator the right to determine whether or not an issue is arbitratable or not. In turn, the courts may determine the arbitratability of an issue if not provided in the contract. However, the courts may rule an issue nonarbitratable if the parties have specially excluded it from the contract. Otherwise, the issue may be arbitratable. Furthermore, if the contract provides for arbitration of all issues arising under the contract, the courts must order arbitration of the issues regardless of the merits of the particular case. Lastly, arbitration awards usually are not to be set aside unless an obligation under the law has not been considered.[11]

Preventive Arbitration

Labor and management sometimes tend to ignore potential problem areas in the relationship until it is too late. The result can be an explosive dispute that does much more harm than good. A preventive arbitrator can minimize this sort of difficulty.[12]

It is the duty of a preventive arbitrator to meet periodically, at least monthly, with union and management representatives to discuss areas of potential trouble between the parties. Although the use of a preventive arbitrator is not a panacea for resolving difficulties in labor/management relations, it can be a potentially useful tool. The plan calls for unilateral adherence to the arbitrator's recommendations during a 60-day period. During that time the problem is to be solved calmly and coolly.

Arbitration's Shortcomings

Several problems exist in grievance arbitration. It has been criticized as being too costly, too legalistic, and too time-consuming. Additional problems involve the availability of new and acceptable arbitrators, due process in arbitration, and the difficult question of individual rights in the grievance process.[13]

Can you define and discuss grievance arbitration?

RESOLUTIONS OF COMMON GRIEVANCE PROBLEMS BY ARBITRATION

Grievance procedures are subject to problems of contract interpretation. Many of the same problems appear again and again. It is useful to look at some of these common problems and their usual resolution through the arbitration process. The following summary of some common problems of application are found in the *BNA Grievance Guide.*[14]

Time Limits

Time pressure is one of the important problems of application with the grievance procedure. Failure to settle grievances quickly will lead to negative employee reaction. Many contracts provide time limits for each step in the grievance procedure, with the idea that time limits provide a safeguard against stalling and backlogging of old complaints. Others feel that time limits encourage an uncooperative party to stall to the maximum time limit. If the contract does contain clear time limits, however, failure to observe them generally will result in dismissal of the grievance from arbitration. Exceptions to this have occurred when both the parties violated the contract with respect to the grievance procedure, or when the existence of the grievance was not known until sometime after the event occurred. In such cases, arbitrators usually hold that the time limit does not start until the individual is aware of the existence of agreements.

Bypassing the First Step

In a grievance procedure, unions may seek to by-pass first line supervisors because of these supervisors' lack of authority to make decisions. Arbitrators usually permit this only under certain circumstances, for example, if the grievance is of a very general nature, which can be resolved only at high union management levels. But, for the most part, the steps in the grievance procedure should be followed.

Right to Union Representation

Unions and managements may disagree as to whether the employee grievances should be taken directly to the foreman or first to the union steward and then to the foreman. Management may argue that bringing the union in at this stage makes the grievance appear more serious than it really is. But, the unions may argue that the steward should be in from the start so that the employee has adequate representation. Arbitrators' rulings have varied, but generally the arbitrators recognize that the employee's right to union representation begins with the first step of the grievance procedure.

Grievance Investigation

Many agreements give union representatives the right to "reasonable access" to the plant to investigate grievances. It has been held that such provisions do not give the union representative the right to roam the plant at will.

Pay for Grievance Time

The extent to which stewards are entitled to be paid for the time they spend adjusting grievances depends upon the particular contract provisions or upon past practice. Under the wage and hour act, such time may be regarded as working time to determine when overtime payment is due. As a general rule, this time is presumed to be working time unless a contrary tension appears in the contract or from the parties' past practices.

"Just Cause"

Another issue commonly involved in grievance procedure is "just cause." Generally, management must have "just cause" for imposing discipline. This is often written in the union contract, and even in the absence of the contract, it is the rule of thumb used by employees in judging whether management acted fairly in enforcing company rulings.

Determining "just cause." The definition of "just cause" obviously varies from case to case. But one arbitrator listed the following questions for determining whether a company has "just cause" for disciplining an employee:[15]

"Was the employee adequately warned of the consequences of his conduct?" The warning may be given orally or in printed form. An exception must be made for certain conduct such as insubordination, coming to work drunk, drinking on the job, or stealing company property, because these actions are so serious that employees are expected to know they will be punished.

"Was the company's rule reasonably related to conditions and safe operation? Did management investigate before administering the discipline?" An incident is normally investigated before the decision to discipline is made. Where immediate action is required, however, the best course is to suspend the employee pending investigation with the understanding that the employee can come back to work and receive pay for the time lost if found not guilty.

"Was the investigation fair and objective? Did the investigation produce substantial evidence or proof of guilt?" The evidence need not be preponderant, inclusive, or beyond reasonable doubt, except where the alleged misconduct is of such a criminal or reprehensible nature which can stigmatize the employee and seriously impair chances for future employment.

"Were the rules, orders, and penalties applied even-handedly and without discrimination?" If enforcement has been lax in the past, management cannot suddenly reverse its course and begin to crack down without first warning the employees of its intent.

"Was the penalty related to the seriousness of the offense in the past record?" If employee A's past record is significantly better than that of employee B, the company probably may give A a lighter punishment than B for the same offense.

What are four grievance problems?

LEGAL vs. BEHAVIORAL
GRIEVANCE RESOLUTION

The inclusion of a union in a formal grievance procedure sometimes leads management to conclude that the proper way to handle grievances is to abide by the "letter of the law." This means management will do no more or no less than what is called for in the contract. Such an approach can be labeled the *legal approach* to the resolution of grievances. A much more realistic approach, the *behavioral approach*, recognizes that a grievance may be a symptom of an underlying problem which management might investigate and rectify.

The difference is apparent in the following example. At Acme Bolt Company a union has recently been voted in to represent the employees. One of the first actions the union took was to insist on having a formal grievance procedure recorded in the contract. One of the clauses in the grievance procedure states that a grievance cannot be reopened once it has been resolved to the satisfaction of both management and the union.

Ed Dyl, a custodian for the Acme Bolt Company, filed a grievance about the danger involved in working around some of the machinery. Dyl felt the machinery was not sufficiently safe so that he could get close enough to clean around it. As a result, the workplace was not very clean. Dyl's grievance was that his performance was being hurt by the situation and had resulted in a warning for poor work from his supervisor. The grievance was resolved at the second level in the grievance procedure. The union "traded" Dyl's case for another, involving an employee who had taken extra days of leave for a funeral. The union felt that the second case was more important to the employees at large than Dyl's.

Dyl has *again* filed a grievance that management is rejecting under a contract clause which says a second grievance cannot be filed on the same issue. Management's *legalistic* approach in this case is hiding a very real problem: the employee is concerned about safety. Management has a duty to provide safe working conditions for its employees; if it fails to recognize that there is a problem here, the federal government can become involved through the Occupational Safety and Health Administration.

Management should consider a grievance a *behavioral* expression of some underlying problem. This statement does not mean that every grievance is symptomatic of something radically wrong. Employees file grievances over petty matters, as well as important concerns, and management must be able to differentiate between the two. However, to ignore a repeated problem and take a legalistic approach to grievance resolution is to miss much of what the grievance procedure can do for management.

GRIEVANCES AND LEADER BEHAVIOR

In a study done at International Harvester Company, two researchers discovered a relationship between the number of grievances filed and the leader behavior of the supervisors involved. In Chapter 3, the two dimensions of leadership used in this study (consideration and structure) were discussed. But to review what each means:

1. *Consideration* includes behavior which indicates a mutual trust, respect, and certain warmth and rapport between the supervisor and the work group. This dimension appears to emphasize a deeper concern for group members' needs and includes such behaviors as allowing subordinates more participation in decision making and encouraging more two-way communication.

2. *Structure*, on the other hand, includes behavior in which the supervisor organizes and defines group activities in direct relations with the groups. The supervisor defines the role expected of each member. The leader assigns tasks, plans ahead, establishes ways of getting things done, and pushes for production. This dimension seems to emphasize overt attempts to achieve organizational goals.[16]

Figure 19–4 depicts the relationship between leader behaviors and

FIGURE 19–4   Grievance rates and leader behavior.

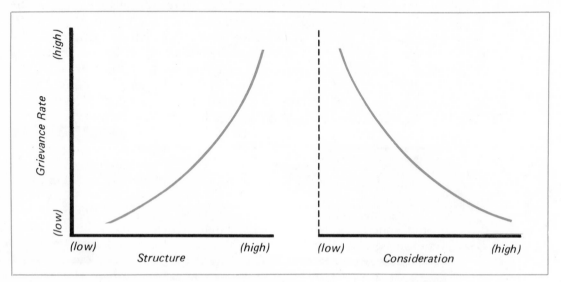

(Source: E. A. Fleishman and E. F. Harris, "Patterns of Leadership Behavior Related to Employee Grievances and Turnover," *Personnel Psychology,* 15 (Spring 1962). Used with permission.)

grievance rates. The curves show that as the leader's behavior becomes more structured, the grievance rate tends to increase; as the leader's behavior becomes more considerate, the grievance rate drops substantially.

But how do different combinations of consideration and structure relate to grievances? Some supervisors score high on both dimensions, and some supervisors score low on both dimensions. Figure 19–5 shows the relationship between structure, consideration, and grievances.

In Figure 19–5, notice that for high-consideration supervisors (those represented by the lowest of the three lines), the amount of structure they use can be increased without substantially increasing the rate of grievances. However, *the reverse is not true.* For supervisors who were low in consideration (the top line), reducing structure did not reduce their griev-

FIGURE 19–5   Combined effect of structure and consideration on grievance rates.

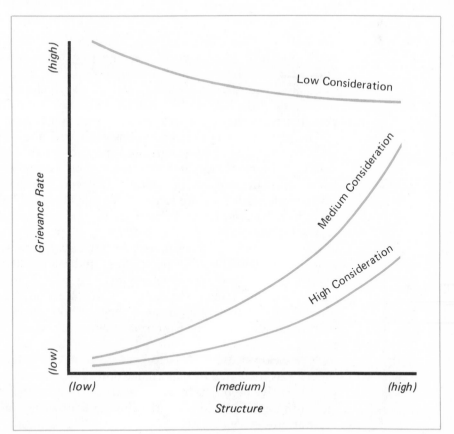

(Source: E. A. Fleishman and E. F. Harris, "Patterns of Leadership Behavior Related to Employee Grievances and Turnover," *Personnel Psychology*, 15 (Spring 1962). Used with permission.)

ance rate by very much. For those supervisors who were average or medium on consideration (middle line), grievances were lowest where structure was the lowest and increased as structure increased. Apparently, high consideration can compensate for high structure, but low structure will not offset low consideration.[17]

In summary, this study found that a supervisor's leader behavior can affect the number of grievances received from the work unit. High structure supervisors receive more grievances, and high consideration supervisors receive fewer grievances.

Can you discuss the legal and behavioral approaches to grievance resolution?

REVIEW AND PREVIEW

The nature of union/management relations that follow certification has been examined in this chapter. Collective bargaining is a process in which management and union representatives attempt to reach a contractual agreement. An employer can take several approaches to collective bargaining. If these approaches fail, then the firm must rely on conciliation/mediation or arbitration to reach a contract.

The second part of the chapter has dealt with the nature of the grievance procedure, its background, and specifics regarding its use. It is not necessary for employees to be represented by a union for an employer to have a formal grievance procedure. However, many employers wait to initiate one until they are *forced* to do so. The existence of a grievance procedure is viewed as a detriment to organizing employees by union representatives.

Management's attitude toward the grievance process is quite important. It can fight the grievance process and assume that its "open-door policy" is sufficient to resolve employee dissatisfactions. But this policy simply does not reflect the realities of organizational life. People do not always present their grievances if they do not have a representative to help them, or if they feel a formal mechanism does not exist for that purpose.

Arbitration, which has been called a form of "industrial self-government," has increased in importance during the past 35 years. Arbitration can help solve problems by acting as the ultimate decision-making mechanism in a grievance procedure. There are, however, problems with the arbitration device.

The final chapter speculates on the future of personnel management. Several emerging dimensions are identified.

Review Questions

1. What is collective bargaining? What are three bargaining relation-ships that can be used? What are some deadlocks that can be reached in collective bargaining?
2. Briefly describe a typical collective bargaining process.
3. Define a grievance and identify the basic steps in a grievance proce-dure.
4. Recent problems with unions in the public sector have led to increased interest in arbitration. What is arbitration and how does it work? What are some problems with using arbitration to resolve grievances?
5. Identify and compare the legal and behavioral approaches to resolv-ing grievances.
6. Discuss the statement: "A leader's behavior can affect the number of grievances."

OPENING CASE FOLLOW-UP

This case points out how minor incidents can result in a grievance being filed. The vagueness of the contract provision is a major problem. What is reasonable?

A key factor to be considered in resolving the grievance is precedent. Questions that would be important include: What have been the past practices regarding clean-up time? Have there been other grievances filed on clean-up time? What were the final outcomes of those grievances?

The patterns established by precedents such as these would form the basis for resolving this grievance at some point. If the grievance reached arbitration, precedent factors would be the major grounds used by an arbitrator in making an award.

Case: The Wilson County Hospital

The Wilson County Hospital has just recently seen its nurses organized after a long and bitter struggle that included dismissal and forced rehiring of some of the organizers. The nurses contended all along that the only reason that they needed to organize was to force the hospital administration to listen to important complaints. The complaints were primarily about poor working conditions and inappropriate patient care brought on by lack of proper facilities. The administration long ignored the nurses' pleas, claiming that available funds precluded them from doing anything about the facilities and working conditions.

The nurses have asked for a 7 percent cost-of-living increase in salary for each of the next three years. The hospital has steadfastly refused to offer any kind of increase in salary, claiming that it simply does not have the money available to pay for increased salaries. Further, since it has no money available, the hospital administration has declined to bargain with the nurses' union about salary. The nurses' union has been designated official bargaining agent for the nurses at Wilson County Hospital by the NLRB after the election. Vernon Cohn, the hospital administrator, was quoted as saying, "Hell, it makes no difference what they want to talk about. There's nothing I can do. We have no more money for salaries and therefore, there's no sense in talking about it. I will not meet with the nurses to discuss salary."

Wilma Jones, the president of the local union, was reinstated in her job with the hospital after having been fired prior to the election. The NLRB found that Wilma had been fired for her organizing activities. In addition to a cost-of-living adjustment, Wilma feels very strongly that the nurses have several ideas on improving conditions and facilities for patient care (if only management would listen). Some method for presenting these ideas is needed because many of the nurses feel even more concerned about these issues than about salary increases.

QUESTIONS

1. Discuss the hospital administrator's refusal to bargain from both his viewpoint and a legal viewpoint.
2. If you were chairman of the board of directors for the hospital, what actions would you suggest to deal with the problems present in the case?

Notes

1. Arthur A. Sloane and Fred Whitney, *Labor Relations*, 2d ed. © 1972, pp. 32–37. Reprinted by permission of Prentice-Hall, Inc., Englewood Cliffs, New Jersey.

2. K. O. Alexander, "Union Structure and Bargaining Structure," *Labor Law Journal* (March 1973), p. 166.

3. *Ibid.*, p. 167.

4. W. J. Usery, Jr., "Some Attempts to Reduce Arbitration Costs and Delays," *Monthly Labor Review*, 95 (November 1972).

5. Richard V. Miller, "Arbitration of New Contract Wage Disputes: Some Recent Trends," *Industrial and Labor Relations Review* (January 1967).

6. James Wilson, "Thoughts on Union Avoidance," *The Personnel Administrator* (June 1977), pp. 14–184.

7. D. Dolnick, "The Settlement of Grievances and the Job Conscious Theory," *Labor Law Journal*, 23 (April 1970), p. 244.

8. *Ibid.*, pp. 244–245.

9. M. S. Wortman, C. E. Overton, and C. E. Block, "Arbitration Enforcement and Individual Rights," *Labor Law Journal*, 27 (February 1974), p. 81.

10. *Ibid.*, p. 84.

11. From Wortman, Overton, and Black, "Arbitration Enforcement," the February 1974 *Labor Law Journal*, published and copyrighted 1974 by Commerce Clearing House, Inc., 4025 W. Peterson Ave., Chicago, Ill. 60646.

12. J. J. Shutkin, "Preventive Arbitration: A Path to Perpetual Labor Peace and Prosperity," *Labor Law Journal*, 21 (September 1968), pp. 539–543.

13. R. W. Fleming, *Labor Arbitration Process* (Urbana: University of Illinois Press, 1967), p. 199.

14. BNA Editorial Staff, *Grievance Guide*, 4th ed. (Washington, D.C.: Bureau of National Affairs, 1972), pp. 1–7.

15. The following is a summary of material appearing in the *BNA Grievance Guide*.

16. E. A. Fleishman and E. F. Harris, "Patterns of Leadership Behavior Related to Employees' Grievances and Turnover," *Personnel Psychology*, 15 (Spring 1962), 43–56.

17. *Ibid.*

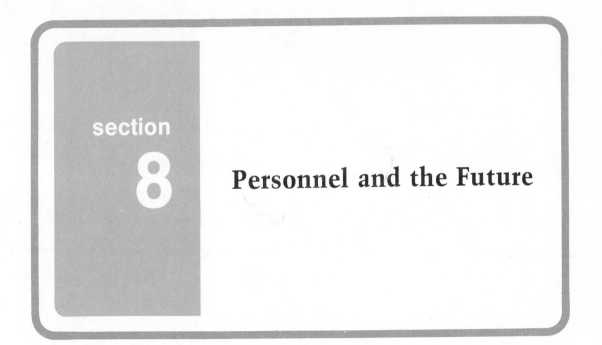

section

8

Personnel and the Future

In order to keep abreast of progress and change, managers must anticipate the impact of future changes on personnel activities. The last chapter looks at personnel management in the future and examines some forces that will significantly affect it. Also, there is a brief discussion of personnel as a career specialization and the continuing need for people knowledgeable in the management of personnel activities.

Personnel and the Future

When you have read this chapter, you should be able to:

1. Identify some reasons why more knowledgeable managers and personnel professionals will be needed in the future.

2. Discuss the nature of personnel as a career specialization.

Who Wears the Pants?

Mark Minsky is a 60 year-old supervisor who has been with the company for 40 years, and does his job very, very well. He supervises a group of assemblers, mostly women, working on the production line. One of Mark's longstanding rules has been that if women are going to work for him, they are going to dress in an appropriate fashion. For his women assemblers, this means neat grooming and wearing a dress. Mark does not tolerate pants of any kind in his unit; even expensive slack suits are unacceptable and anyone wearing this sort of attire on the job is sent home to change. This "dress code," as the employees call it, has never presented any problem for Mark until recently.

Over the past four years many of the older employees have retired and been replaced with younger employees. The turnover in the unit is not very high, and unless somebody retires, employees generally stay with the company. One of the main reasons that this low turnover exists is because the company pays quite a bit more than the prevailing wage rate in the community. Also, the company offers it employees profit-sharing schemes and excellent benefits.

Recently among the younger group of assemblers the rule about wearing a dress to work has become a point of contention. Many of the younger women feel that pant suits are acceptable attire anywhere today, and that it should be acceptable attire at work as well. The issue came to a head last Wednesday when Margaret Breland, one of the better assemblers, came to work in a fashionable pant suit and refused to go home when Mark suggested she do so. Mark told her she could stay but she would not be paid for the time she was at work in a pant suit. Margaret wrote a letter to the personnel director criticizing Mark Minsky, contending that the rule was an infringement upon her freedom to dress as she chose and had nothing to do with her ability to perform the job.

The letter is now on the desk of the personnel manager, Wayne Phillips, who must respond to it before the end of the week. On one hand, the personnel manager feels a need to support a management employee in his right to run his unit the way he sees fit. On the other hand, Wayne knows that societal attitudes toward dress have changed in the last ten years and that Mark is hopelessly behind the times. The personnel director mentally notes that this is the fifth problem he has had to deal with this year that in some way reflects new values and attitudes held by the employees. Wayne sighs and starts drafting his response.

514

The scope and complexity of personnel management have been emphasized throughout this book. Yet, only within the last decade has personnel management truly come into the mainstream of organizational life. The management of human resources in organizations is much more complex now than in the recent past because the external environment is placing more demands on managers and personnel specialists. To illustrate, consider just three areas that may "complicate" the way personnel management activities are performed in organizations: (1) governmental regulation, (2) changes in social values, and (3) shifts in unionization efforts.

GOVERNMENTAL REGULATION

Today, managers of organizations are confronted with an expanding and often bewildering array of governmental rules and restrictions that have a tremendous effect on the management of human resources. Although government regulation of personnel activities has occurred for many years, the last few years have seen the passage of laws that restrict an employer's flexibility. EEOC, OSHA, and ERISA are acronyms familiar to many managers; a discussion of each relative to its impact on personnel is in order, and will serve as a review of these three major personnel changes.

Equal Employment Opportunities

Equal Employment Opportunity as a desirable social goal received formal impetus with the passage of the Civil Rights Act of 1964. The Equal Employment Opportunity Commission (EEOC) was established to oversee the enforcement of this act. EEOC can require employers to alter their hiring and promotion practices to assure that certain groups of people are provided equal chances for employment. Recently (and with good reason) emphasis has been placed on providing equal opportunities to women. The increasing concern about equal opportunities for women and the continuing concern for equal opportunities for racial minorities have had and will have a significant and vital effect on organizations in years to come.

The authors are familiar with one employer having 6000 employees who has agreed to fill 15 percent of its management positions with women in the next five years. Currently the employer has only 15 women supervisors out of 800 managerial slots. To fulfill its promise in five years, the organization must have 105 more women in management jobs at a variety of levels. This is an increase of 700 percent! But even then, only one out of eight management jobs will be held by a woman. Pressure to provide women with more equal opportunity has caused this organization to restructure its recruiting, selection, and training practices drastically.

EEOC enforces the act to such an extent that some EEOC officers now require organizations to tell them how many employees are of American Indian descent, including the tribal affiliation of each person claiming at least one-sixteenth Indian descent. Affirmative Action programs to insure meaningful equal opportunity and the related problems of "reverse discrimination" are destined to receive increasing attention in personnel management.

Occupational Safety and Health

Passage of the Occupational Safety and Health Act of 1970 (OSHA) has resulted in intensified pressure on employers to provide safe working conditions. A survey of 105 organizations revealed that safety and health was the area of personnel management receiving the largest increase in attention—primarily because of OSHA efforts.[1]

OSHA has changed its emphasis and tactics somewhat since its inception. The emphasis seems to be shifting somewhat from safety to occupational health. The work-related illnesses that may be contracted by working around certain chemicals and materials are a source of major national concern. Certainly the interest in safety will continue and new more helpful and acceptable ways of impressing this fact on employers will be forthcoming.

As OSHA rules have been enforced, employers have a larger responsibility to know about safety and health provisions and to comply with them. Revision of work procedures, replacement of machines, and changes in employee practices are all possibilities that employers may face as a result of greater OSHA enforcement efforts.

Employee Retirement Income Security

Passage of the Employee Retirement Income Security Act (1974) has placed another burden on the management of human resources. Now managers must not only hire and promote equitably (EEOC), and provide safe working conditions (OSHA), but they also must provide greater benefits for employees who retire. In Chapter 14 it was pointed out that funding and disclosure provisions of ERISA will place more and more financial responsibility and commitment on many employers.

The change in mandatory retirement age will have a major impact as well. For the most part, people may work until age 70 if they choose. This continuation will have a major impact on appraisal, promotion, career planning, and manpower planning systems.

It is clear that governmental regulations currently have an important effect on personnel management. These pressures will continue to affect personnel management markedly in the future. More organization time, money, and effort will have to be allocated to comply with government regulations. The net effect of all these government interventions into personnel management will be to increase its importance in the organization.

CHANGES IN SOCIAL VALUES

Changes in social values about work and what a job should be, place more pressure on the management of people in work situations. Increasing concern about the "quality of life" at work is likely. News media discussions of job boredom and the monotony of assembly lines are evidence of this concern. Interest in flexible scheduling and the four-day workweek reflects changing views about work scheduling and work's relationship to leisure.

Instead of attempting to force employees to conform to a "corporate mold," future managers may well have to allow for individual differences in people. Consider the problems caused by employers hiring more highly educated workers. Workers with more education may not be as willing to "mark time" in their jobs and wait patiently for promotions. Organizations that do not change their internal systems to accommodate this impatience may well see their turnover rates balloon. It has been advocated that personnel management strategies will have to be shaped to fit a variety of value systems.[2]

The influx of women into the workforce represents another major social value change that has a major impact on personnel management. A *much* higher percentage of the workforce now is female, as women choose to seek careers outside the home. This shift leads to pressure to provide effective career paths for women and men and to reduce the distinction between "male" and "female" jobs. Hiring, training, and wage and salary systems are all affected.

SHIFTS IN UNIONIZATION EFFORTS

Public sector and white-collar unions are the fastest growing segments of the labor movement. Employees who previously saw unions as villains are "seeing the light" and joining unions (see Chapter 18). School teachers, university professors, fire fighters, police officers, and nurses are just a few of the professionals who have experienced the increased appeal of organizing.

Numerous managers in a variety of organizations will have to adjust to dealing with unionized employees. Also, established unions and their leaders will be facing internal challenges from younger workers. New bargaining relationships, such as the inclusion of no-strike clauses and compulsory arbitration in contracts, will have to be considered by both employers and unions. These two important clauses are actively being considered by employers and unions representing employees in the public sector.

A year long study of future trends in the employee relations field focused on opinions of more than 100 leaders from industry, education, and government.[3] Among other interesting predictions this study forecasts is a stronger role in the public sector for arbitration/mediation services. This growth will be forthcoming because of a tremendous increase in unionization by public employees. The study also predicts growth in union members in all sectors and new and better-educated union leadership. The net result of such a trend will be to put additional pressure on personnel systems.

Unions typically have had the effect of causing organizations to be more professional and careful about their personnel policies and practices. Especially in certain white-collar and professional occupations, a major re-analysis of personnel management will be required if the predicted trend does indeed occur.

EFFECTIVE PERSONNEL MANAGEMENT IN THE FUTURE

Throughout this book it has been stressed that personnel management is a series of activities that must be performed in organizations. Coordination between personnel specialists and other managers is vital. The three areas discussed earlier illustrate the challenges managers and personnel specialists are going to face in the future.

Why will more knowledgeable personnel specialists be needed in the future?

Emphasis on personnel management as a set of activities does not ignore the fact that effective personnel management requires professional personnel specialists. Personnel activities will become more and more important, which will increase the demand for a greater number of competent individuals to make personnel their career specialty.

This book has stressed the concept of "interfaces" between the personnel unit and other managers. As the changes noted above suggest, the days when personnel activities can be ignored or relegated to one part of the organization exclusively are gone. All managers will have to understand the basic issues and problems associated with personnel management if the organization is to be effective. A brief summary of each of these critical activities follows.

Work

A good working relationship between people and their jobs does not just happen. It requires analysis of the job to be done and proper design of the work people do. Job analysis, job descriptions, and job specifications that consider the behavioral aspects of people of the work will become increasingly important.

Staffing

Manpower planning, Affirmative Action, EEO, and test validity are terms lightly used 20 years ago. Yet, these concepts form the cornerstone of modern staffing practices. They affect personnel managers, as well as production, marketing, and finance managers. All of these managers have to staff their jobs with people in such a way as to live with current legal and social expectations.

Training and Development

Training needs assessment, training evaluation, career planning, and organization development have grown in importance. However, training costs—like everything else—are increasing, and management has a right to know whether or not it is receiving a dollar's benefit for a dollar spent in this area. Further, as women and minorities with special training needs become more predominant in organizations of all kinds, a greater need for specialized types of training and development will continue to grow.

Appraisal

Performance appraisal has typically been very poorly done in most organizations. Yet, as the cost of keeping poor employees continues to grow, performance appraisal will increase in importance. The cost associated with having unrecognized excellence and potential is at least as great. Well-designed, properly implemented appraisal systems, perhaps more than any of the other activities, require the cooperative efforts of the personnel unit and operating managers in an organization.

Compensation

Productivity has been a national concern for some time. One possible way to increase productivity is to tie compensation to production. Yet, compensation administration is becoming increasingly complex. ERISA has greatly changed benefit plans, and increasing unionization in white-collar jobs will make the tie between productivity and compensation even more complex. New approaches, new ideas, and a professional approach to compensation and benefits are vital if strides are to be made in this area.

Maintenance

Largely because of OSHA, but also because of increasing management awareness of its social responsibilities to the public and its employees, personnel health and safety will continue to grow in importance. Further, the updating of personnel policies and rules must occur if organizations are to remain viable and competitive.

Union

Finally, the interface with labor organizations will increase in importance for some organizations. In other organizations and industries a rethinking and reformulation of existing relationships may be necessary for the industries to grow and remain viable. The construction industry is an example of an industry where this reexamination appears to be occurring.

Why will more knowledgeable managers in the personnel area be needed in the future?

The need for personnel specialists certainly will not diminish in the next several years. Personnel as a career specialization is both attractive and challenging.

PERSONNEL AS A CAREER SPECIALIZATION

A wide variety of jobs are performed by career professionals. The common jobs and job titles listed in Figure 20–1 illustrate the number of areas in which career personnel professionals can work. There are job opportunities in specific personnel areas and for personnel generalists who are knowledgeable in several areas.

Knowledge of salary information may be useful for those individuals who aspire to executive jobs such as personnel director, vice-president of human resources, or director of industrial relations. One study found that personnel executives in many organizations, who once received about 70 percent of the salary of their marketing and finance counterparts, now command comparable salaries.[4]

Another study surveyed the job satisfaction of American personnel managers. As a group, personnel managers were found to be relatively satisfied with their personal lives, social relationships, and with most aspects of their jobs.[5] Employee relations, employee counseling, union contract negotiation, management development, and wage and salary administration were the top five job content items in terms of satisfaction.

What are several aspects of personnel as a career specialization?

CONCLUSION

A major perspective of this book is that, to a certain extent, all managers are personnel managers. All managers, including career personnel professionals, must expand their knowledge of activities that focus on the management of human resources. In addition to a basic familiarity with the many ideas and issues contained in this text, managers and personnel professionals must continually develop their knowledge of general management and human behavior.

In the future, personnel management will play an increasingly important role in the destiny of organizations. This book has attempted to

FIGURE 20–1   Sample job titles of personnel professionals.

Personnel Director	Safety Coordinator
Director of Industrial Relations	Employee Relations Counselor
Employment Manager	Corporate Ombudsman
Compensation Analyst	EEO Compliance Manager
Benefits Coordinator	Training Director
Job Analyst	Manager of Organization
Personnel Interviewer	Development
Personnel Research Analyst	Pension Analyst
Labor Relations Specialist	Employee Services Coordinator
	Testing Consultant

capture the essence and challenge of personnel management today, so that readers will be better prepared for the organizations of tomorrow.

Concluding Question

1. You have completed a book about personnel management. How will your knowledge of personnel management make you a better manager?

OPENING CASE FOLLOW-UP

This case demonstrates some of the emerging problems that personnel managers often face. The workforce is changing and has changed considerably in its nature over the last several years. As a result, many of the rules, policies, procedures, and practices used in the past are no longer appropriate.

The case demonstrates the necessity for a broad perspective on the part of personnel managers and operating managers. It shows some of the types of problems career personnel professionals are likely to confront. In addition to day-to-day, mundane operating problems, larger problems exist as well. Many times the resolution of problems such as this one requires a balance of interests, rather than any one right answer or decision. If the personnel director supports Margaret, he may undermine Mark's effectiveness as a supervisor. If he supports Mark, he may face severe resistance from the assemblers. Discovering ways to "solve" the problem without causing more problems illustrates the challenges of personnel management.

Notes

1. ASPA-BNA Survey #18, "Trends in Personnel Management: 1971–1972," *Bulletin to Management*, June 7, 1973.

2. Charles L. Hughes and Vincent S. Flowers, "Shaping Personnel Strategies to Disparate Value-Systems," *Personnel* (March-April 1973), pp. 8–23.

3. M. R. Schiavoni, "Employee Relations: Where Will it be in 1985?", *The Personnel Administrator* (March 1978), pp. 25–27.

4. *Wall Street Journal*, December 13, 1977, p. 1.

5. J. L. Rettig and R. F. McCain, "Job Satisfactions of Personnel Managers," *The Personnel Administrator*, (September, 1978), pp. 23–26.

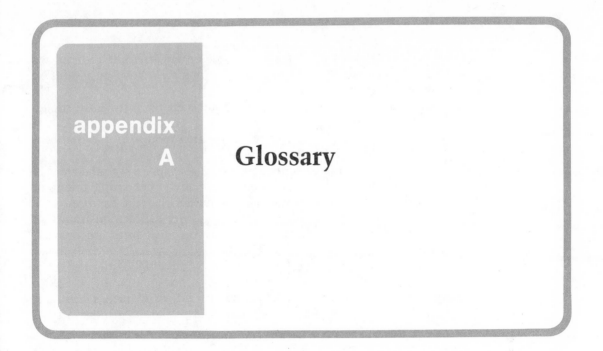

appendix A

Glossary

Adverse impact action which results in the underrepresentation of protected minorities.

Affirmative action an effort by an organization to identify and analyze problem areas in their minority employment, and then to identify goals to overcome those problems.

Arbitration process whereby an impartial entity determines the relative merit of different viewpoints and makes a decision called an *award*.

Authority the right to use resources to accomplish goals derived through formal or informal designation.

Benefits rewards available to employees as a part of organizational membership.

B.F.O.Q. (Bonafide Occupational Qualification)—legitimate reason why employment can be reasonably restricted to exclude persons on otherwise illegal bases of consideration.

Co-determination a concept whereby union or worker representatives are given positions on a company's board of directors.

Collective bargaining the process whereby representatives of management and representatives of the workers meet and negotiate over items such as wages, hours, and conditions of employment.

523

Conciliation   process in which an outside entity attempts to help two deadlocked parties continue negotiations and arrive at a solution (also called *mediation*).

Consideration   behavior from a leader indicating warmth, trust, friendship and respect to group members.

Contributory plan   a retirement plan in which money for pension benefits is paid by both employees and the employer.

Discrimination   (E.E.O.C. definition)—the use of any test that adversely affects hiring, promotion, transfer or any other employment or membership opportunity of classes unless the test has been validated and is job related, and/or an employer can demonstrate that alternative hiring, transfer, or promotion procedures are unavailable.

Duty   a work segment performed by an individual composed of a number of tasks.

Equal employment   offering individuals regardless of race, creed, age, sex, religion, or handicaps, fair and equal treatment in all employment-related actions.

Equity   the perceived fairness of what a person does compared to what he/she receives.

Ergonomics   field of study that examines the interaction among workers, jobs, and work environments.

Flexitime   a work scheduling arrangement whereby employees may vary their starting and quitting time, but work a constant number of hours.

Grievance   a specific, formal dissatisfaction expressed through an identified procedure.

Halo effect   one characteristic or factor carries an inordinate weight when appraising or selecting an individual.

Health   a general state of physical, mental, and emotional well-being.

Human resource accounting   a specialized personnel research format which continually attempts to quantify the value of an organization's human resources.

Incentives   rewards designed to encourage and reimburse employees for efforts beyond normal expectations.

Initiating structure   an effort on the part of the leader to get the job done through group members.

Interfaces   an area of contact between the personnel unit and other managers in an organization.

Job   an organizational unit of work composed of tasks, duties, and responsibilities.

Job analysis   a systematic investigation of the tasks, duties, and responsibilities of a job, and the necessary knowledge, skills, and abilities a person needs to perform the job adequately.

Job depth   concept referring to the amount of planning and control an employee has in a job.

Job description   a summary of the tasks, duties, and responsibilities in a job.

Job design   refers to conscious efforts to organize tasks, duties, and responsibilities into a unit of work to achieve a certain objective.

Job enlargement   the concept of broadening the scope and/or depth of a job.

Job evaluation   the systematic determination of the relative worth of jobs within an organization.

Job rotation   a process of shifting a person from job to job.

Job scope   a concept referring to the number and variety of tasks performed by the job holder.

Job specification   listing of the various knowledge, skills, and abilities an individual needs to do a job satisfactorily.

Labor grades   the grouping of individual jobs having approximately the same job work together.

Manpower planning   process of estimating the number, type, and sources of employees required for an organization to meet its overall objectives.

Matrix organization   an organization in which two structures exist at the same time.

Motivation   an emotion or desire operating on a person's will and causing that person to act.

Norms   expected standards of behavior, usually unwritten and often unspoken, that are generally understood by all members of the group.

Open system   a living entity which takes energy from its environment, processes it, and returns output to the environment.

Organization   a set of stable social relations deliberately created with the explicit intention of accomplishing some goal or purpose, generally existing within an authority structure, and influenced considerably by the technology and the environment in which it operates.

Organization development   a value-based process of self-assessment and planned change, involving specific strategies and technology, aimed at improving the overall effectiveness of an organizational system.

Orientation   the planned introduction of employees to their jobs, their co-workers, and the organization.

Pay   basic compensation employees receive, usually a wage or salary.

Performance appraisal   activities related to the determination of how well employees do their jobs.

Personnel audit   a formal research effort to evaluate the current state of personnel management in an organization.

Personnel development   activities concerned with increasing the capabilities of employees for continuing growth in the organization.

Personnel information system   an integrated man/machine system that is designed to provide information to be used in making personnel decisions.

Personnel management   the effective use of human resources in an organization through the management of people-related activities.

Personnel research   analyzes problems and success methods by comparing past and present practices with criteria or standards.

Policies   general guidelines that regulate organizational actions by providing a framework for managerial actions.

Portability   a pension right allowing employees to move pension benefit rights from one employer to another.

Position   a collection of tasks, duties, and responsibilities performed by one person.

Recruiting   process of generating a pool of qualified applicants for organizational positions.

Red circle rate   a job whose current occupant's pay is out of grade or range.

Reliability   the consistency with which a test measures an item.

Responsibilities   obligations to perform accepted tasks and duties.

Rules   specific guidelines that regulate and restrict the behavior of individuals.

Safety   protection of the physical health of people.

Salary   compensation that is consistent from period to period and is not directly related to the amount of hours worked by the individual.

Selection   process of picking individuals who have the necessary and relevant qualifications to fill jobs in the organization.

Self-actualization   the striving of an individual to reach his highest level of potential.

Status   the relative social ranking an individual has in a group or organization.

Systems approach   an organization is viewed as a whole comprised of subsystems.

Task   a distinct identifiable work activity composed of motions.

Technology   types and patterns of activity, equipment, materials, and knowledge or experience used to perform tasks.

Title VII   that portion of the 1964 Civil Rights Act prohibiting discrimination in employment.

Training   a learning process whereby people acquire skills, concepts, attitudes, or knowledge to aid in the achievement of goals.

Turnover   process of employees leaving an organization and having to be replaced.

Unfunded plan   a retirement plan which pays pension benefits out of current income to the organization.

Validity   actually measuring what a test says it will measure.

Vesting   right of employees to receive benefits from their pension plan.

Wages   pay directly calculated on the amount of time worked.

Work group   a collection of individuals brought together to perform organizational work.

appendix B

Important Organizations in Personnel Management

1. AFL-CIO
   815 16th Street N.W.
   Washington, D.C.   20006

2. American Management Association
   (AMA)
   135 West 50th Street
   New York City, New York   10020

3. American Society for Personnel
   Administration (ASPA)
   30 Park Avenue
   Berea, Ohio   44017

4. American Society for Training and
   Development (ASTD)
   P.O. Box 5307
   Madison, Wisconsin   53705

5. Bureau of Industrial Relations
   (University of Michigan)
   Ann Arbor, Michigan   48104

6. Bureau of Labor Statistics (BLS)
   Department of Labor
   3rd Street & Constitution Ave, N.W.
   Washington, D.C.   20210

7. Bureau of National Affairs (BNA)
   1231 25th Street, N.W.
   Washington, D.C.   20037

8. Department of Labor
   3rd Street & Constitution Ave., N.W.
   Washington, D.C.   20210

9. Equal Employment Opportunity
   Commission (EEOC)
   2401 E. Street, N.W.
   Washington, D.C.   20506

10. Internal Revenue Service (IRS)
    111 Constitution Ave., N.W.
    Washington, D.C.   20224

11. International Personnel Management
    Association (IPMA)
    1313 E. 60th Street
    Chicago, Illinois   60637

12. Labor/Management Mediation Service
    1620 I Street, N.W., Suite 616
    Washington, D.C.   20006

13. National Association for the
    Advancement of Colored People
    (NAACP)
    1790 Broadway
    New York, New York   10019

14. National Association of Manufacturers
    (NAM)
    1776 F. Street
    Washington, D.C.   20006

15. Occupational Safety and Health
    Administration (OSHA)
    200 Constitution Ave., N.W.
    Washington, D.C.   20210

16. Office of Federal Contract Compliance
    (OFCC)
    200 Constitution Ave., N.W.
    Washington, D.C.   20210

17. Pension Benefit Guaranty Corporation
    P.O. Box 7119
    Washington, D.C.   20044

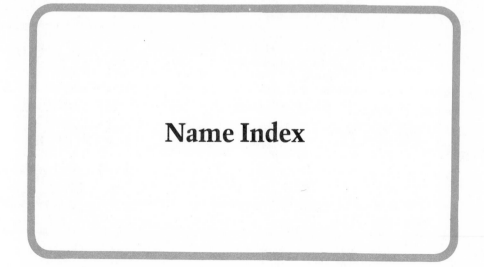

Name Index

Subject Index